Also in the Variorum Collected Studies Series:

ALLAN CHAPMAN
Astronomical Instruments and their Users
Tycho Brahe to William Lassell

A.W. SKEMPTON
Civil Engineers and Engineering in Britain, 1600–1830

ROY M. MacLEOD
Public Science and Public Policy in Victorian England

WILLIAM H. BROCK
Science for All
Studies in the History of Victorian Science and Education

P.M. HARMAN
After Newton: Essays on Natural Phliosophy

CURTIS WILSON
Astronomy from Kepler to Newton

ALLEN G. DEBUS
Chemistry, Alchemy and the New Philosophy, 1550–1700
Studies in the History of Science and Medicine

TREVOR H. LEVERE
Chemists and Chemistry in Nature and Society, 1770–1878

ROBERT FOX
The Culture of Science in France, 1700–1900

R.W. HOME
Electricity and Experimental Physics in 18th-Century Europe

A. RUPERT HALL
Science and Society
Historical Essays on the Relations of Science, Technology and Medicine

ROBERT FOX
Science, Industry and the Social Order in Post-Revolutionary France

MAURICE CROSLAND
Studies in the Culture of Science in France and Britain since the Enlightenment

JOHN HEDLEY BROOKE
Thinking about Matter
Studies in the History of Chemical Philosophy

COLLECTED STUDIES SERIES

Science, Culture and Politics in Britain, 1750–1870

Jack Morrell

Science, Culture and Politics in Britain, 1750–1870

VARIORUM
1997

Published by VARIORUM
Ashgate Publishing Limited
Gower House, Croft Road,
Aldershot, Hampshire GU11 3HR
Great Britain

Ashgate Publishing Company
Old Post Road,
Brookfield, Vermont 05036–9704
USA

ISBN 0–86078–633–1

British Library CIP Data
Morrell, Jack.
Science, Culture and Politics in Britain, 1750–1870.—(Variorum Collected Studies Series: 567)
1. Science and civilization. 2. Philosophy, modern—18th century.
3. Philosophy and science—Great Britain. 4. Science—Great Britain—History. I. Title. II. Series: Variorum Collected Studies Series: CS567.
509.4'1

US Library of Congress CIP Data
Morrell, Jack.
Science, Culture and Politics in Britain, 1750–1870 / Jack Morrell.
p. cm. — (Variorum Collected Studies Series: CS567)
Includes index.
1. Science—Great Britain—History—18th Century. 2. Science— Great Britain—History—19th Century. 3. Science—Scotland—Edinburgh—History—18th Century. 4. Science—Scotland—Edinburgh—History—19th Century. 5. University of Edinburgh—History. I. Title.
II. Series: Collected Studies: CS567.
Q127.G4M67 1997 96-52706
509.41'09'033—dc21 CIP

The paper used in this publication meets the minimum requirements of the American National Standard for Information Sciences - Permanence of Paper for Printed Library Materials, ANSI Z39.48-1984. ∞ ™

Printed by Galliard (Printers) Ltd
Great Yarmouth, Norfolk, Great Britain

VARIORUM COLLECTED STUDIES SERIES CS567

CONTENTS

This volume contains xii + 336 pages

PREFACE

The publication of a selection of one's papers provides an irreproachable occasion for auto-aggrandisement. Simultaneously the passage of time has made me, to my surprise, an object of historical enquiry. It seems that in the 1970s some of my papers integrated the various contexts of science with its content and one of them, essay VIII, has been praised for its genius. In this preface I acknowledge my early intellectual debts partly for the record and partly to rebut the proposition that nothing done in social history of science before 1980 is now worth reading. I mention only those scholars whom I met before 1972. Most of them were by then examining science as an activity and not just as published knowledge. Their publications of the 1970s and thereafter are so well-known that it is otiose to give references.

At school I liked history, English, and chemistry equally but specialised in science in the sixth form. I read chemistry at Birmingham where I discovered that I was not a great researcher. As I spent far more time in the laboratory than in the lecture room in my final year, I wondered what the purposes of laboratory experience were, because for me the intellectual gains seemed disproportionately meagre. I then read English at Oxford where I knew about A.C. Crombie's classes in history of science but did not attend them. From my two tutors, Ian Jack and Brian Miller, I learned about the importance of authors' intentions, the difference between intent and achievement, the significance of genre (discourse [sic] etc), and how to combine textual analysis with contextual history. I discovered that assertion does not constitute an argument and, by producing ten to fourteen essays a term, acquired a concern for written language. Through writing on successive weeks an essay attacking Milton and one defending him, I understood what might now be called historiographical symmetry.

In my teaching-diploma year at Bristol I bought and read Butterfield, *Origins of Modern Science*. This mild interest in history of science was strengthened from 1959 to 1963 when I taught mainly chemistry at Queen Elizabeth Grammar School, Wakefield. Its headmaster took all the third-year sixth form through Butterfield's book. On occasion I deputised for him. Feeling ignorant I bought in 1961 Crombie's *Augustine to Galileo*. In autumn 1963 I was appointed as lecturer in history of science at what soon became the University of Bradford. I applied for the post because the subject interested me but also because travelling six days a week between Wakefield and Bradford (where I lived), and teaching 35 out of 37 periods a week, were unsustainable.

I began my stint at Bradford in January 1964, knowing little about my subject and having heard only one historian of science, Jerry Ravetz, who had come from Leeds University to Wakefield to address a boy' society. He advised me to read Dijksterhuis's *Mechanization of the World Picture,* which I did. My Bradford colleague, Harold Jones, was mainly an editor and bibliographer of seventeenth-century texts so I had to be an auto-didact. One of my responsibilities, was to teach a finals paper on philosophy of science set by the London School of Economics group for the demanding London BSc (Econ) external degree. I took my students and myself through the set-books, and concluded that most of them bore little relation to the laboratory life I had experienced or to the mundane activities of dead scientists.

About 1967 I made contact with historians of science at the Universities of Leeds and Manchester. These northern colleagues helped to clarify and consolidate my approach to history of science. At Leeds, Jerry Ravetz analysed science as a craft activity concerned with setting and solving problems about the natural world, the value of the problems and the adequacy of the answers being subject to dispute. Maurice Crosland gave seminars on French science which revealed the importance of research programmes, careers, and politics. Charles Webster gave an example of penetrating social history of science in his seminar on mid-seventeenth century science. Slightly later Charles Schmitt's research on Aristotelianism in late medieval universities confirmed my view that universities constituted a strategic research site. At Leeds I met Robert Fox with whom I must have discussed aspects of his well-known paper on Laplacian physics. At Manchester the focus was on the history of modern science and technology construed as related activities. Donald Cardwell had published a pioneering book on *The Organisation of Science in England* (1957) and introduced me to the scientific life pursued in both upper and nether Grimedale. Wilfred Farrar was a mine of information about pure and applied chemistry, especially in Manchester and Germany. Arnold Pacey was developing an approach to history of technology which led to his recent and widely acclaimed books. At Manchester gudgeon-pins and locality were of more interest than metaphysics.

Also in 1967, I met Arnold Thackray through a common interest in Dalton's chemical atomic theory, first published by Thomas Thomson. Arnold encouraged me to continue analysing Thomson's career, and introduced me to Robert Merton's ideas about foci of interest and the utilities of science at a time when for most historians Merton meant no more than the puritan-ethic theory. By 1969 I had published my first two articles (VI, IX). They were unpopular in some quarters because they showed that the fates of chemistry in two Scottish universities at the same time depended on institutional faction-fighting, especially about money, as well as intellectual matters. On this slim basis, Arnold invited me for six months in 1970 as a visitor to the University of Pennsylvania, where I gave a seminar on Science in the Scottish Enlightenment and began to think about writing a book on the history of science and medicine at the University of Edinburgh, an unfulfilled project which led to several articles (I, II, V, VII, X). Before the start of an early seminar at Penn I was stopped in a corridor by a burly mature student, already balding, who said to me out of the blue, 'Do you know what? Knowledge is power.' I was so startled by his question and aphorism that I failed to give the standard Noel Coward answer, 'Of course it is, my dear'. That was my first meeting with Steven Shapin, later the social historian of truth. At Penn Arnold and I began a long collaboration which culminated in our two volumes on the early British Association for the Advancement of Science (1981, 1984). From Russell McCormmach I learned much about disciplinary history. In exchange I wrote for his journal article XI, the title of which pays homage to Lewis Namier's *The Structure of Politics at the Accession of George III*. From Namier I learned much about coteries and interests, years before sociologists of science at Bath and Edinburgh wrote about them, though I regretted that for him ideas could not be interests. At Penn I also wrote articles III and IV, my interest in the comparison made in the latter having been stimulated by Anand Chitnis whose PhD led to his two interesting books on the Scottish Enlightenment. At Penn I met Charles Rosenberg, whose writings on history of medicine continue to provide an inspiring model, and Whitfield Bell who wrote about medical networks and transfers decades before Bruno Latour became a cult figure. On returning to Bradford I began to think about research schools, one product being article VIII which had the benefit of Bill Brock's editorial generosity and care and his knowledge of German university laboratory life.

By 1972 I had met a cohort of historians, whose new approaches to the history of science, technology, and medicine had greatly encouraged me. After that I was to learn from others, but that phase falls outside the scope of this preface. I incurred, however, one general debt which should not be forgotten. This was to Sir John Barbirolli, conductor of the Hallé Orchestra. In the 1960s at his concerts in Bradford, Leeds and Manchester, he provided an inspiring example of an original approach, technical competence, total commitment and expressive intensity. He showed that great achievements were possible in the north of England. My debt to Glorious John has been revealed only once – at the end of article XV, which in spoken form was delivered in Manchester, the home of the Hallé.

Bradford, West Yorkshire
September 1996

JACK MORRELL

ACKNOWLEDGEMENTS

I am grateful to the following editors and publishers for permission to reproduce the articles included here: Professor R. S. Porter (I); Dr Robert Anderson and the trustees of the National Museums of Scotland, Edinburgh (II, XIII); Dr M. Rossiter, the History of Science Society, and the University of Chicago Press (III); the Royal Society of London (IV); Professor S. J. Brown and *The Scottish Historical Review* (V); Dr J. Browne and the British Society for the History of Science (VI, VII, XII, XV); Dr G. K. Roberts and the Society for the History of Alchemy and Chemistry (VIII, IX); Dr D. Edge, *Social Studies of Science*, and Sage Publications, London (X); the Regents of the University of California (XI); and Professor I. Inkster (XIV).

PUBLISHER'S NOTE

The articles in this volume, as in all others in the Collected Studies Series, have not been given a new, continuous pagination. In order to avoid confusion, and to facilitate their use where these same studies have been referred to elsewhere, the original pagination has been maintained wherever possible.

Each article has been given a Roman number in order of appearance, as listed in the Contents. This number is repeated on each page and quoted in the index entries.

I

REFLECTIONS ON THE HISTORY OF SCOTTISH SCIENCE*

In a characteristically captivating essay, Charles Rosenberg has recently pointed out that the historian of American science faces the danger of falling between two stools: that is, he or she may not be fully accepted either as an American historian or as a historian of science.[1] This is, of course, the possible fate of any historian of national science. Indeed the very attempt to write history of national science may strike some sceptics as being fundamentally ridiculous. These sceptics will argue that science was an international endeavour which successfully devoted itself to the production of eternal truth about nature, using that unique tool known as scientific method. Such a noble and transcendental view of science offers little to the historian of national science. Indeed it implies that his efforts cannot rise above the merely local and peripheral.

Fortunately we can reject an exclusively internal historiography as being too simplifying without falling into the alternative trap of that vulgar Marxism which asserts that the economic substructure determines the superstructure of which science is a part. The work of Kuhn, of Ziman, and of Ravetz, has confirmed that science was and is the socially organized attempt to set and to solve problems concerning nature, the character of the problems and the acceptability of the solutions being in constant evolution.[2] This view of science offers many enticing prospects to the historian of national science. It invites us to see the development of scientific roles in reciprocal relation with the social, educational, political, religious, and economic systems of different countries and places.[3] In this connection Scotland, especially after the Union of 1707 with England, is particularly interesting: though a part of the United Kingdom, she still retained considerable independence via her educational, legal, and ecclesiastical systems.[4] The view of science as socially organized problem-solving also draws attention to institutions devoted *inter alia* to scientific activity because it was in these that the intellectual activity called science was quite deliberately socially fostered and

* This paper, and the two that follow it, have been developed out of papers given on 24 February 1973 at a conference on Scottish Science in the Eighteenth Century, organized by Dr N. T. Phillipson under the joint auspices of the Science Studies Unit and the Institute for Advanced Studies in Humanities of the University of Edinburgh. Thanks are due to Dr Phillipson for encouraging the publication of the papers jointly in this form.

legitimated. Here again Scotland offers prospectively a rich harvest from universities to ephemeral societies. Hence the study of Scottish scientific roles and institutions can be the opposite of the merely peripheral. At the least such work would help to fill the many gaps in our knowledge of the variegated structure of British science.[5] It ought to contribute to our understanding of the general development of science as a profession. It might reveal how science, before it became self-evidently a good thing, had to justify itself in terms of values other than those of scientific knowledge *per se*. It offers good prospects of achieving a rotund history of science from which the fruitless distinction between internal and external historiographies would be banished. For all these reasons the history of Scottish science is potentially rewarding, apart from the obvious fact that in some subjects Scots made considerable and sometimes decisive contributions to European science.

We have recently been favoured with some welcome studies which offer competent analytical intellectual history of Scottish science.[6] In this essay I shall resist the temptation to appraise recent work in this genre because I wish to concentrate on the history of institutionalized science using Scottish examples. In order to avoid merely ritualist historiographical gestures, my discussion will be limited to four related themes: the development of scientific disciplines; the importance of organizational features; the use of models; and the significance of localism. Most, though not all, of the supporting illustrations will be drawn from the University of Edinburgh because from the late seventeenth century it has always been one of the most important of Scottish scientific institutions. No apology is required for offering substantive concrete examples. Without these, there is a danger that one merely debates desiderata and avoids doing history.

I

Perhaps one of the most important problems awaiting attack is the birth, the maintenance, the expansion, and sometimes the decline of scientific disciplines within institutions.[7] A particularly fascinating study of this type would be natural philosophy at the University of Edinburgh. The challenge of the problem may be gauged if we recall the names of the five professors of natural philosophy between 1774 and 1901: John Robison, John Playfair, John Leslie, James David Forbes, and Peter Guthrie Tait. Such discipline-orientated study is necessary because, in utopian circumstances, it is the discipline which "prescribes the scientist's problems and methods, channels his personal ambition, rewards his achievements, and conditions his attitudes, values, and behavior".[8] Such an affirmation may, however, be too simplifying in the case of scientists working in institutions. Indeed the nature of the work done by an institutionalized scientist may be most fully understood in terms of the way in which his disciplinary ambitions were tempered or frustrated by institutional restraints. For example, the features of natural philosophy at Edinburgh during Tait's incumbency cannot be explained solely in terms of the state of his discipline at that time and his own intentions. It is abundantly clear that the extreme poverty of his institution and the clerical nature of his students prevented him from achieving some but not all of his aims.[9] If we turn to the question of what happened to chemistry at the leading Scottish universities after the halcyon days of Joseph Black, we find that institutional choices and restraints were again significant. At Edinburgh, Thomas Charles Hope, a protégé of Black, was faced with certain institutional demands and opportunities. After an initial period in which he maintained his research, Hope chose to devote his time and effort to teaching. Subsequently he responded to his institutional monopoly of his subject by resisting developments concerned with practical chemistry for which his Edinburgh contemporaries and some students were calling.[10] At Glasgow, however, Thomas Thomson, another pupil of Black, maintained his research vision and activities but institutional demands and irritants severely limited his achievement.[11] These examples suggest, I think, that it is useful to look at the development or decline of disciplines within an institution in terms of the ways in which disciplinary aims, methods, and ambitions were related to institutional supports and hindrances.

II

This last point is closely related to another desideratum for the history of institutionalized science, *i.e.* that greater attention might be paid to organizational changes, including the drafting of pertinent documents. In saying this I am not advocating what might be called the Whig interpretation of the social history of science. This simplistic view assumes that organizational changes simply and inevitably followed antecedent intellectual ones. It seems to me to be more profitable, however, to assume as a working hypothesis that intellectual and organizational changes were mutually related; in other words, that their relation may have been symbiotic and not just consequential. Such an assumption is in harmony with the view of scientists as comprising a mandarinate or a clerisy, because organizational arrangements and changes can isolate scientists from social pressures.[12] It is insufficient to regard these organizational features as simply transmitting economic and social forces; astute scientists may use these features to deflect, repel, or metamorphose social demands.

Even apparently mundane organizational changes deserve scrutiny. For instance, the abolition of regenting in Arts subjects at the University of Edinburgh in 1708 seems unstartling. What happened at the administrative level was that specialist professors replaced the transient young regents who previously had carried their particular class through all the subjects of the arts curriculum. This change was clearly engineered by Principal William

Carstares who was concerned to raise the level of instruction available to future Scottish divines. His model was patently the Universities of Utrecht and of Leyden.[13] The intellectual possibilities created by this administrative change soon became apparent. In the case of students, they lost that close supervision which the regenting system offered at its best; but they gained *Lernfreiheit* which allowed them to study those scientific subjects which were prospectively or actually appealing. Not surprisingly graduation in arts declined rapidly. For professors the new system introduced a good deal of *Lehrfreiheit* and encouraged them to be specialists in a particular discipline. At the same time, the class-fee system encouraged, though it did not oblige, professors to be student-orientated as well. Compared with a regent, a permanent professor who enjoyed legal monopoly of his subject carried at best more intellectual responsibility and possessed more scope for intellectual manoeuvre and innovation within his subject. Indeed the advantage for science of having a professor, who did not also function as a regent, had been perceived in 1674 when James Gregory (1638–75) was elected to the chair of mathematics and was officially relieved of the burden of regenting.[14] Edinburgh was the first of the Scottish universities to abolish regenting. Glasgow officially followed suit in 1727, St Andrews in 1747, Marischal College Aberdeen in 1753, and King's College Aberdeen in 1799. Though Edinburgh created and enjoyed many advantages compared with its rivals, the sweeping administrative change introduced largely by Carstares was a long-term condition of the University's subsequent rise to international eminence in medicine and in science. Carstares's innovation ensured that the creation and expansion of the medical faculty in the early eighteenth century would be accomplished via the differentiation of pedagogic areas which established specialised teaching provinces.

Proposed as well as actual organizational changes merit attention because they may reveal underlying issues and choices. A very significant example is again provided by the University of Edinburgh at which during the early 1830s laboratory training was available in only anatomy and chemistry. Each of these classes was taught, not by the respective professor, but by an assistant appointed and supervised by the professor. By 1833, however, both William MacKenzie and David Boswell Reid clearly felt that practical anatomy and practical chemistry were no longer optional luxuries for students: each therefore petitioned the Town Council of Edinburgh, the patrons of the University, to create a separate independent post for himself.[15] From studying the ensuing controversies, it becomes clear that from the 1820s neither Monro III (professor of anatomy, 1798–1846) nor Hope (professor of chemistry, 1795–1843) appeared even occasionally in his laboratory to teach his own subject practically to his students. The absence from their teaching laboratories of the professors of anatomy and of chemistry is a telling symptom of the University's declining reputation in science at that time.

Sometimes the detailed drafting of documents may reveal or highlight motives which might otherwise remain unnoticed. A choice case is provided by the appointment of Colin MacLaurin to the chair of mathematics at the University of Edinburgh on 3 November 1725. The relevant Town Council Minute gives an apparently obvious reason for this appointment, that it was impossible to do "a thing more honourable and advantageous for the city, that would contribute more to the reputation of the university, and advance the interest of learning in this country, than the giving Mr. M'Laurin suitable encouragement to settle among us".[16] Now MacLaurin had been professor of mathematics at Marischal College, Aberdeen, from 1717; and Edinburgh Town Council, when appointing a practising teacher to a chair, usually justified its decision by referring to his previous success as a teacher. In MacLaurin's case, however, the appropriate minute ignored MacLaurin's teaching at Aberdeen. The explanation of this discreet silence is simply that at Aberdeen MacLaurin had been an absentee professor from autumn 1722 to early 1725 as tutor to the eldest son of Lord Polwarth. When he returned to Aberdeen in January 1725, a Committee of Aberdeen Town Council, then the patrons of the Marischal mathematics chair, was appointed to discuss with MacLaurin "1st His going away without Liberty from the Counsell, 2nd His being so long absent from his charge". By April 1725 MacLaurin had wisely appeared before the Aberdeen Town Council, expressed his regret for his misdemeanours and was accordingly reponed. When he had been appointed to the Edinburgh chair in November 1725, MacLaurin once again treated the Aberdeen Town Council in a cavalier way: he did not resign his Aberdeen chair immediately, but left the Aberdeen Council to discover from "publict news prints" that he was by then an Edinburgh professor. Indeed the Aberdeen Council declared his chair vacant on 12 January 1726 before MacLaurin bothered to intimate his resignation on 23 February 1726.[17] The Edinburgh Town Council was surely aware of one unattractive feature in MacLaurin's curriculum vitae, yet it risked appointing him because it was keen to acquire a man already eminent by his publications and one strongly supported by leading mathematicians such as Newton.[18] Irrespective of who engineered the election of MacLaurin, it is clear that he was appointed not because of his dependability as a teacher but on account of his demonstrated brilliance in research. Judged by eighteenth century mercantilist and pedagogic criteria, MacLaurin's appointment was unusual. Generally speaking, their proved skill as teachers, their general intellectual reputation, and demonstrated institutional loyalty were basic reasons for the appointment of professors in European universities during the eighteenth century.[19] It was, of course, only in the next century that in these universities professors began to be appointed primarily because of their proved brilliance in specialized research. Yet at Edinburgh in 1725 a brilliant researcher was deliberately recruited by the

Town Council and his previous unreliability as a teacher discretely ignored. It is widely and rightly assumed that it was in the nineteenth century that universities began to function as nationalist showpieces via their scholarship and research. But at Edinburgh in 1725 MacLaurin was appointed with just this purpose in mind. The result of his election was, of course, that the University of Edinburgh became an acknowledged centre for the diffusion of Newtonian mathematics, astronomy, and natural philosophy by the most gifted and accomplished British disciple of his generation.

III

One way in which the history of institutionalized science might be furthered is by the use of explicit frameworks or models whether of the heuristic or the substantive kind. Without these it is easy for the historian to slip into myopic piecemeal empiricism, and even into rampant antiquarianism. Frames of reference provide continuity of themes and of approach; they force one to examine one's own presuppositions in writing history; and they compel one to examine features and relations which otherwise might be overlooked. They bring into one focus a good deal of scattered information; and by so doing they convert such information into evidence.

One obvious frame of reference or sociological theory which might be exploited is structural functionalism which explains institutional change in terms of response and adaptation to social 'needs'. Where 'needs' can be made historically specific and concrete, the functionalist approach yields dividends, because it exposes the roles which institutions play, the expectations surrounding them, and the norms controlling their behaviour. But often 'needs' remain historically-speaking nebulous. A further weakness of the functionalist approach is that it is vague about the timing of adaptation and the chronology of change. Its most glaring defects are, however, that it ignores conflict about and within institutions, the exertions of pressure groups, and the triggering effect of individual initiative. After all, some men create opportunities besides responding to existing needs.[20]

A second sociological theory which relatively few historians have employed is Marxism. In contrast with functionalism, this approach does focus on conflict about and in institutions; but it explains such conflict as merely an aspect of economic class-conflict and of the economic substructure. Like the functionalist approach, in its cruder forms it diminishes the importance of ideas, of debate, and of individual initiative. It faces considerable difficulties in explaining how the 'superstructure' has sometimes successfully resisted the pressures generated by economic change. The Marxist approach is useful in that it sees conflict as the cause of institutional change. Yet it is restricting in that *inter alia* it fails to take into account the effects achieved by groups other than classes.

A third frame of reference has been provided by the work of Namier and his followers who stress the importance of self interest in explaining political change. If it is crudely handled this approach tends to devalue the importance of ideologies, and of articulated intellectual systems.[21] The related technique of prosopography which Namier pioneered is receiving critical evaluation in this journal, and its power in the study of institutionalized science has been revealed by Thackray's work on the Manchester Literary and Philosophical Society.[22] The only point I wish to make about Namier's approach is that it reminds us that professed ideals and rhetorical programmes may be just attempts to rationalize and legitimate the intended or actual results of machinating self-interest. His approach pricks the bubble of idealism. In the field of history of institutionalized science, the Namierite view invites us to examine the administrative mechanisms and personal ties which may have been important in allowing certain aims and changes to be achieved. For instance, it is no doubt true that the search for prestige explains why some scientific institutions were created and maintained. But the notion of prestige *per se* is inadequate unless it is supplemented by analysis of the detailed mechanics by which institutional change took place.[23] Namier's approach is an essential component of my own which assumes that both stability and change in scientific institutions may be explained in terms of the *interests* and/or the *ideas* of various groups competing for control of those institutions. Of course only detailed scrutiny of the widest possible range of published and unpublished sources can reveal the nature of those interests and ideas and the identities of the competing groups.

Models, like frameworks, have become fashionable in history. It seems that they were first developed by economists who hoped to create comprehensive systems of inter-related quantifiable parameters which would describe accurately given economic situations. From these systems or models it was hoped that predictive quantitative power would flow. As historians are not concerned with prediction about the future but with rational reconstruction of the past, they use models differently. Generally there seem to be two chief types, the substantive and the heuristic. The former claims that it comprehends the chief parameters which were actually responsible for a given historical situation; the latter draws attention to the possible parameters which may have been responsible for it. In old-fashioned terms the former is a substantive theory, and the latter a working hypothesis.

One obvious difficulty inherent in using a model is that it can tend to be an idealizing rationalization or even a pretentious restatement of widely accepted historical facts and interpretations. Certainly a recently published model of a successful laboratory-based research school may be assailed as being nothing more than a restatement of Liebig's success as a supervisor of research.[24] Yet the model does reveal why and how both Liebig and Thomson operated in their laboratories and in their universities. Because it includes intellectual, institutional, technical, psychological, and financial components, it forced one to ask questions about Thomson's research programme; his early inspirations; the recruitment, training, and employment of his students; the laboratory techniques they used; publication opportunities; his limited institutional power *qua* Regius professor; his sardonic personality; his laboratory accommodation; and the financial support given to him by his University. The answers provide a pluri-causal explanation of Thomson's failure to realize the aims he deeply cherished. In the case of Liebig, the model stresses how Liebig established a 'self-expanding' cycle comprising recruitment of students, laboratory techniques, publications, reputation, recruitment of more students, etc. A part of the model also posits that the features of Liebig's research programme may be understood by considering Liebig's evaluation of the repellent frustrations he endured, of the positive inspirations he enjoyed, and of the state and potentialities of chemistry. It thereby avoids the vacuous notion of 'influence', *i.e.* that 'influential' men exude an all-suffusing miasma which inevitably 'influences' their contemporaries and even the unborn. If this part of the model is generalized, it encourages us to examine the *indebtedness* which scientists feel to others for subject matter, problem area, explicit attitudes, tacit assumptions, theoretical and practical techniques, and simple facts. The model as a whole has heuristic possibilities. For example the failure of Lyon Playfair, professor of chemistry at the University of Edinburgh from 1858 to 1869, to establish a research school on the Liebig-Bunsen pattern is *prima-facie* rather surprising.[25] If the model is applied, however, it reveals that Playfair did not devise a set of appropriate techniques with which a considerable cohort of average students could do competent research. Hence his laboratory was devoted just to teaching chemical manipulation and analysis. One also suspects that he had no large research programme in his mind; perhaps his previous career as a consultant and administrator put such emphasis on commissioned *ad hoc* research that he lost the art of creating for himself and for others an area of research so large that no single individual could effectively attack it.

IV

It is a truism that the pattern of organized British science during the first industrial revolution seems variegated and haphazard. This diversity frequently emanated from local initiative which was exercised partly in response to local conditions and pressures. Hence, as long as centralizing forces were relatively powerless, one expects to find that many industrializing cities and traditional regional centres nourished an institutionalized scientific life *sui generis*. A most obvious but yet unappreciated example of such localism is provided by the different histories of the general scientific societies of Edinburgh and of Glasgow.

The Royal Society of Edinburgh was chartered in 1783 as a result of conflict between three institutions. During Hanoverian times it gained intellectually and socially from the contributions made by the University professoriate, the medicals, the lawyers, and the lowland landed gentry.[26] Unlike many scientific societies of the time, it met regularly, enjoyed a continuous existence, and rapidly established the importance of its *Transactions*. But what was happening only fifty miles westwards in Glasgow, a city which experienced a five-fold growth in population from 40,000 to 200,000 between 1780 and 1830? In that period, as Smout has recently confirmed, the structure of the middle class in Glasgow was quite different from that of Edinburgh.[27] Compared with the Athens of the North, Glasgow was not a magnet for gentry and tourists; and its business men were more prominent than its professional men. Smout has pointed out that, if the street directories are accurate guides, in Edinburgh one entrant in three was a professional man and one in eight a business man; whereas in Glasgow one in three was a business man and one in eight a professional man.

Glasgow's expansion was based on the entrepreneurial skill of her businessmen, whether merchants or manufacturers. Not surprisingly, therefore, the Philosophical Society of Glasgow was founded in 1802 by three laymen interested "in the prosperity of the trade and manufactures of their country, and anxious for the improvement of the Arts and Sciences".[28] The members of the Society were mainly manufacturers, artisans, and merchants, whose behaviour was redolent of both the Lunar Society and the Pickwick Club.[29] Like many ambitious societies at that time, it immediately met difficulties: no papers, no speakers, no publication, and irregular meetings. Thirty years after its foundation it was still dominated in its membership by intellectually isolated craftsmen and manufacturers, who generally neither offered papers nor attended meetings. Out of the fortyseven members registered in February 1832, no less than twentyfive were directly engaged in manufactures of some kind.[30] The next group in size comprised five merchants. In sharp contrast with the Royal Society of Edinburgh, the Glasgow Society mustered only two professors, two medicals, four lawyers, and one teacher.[31] The nobility, the gentry, and the clergy were totally unrepresented. No wonder that particularly from 1830 the Glasgow Society slid from crisis to crisis until in 1834 it was renovated in an apparently strange way. In that year, distinguished professors from the University of Glasgow and Anderson's University who had previously ignored the Society took it over by being elected to membership and immediate office. Renovation took the form of regular meetings, advertisements in the press, an effective council, and an obvious bias towards chemistry pure and applied. Even so, it was not until 1842 that the Society became so effective that it began to publish its *Transactions*.

The early career of the Philosophical Society of Glasgow between 1802 and 1834 is instructive. Until 1834 it was ignored by the elite of the scientific professoriate of the University of Glasgow such as Thomas Thomson (chemistry), William Jackson Hooker (botany), James Thomson (mathematics), and John Burns (surgery). It was mainly ignored before 1834 by the staff of Anderson's University such as Thomas Graham (chemistry) and Andrew Buchanan (materia medica). Apparently it was totally ignored by the ancient medical corporation of Glasgow, the Glasgow Faculty of Physicians and Surgeons. Among the few merchants with scientific capacity, the geologist James Smith of Jordanhill remained aloof until 1834. So did the eminent chemist and calico-printer Walter Crum. Again only in 1834 did the well-known chemist, bookseller, and instrument maker, J. J. Griffin, join the Society. It seems then that Glasgow's dominant scientific institutions and individuals deliberately avoided the Philosophical Society until 1834 when they saw it could serve their purposes.

Such aloofness seems at first sight rather surprising. One might have expected that in Glasgow between 1800 and 1830 the professoriate, the medicals, the new manufacturers, maybe supported by enlightened merchants, would have formed a vigorous and effective organisation. That, however, did not happen. Here is a pointed contrast with Manchester, where the Literary and Philosophical Society (founded 1781) was run largely by the town's medicals and teachers (such as Thomas Percival and John Dalton), and by livelier manufacturers (such as the Henrys). But Manchester was a *parvenu* town with few established institutions; Glasgow was an ancient city with old academic and medical corporations. This difference is, I think, crucial to explaining the contrast between the fortunes of the Glasgow and Manchester Societies.

Until 1834 the brighter scientific academics and the medicals largely ignored the Glasgow Society. Their absence was telling, because by the early nineteenth century both these groups generally possessed attributes and skills vital to the success of scientific societies. Both enjoyed some though variable status. Both had usually experienced some form of scientific training and were likely to be as well qualified as any other group to act as scientific leaders. In some cases, their permanent job, as say professor or hospital physician, provided scientific problems to solve. If anyone was likely to have a paper in his brief-case, ready to buttress a list of speakers or to fill a gap at short notice, it was the academic or the physician. Compared with other groups they were never less than literate. As the result of their daily experience in the university or the hospital, they were likely to possess a modicum of administrative competence which when applied within scientific societies produced at best systematic organisation of meetings and regular publication. They were unlikely to be socially gauche; some indeed positively revelled in clubability.

At Glasgow before 1834 the manufacturers and merchants intermittently formed an audience, but the best scientific performers including academics and medicals kept themselves aloof. Perhaps they despised the dominant social tone of the Society, and scorned its intellectual incompetence. More positively the non-decrepit university academics and medical men already enjoyed sufficient opportunities and outlets for scientific research, discussion, and publication. In the case of the academics, from 1819 until 1834 Thomson's scientific life revolved around his university chemistry laboratory, just as Hooker's was focused on the Botanic Gardens, and Burns's on the Infirmary. For the medicals the institutional foci were the Infirmary, the Faculty of Physicians and Surgeons (the medical licensing body for West Scotland until 1858), and the Glasgow Medico-Chirurgical Society. Nor must we forget that, for much of the first half of the nineteenth century, the University and the Glasgow Faculty of Physicians and Surgeons were on such bad terms that lengthy litigation was the sad result. During the 1820s and 1830s these disputes about whether Glasgow medical and surgical graduates could practise within the territory 'governed' by the Glasgow Faculty were particularly intense.[32] One suspects that during those years university academics and members of the local medical corporation simply did not wish to collaborate in any activity.

Why, then, did the academics bother to revive and transform the Society in 1834? Partly the answer lies in that local pride which felt that the Glasgow Philosophical Society should not be merely an also-ran at a time when philosophical societies were burgeoning elsewhere in Britain. It also lies in the contingent fact that by 1834 Thomson's productive research career had come to an end. Here was a savant of European reputation waiting in the wings ready to assume a new role as Glasgow's scientific elder statesman, with one of his protégés, Thomas Graham, as his right-hand man. And, of course, the existing Society did not resist the take-over. In 1833 it had virtually collapsed: only one meeting took place that year, and it was abandoned for lack of a quorum. Two concerned members, a baker and an ironmonger of considerable local standing, decided to save the Society from extinction by inviting many of Glasgow's scientific savants to join it. The Thomsons and Grahams were therefore invited to invade and govern it without jealousy and without conflict. Such was Thomson's importance to the Society that he was elected to membership and life-long Presidency at the same meeting on 12 November 1834. In making this contrast between the Society before and after 1834 I am not denigrating the first phase of its history. But I am stressing that local conditions and contingencies shaped its otherwise strange career.

Perhaps we may hazard a few mundane generalizations about scientific societies on the basis of the particular example of Glasgow. It is tempting to see the composition and interests of scientific societies as reflecting *tout court* the social structure of their locality. This notion is useful heuristically in that it focuses attention on *all* the groups and elements in a locality which might have contributed to institutionalized science. But further queries have still to be raised. Why did any particular group or element choose science as an intellectual and cultural pursuit? Was it active in scientific performance or in appreciation? Why did any specific group and its individual members choose a local scientific society when faced with alternative and possibly competing institutional outlets? How was the timing and nature of change in a scientific society related to the ambitions and career prospects of its members? All these questions must be asked and answered in order to supplement the simple functionalist view of scientific societies. If they are not asked, it is likely that the study of scientific societies in their local context will decline into despicable drabness.

Acknowledgements

For permission to use materials under their charge, I am grateful to Mr C. P. Finlayson, Keeper of Manuscripts, Edinburgh University Library and to Professor J. M. A. Lenihan, Secretary of the Royal Philosophical Society of Glasgow.

REFERENCES

1. Charles E. Rosenberg, "On writing the history of American science", in Herbert J. Bass (ed.), *The state of American history* (Chicago, 1970), 183–96. I wish to acknowledge my debt to this article which renders explicit much that I had tacitly assumed.
2. Thomas S. Kuhn, *The structure of scientific revolutions* (Chicago, 1962); John Ziman, *Public knowledge* (Cambridge, 1968); Jerome R. Ravetz, *Scientific knowledge and its social problems* (Oxford, 1971).
3. Joseph Ben-David, *The scientist's role in society : a comparative study* (Englewood Cliffs, New Jersey, 1971).
4. N. T. Phillipson and Rosalind Mitchison (eds), *Scotland in the age of improvement* (Edinburgh, 1970) is the best recent survey of eighteenth century Scotland.
5. The enviably impressive range of work being done on American scientific institutions may be gauged from George H. Daniels (ed.), *Nineteenth-century American science : a reappraisal* (Evanston, 1972).
6. Richard Olson, "Scottish philosophy and mathematics: 1750–1830", *Journal of the history of ideas,* xxxii (1971), 29–44; George Elder Davie, *The democratic intellect : Scotland and her universities in the nineteenth century* (Edinburgh, 1964); G. N. Cantor, "Henry Brougham and the Scottish methodological tradition", *Studies in the history and philosophy of science,* ii (1971), 69–89; P. M. Heimann and J. E. McGuire, "Newtonian forces and Lockean powers: concepts of matter in eighteenth-century thought", *Historical studies in the physical sciences,* iii (1971), 233–306; Patsy A. Gerstner, "The reaction to James Hutton's use of heat as a geological agent", *The British journal for the history of science,* v (1971), 353–62; Gordon L. Davies, *The earth in decay : a history of British geomorphology 1578–1878* (London, 1969).
7. A useful demonstration is provided by Charles E. Rosenberg, "Factors in the development of genetics in the United States", *Journal of the history of medicine,* xxii (1967), 27–46.
8. Russell McCormmach, "Editor's Foreword", *Historical studies in the physical sciences,* iii (1971), ix–xxiv, p. ix.

9. Cargill Gilston Knott, *Life and scientific work of Peter Guthrie Tait* (Cambridge, 1911), 64–97 and 248.
10. J. B. Morrell, "Practical chemistry in the University of Edinburgh, 1799–1843", *Ambix*, xvi (1969), 66–80.
11. J. B. Morrell, "Thomas Thomson: professor of chemistry and university reformer", *The British journal for the history of science*, iv (1969), 245–65.
12. Roy Porter, "The industrial revolution and the rise of the science of geology" in M. Teich and R. M. Young (eds), *Changing perspectives in the history of science* (London, 1973), 320–43, p. 342.
13. Alexander Grant, *The story of the University of Edinburgh during its first three hundred years* (London, 1884), i, 147–8 and 259–63.
14. Grant, *University of Edinburgh*, 216.
15. Reported in Senate Minutes, 25 June 1833 and 30 April 1833.
16. Alexander Bower, *The history of the University of Edinburgh* (Edinburgh, 1817), ii, 223.
17. Peter John Anderson (ed.), *Fasti Academiae Mariscallanae Aberdonensis: selections from the records of the Marischal College and University MDXCII-MDCCCLX* (Aberdeen, 1889), 147–8.
18. "An account of the life and writings of the author" in Colin MacLaurin, *An account of Sir Isaac Newton's philosophical discoveries* (London, 1748), i–xx, pp. iv–v, xiii.
19. R. Steven Turner, "The growth of professorial research in Prussia, 1818 to 1848—causes and context", *Historical studies in the physical sciences*, iii (1971), 137–82, p. 157. In 1722 Monro *primus* became the first Edinburgh professor who gained tenure *ad vitam aut culpam*. Quite characteristically the Town Council rewarded his diligence and assiduity as a teacher: Bower, *University of Edinburgh*, ii, 182.
20. Roger Hahn, *The anatomy of a scientific institution: the Paris Academy of Sciences, 1666–1803* (Berkeley, 1971) uses a functional approach in which his theme of the double loyalty of the academicians to science and to the state allows him to give due consideration to conflicts and ideologies.
21. J. E. McGuire, "Newton and the demonic furies: some current problems and approaches in history of science", *History of science*, xi (1973), 21–48, pp. 23–27.
22. Steven Shapin and Arnold Thackray, "Prosopography as a research tool in the history of science: the British scientific community, 1700–1900", *History of science*, xii (1974), 1–28; Arnold Thackray, "Natural knowledge in cultural context: the Manchester model", *American historical review*, lxxix (1974), 672–709.
23. Steven Shapin, "Property, patronage and the politics of science: the founding of the Royal Society of Edinburgh", *The British journal for the history of science*, vii (1974), 1–41.
24. J. B. Morrell, "The chemist breeders: the research schools of Liebig and Thomas Thomson", *Ambix*, xix (1972), 1–46.
25. J. B. Morrell, "The patronage of mid-Victorian science in the University of Edinburgh", *Science studies*, iii (1973), 353–88. Playfair's inability to respond to the German challenge indicates as well as anything else when the Scottish Enlightenment began to fade into the Celtic Twilight.
26. Steven A. Shapin, *The Royal Society of Edinburgh: A study of the social context of Hanoverian science* (unpublished Ph.D. thesis, University of Pennsylvania, 1971).
27. T. C. Smout, *A history of the Scottish people 1560–1830* (London, 1969), 379–90.

28. Andrew Fergus, "Sketch of the early years of the Society", *Proceedings of the Philosophical Society of Glasgow,* xiii (1882), 1–20, p. 2.
29. This apt comparison is made by Andrew Kent, "The Royal Philosophical Society of Glasgow", *The philosophical journal,* iv (1967), 43–50, p. 44. Dr Kent was the first to stress the near-extinction of the Society in 1833 and its revival the next year.
30. The minute of the agreement made on 27 February 1832 between a committee of the Managers of Anderson's University and the Society gives a list of the fortyseven registered members of the Society, and is contained in the Society Minute Book, vol. i. My account of the Society draws on this Minute Book and on Dr Kent's article.
31. The two inactive professors were William Meikleham (professor of natural philosophy at the University of Glasgow, 1803–46) and William Couper (professor of natural history, 1829–57).
32. James Coutts, *A history of the University of Glasgow* (Glasgow, 1909), 545–53 gives a detailed account of this struggle for power.

II

The Edinburgh Town Council and its University, 1717–66

It is a just commonplace that for Scotland the eighteenth century was an age of improvement, when compared with the cultural isolation, the economic deprivation, the political anarchy, and the religious barbarism, which she had endured during the previous century.[1] One of the most conspicuous examples of this improvement was the transformation of the University of Edinburgh. In the seventeenth century it had been merely a local moderately prosperous arts and divinity college; but, by at least the mid-eighteenth century, it had become one of the leading universities of Europe. This was a remarkable metamorphosis, especially so because universities did not generally prosper in the eighteenth century. Recent work on the size of the student body at both Oxford and Cambridge has confirmed that in the 1750s it was slightly less than half its value eighty years earlier; indeed the larger period 1670–1809 seems to have been characterized by low enrolment of students compared with 1620–40.[2] Some Scottish universities fared little better: the fusion in 1747 of the previously separate colleges of St Salvator's and St Leonard's to form the United College confirmed the lamentable financial condition of St Andrews.[3] Further north at Aberdeen, attempts made in the 1750s to unite the two universities there, situated barely a mile from each other, ground to a halt on the question of location; King's and Marischal Colleges 'continued to scratch out a somewhat meagre and cheerless existence' until their union in 1860.[4] In France the universities declined so much that after the Terror they were effectively replaced by *les grandes écoles*. Likewise in Germany, the declining attractions of most of the universities were shown in static expenditure on them by their respective governments, and by falling student enrolment between 1740 and 1800.[5]

Universities such as Edinburgh and Göttingen which prospered during a century of widespread stagnation and decline were clearly uncommon and exceptional. At a time when survival was the aim of many universities, Edinburgh expanded mainly on the basis of its medical school which recruited non-Scottish students as well as native ones. That ability to recruit from south of the border and elsewhere has to be explained, because it was unusual. Recent work has confirmed that up to about 1850 the three medieval Scottish universities (St Andrews f. 1411, Glasgow f. 1451, King's College Aberdeen f. 1494) and the two post-Reformation ones (Edinburgh f. 1582, Marischal College Aberdeen f. 1593) functioned mainly as regional universities which recruited local students for the four faculties of arts, law, theology, and medicine.[6] To that generalization the faculty of medicine at Edinburgh was an outstanding exception. Though it would be foolish to ignore the attendance of English dissenters for a general education at Edinburgh and Glasgow, it seems undeniable that of the twenty university faculties available *in actu* or *in potentia* in eighteenth-century Scotland, Edinburgh's faculty of medicine was unique in the conspicuously 'international' composition of its students. Such success in attracting students did not simply happen and it requires explanation.

Edinburgh was unique among the Scottish universities in that it was municipally supported and controlled: the Town Council founded chairs, appointed men to them, paid salaries to some of them, maintained the University buildings, provided teaching aids, and was generally responsible for the supervision of the University. This was the case from 1582 until 1858 when the Universities (Scotland) Act abolished municipal patronage of the University. Elsewhere in Scotland formal municipal involvement in the universities was slight. The Edinburgh Town Council tended to be a self-perpetuating oligarchy; it was composed of 33 members, mainly merchants and artisans, who represented primarily merchant and trade guild interests. This basic orientation was not disturbed until 1833 when reform of the Scottish burghs took place. It would be wrong, however, to think of the Town Council in the eighteenth century as being necessarily corrupt and limited. It is too easy to extrapolate backwards from Henry Cockburn's vivid vignette of the Town Council in the 1820s: its members, he claimed, were 'omnipotent, corrupt, impenetrable . . . Silent, powerful, submissive, mysterious, and irresponsible, they might have been sitting in Venice'.[7] Though this analysis may be useful for the 1820s, it is entirely inappropriate for the 1720s when the Town Council was anything but submissive and irresponsible in its supervision of the University. Indeed the main thrust of this paper will be to try to explain the relation between two of Edinburgh's unique features, namely, the conspicuous success of the University's medical school from the 1720s, and the municipal patronage of the University. In particular I shall suggest that the Town Council's ambition for its University reached its zenith during the epoch of George Drummond who used his financial acumen and political ability to implement his related visions of a transformed university, of a municipal revival, and of national improvement.

I

In almost a century after its official foundation, the University had enjoyed little growth in its teaching staff. In 1674, for instance, it mustered a Principal who was nominally professor of theology, a professor of divinity, a professor of hebrew, and James Gregory who in that year had been appointed as the first substantive professor of mathematics; the brunt of the teaching, however, was carried by five regents who covered various branches of philosophy and humanity (latin). The dominance of arts and theology was not surprising, nor was the total absence of medicine. At this time Edinburgh functioned as a local college, teaching arts and divinity, which were not the fields in which the University gained its greatest reputation during the eighteenth century. Somehow, therefore, between the 1670s and 1726, the local college was transformed into an international university; and concomitantly, medicine displaced arts/theology as the University's leading pedagogic sector. This double modification took half a century to achieve, and for that reason alone cannot be seen as being sustained and continuous. Rather it was slow, intermittent, and discontinuous. Indeed, as I shall claim, by 1719 medicine at Edinburgh was foundering badly and apparently due to expire. Nevertheless from 1676 onwards, the University was being changed in ways that were immediately or subsequently connected with the teaching of medicine. These changes may be considered quite arbitrarily under three heads or phases.[8]

The first phase was initiated by leading Fellows of the Royal College of Physicians of Edinburgh, especially Robert Sibbald. Firstly, in 1670, Sibbald and Andrew Balfour engineered the appointment of James Sutherland as Keeper of the Holyrood Garden. By 1675, they persuaded the Town Council to grant a lease to Sutherland of the Trinity Hospital Garden. Next year the Town Council appointed him to teach botany in the Town's College at a salary of £20 per annum. The Council intended Sutherland's teaching to be concerned with 'that most necessary though hitherto much neglected part of the naturall historie and knowledge wherein the health of all persones whether it be for food or medecine is so nearlie concerned'.[9] Whether he taught is doubtful, and this very uncertainty reveals that at this period the Town Council did not always insist on its decisions *á propos* the College being implemented. In the next decade, Sibbald's second innovation was to gain for the Royal College of Physicians of Edinburgh in 1681 a charter in which after long negotiation, and no doubt horse-trading, it was agreed that the College of Physicians should have no power to erect a medical school or to confer degrees. Irrespective of the reasons for this agreement, it did confirm the allocation of licensing and teaching functions to the College of Physicians and to the University respectively. Sibbald's third contribution was to have himself appointed in 1685 by the Town Council as one of three joint professors of medicine, in harness with Archibald Pitcairne and James Halket. These leading Fellows of the College of Physicians were granted no salaries and their duties remain unspecified. Not surprisingly these three chairs were titular; and, in any case, Sibbald's religious difficulties, the 1688 revolution, and the purging in 1690 of catholics and episcopalians, hardly furthered the cause of medical teaching in the University. In sum, the 'Sibbald' phase did not succeed in establishing regular medical teaching, yet in principle the university was free from 1681 to develop medical teaching without arousing overt hostility from the College of Physicians. A similar sort of ambiguity was shown by the Town Council which recognised the need for medical teaching, yet lacked any consistent attitude to specialisation in that intended teaching.

The second phase in the transformation of the University was initiated by the College of Surgeons in Edinburgh. Revived by its new royal charter granted in 1697, the College of Surgeons took up the running after the 'Sibbald' phase had proved largely abortive. The Surgeons at this time seem to have had close formal connections with the Town Council not only through their Deacon (President) being a member of the Town Council but also through their joint interest in the supply of bodies for dissection. In 1705 the College of Surgeons took the iniative of appointing Robert Eliot, one of its Fellows, as public dissector in anatomy to ensure that regular teaching took place. Eliot then petitioned the Town Council to support his expensive venture, to which the Town Council responded by appointing him in 1705 as professor of anatomy at a salary of £15 per year.[10] For the next fifteen years, Eliot and his two successors gave public dissections intermittently, not however in the University but in the Surgeons' Hall. Eliot's appointment signified that the Town Council saw the importance of teaching a medical speciality, especially at a time of extended warfare, and resented the needless expense incurred by students who studied abroad.

From 1703 to 1715 the Reverend William Carstares was Principal of the University. A very experienced and powerful politician, Carstares while Principal adeptly manipulated both the Edinburgh Town Council and the General Assembly of the Church of Scotland. Though undoubtedly 'one of the most consummate politicians of modern Europe', Carstares was deeply concerned about the Scottish universities whose teaching of potential clerics was in his view not up to par.[11] Having himself been a student at Utrecht, from the 1680s he nourished the vision of improving the standard of divinity teaching by either importing Dutch professors or by modelling the teaching on Dutch lines.[12] When he become Principal, he attempted to implement this vision and was thereby largely responsible for the third phase of the University's transformation. At the time of the Union with England in 1707, Carstares tried to make Edinburgh the mecca and the metropolis of English dissent by negotiating with Calamy and others to bring English nonconformists to the University of Edinburgh where they would live in a collegiate hall. Ultimately, though a good subscription was raised, the English dissenters dropped the scheme and Carstares died. Yet that failed scheme shows that Carstares was very conscious of student enrolment: he saw that there was a potential market of English dissenters to be exploited; and that through them Edinburgh could be more than a merely local college. More basically Carstares worked hard, in appropriate quarters, to convince parents that the University could offer more than a family tutor or a private school. He realized perceptively that because parents had chosen the close supervision and pastoral care offered by domestic tuition and by private academies, 'universities have fallen into decay, the improvement of youth is greatly obstructed, and the general state of learning visibly threatened'.[13]

Perhaps Carstares' major attempt to improve the general state of learning was his engineering in 1708 of the abolition of regenting in arts subjects. This meant that specialist professors replaced the transient young regents, destined for a church living, who previously had carried their particular class through all the subjects of the arts curriculum: chairs were instituted in humanity, greek, logic, natural philosophy, and moral philosophy, on the model of the Universities of Utrecht and Leiden. This change was effected primarily to produce better education of prospective clergymen for the presbyterian Church of Scotland, but the consequences were considerable. Of these the chief was to ensure that the creation of the medical faculty would be accomplished via the differentiation of pedagogic areas which established specialised teaching provinces taught by professors who could move during their careers from one area to another.[14] This was patently shown in 1713 when the Town Council appointed James Crawford to the new chair of medicine and chemistry. His election and the chair were almost certainly arranged by Carstares who saw in Crawford, a pupil of Boerhaave (MD Leiden 1707), the next best thing to a Dutchman. In this instance the Town Council gave the impression that the initiative came from Crawford probably because it wished to justify its parsimony in paying no salary to him. As with the chair of anatomy, the proferred reason for Crawford's appointment was the expense and inconvenience of students going abroad to study medicine. His tenure was not an unqualified success; he seems to have lectured intermittently; in any event, he probably resigned his chair in 1719 when he was elected professor of hebrew. Crawford's career shows that in the 1710s the creation of a specialised chair within medicine did not automatically create a new race of active professors committed for years to a given speciality. Nevertheless Carstares did succeed in consolidating the professorial system as the basis for the University's future expansion; and he canvassed the possibility of recruiting large numbers of students from England and Ireland. Though Carstares perhaps hoped that Crawford would be Edinburgh's answer to Leiden's Boerhaave, such was patently not the case: Crawford's chemical career simply evanesced.

By 1719, after some 45 years in which various attempts to establish medical teaching had been made, what was the position? The professor of botany, by that time George Preston, was chiefly Keeper of the Trinity Hospital Garden where he did no more than regularly exhibit plants. Of the three professors of medicine appointed in 1685, Halket and Pitcairne were dead and their chairs had not been continued; Sibbald, the only survivor, enjoyed a merely titular chair. In chemistry there had been only sporadic teaching from 1713 by Crawford who in 1719 transferred to a non-medical chair. Anatomy, however, was periodically taught by two joint professors of anatomy, Adam Drummond and John McGill, who did not between them perform every session. Their anatomical dissections constituted the solitary example of moderately sustained medical teaching associated loosely with the University. As they taught in the Surgeons' anatomy theatre, not even one medical lecture, let alone course, was delivered it seems within the University walls during session 1719–20. The attempts to establish university medical teaching seemed to have failed dismally after 45 years of sporadic endeavour. This desperate situation called for an original and drastic answer to this lacuna in the University's teaching.

II

The solution was provided, as we all know, by John Monro (1670–1740) who had attended Leiden 1692–94 and eventually settled in 1700 as an apothecary-surgeon in Edinburgh. As a former Deacon of the Surgeons and *ex officio* a member of the Town Council, by the late 1710s he had developed sufficient connection with the Council to realise his aim of having in Edinburgh a medical school like that of Leiden. With outrageous optimism and bizarre paternity, he dedicated his only son Alexander to the project and educated him accordingly at Edinburgh, London, Paris, and Leiden. Early in 1720 he used his power in the College of Surgeons to force the two demonstrators in anatomy to resign in favour of his son who was appointed by the Town Council as professor of anatomy on 29 January 1720. In the summer of that year the Monros took good care to secure public approval of Monro *primus*' imminent venture by courting the Colleges of Physicians and of Surgeons and the Town Council. These representations made to the Council on Monro *primus*' behalf revealed the three chief arguments in favour of the Monros' scheme: cheaper anatomy teaching than before for Scots; 'bring straingers to this Citie from other pairts for their improvement'; and increasing 'the honour and advantage of this Citie'.[15] In October 1720 Monro *primus* began teaching in the Surgeons' Hall, attracting 57 students, and henceforth he taught regularly and in the vernacular. Monro *primus*' second session, 1721–1722, was even more successful: of his 68 students, some had travelled from England and Ireland. Encouraged by his success in acting as a medical magnet, Monro *primus* petitioned the Town Council in March 1722 to give him life tenure if it wished to consolidate his pioneering attempt to establish a famous school of anatomy as the basis of 'a compleat Systeme of Medicine'. The Town Council responded by departing from its former custom of appointing professors at its pleasure because of Monro *primus*' success and promise. In so doing it inaugurated at Edinburgh the system of life-tenure which increased the quality of applicants for chairs, and discouraged neglect of professorial duty; above all, it gave security, independence, and respectability to professors. The fact that Monro *primus* was the first beneficiary of this system shows that by 1722 the Town Council was seriously committed to establishing medicine in the University for the 'advantage and honour of this Citie', though at this time Monro *primus* was still teaching in the Surgeons' Hall.[16]

The final establishment of the medical faculty in 1726 was based on a fortunate accident which occurred in 1725. Following alleged grave robbing for dissection purposes, there was public rioting which made Monro *primus* feel unsafe while lecturing in the Surgeons' Hall. He therefore persuaded the Town Council to transfer the location of his teaching to the safer precincts of the University where an anatomical theatre of sorts was made for him. In November 1725, therefore, serious medical teaching within the University walls was at last begun. Monro's departure from the Surgeons' Hall left a gap which William Graeme and George Martine filled in late 1725 when they begall to teach medicine there. Their rivals were John Rutherford, Andrew St Clair, Andrew Plummer and John Innes, who had begun teaching medicine and pharmacy in February 1725 in the previously neglected University garden. Clearly these four men wished to join Monro *primus* in the University because they petitioned the Town Council on the basis that they had already proved their success as medical teachers. The Town Council, ignoring the existence of the sinecurist William Porterfield whom it had appointed as professor of medicine in 1724 without life-tenure, appointed them professors of medicine *ad vitam aut culpam* and, as expected, without salary. Clearly the Town Council aimed to esablish a group of 'able professors', sufficiently large to cover the important branches of medicine and to conduct students to graduation. The Town Council minute of 9 February 1726 was quite explicit about these aims:

> it would be of great advantage to this Colledge, city, and country that Medicine in *all its branches* be taught and professed here by *such a number* of Professors of that science as may *by themselves* promote students to their Degrees with as great solemnity as is done in any other Colledge or University at home or abroad.[17]

By 1726 then, the University housed five medical professors all of whom had been students of Boerhaave at Leiden. As Christie has rightly stressed, the minor and occasional teaching functions of the Colleges of Physicians and of Surgeons had been hived off to the University which in the future was to be the main locus of medical teaching, leaving the Colleges to their primary business of protecting the rights of their Fellows and trying to control practice.[18]

The model used in Edinburgh to establish a complete and regular system of medical education was that of Leiden. Such a statement is old-hat, but it is worth making because in at least six ways Edinburgh was indebted to Leiden.[19] Firstly Leiden provided a model of lay control and innovation through its Board of Curators who from time to time imposed its policy on the professoriate as when Boerhaave himself was appointed professor of botany in 1709. Only Edinburgh of the five Scottish universities was in a position to copy this pattern of lay and municipal involvement and innovation. Secondly, Boerhaave had demonstrated the catalytic effect one man could have in a medical faculty; indeed, as a medical polymath covering botany, chemistry, physiology, pathology, pharmacy, and clinical medicine, Boerhaave was almost a medical faculty in himself. This practice of building a medical faculty around one key man was copied at Edinburgh, Monro *primus* being the lynch-pin figure; but, sensing the precariousness of laying so much responsibility on one man, the Edinburgh plan was to build a strong teaching faculty around Monro, supporting and complementing his work. Thirdly, after a period of relative stagnation in the 1690s, Leiden in the early eighteenth century began to attract more foreign medical students of varying religious persuasions, without the town having any metropolitan advantages. As one of Europe's largest cities, Edinburgh had advantages in attracting non-Scottish students which were denied to Leiden. Fourthly, as the promoter of students to their medical degrees at Leiden, compared with the other professors, Boerhaave provided a model of medical graduation. Fifthly, through his text-books and his students, Boerhaave had shown how a reputation as a medical educator could be fostered; one suspects this example was not lost on Monro *primus* who by 1726 had published his osteological textbook on *The Anatomy of the Humane Bones*. Sixthly, Boerhaave provided a model curriculum in his insistence on medical sciences being taught first, followed by clinical teaching essentially Hippocratic in approach. In all these ways Edinburgh was indebted to Boerhaave and to Leiden, yet the timing of the indebtedness was extraordinary: only Edinburgh successfully imitated the Dutch model during Boerhaave's own life-time. Other medical schools derived from Leiden, such as Göttingen under Haller and Vienna under van Swieten, flourished only after Boerhaave's death in 1738. Edinburgh was peculiarly speedy in perceiving Leiden as a useful model. The rapid implementation in the 1720s of John Monro's vision, and of the ambitions of his son, indicates that in this decade peculiarly effective motives came into play in Edinburgh.

III

The formal agent which established the medical faculty in 1726 was the Town Council in which the leading figure at that time was George Drummond (1687–1766) a close friend of the Monro family. He first appeared on the Town Council in 1717 as Treasurer, and between 1725 and 1764 was Lord Provost no less than six times.[20] From 1717 until his death, Drummond was Edinburgh's outstanding politician; and, with extraordinary tactical skill, he usually worked in harmony with the various political managers of Scotland. It is significant that so many of the outstanding changes in the University, such as the founding of the medical faculty and many remarkable appointments to chairs, took place while he was Provost. Drummond represented therefore the zenith of the Town Council's ambition for its University; Bower recognized this by describing Drummond as 'the greatest benefactor which the University ever had'.

When he first rose to power in Edinburgh in the late 1710s, Edinburgh was in a depressed economic condition. Like Scotland as a whole, Edinburgh then lacked the means to exploit the potential economic opportunities provided by the incorporating Union of 1707. By the late 1710s Edinburgh Town Council was economically in a desperate situation; it was burdened with mounting debts and the indigent, while its revenue was shrinking. No longer the capital of a Kingdom, stripped of the Scottish Parliament, of the Privy Council, and of the Treasury, Edinburgh had suffered a decline in fashionability and trade as the merchant and trade guilds noted frequently and sadly.[22] The greater nobility and gentry were disappearing from Edinburgh so that the lodglngs once filled with people of quality were left empty: apparently many decayed for lack of tenants, and some fell almost into ruin. In short, by the late 1710s, the town was deprived of national dignity, its municipal pride was hurt, and its Council faced mounting debt. How did Drummond react to this depressing state of affairs? He simply refused to accept that Edinburgh, a major European city with a population of about 30,000, was a fading superceded capital. His life's work was indeed to revive national dignity, to develop municipal pride, and to encourage trade and manufacture throughout Scotland. Accordingly he had a finger in many pies: a director of the British Linen Bank and the Royal Bank of Scotland; a Commissioner for improving fisheries and manufactures in Scotland; a grand master of the Scottish freemasons; a trustee of the forfeited estates; a manager of the Edinburgh Society for the Encouragement of the Arts, Sciences, Manufactures, and Agriculture; a member of the Edinburgh Literary Society; deputy governor of the Music Society; a representative of the annual convention of Scottish royal boroughs; and, not least, the Edinburgh Town Council. Such comprehensive involvement in Scottish affairs shows that Drummond was more than an expert accountant and man of business. Using his extraordinary skills of political prestidigitation, Drummond implemented his vision of a splendid and magnificent city to replace the ruinous and neglected buildings endemic in the 1710s. By concerning himself with buildings, he changed the face of the Scottish metropolis: he was primarily responsible for the new Infirmary opened in 1741, the Royal Exchange, and of course for the expansion of Edinburgh northwards. With symbolic justice one of his last public acts was to lay the foundation stone of the North Bridge in 1763.[23]

Drummond's interest in the University was, therefore, an important aspect of his larger concern for Edinburgh's prosperity and dignity. Negatively, Drummond with others resented the expense of having students trained abroad in law and medicine. Positively, however, Drummond hoped to bring cultural renown and financial gain to Edinburgh by attracting students to it not only from Scotland but also from England, Ireland, and the colonies. Accommodation was no problem because lodgings were conspicuously vacant in the late 1710s, but that of attracting students at all remained unsolved: Drummond presumably realised in 1719 that medical teaching in the University was non existent. It was, however, in this year that Monro primus returned from his medical training on the continent. Perhaps his tributes to Boerhaave's success at Leiden, especially in attracting the English, convinced Drummond that John Monro's plan for an Edinburgh competitor to Leiden's medical school was not a pipe-dream. Perhaps, too, Monro *primus*' success in his first two sessions of teaching demonstrated to Drummond that he was Edinburgh's answer to Boerhaave; hence Drummond was prepared to grant life-tenure to Monro *primus* to encourage him and to see whether he would continue to attract non-Scottish students. Drummond was always a keen Hanoverian, and supporter of a united Britain. As an astute accountant, professionally concerned with excise matters, perhaps Drummond realised that medical students could be imported, processed, and then exported like other economic commodities. Drummond always gave his best attention to the medical faculty of the University, as his interests in the new Infirmary and the clinical teaching there abundantly confirm. Edinburgh-trained medical students were potentially exportable in large numbers, theologians less so, and lawyers hardly at all, owing to the distinctness of Scotland's ecclesiastical and legal systems. The Drummond-Monros axis had therefore a different plan from Carstares: all worked on the Dutch model, Carstares being primarily concerned with producing clergymen from Scottish students and English dissenters; but Drummond and the Monros were intent on importing any student irrespective of his religion and provenance, processing him in Edinburgh by teaching him medicine, and exporting him as an advert for the medical school.

Drummond's political career in Edinburgh fell into two well defined phases. First, between autumn 1717 and autumn 1727, he held office for a total of seven years as Treasurer (2 years), Second Bailie (1 year), Dean of Guild (2 years), and Lord Provost (2 years). At that time, Drummond supported the medical school as an experimental venture which would not necessarily be successful. Second, between autumn 1746 and autumn 1764, Drummond was Lord Provost every alternate pair of years for a total of 10 years; and, when formally out of office, clearly he remained the *eminence grise* of the Town Council. In this second phase of his career, Drummond had to replace the founding medical professors of the 1720s who grew old together; but by the 1750s the medical school, in Drummond's opinion, was a proved success, and demonstrably, 'an immense benefit to the community'.[24]

It has often been noted that when Drummond held office the Town Council made many of its most famous appointments to chairs. I think it is a reasonable hypothesis to suggest that there was a Drummond policy for appointing to chairs, one which was adopted tentatively in the 1720s, and firmly between 1746 and 1764. A complete list of appointments made during Drummond's periods of office is given in Appendix A. It excludes distinguished appointments, such as that of William Robertson as Principal in 1762, in which Drummond probably had a strong say.[25] Irrespective of who pulled the patronage strings and for what reasons, two categories of professor seem to have been appointed especially to medical chairs under Drummond's aegis.

The first and more prevalent category was that of the proved teacher. In 1726 the medical faculty had been established by conferring the title of professor on four physicians who were already teaching successfully in Edinburgh. The Town Council minute was quite explicit that Rutherford, St Clair, Plummer, and Innes:

> have given the clearest proof of their capacity and ability to reach the above valuable ends and purposes, they having already professed and taught Medicine with good success and advantage and with the approbation of all the learned in that science here . . . .[26]

Subsequently the Town Council continued this policy by appointing such proved teachers as Robert Whytt, Monro *secundus*, and Hugh Blair; it also expanded this notion of appointing proved local teachers to that of attracting professors of known teaching ability from other Scottish universities. The appointment in 1755 of William Cullen to the chair of chemistry inaugurated the brain-drain of professors from Glasgow and Aberdeen to Edinburgh. When Drummond told Cullen that it was the Town Council's responsibility to fill chairs 'with professors of established reputation', he probably had Cullen's teaching record at Glasgow primarily in mind.[27]

The second category was of proved specialist scholars, preferably of international reputation, who were appointed to bring renown to the University through their specialised published research. Though this type of appointment became more prevalent in the 1760s, it was first explicitly made in the case of Colin MacLaurin. As the Town Council minute has it:

> It was impossible for us to hope for any opportunity of doing a thing more honourable and advantageous for the city that could contribute more to the reputation of the university and advance the interest of learning in this country, than the giving Mr MacLaurin suitable encouragement to settle among us.[28]

MacLaurin was certainly not appointed because of his demonstrated diligence, assiduity, and dependability as a teacher. As professor of mathematics at Marischal College, Aberdeen, he had been absent without leave for two and a half years as a private tutor. This apparently damning feature in MacLaurin's curriculum vitae was ignored by the Town Council which wanted to use him as a national and municipal showpiece via his specialist research.[29]

Granted these were the two chief categories of well-known appointments to chairs, fiendishly complex patronage had to be employed to gain the desired result. Much remains to be discovered about the patronage of eighteenth-century Scottish universities in that though its main lines are clear the supporting detailed and direct documentary evidence is hard to obtain. Even the sequence of letters from Drummond to Lord Milton, covering fifteen years, contains only one item directly concerned with university patronage, namely, the election of Ferguson to the chair of natural philosophy in 1759; but it is a gem. Drummond's aim was to improve the teaching of philosophy in the University. An opportunity presented itself in 1759 when through the death of John Stewart the chair of natural philosophy fell vacant, the chair of moral philosophy being held by the relatively incompetent James Balfour. Two close friends were waiting in the wings for a chair: James Russell for natural philosophy; and Adam Ferguson for moral philosophy. The obvious answer ('the double scheme') was to elect Russell to the natural philosophy chair for which he was appropriate; and to buy out Balfour, or force him to resign, when Ferguson would be elected in his stead. But Drummond, acting in harmony with Lord Milton, ordered things differently: Ferguson, ultimately destined for the moral philosophy chair, was appointed to that of natural philosophy in order to get him into the professoriate. Drummond regaled Lord Milton with the details of the negotiations as follows:

> On Friday Alston [William] brought me your letter . . . which, speaking honestly, is a masterpiece. You know I devote Saturday and Monday to our freinds of the town to strengthen our harmony in the Councill. On the

> Saturday I mix some other folks with them. This Saturday I had 9 of the Councill some of whom I had talk't to separately. I found an opportunity to read your letter to them in a body and explained the several paragraphs thereof. Russell has the caracter of being the best natural philosopher in the country and, to do him justice, his succeeding Stewart in that profession would raise the reputation of our University. This made several of our freinds point at delaying the naming Fergusone for some time, in order to bring about the double scheme, being informed that Mr Balfour was to come to me with proposals. But a very little reasoning convinced them that the way to do good to the Colledge and to get Russell was, in the first place, to possess ourselves of Ferguson with unanimity and dispatch. Yesterday we were 17 here who all of them heartily agreed in this measure, so tomorrow I am to move the Council to call our clergy together for their avisamentum on Friday next, and the Wensday following we will elect Fergusone unanimously by the merchants, and I imagine even by the trades too.[30]

The election of Ferguson went according to plan because of the meticulous 'fixing' done by Drummond not only for his personal advantage but also for the good of the University. Whether Balfour came in 1759 with proposals, presumably to resign, is not known; but in 1764 a dexterous game of professorial chairs took place under the connivance of the Lord Advocate and the Town Council. As Hugh Blair told David Hume:

> In our College we are making a great improvement. In consequence of a bargain made with James Russell, Bruce, the Professor of the Law of Nature and Nations, goes out, Balfour of Pilrig moves into his place, Ferguson into the Chair of Moral Philosophy, and Russell into that of Natural. Is not this clever?[31]

The point of this deft arrangement was that the well-endowed chair of law was a sinecure which had been bought and sold. The Town Council and Drummond were presumably prepared to permit this chair of law to remain a sinecure because it functioned as a convenient dust-bin to accommodate an inefficient man, thus permitting Ferguson to move sideways into the moral philosophy chair and Russell to gain at last the natural philosophy one. Though Milton was clearly at work in the 1759 election, it remains true, as the 1759 and 1764 elections confirm, that the Town Council, especially under 'Doge' Drummond, was concerned with the reputation of its university; and had a scale of priorities which involved a golden-handshake to an incompetent man. In an age dominated by wheeling-and-dealing and the making of 'interest', Drummond used his undoubted abilities in these fields to serve his vision of a glorious city and university. In short, as part of a programme of municipal improvement, the University was necessarily subject to lay evaluation and innovation: it thereby escaped from the worst features which characterised closed academic corporations in the eighteenth century.

It is in this respect that Edinburgh differed so conspicuously from the other Scottish universities and from Oxford and Cambridge, especially with regard to medical education. Glasgow, potentially a rival, did not become so until the nineteenth century: in the eighteenth century Glasgow was primarily an arts and divinity college of the type Edinburgh had been late in the previous century. There was at Glasgow no formal lay patronage, nobody analogous to Drummond, to impress change on the University and to induce co-operation from the surgeons and physicians. The vision of a Glasgow medical school had to come from the academic staff: it appeared first through Cullen when he was appointed lecturer in chemistry at Glasgow in 1747, the year in which Whytt's appointment inaugurated the second generation of Edinburgh's medical professoriate. By 1800, the Glasgow medical professoriate numbered only two men aided by three untenured lecturers; and clinical facilities became available only in 1794, some fifty years after Edinburgh.[32] Until the nineteenth century, the University of Glasgow lacked two key components of the Monros-Drummond programme, namely, a sufficient number of tenured medical professors, and clinical teaching. The situations at Aberdeen and St Andrews offered not even a toehold for such a programme: at these three impoverished local universities, with small student enrolments, survival and not expansion was the chief aim. Oxford and Cambridge enjoyed enormous aggregate wealth compared with all the Scottish universities and, of course, in principle taught medicine. Their course involved a far longer period of residential study, making Edinburgh much cheaper. No clinical teaching existed in the eighteenth century, and the lecturing was irregular. An ironic contrast was provided by anatomy teaching at Edinburgh and Cambridge in 1728. Monro *primus*, whose assiduity had been rewarded by the Town Council, attracted 70 students including foreigners in session 1728–29, and by 1732–33 had topped a hundred for the first time: that great anatomical oracle was well launched by 1728. In Cambridge, however, George Rolfe, the first professor of anatomy, was deprived of his office in 1728 for continued absence.[33]

At its best the relation between town and gown was symbiotic. That was well shown by the way in which Drummond and Monro *primus* were the twin motors of the successful movement to build the new Infirmary opened in 1741. In the case of Monro *secundus* and Drummond it was palpably displayed in the negotiations which led to the building of the new anatomy lecture-theatre in 1764.[34] In September 1758 Monro *primus* and *secundus*, keen to improve the anatomy theatre, petitioned the Town Council which remitted the matter to its College Committee. The desired changes were probably not made. In February 1764, probably in collusion with Drummond, Monro *secundus* brought a second attempt to a climax with a long petition submitted on 18 June to the Town Council. It is reproduced in Appendix B. In it Monro secundus drew attention first to the difficulties produced by his present small lecture theatre: his excessive lecturing load of 15 hours a week, his consequent lack of time for research, and the pedagogic inadequacies caused by bad lighting. He then adumbrated the advantages to be enjoyed from a new lecture theatre, but he was careful to buttress these claims with arguments likely to carry weight with the Town Council. He put the economic argument quantitatively by stressing that since 1725 the town had received from anatomy students at least £300,000. He also put the competition argument, emphasising that in particular Edinburgh's provision for anatomy teaching had fallen behind that of other universities and that in general the professors needed the assistance of the Council to preserve the University's reputation. Moreover, Monro *secundus* was so determined to sharpen his competitive edge and to increase his class fees that he dangled two irresistible pieces of bait before the Town Council. Firstly he offered to lend the Council a maximum of £300 to pay for the new theatre; and secondly, he undertook to bequeath to the university for the use of his successors the anatomical collection worth almost £1,000 built up over many years by his father and himself. The Town Council had also received a petition from Russell for better accommodation for the natural philosophy class, but preference was given to Monro *secundus*' claims: Monro *primus*, Robertson, and Drummond gave their crucial support for a new anatomy theatre on the grounds of the central importance of anatomy to the reputation of the University, especially with respect to recruitment of students. The prescience of their preference in 1764 for anatomy was, of course, subsequently confirmed by the increasing size of the anatomy class which reached its peak of 436 students in 1783. It must be stressed that the Town Council acted not only shrewdly but generously in 1764. It accepted Monro's loan of £300 on the condition that if the cost of the new theatre were eventually to exceed £300, the excess would be met by him. In the event the total cost was £389, the whole of which was refunded by the Town Council to Monro *secundus*.

IV

This whole episode encapsulated the central theme of this paper. Monro *secundus* and Russell were compelled to state publicly their aims for their respective subjects, and to justify their cases; Robertson, aided by four medical professors, acted as a referee, an academic court of appeal, with respect to these two competing petitions; and the Town Council, advised by the academics and by its specialist College Committee, was forced to decide its priorities for its University in choosing one of them and postponing the other. All this has a modern bureaucratic ring about it; certainly it was very different from the usual small change of the academic politics and preferment so prevalent in the eighteenth century. Under the Edinburgh arrangements both gown and town were kept alert to their responsibilities. On the gown side, the medical professors were paid either a low salary or none at all.[35] Most of their emolument came from the fees paid to them by members of their class. Professors were encouraged by this system of remuneration to increase the size of their class by developing teaching aids and to transfer to larger classes. If the second possibility was not feasible, then professors were induced to exert themselves to keep themselves in flourishing business as teachers. This testing system did not go un-noticed at Leiden. Oliver Goldsmith, who studied at both Edinburgh and Leiden, recorded in the late 1750s:

> Happening once in conversation with Gaubius [Boerhaave's successor as professor of chemistry] of Leyden, to mention the college of Edinburgh, he began by complaining, that all the English students, which formerly came to his university, now went entirely there; and the fact surprised him more, as Leyden was now as well as ever furnished with masters excellent in their respective professions. He concluded by asking, if the professors of Edinburgh were rich. I reply'd, that the salary of a professor there seldom amounted to more than thirty pounds a year. Poor men, says he, I heartily wish they were better provided for, until they become rich, we can have no expectation of English students at Leyden.[36]

No wonder that ambitious Edinburgh professors pestered the Town Council for better classrooms and equipment, a form of lobbying which during Drummond's reign reached its apogee with Monro *secundus*' petition of 1764.

On the town side, the Council subjected to lay evaluation the proposals emanating from the University and from ambitious individuals. Under Drummond it seems to have judged them according to the extent to which they were likely to contribute to the benefit of the good town and the advantage of the University. This policy was first operated with respect to medicine in the 1720s when the Drummond-Monros programme was tentatively implemented with the aim of helping to revive the town by establishing proper medical teaching in the University. From then onwards the medical faculty was carefully nurtured by Drummond as the University's leading sector. In office, he established the medical faculty in the 1720s, and then after the '45 he renewed it. Out of formal office, he expended his best efforts on the building of the new Infirmary in order to strengthen the University's medical teaching. We see more than vestiges of an appointments policy, tentatively pursued in the 1720s and firmly implemented after 1746. With some other universities at this period it would be ridiculous to talk of an appointments policy developed for the reputation of the university: mere patronage, based exclusively on 'kinship and kindness', was the order of the day.

Of course Islay, Bute and Milton on occasion wielded power in elections to Edinburgh chairs. As Somerville recollected:

> I know it to be a fact, that Provost Drummond, the most meritorious benefactor of the community over which he presided, did not find himself at liberty to promise any deferment at the disposal of the Town Council of Edinburgh, without the previous consent of Lord Milton, the delegate and political agent of Archibald, duke of Argyle.

Indeed the election of Cullen, owing to Argyll's crucial support, exemplifies this point. But Somerville also stressed that the Town Council under Drummond was not merely passive but had a policy on academic appointments:

> It was fortunate that, in the enlightened scheme for filling the chairs in the University with the ablest candidates, the Duke of Argyle concurred with Provost Drummond.[37]

At least the existence of such a scheme introduced academic considerations to countervail the mere political jobbing so endemic in most academic corporations during the eighteenth century. It was equally important that an able professor could lobby the Town Council for teaching aids and the like, knowing that under Drummond his petition would be carefully evaluated according to the criteria of the honour and advantage of both gown and town. In short, though it was not an entirely autonomous or unanimous body, the Town Council, composed of merchants and tradesmen not especially knowledgeable about higher education, saved its University from the usual effects of eighteenth-century patronage by adopting policies of appointment and of provision, especially with respect to medical teaching, orchestrated by Drummond as part of his wider programme of restoring 'the guilt of the city absolutely'.[38]

References

For permission to cite and to quote from manuscripts in their care I am grateful to Edinburgh Corporation, the Trustees of the National Library of Scotland, and the University of Edinburgh. For valuable comment I am indebted to Geoffrey Cantor and John Christie.

1. N.T. Phillipson and R. Michison (eds), *Scotland in the Age of Improvement* (Edinburgh, 1970), especially 1–4.
2. L. Stone, 'The Size and Composition of the Oxford Student Body 1580–1909', L. Stone (ed.), *The University in Society* (Princeton, 1975), I, 3–110 especially 37–59.
3. R.G. Cant, *The University of St Andrews: a Short History* (Edinburgh, 1946), 87–88.

4. D.J. Withrington, 'Education and Society in the Eighteenth Century' *op.cit.* (1), 169–199 (189).
5. R.S. Turner, 'University Reformers and Professorial Scholarship in Germany 1760–1806', *op.cit.* (2), II, 495–531, especially 498–500.
6. R.N. Smart, 'Some Observations on the Provinces of the Scottish Universities, 1560–1850', F.W.S. Barrow (ed.), *The Scottish Tradition. Essays in Honour of Ronald Gordon Cant* (Edinburgh, 1974), 91–106.
7. H. Cockburn, *Memorials of His Time, 1779-1830* (Edinburgh and London, 1910), 87
8. My account leans heavily on J.R.R. Christie, 'The Origins and Development of the Scottish Scientific Community, 1680–1760', *Historyof Science* 12 (1974), 122–141; A. Grant, *The Story of the University of Edinburgh* (London, 1884); R.E. Wright-St Clair, *Doctors Monro. A Medical Saga* (London, 1964).
9. Town Council Minute of 5 January 1677 quoted by J.M. Cowan, 'The History of the Royal Botanic Garden, Edinburgh', *Notes from the Royal Botanic Garden, Edinburgh* 19 (1933–38), 1–62 (15).
10. A. Bower, *The History of the University of Edinburgh* (Edinburgh, 1817) II, 161, quoting Town Council Minute of 29 August 1705.
11. Bower, *op. cit.* (10), II, 44.
12. E. Calamy, *An Historical Account of my own Life, with some Reflections on the Times I have lived in* (London, 1829) I, 172.
13. W. Carstares, 'Considerations and proposealls for encouraging of parents in sending their sons to the University of Edinburgh 1709', Edinburgh University Library, La.II.407,f6.
14. This point is rightly stressed by Christie, *op.cit.* (8), 127.
15. Bower, *op.cit.* (10), II, 177, quoting Town Council Minute of 24 August 1720.
16. Ibid. II, 181–182, quoting Town Council Minute of 14 March 1722.
17. Ibid. II, 205–208. This minute of 9 February 1726 was omitted from the minutes of that date, but was inserted in those of 26 August 1747. The italics are mine.
18. Christie, *op. cit.* (8), 130.
19. G.A. Lindeboom, *Hermann Boerhaave: The Man and His Work* (London, 1968) ,360–74.
20. W. Baird, 'George Drummond: an eighteenth century Lord Provost', *The Book of the Old Edinburgh Club* 4 (1911) 1–54, 'Biographical Sketch of the late George Drummond', *The Scots Magazine* 64 (1802), 375–384, 466–470. Drummond occupied the following offices in the Town Council: 1717–19, Treasurer; 1721–22, Second Bailie; 1722–24, Lord Dean of Guild; 1725–27, 1746–48, 1750–52, 1754–56, 1758–60, and 1762–64, Lord Provost.
21. Bower, *op. cit.* (10), II, 185.
22. H Armet (ed.), *Extracts from the Records of the Burgh of Edinburgh, 1701–1718* (Edinburgh, 1967), Introduction.
23. A.J. Youngson, *The Making of Classical Edinburgh 1750–1840* (Edinburgh, 1966), 13–17, 60.
24. J. Thomson, *An Account of the Life, Lectures, and Writings of William Cullen, MD* (Edinburgh and London,1859), I, 95, quoting Drummond to Cullen, 3 February 1756.
25. J.J. Cater, 'The Making of Principal Robertson in 1762: Politics and the University of Edinburgh in the second half of the eighteenth century', *The Scottish Historical Review* 49 (1970), 60–84.
26. Bower, *op.cit.* (10), II, 206, quoting Town Council Minute of 9 February 1726.
27. Thomson, *op. cit.* (24), I, 95.
28. Bower, *op.cit.* (10), II, 223, quoting Town Council Minute of 3 November 1725.
29. J.B. Morrell, 'Reflections on the History of Scottish Science', *History of Science* 12 (1974), 81–94 (85–86).

30. Drummond to Milton, 26 June 1759 [Tuesday], National Library of Scotland, Saltoun papers, SC205, ff 252–53. It was a dilemma that Ferguson, supported by Milton, needed the chair financially far more than Russell but was less qualified for it. See Hume to Robertson, 29 May 1759, in R. Klibansky and E.C. Mossner (eds), *New Letters of David Hume* (Oxford,1954), 55–58.
31. Grant, *op.cit.* (8), II, 315; and Klibansky, *op. cit.* (30) 56 (footnote 2). See also Ferguson to Drummond, 18 May 1764, City of Edinburgh District Council Archives, Bundle 11, Shelf 36, Bay C, which begins: 'Being informed of an intention to appoint me Professor of Moral Philosophy in the place of Mr Balfour who has resigned in order to make way for Mr Russell to succeed me in the Professorship of Natural Philosophy: I hereby give my full consent to the part of this arrangement which depends on me . . . '.
32. J.D. Mackie, *The University of Glasgow 1451–1951* (Glasgow, 1954), 224–226.
33. R.G. Frank, 'Science, Medicine and the Universities of early modern England', *History of Science* 11 (1973), 194–216, 239–269 (241).
34. D.B. Horn, 'The Anatomy Classrooms in the present Old College, 1725–1880', *The University of Edinburgh Journal* 22 (1965–66), 65–71.
35. J.B. Morrell, 'The University of Edinburgh in the late eighteenth century: its scientific eminence and academic structure', *Isis* 62 (1971), 158–171.
36. O. Goldsmith, 'An Enquiry into the Present State of Polite Learning in Europe [1759]', A. Friedman (ed.), *Collected Works of Oliver Goldsmith* (Oxford, 1966), I, 253–341 (309).
37. T. Somerville, *My Own Life and Times* (Edinburgh, 1861) 380, is the source of both quotations.
38. Drummond to Milton, 4 April 1761, National Library of Scotland, Saltoun papers, SC 215, f 213.

APPENDIX A

Appointments made during George Drummond's tenure of official office in the Town Council.

Professor	*Subject*	*Date of appointment*
Crawford, James	Hebrew	21 August 1719
Mackie, Charles	Universal History	28 August 1719
Monro, Alexander, *primus*	Anatomy	14 March 1722
Bayne, Alexander	Scots Law	28 November 1722
Porterfield, William	Medicine	12 August 1724
McLaurin, Colin	Mathematics	3 November 1725
St Clair, Andrew	Theory and Practice of Medicine	9 February 1726
Rutherford, John	Theory and Practice of Medicine	9 February 1726
Plummer, Andrew	Medicine and Chemistry	9 February 1726
Innes, John	Medicine and Chemistry	9 February 1726
Gibson, Joseph	Midwifery	9 February 1726
Whytt, Robert	Medicine	26 August 1747
Stewart, Matthew	Mathematics	2 September 1747
Robertson, James	Hebrew	26 June 1751
Wallace, William	Universal History	23 December 1754
Dick, Robert	Civil Law	22 January 1755
Cullen, William	Medicine and Chemistry	19 November 1755
Young, Thomas	Midwifery	18 February 1756
Ferguson, Adam	Natural Philosophy	4 July 1759
Blair, Hugh	Rhetoric	27 June 1760
Balfour, James	Law of Nature and Nations	23 May 1764
Russell, James	Natural Philosophy	23 May 1764
Ferguson, Adam	Moral Philosophy	23 May 1764

APPENDIX B

Monro *secundus*' petition to the Town Council of 18 June 1764 is faithfully reproduced in Edinburgh Town Council Minutes (16 May 1764–20 February 1765) volume 80, minutes for 4 July 1764, pp. 47–58. As the chief concern of my paper is the Town Council's view of its University, this Appendix reproduces the Town Council minute.

Anent the petition given in and presented by Dr. Alexander Monro, jnr. Professor of Anatomy in this Citys University, setting furth that the Petitioner unwilling to be troublesome to the honble Patrons of the University or to put the Town of Edin^{r}. to expence has for several [years] past struggled with many great inconveniences in the teaching his branch in the University but these at last became so intolerable to him, and so loudly complained of by the students, as preventing them from acquiring sufficient knowledge in this fundamental part of physic and surgery, and are therefore so prejudicial to the reputation of the University, and of course so hurtfull to the Interest of the Town, that the Petitioner flattered himself, he would be excused for takeing the liberty, to represent them, and to beg relief which the Town could grant at small expence – – – – The grievances chiefly to be complained of are, – That the present teaching room is not large enough to contain above two thirds of the students of anatomy so that the Petitioner was under the necessity of dividing them into two classes, and of repeating every Lecture, twice over, a hardship which no Professor in this or in any University is forced to undergo, and which was the more insupportable, that from the extensive nature of this branch of science, in place of one hour's lecture which is all the other Professors of Physic give, he has for two years past been obliged to lecture to each class an hour and a half at least sometimes two hours, and yet withall cannot conclude his course so soon as the other medical Professors do, by which many of his students are every year contrary to their inclination, called away on different accounts before the end of it. He is likewise oblidged through want of time & strength to cut short several parts of his course, which it would be greatly for the advantage of the students to have more fully explained[.] Besides by so much time being consumed in lectureing he has little or none left for the improvement of his art in the winter, which is the season best fitted for such inquiries, and as at present in the vigour of life, he finds his labour extremely fatiguing and exhausting, and that a very slight indisposition altogether unfits him for so great a task, he foresees the impossibility there will be under the present disadvantages of his or any persons continuing for any great number of years, to teach Anatomy in that accurate and extensive way which is nowadays practised and become necessary, from it being found usefull _____ In the next place the students who attend the Petitioners second class have not a room to wait in, till the first class are dismissed, large enough to contain above a third part of their number, the room allotted for that purpose being only twelve feet square and as the petitioner cannot possibly dismiss his first class exactly at the very same time every day, many of the students are obliged to wait in the open area of the University. – The numerous preparations and instruments which the petitioner and his father have made & collected with very great labour and expence, and to which the Petitioner proposes to add yearlie, are partly huddled together in a room of the above dimensions and are partly lodged in dark corners below the seats of the teaching room by which they suffer great damage and add no ornament to the University which they might do if properly disposed. That of late years, the Petitioner has been frequently disturbed by the noise of the students in the university Library which is now overhead of his teaching room an inconvenience that cannot well be remedied, and which as the Library is every day more and more frequented will increase – But a more material inconvenience than any of these still remains to be mentioned, and which although the others could be removed, would alone render it impracticable for the Petitioner to teach anatomy with that distinctness and accuracy which is necessary, and which is at present practised in every University of eminence in Europe, To witt that the teaching room is dully lighted by its floor being sunk several feet underground, and by having the Principals house near and directly opposite to its windows, and then that the light comes in at the side of tlle room, which way of lighting tho' it may be abundantly convenient for the demonstrations of most of the other Professors, is altogether unfit for the purposes of anatomy, because the subject must be brought close to the window to have the light to fall on it, by which there can be only half a circle of students around the table, and even to them the light falls on the wrong side of the subject, and in fact the Petitioner has found this light so unfit and insufficient for his Demonstrations, that for three fourths of his course, he has shut it out entirely and tried to make a shift with candlelight, but to say nothing of the increase of labour and loss of time in this way the students are dissatisfied with it as the candles must be placed between them and the subject, and therefore intercept their view, whilst they at the same time give but a false and very faint light by no means sufficient for a large audience – All these inconveniences would be removed if the honble Patrons of the University would be pleased to build a single additional room large enough to contain all the students of anatomy and properly lighted adjoining to the present teaching room. By this means the Petitioner will be enabled to demonstrate his subject, preparations and instruments with the necessary clearness and accuracy[.] by being able to demonstrate to a greater number of students at once he will considerably shorten the time hitherto employed in his demonstrations, and hence have more time to bestow in lectureing and pointing out the application of Anatomy to physic and surgery – By not being obliged to Lecture the same thing twice over he will be able to go through his task with more spirit and advantage to his students – By generally conveening all his students together and lectureing to them two hours in place of an hour and a half which he at present bestows on each class, he will be able to render his Lectures still more extensive and usefull, and to finish them at the same time with the other professors of physic – As so much time will not be needed when all his students are convened together, he will perhaps be able to spare an hour to some of the other Professors of physic who at present are obliged to meet at an inconvenient hour. The few times the students must be divided into two Classes on account of demonstration of some very minute parts, the present teaching room will serve as a very convenient waiting room[.] The present teaching room will likewise make a very fitt place for lodgeing the preparations, which properly put up, will be an ornament to the University, and serve to give strangers a more favourable idea of it whilst by making the waiting and Preparation room the same, the students will have the opportunity of examining, at their leisure, the preparations of any organ they wish to be more particularly acquainted [with]. The Petitioner therefore though he were to draw no inference from the singular hardships he labours under, persuades himself that the honble Magistrates and Council would find it highly for the interest of the Town to order a proper room to be built, as the money required for that purpose cannot be laid out in any [way] whatsoever that will return so much profit to the Town, for the petitioner can show to their satisfaction, that within these fourty years the Town of Edin^{r} has received from the students of anatomy alone, on the lowest computation above £300000 sterling and that for the last twenty years, the town has received from the students of anatomy alone above £10000 str per annum. – That the other Medical Colleges and the benefite of seeing the practice of physic and surgery in the Infirmary have increased the number of students in the College of Anatomy, is unquestionably true but that this College alone has great effect in bringing students to Town appears not merely from the nature of the thing, but has been proved in fact from the very considerable confluence of students on account of the anatomy, before any of the other Medical Colleges were taught – Further in those Universities that are most likely to rival that of Edinburgh, to witt in Gottingen, Leyden, Cambridge Oxford & Dublin, the Patrons have not only erected buildings for the Professor of anatomy much more spacious and convenient than what the Petitioner asks, but have besides in some of those Universities, taken measures to supply the Anatomical Theatre with such a number of subjects, that the students have the benefite of dissection – That as the honble Patrons of this University have made no provision of the latter kind it is particularly necessary that they should furnish a place for their Professors of Anatomy in which the Petitioner can demonstrate the few subjects the students have opportunity to see in a clear and accurate manner – Nay it is consistent with the knowledge of some of the other Professors of physic as well as of the Petitioner, that some students who intended to pass several years in this University, have for want of such a place, left the University after one years study, and that the same circumstance has prevented many students from comeing to it – Lastly, as of late years many more attempts than formerly have been made, to teach the severall branches of physic, and particularly Anatomy in London and other parts of his Majesties Dominions, and even in America It is at present highly necessary, that the Patrons of this University should exert themselves, since, without their assistance, the outmost diligence and activity of the Professors will not be able to mentean the reputation this University has acquired, nor prevent its falling into decline – The Petitioner therefore humbly hopd that all things considered the honble patrons would grant his Petition . . . which being read in Council . . . was remitted . . . to the College Committee which reported that being very sensible of the many advantages ariseing to this City from the students of Anatomy, and that the place where Mr Munro at present gives his Lectures is very improper for that purpose, as it is very badly lighted, and only contains about one half of the students who usually attend his lectures which obliges him to give double lectures upon every subject, a piece of fatigue and labour unknown to any other professor, and which very soon must greatly affect Mr Munros health and that he has offered to leave for the use of College at his death the whole anatomical preparations he is now and shall then be possest of which are of very great value, and must be extremely beneficial to whoever shall be his successor, and add great reputation to the University; Therefore the Committee were humbly of opinion that as Mr Munro desrved all manner of encouragement from the good Town he should be allowed to build a proper room upon the ground to the eastward of his present teaching room for teaching his class conform to the plan produced & signed by him, and to fitt up the present teaching room with shelves and presses for holding the preparations conveniently, the expence whereof not to exceed the sum of three hundred pounds sterling, and that as he proposed to advance the said sum himself That the Council should recommend it to their successors in office to repay the sum in three annual & equal payments, the first payment thereof to commence in June next, the second in June thereafter, and the third payment in the month of June seventeen hundred & sixty seven, and that so soon as the work is fully executed, Mr Monro should lay the accompts of the expence thereof before the Council to be audited, Declareing that if the executing of these works shall cost less than the said sum of £300 Dr Monro shall not be entitled to ask more than repayment of the sum actually expended, and that if the executing thereof, shall cost more than the foresaid sum, in that case he shall be at the expense of the superplus, And that the obligation granted by Mr Monro to leave to the College at his death his anatomical preparations before mentioned should be regisred in the burrow Court Books and an extract thereof given to the College Treasurer . . . Which Report being considered by the Magistrates & Council they . . . approvd thereof, and authorize & allow the Petitioner Dr. Monro to build a proper room upon the aforesaid piece of ground conform to the plan produced & signed by him, and did and hereby do enact and recommend in terms of and agreeable to the said report.

The following thirteen letters, petitions, and reports in the Monro Documents, City of Edinburgh District Council Archives, Bundle 1, Shelf 16, Bay A, are pertinent to the minute reproduced above

- a Petition of Monros *primus* and *secundus* to Town Council, 5 September 1758, for improvements to the anatomy theatre. This petition is much shorter than (e) and was unsuccessful.
- b Letter of Monro *secundus* to Drummond, 11 February 1764, showing that Drummond had given a petition prior approval and had orchestrated Monro's lobbying of Town Council members. This letter probably refers to the 'inclosed Petition'(c), and not to (e)
- c Petition of Monro *secundus* to Town Council, 13 February 1764, requesting that his dissector, John Innes, be given a salary by the Town Council. On 15 February 1764 the Council agreed to do so.
- d Letter of Principal Robertson and professors Stevenson, Stuart, Balfour, Ferguson, and Hunter, to Town Council, 13 February 1764, supporting petition (c).
- e Petition of Monro *secundus* to Town Council, 18 June 1764, concerning a new anatomy theatre.
- f Letter of Monro *secundus* to Town Council, 18 June 1764, 'To be presented after reading the Petition of Dr Monro jr' [i.e. petition (e)], offering to bequeath his anatomical specimens to the University provided the Town Council grants his petition [(e)].
- g Estimate by Monro *secundus* to Town Council, n.d., containing twenty six items relative to the proposed new anatomy theatre which will cost £300.
- h Letter of Principal Robertson and professors Whytt, Hope, Rutherford, and Cullen, to Town Council, n.d., supporting petition (e) which they have read, corroborated, and discussed with students.
- i Letter of Monro *primus* to Drummond, 25 June 1764, supporting a new anatomy theatre in preference to an improved natural philosophy class room on grounds of greater necessity, smaller cost, greater attraction to students, and offer of loan by Monro *secundus*. Monro *primus* states explicitlv that he has frequently advised Drummond.
- j Report of College Committee of Town Council, 28 June 1744, supporting petition (e), and faithfully reproduced in Town Council minute of 4 July 1764.
- k Letter of Monro *secundus* to Town Council, 30 June 1764, offering to the Council a loan of £300 according to his estimated cost, and agreeing to pay any extra expense.
- l Petition of Monro *secundus* to Town Council, n.d. probably November 1764, giving details of chief items of expense additional to the estimated £300 and asking Council to meet this extra cost. On 19 December 1764 the Council agreed to do so.
- m Memorial of Monro *secundus* to Town Council, 14 July 1777, concerning teaching of surgery, shows *inter alia* that from session 1759–60 (when Monro *secundus* entirely replaced his father) to 1763–74, the size of the anatomy class grew rapidly: 1759–60, 134 students; 1760–61, 160; 1761–62, 174; 1762–63, 180;

II

26

1763–64, 187. This expansion provided a dire accommodation problem for Monro but convinced the Town Council of his effectiveness.

III

The University of Edinburgh in the Late Eighteenth Century: Its Scientific Eminence and Academic Structure

I

SINCE THE SECOND WORLD WAR the history of science as an autonomous discipline has steadily expanded, mainly through institutional recognition, yet much of its undeniably vigorous activity remains regrettably unknown to general historians. The chief source of this inaccessibility is clear. As long as it is assumed that science is just recorded positive public knowledge, then its history is likely to be concerned with mere technical accounts of scientific ideas and results *per se*. If, however, it is considered as a socially organized and supported intellectual enterprise engaged in understanding and controlling nature, its history should demonstrate a synthesis of social and intellectual elements from which the fruitless distinction between externalist and internalist historiographies would be excluded.

Praticularly in Britain has science been countenanced by a great variety of institutions. Of these the universities seem the most apposite for study because their ostensible aims, organizational structure, financial arrangements, and teaching styles have often been well defined. Among the older British universities the collegiate structure of Oxford and Cambridge renders them historically fascinating and frustrating. The University of Edinburgh, however, being noncollegiate and professorial in its organization, was less diffuse and more compact. Moreover, in the late eighteenth century it achieved a notable preeminence in science which gained for it the reputation of being the best university for science in Europe and in the English-speaking world. It would seem therefore that the social history of late-eighteenth-century science in the University of Edinburgh could be both illuminating and suggestive.

The qualitative impression of Edinburgh's scientific importance has been quantitatively confirmed by Nicholas Hans, who analyzed into age groups the university careers of 680 British scientists who made original contributions in the seventeenth

I am grateful to the University of Pennsylvania for the tenure of a visiting professorship in Spring 1970. For help and encouragement I am indebted to the faculty and students of its Department of History and Philosophy of Science, particularly Dr. A.W. Thackray, and to Dr. A.C. Chitnis of the University of Stirling, and my Bradford colleague, Professor F. Musgrove.

Reprinted from Isis, Vol. 62, Part 2, No. 212

Table 1

When born	1726–1745	1746–1765	1766–1785
Total number of scientists	128	106	88
Oxford	14	17	7
Cambridge	23	14	11
Edinburgh	26	25	15
Other British	5	7	8
% total at Oxford	11	16	8
% total at Cambridge	18	13	12
% total at Edinburgh	20	24	17
% total at other British	4	7	9

and eighteenth centuries. Part of one of his tables, to which I have added the last four rows calculated from his data, is set out in Table 1.[1] These figures show that in the late eighteenth century the University of Edinburgh was remarkably productive of students who attained eminence in science partly as a result of their deliberate sojourn in the city. No wonder then that two great American polymaths recognized the specific vigor of Scotland's metropolitan university. Shortly before the Declaration of Independence Benjamin Franklin could still remark that the University of Edinburgh possessed "a set of as truly great men, Professors of the Several Branches of Knowledge, as have ever appeared in any Age or Country."[2] A generation later the equally travelled Thomas Jefferson was similarly convinced that for science "no place in the world can pretend to a competition with Edinburgh."[3]

The preeminence in science of the University of Edinburgh in the late eighteenth century was of course the result of many elements acting in perpetually shifting and dynamic equilibria. In order to embrace the Scottish Enlightenment, of which the University's scientific superiority was a crucial component, one must duly consider the crisis of Scottish identity which manifested itself in institutionalized educational nationalism, the secularization of zealous Scottish Calvinism by the accommodating and dominant Moderate party of the Church of Scotland, the general literacy produced in Lowland Scotland by the much vaunted system of parish and burgh schools, the cultural patronage exerted by the landed classes, and not least the attractions of Scotland's capital, which Henry Cockburn so nostalgically conveyed.[4] Within this larger pattern, however, the peculiarly Scottish internal structure of the University

[1] Nicholas Hans, *New Trends in Education in the Eighteenth Century* (London: Routledge & Kegan Paul, 1951), p. 32.

[2] J. Bennett Nolan, *Benjamin Franklin in Scotland and Ireland, 1759 and 1771* (Philadelphia: Univ. Pennsylvania Press, 1938), p. 50.

[3] Letter of June 21, 1789, from Jefferson to Dugald Stewart written from Paris, a center for chemistry and physics, cited by D. B. Horn, *A Short History of the University of Edinburgh 1556–1889* (Edinburgh: Edinburgh Univ. Press, 1967), p. 64.

[4] The general history of 18th-century Scotland is well covered in T. C. Smout, *A History of the Scottish People 1560–1830* (London: Collins, 1969), and W. Ferguson, *Scotland 1689 to the Present* (Edinburgh: Oliver & Boyd, 1968). The cultural nationalism which burgeoned after the 1745 rebellion is stressed by H. J. Hanham, *Scottish Nationalism* (Cambridge, Mass.: Harvard Univ. Press, 1969), and G. E. Davie, "Hume, Reid and the Passion for Ideas" in Douglas Young *et al.*, *Edinburgh in the Age of Reason: A Commemoration* (Edinburgh: Edinburgh Univ. Press, 1967). Henry Cockburn, *Memorials of his Time* (Edinburgh/London: Foulis, 1910), remains signally illuminating.

constituted an important element, the significance of which seems to have been generally underestimated.

My aim in this paper is to add another dimension to our understanding of the peak of scientific distinction which the University of Edinburgh enjoyed in the late eighteenth century by analyzing this internal structure. In particular I shall draw attention to the aspirations, opportunities, and restraints which professors and students experienced within it instead of attempting yet another chronological history of the University during one of its greatest periods. As my discussion is deliberately focused on the University's institutional characteristics as they related to science, I shall refrain from considering the important question of the distinctive content and approach of its teaching. To facilitate discussion, information about the Edinburgh professoriate between 1750 and 1800 is arranged by faculty and given in Table 2.

II

When an Edinburgh science professor was nominated to his chair, usually by the local Town Council, which controlled appointments to most posts, or less often by the Crown, he was generally no stranger to the University: as a native Scot born into at least a middle-class family, he had often enjoyed the whole or part of an undergraduate career there.[5] Of the late-eighteenth-century science professoriate only John Robison and John Hope, both graduates of the University of Glasgow, were not Edinburgh alumni. Once the Edinburgh professor was ensconced in his chair, he could eagerly anticipate the legal monopoly of his subject. As intramural competition within a field was not permitted, professors lacked the bracing rivalry which the *privat dozents* provided in the German universities. Even extramural competition was regarded as a threat partly to academic standards and partly to professorial remuneration. So strong was the tradition of professorial engrossment that when an assistant was employed he was totally subject to the professor's whim and pocket.

Such exclusive possession of a subject was closely related to the system of remuneration which was generally adopted in the Scottish universities and in an extreme form at Edinburgh. An Edinburgh professor derived his emolument, out of which he met the expenses associated with mounting his class, mainly from class fees and secondarily from examining. His basic annual stipend was inevitably low; indeed five Edinburgh medical professors received no salary whatsoever, which acted as a strong stimulus to erect and maintain not only a large class but also a lucrative and time-consuming private practice, which could interfere with teaching duties. At the beginning of an

[5] This and other paragraphs are partly based on retrospective reconstruction from *Report of the Royal Commission of Inquiry into the State of the Universities of Scotland, British Parliamentary Papers*, 1831, *12*, and particularly *Evidence, Oral and Documentary, taken and received by the Commissioners for visiting the Universities of Scotland: The University of Edinburgh, British Parliamentary Papers*, 1837, *35*. In future references these volumes will be called *Report* and *Edinburgh Evidence*. Other sources used intermittently are Alexander Grant, *The Story of the University of Edinburgh* (London: Longmans Green, 1884); Horn, *A Short History;* A. Bower, *The History of the University of Edinburgh* (Edinburgh: Oliphant, Waugh & Innes, 1817); biographies of professors, a guide to which is jointly provided by the *Dictionary of National Biography* and the *British Museum Catalogue of Printed Books*; biographies and autobiographies of students such as Alexander Bain, *James Mill: A Biography* (London: Longmans Green, 1882) and Leonard Horner, ed., *Memoirs and Correspondence of Francis Horner* (London: Murray, 1843).

academic session each professor received a salutary reminder about a basic source of his livelihood when he collected two or three guineas, depending on the class, from every prospective member. Clearly this testing system, analogous to that in the German universities, stressed payment by results and by popularity. As Adam Smith noted, it contrasted sharply with the comfortable situation at the universities of Oxford and Cambridge, where professors gladly received fixed and adequate salaries irrespective of the number of their students.[6]

As professors were so dependent on student fees for their livelihood, their own classes were likely to be their chief interest, the total program followed by students who intended to graduate being relegated to secondary importance. This emphasis was quite in accord with the Edinburgh arrangement in which essentially free-lance independent professors were permitted by the Senate and Town Council to teach in what may be called a pre-bureaucratic situation. Yet the class fee system encouraged professors to be as concerned with the occasional students who had no intention of graduating as with the regular ones who were pursuing a degree.[7] Correspondingly, professors were reluctant to introduce pedagogic methods from which the occasional students might recoil; examinations and oral testing were hardly pervasive at Edinburgh.

The nature of his subject affected each professor profoundly. If he taught anatomy or chemistry—subjects which were popular, vocational, and compulsory for graduating purposes—then happily he possessed a guaranteed audience whose size he could hopefully increase from year to year. Even within one field different solutions to this problem were produced: Joseph Black supported his lucid, simple, and elegant lectures with impeccably neat lecture demonstrations displayed in his prime to classes of about two hundred; whereas his pupil and successor Thomas Charles Hope eventually became the richest Scottish professor of his time by attracting in the 1820s audiences of over five hundred who reveled in his glittering showmanship.[8] If, however, a professor's subject was not obviously utilitarian, not compulsory for graduation, and seemed difficult or obscure to his potential audience, his remuneration could be distressingly low. For instance, though Robison realized that his students were inadequately equipped in mathematics, he refused on principle to be an academic clown purveying frivolous amusement to his class[9]: as he deliberately made little use of lecture demonstrations of experiments on the strict Baconian tenet that a particular experiment merely illustrates a particular truth, his class—of about one hundred at best—was predictably small.[10]

It is apparent that the wide disparity of remuneration, which was approximately calculable and publicly known from year to year, usually spurred ambitious professors to produce or to transfer to a class of adequate size. It could equally engender inter-

[6] Adam Smith, *The Nature and Causes of the Wealth of Nations* in *The Works of Adam Smith* (London: Cadell & Davies, 1811), Vol. IV, pp. 151–155, 169–170.

[7] *Report*, pp. 9–10.

[8] Black's last course of lectures is euphorically described by Thomas Thomson, *The History of Chemistry* (London: Colburn & Bentley, 1831), Vol. I, pp. 325–327. On Hope see J. B. Morrell, "Practical Chemistry in the University of Edinburgh, 1799–1843," *Ambix*, 1969, *16*:66–80.

[9] E. Robinson and D. McKie, *Partners in Science: Letters of James Watt and Joseph Black* (London: Constable, 1970), p. 130.

[10] John Playfair, "Biographical Account of John Robison LL.D." in *The Works of John Playfair* (Edinburgh: Constable, 1822), Vol. IV, pp. 121–178 (pp. 146–147).

*Table 2**

Chair	Faculty	Founded	Patron	Incumbents 1750–1800
Mathematics	Arts	1674	Town Council	Matthew Stewart 1746–1775 Dugald Stewart 1775–1785 John Playfair 1785–1805
Latin	Arts	1597	Town Council	George Hunt 1741–1775 John Hill 1775–1805
Greek	Arts	1708	Town Council	Robert Hunter 1741–1772 Andrew Dalzell 1772–1806
Logic and Metaphysics	Arts	1708	Town Council	John Stevenson 1730–1775 John Bruce 1775–1792 James Finlayson 1792–1808
Moral Philosophy	Arts	1708	Town Council	William Cleghorn 1745–1754 James Balfour 1754–1764 Adam Ferguson 1764–1785 Dugald Stewart 1785–1810
Natural Philosophy	Arts	1708	Town Council	Adam Ferguson 1759–1764 James Russell 1764–1773 John Robison 1774–1805
Universal History	Arts	1719	Town Council	Charles Mackie 1719–1765 John Pringle 1765–1780 Alexander Fraser Tytler 1780–1801
Rhetoric	Arts	1762	Crown	Hugh Blair 1762–1784 William Greenfield 1784–1801
Natural History	Arts	1767	Crown	Robert Ramsay 1767–1779 John Walker 1779–1804
Practical Astronomy	Arts	1786	Crown	Robert Blair 1786–1828
Agriculture	Arts?	1790	Sir W. Pulteney	Andrew Coventry 1790–1831
Public Law	Law	1707	Crown	George Abercromby 1735–1759 Robert Bruce 1759–1764 James Balfour 1764–1779 Allan Maconochie 1779–1796 Robert Hamilton 1796–1831
Civil Law	Law	1710	Town Council	Kenneth McKenzie 1745–1754 Robert Dick 1755–1792 John Wilde 1792–1800
Scots Law	Law	1722	Town Council	John Erskine 1737–1765 William Wallace 1765–1786 David Hume 1786–1822

Chair	Faculty	Founded	Patron	Incumbents 1750–1800
Principal	Theology	1586	Town Council	William Wishart 1737–1754 John Gowdie 1754–1762 William Robertson 1762–1793 George Husband Baird 1793–1840
Divinity	Theology	1587	Town Council	John Gowdie 1733–1754 Robert Hamilton 1754–1779 Andrew Hunter 1779–1809
Hebrew	Theology	1642	Town Council	James Robertson 1751–1792 William Moodie 1793–1812
Ecclesiastical History	Theology	1695	Crown	Patrick Cumming 1737–1762 Robert Cumming 1762–1788 Thomas Hardy 1788–1798 Hugh Meiklejohn 1799–1831
Botany	Medicine	1676	Town Council and Crown	Charles Alston 1738–1761 John Hope 1761–1786 Daniel Rutherford 1786–1819
Institutes (theory) of Medicine	Medicine	1685	Town Council	Robert Whytt 1747–1766 William Cullen 1766–1773 James Gregory 1776–1789 Andrew Duncan 1790–1819
Practice of Medicine	Medicine	1685	Town Council	John Rutherford 1726–1766 John Gregory 1766–1773 William Cullen 1773–1790 James Gregory 1790–1821
Anatomy	Medicine	1705	Town Council	Alexander Monro 1 1720–1758 Alexander Monro 2 1758–1798 Alexander Monro 3 1798–1846
Medicine and Chemistry	Medicine	1713	Town Council	Andrew Plummer 1726–1755 William Cullen 1755–1766 Joseph Black 1766–1796 Thomas Charles Hope 1796–1843
Midwifery	Medicine	1726	Town Council	Robert Smith 1739–1756 Thomas Young 1756–1780 Alexander Hamilton 1780–1800
Materia Medica	Medicine	1768	Town Council	Francis Home 1768–1798 James Home 1798–1821

* Source: Alexander Grant, *The Story of the University of Edinburgh* (London: Longmans Green, 1884), passim.

necine jealousy and acute depression in their uncompromising or unpopular colleagues. Table 3 demonstrates with striking clarity the identities of the more popular and more remunerative classes for three arbitrarily chosen years in the 1790s. Though the figures for class sizes are generally reliable, those for class emoluments are not necessarily exact; in the late eighteenth century neither the Town Council, which was responsible for the supervision of the University, nor the Senate controlled class fees. These were fixed by individual professors who in any event varied their rates: repeating students received discounts; poor students or those reading divinity sometimes attended gratis depending on the professor involved.

When a professor grew old he could not look forward to a pension or superannuation—a deficiency which was mitigated by various devices. If like Robison he was badly placed financially, he held his chair until he died, irrespective of his intellectual competence. The more affluent professor often made a private arrangement for his classes to be taught by an assistant eager to succeed him, as Black's employment of Hope for 1796–1799 shows. Lastly a professor who was keen to maintain or begin an academic dynasty could put his son in charge of his class with the hope that successful discharge of duty would endear him to the patrons of the chair. This nepotism, of which two demonstrations occurred in the 1790s alone, is vividly illustrated by Monro secundus' success in placing his son in his chair so that the family monopoly of the anatomy department lasted in toto for 126 years.[11]

An average Edinburgh professor could expect to carry a heavy teaching load during the academic session, which lasted six months from early November to early May with a short bibulous break in late December. He usually lectured one hour on each weekday for about twenty-five weeks.[12] According to his penchant he could spend a few additional hours a week on verbal testing of students, a practice which was not prevalent at Edinburgh owing in part to the large number of students. If he was concerned to illustrate his lectures with specimens and demonstrations of experiments, their preparation and rehearsal could consume hours each day.[13] Additionally, many medical professors spent some time every day on clinical teaching in the infirmary.

At the end of the session, however, the ceaseless demands of teaching gave way to the welcome nirvana of six months' vacation, which the professoriate shared with the top Edinburgh lawyers. Unless a professor chose to deliver a summer course lasting three months, he enjoyed the enviable opportunity of having half the year in which to continue his private practice, to perform consultancy work, to prepare his lectures, to do research, and to publish. Indeed the inadequacy of their low fixed salaries positively encouraged professors to publish, not only for personal profit but also to increase their reputation and the prestige of the University. There was no question of professors having to publish to gain tenure, which along with monopoly they enjoyed from the moment they assumed office. Rather, they readily apprehended that a good teacher's reputation would remain merely local unless he became nationally visible through his published work. Fortunately for them the city's printing and bookselling, like most of the industries which serviced Edinburgh's eminently bulky professional groups, were thriving as never before in the late eighteenth century, and authors were accordingly

[11] Rex Wright-St. Clair, *Doctors Monro: A Medical Saga* (London: Wellcome Historical Medical Library, 1964).

[12] *Edinburgh Evidence*, Appendix, pp. 123–124.

[13] William Ramsay, *The Life and Letters of Joseph Black* (London: Constable, 1918), p. 127.

*Table 3**

Chair	Salary (nearest)	Class fee (guineas)	Class size 1794–1795	Class size 1796–1797	Class size 1798–1799	Class emolument (guineas) 1794–1795	Class emolument (guineas) 1796–1797	Class emolument (guineas) 1798–1799
Mathematics	113	3	72	67	72	216	201	216
Latin	52	2	193	171	189	386	342	378
Greek	52	2	265	237	243	530	474	486
Logic	52	2	87	87	79	174	174	158
Moral Philosophy	102	3	116	95	100	348	285	300
Natural Philosophy	52	3	93	81	85	279	243	255
Universal History	100	3	24	33	22	72	99	66
Rhetoric	100	3	15	13	14	45	39	42
Natural History	100	3	*c.* 50	*c.* 50	*c.* 50	*c.* 150	*c.* 150	*c.* 150
Practical Astronomy	100 not taught	—	—	—	—	—	—	—
Agriculture	50	3	20	39	no record	60	117	—
Public Law	280 not taught	—	—	—	—	—	—	—
Civil Law	100	3	21	48	9	63	142	27
Scots Law	100	3	113	128	113	339	384	339
Principal	111 (no class)	—	—	—	—	—	—	—
Divinity	161	0	146	135	125	0	0	0
Hebrew	80	2		no record		—	—	—
Ecclesiastical History	200	0	*c.* 35	*c.* 35	*c.* 35	0	0	0
Botany	128	3	78	93	97	234	279	291
Institutes of Medicine	0	3	80	97	68	240	291	204
Practice of Medicine	0	3	225	227	232	675	681	696
Anatomy	50	3	307	326	274	921	978	822
Chemistry	0	3	225	253	262	675	759	786
Midwifery	0	3	79	126	144	237	378	432
Materia Medica	0	3	58	66	95	174	198	285

* Source: *Edinburgh Evidence*, Appendix, 51–64 and 130.

rewarded munificently.[14] The publishing opportunities were conveniently varied. Textbooks based on lectures formed the staple didactic genre in which the science professors were notably productive. Perhaps it is significant that Black, Hope, and Monro secundus, all of whom reveled in their exceptionally large classes, conspicuously deviated from this norm. At a less specialized level the *Encyclopaedia Britannica* began to solicit scientific articles from such masters of synopsis as Robison during the publication of its third edition.[15] For research publications the various Edinburgh medical journals, the *Transactions of the Highland Society of Scotland*, and those of the Royal Society of Edinburgh acted in part as house journals for the professoriate. The Royal Society, whose charter was granted in 1783, provided for Edinburgh science professors a polite forum for debate on current research, an enviable facility which their Oxford, Cambridge, and Glasgow equivalents did not enjoy.[16]

The class fee system, by stimulating professors to acquire and maintain large classes, discouraged the sinecuring so endemic at Oxford and Cambridge. Its consequences, however, were not inevitably beneficial: in particular, vested interests within the professoriate, by opposing innovation for reasons of personal finance and not necessarily on intellectual grounds, frequently produced academic conservatism.[17] Hence the paradox that in the late eighteenth century the University Senate consistently resisted the desirable expansion of its medical professoriate even though the medical program was undeniably the primary source of the University's international reputation. Not surprisingly only two new science chairs, practical astronomy and agriculture, were created in the period; and these were externally endowed by the Crown and a private individual, respectively.

Within the field of medicine the most contentious issue was patently the lack of a chair of surgery. The political agility of the Senate had been amply displayed in 1777 when the insistent College of Surgeons of Edinburgh recommended to the Crown that the University have a chair of surgery separate from that of anatomy. This proposal was opposed by the extremely able Monro secundus, the distinguished historian William Robertson, and by their medical colleagues. The Town Council reacted to the dispute with a compromise measure in which Monro was given a new commission which made him joint professor of anatomy and surgery for his lifetime only; and it reserved the right to separate these subjects after his death. Significantly, the Monro dynastic and financial interest remained unimpaired, and indeed it prevailed until 1831, when the Crown intervened by creating a separate chair of surgery.

The two new chairs of practical astronomy and agriculture were characteristically the result of external initiative. Urged by the Town Council's utilitarian arguments, the Crown endowed a chair of practical astronomy in 1785. Though its first incumbent, Robert Blair, received a salary of £100 a year, the Crown allowed him neither observatory nor apparatus. The deprived professor was unable to run an effective class, so he

[14] Smout, *A History*, pp. 361–379.

[15] Playfair, *Robison*, pp. 154–157, stresses that Robison was the first practicing and competent natural philosopher to contribute to the outstanding Scottish encyclopedia.

[16] London lacked a university; the Philosophical Society of Glasgow, the Cambridge Philosophical Society, and the Ashmolean Society (Oxford) were founded in 1802, 1819, and 1828, respectively. In the late 18th century only Edinburgh among English and Scottish centers possessed a thriving university and an active scientific society.

[17] This and the following paragraph are based on Grant, *The Story*, Vol. I, pp. 321–328, 338–341, 344–347, and *Edinburgh Evidence*, passim.

withdrew in a huff to become the solitary sinecurist science professor in the University. More contentious was the endowment in 1790 by an alumnus, Sir William Pulteney, of a chair of agriculture—at that time a subject of great theoretical and practical interest in the Lowlands of Scotland.[18] Not unexpectedly, Pulteney declined Robertson's suggestion that the proposed salary of £50 a year was decidedly low: he wanted exertion and not indolence from Andrew Coventry, the first occupant of his chair. As agriculture potentially impugned natural history and botany, the presentation of Coventry's commission produced the appropriate protests against academic encroachment.

III

The attractions of the University in the late eighteenth century for students were agreeably multifarious. In the first place, like the German universities and in contrast with the two English ones, it was nonecclesiastical: though professors nominally took the oath of allegiance to the Church of Scotland, most classes with the obvious exception of theological ones were taught by laymen.[19] Indeed John Playfair and John Walker, the two ordained science professors, merely followed the practice of the Reverend William Robertson, Principal of the University, in putting scholarship before preaching.[20] This decidedly secular ethos drew a cosmopolitan array of students from Scotland, England, Ireland, and the colonies. Particularly after 1789, English middle-class families, deprived of the European grand tour, increased the already considerable influx of English students among which religious dissenters had been prominent for decades. Edinburgh attracted students from south of the border for much of the century, to the extent that out of its 343 distinguished eighteenth-century alumni no less than 152 were English.[21]

As a result of the operation of the class fee system most graduating students were probably at least of lower-middle-class origin, as Smout has rightly stressed.[22] Yet poor students could attend classes on an ad hoc basis or be admitted gratis by a generous professor. Furthermore, opportunities for part-time teaching and writing were readily available in Edinburgh during term, and in the long vacation temporary jobs could be taken at home. Compared with the expenses necessarily incurred at Oxford and Cambridge, those at Edinburgh could be significantly lower for the abstemious or parsimonious. Though estimates of what constituted sparse but not intolerable subsistence inevitably varied, the total annual cost of an Edinburgh session for a frugal student could be as little as a third of that at Oxford.[23] Even the anglophilic and Tory Scottish Universities Commission (1826–1830) was impressed by the flexibility and social inclusiveness of the institutions they were investigating: "it is essential to keep in view the peculiar and beneficent character of the Scotch Univer-

[18] The importance of agriculture in 18th-century natural philosophy in Scotland may be gleaned from J. E. Handley, *Scottish Farming in the Eighteenth Century* (London: Faber & Faber, 1953).

[19] *Report*, p. 8.

[20] James Playfair, "Biographical Account of the late Professor Playfair" in *The Works of John Playfair*, Vol. I, pp. xi–lxxvi, and John Walker, *Lectures on Geology: Including Hydrography, Mineralogy, and Meteorology with an Introduction to Biology*, ed. Harold W. Scott (Chicago: Univ. Chicago Press, 1966), pp. xvii–xlvi.

[21] Hans, *New Trends*, pp. 18, 24.

[22] Smout, *A History*, pp. 478–479.

[23] Living expenses in the late 18th century could be limited to £15–£20 per session (*Edinburgh Evidence*, pp. 547, 549, 565, 571, 584, 586, 589, 598–599).

sities, that they are intended to place the means of the highest education in Science and Philosophy within the reach of persons in humble ranks of life, while, at the same time, they are equally adapted to educate and enlighten the youth of the highest class of society."[24]

Each university class showed marked variety not only in the provenance and rank of its members but also in intellectual training and age. Quite simply, as a matter of university policy or expediency no entrance qualifications for particular classes were required from students, who additionally enjoyed the privilege of *lernfreiheit.*[25] Provided his pocket allowed him, any person of any age and training could attend any of the classes in whatever number and order best suited his particular preferences and prospects. Neither individual professors nor the Senate interfered with the course or study which any student chose to adopt. Hence, particularly in the arts faculty very few students followed the full degree program. It is therefore rash to assume, for instance, that all students of the natural philosophy class automatically attended that of moral philosophy.[26] On the contrary, the system of open access to any class maximized opportunities for students to study according to their individual interests and aspirations:[27] hence the basis of the old adage that while Oxford taught men how to spend a thousand a year, Edinburgh taught them how to make a thousand a year.

Of course, the absence of admission requirements allowed many professors to recruit classes sufficiently big to ensure adequate remuneration. Though students could be inadequately prepared for attendance at science classes, the low standard of their mathematics being an obvious instance, the Edinburgh and Scottish system had the distinct virtue of at least trying to cope with the problem of mass tertiary education. Accordingly, in one science class there could be found middle-aged men attending for amusement and improvement, professional men present for interest and expertise, nongraduating young students who attended the University for a year or so before entering trade or commerce, as well as that minority of regular students who were intent on graduation.

It must be understood that in the late eighteenth century the only degrees awarded were almost exclusively in medicine.[28] Even in this licensing and vocational faculty, few bothered or could afford the £20 fee necessary to graduate. In any given year toward the end of the century only 12% at best of the total medical student body took the M.D. degree.[29] After all, many opportunities in general practice existed outside

[24] *Report*, p. 9.

[25] *Edinburgh Evidence*, Appendix, p. 121.

[26] The strong support of *lernfreiheit* as one of Edinburgh's great strengths was maintained into the next century. As Andrew Duncan, jr., pointed out to the Scottish Universities Commission, "it is one of the great advantages, not only in this school, but in the best schools in the north of Germany, that the students are left very much to direct their own course of education and I apprehend that they do it much better than by having a fixed curriculum laid down." (*Edinburgh Evidence*, pp. 246–247)' The very welcome recent studies of Davie and Olson underestimate the fragmentation of the full degree program which *lernfreiheit* produced. See G. E. Davie, *The Democratic Intellect: Scotland and Her Universities in the Nineteenth Century* (2nd ed., Edinburgh: Edinburgh Univ. Press, 1964), p. 10; R. Olson, "The Reception of Boscovich's Ideas in Scotland," *Isis*, 1969, *60*:91–103 (p. 102).

[27] Edward Topham, *Letters from Edinburgh written in the years 1774 and 1775* (London: Dodsley, 1776), p. 210.

[28] *Edinburgh Evidence*, Appendix, p. 151. In 1790, for example, there were 32 graduations in medicine, and none whatsoever in arts, divinity, and law.

[29] The figure of 12% has been estimated from the data given in *Edinburgh Evidence*, Appendix, pp. 128 and 151.

metropolitan centers for a medical student who had attended the University's distinguished medical classes without taking a degree. The process by which an Edinburgh M.D. was acquired still bore medieval characteristics.[30] Having attended recognized courses mainly six months in length in anatomy, chemistry, botany, materia medica, institutes of medicine (or having acquired certificates of attendance), for at least three years, of which one had to be passed at Edinburgh, the candidate was given a private *viva voce*. The satisfactory student then submitted his thesis. Next he was exposed to a second oral on the different branches of medicine, and also a written test on two aphorisms of Hippocrates and two case histories. Finally his thesis was published and publicly defended on graduation day. At its worst, the system of graduating in medicine was dangerously ceremonial; at its best, however, the vitality of the system came from the professors' knowledge of a student's clinical work, from the length and closeness of the private examination, and from his thesis, which gave some evidence of capacity to do research.

For individual students the consequences of *lernfreiheit*, when exercised by a total student population of about one thousand of whom about four hundred were medicals, tested their powers of choice, initiative, and self-reliance. Except in medicine where the acquisition of an M.D. licensed a graduate to practice, usually in the non-golden-cane sections of British medicine, graduation was simply unimportant: students extended their loyalty primarily to the separate classes for which they paid and only secondarily to the University. They expected neither the paternalism nor the pastoral care which the more conscientious Oxford and Cambridge colleges sometimes displayed to their students. On the contrary, they tasted the freedom of a nonresidential university and learned how to provide for themselves in the classrooms, lodgings, and the taverns of the expanding and sociable city.[31]

Serious students could easily see that Edinburgh's great advantage over Oxford and Cambridge lay in the wider range of available subjects from which they could choose according to their needs and aspirations. While Oxford and Cambridge stressed classics and mathematics respectively, Edinburgh voraciously spanned professional and liberal education in its characteristic emphasis on medicine and philosophy. Not surprisingly, science at Edinburgh occupied an important position in both the medical and arts faculties. In the latter, natural philosophy, mathematics, agriculture, and natural history were available together with the moral philosophy delivered by Dugald Stewart, who concerned himself *inter alia* with the philosophy and history of science.[32] But the medical courses formed the chief magnet to students interested in science. Generally the medical professors were at least competent and at best charismatic, particularly when compared with their colleagues in law and divinity. In the premedical subjects such as anatomy, botany, and chemistry the University could convincingly boast of Monro secundus, John Hope, Thomas Charles Hope, and their

[30] The regulations in force in 1783 are cited verbatim in *Edinburgh Evidence*, Appendix, p. 137.

[31] The extramural attractions and physical growth of Edinburgh are well described in H. G. Graham, *The Social Life of Scotland in the Eighteenth Century* (2nd ed., London: Black, 1909), and A. J. Youngson, *The Making of Classical Edinburgh 1750–1830* (Edinburgh: Edinburgh Univ. Press, 1966).

[32] J. Veitch, "Memoir of Dugald Stewart" in *Collected Works of Dugald Stewart*, ed. W. Hamilton (Edinburgh: Constable, 1854–1860), Vol. X, pp. vii–clxxvii.

doyen Black, "so pale, so gentle, so elegant, and so illustrious."[33] In medical subjects proper, where Oxford and Cambridge offered no competition, theory of medicine, practice of medicine, midwifery, and materia medica lay in the competent hands of Duncan, Cullen, Gregory, Hamilton, and Home. Though on a small scale, the facilities for clinical teaching in the Edinburgh hospitals were not only outstanding by British standards but were also enthusiastically admired by Cabanis and Pinel, respectively the philosopher and first leader of the Paris clinical school.[34] Their value resided in the measure of empirically based, undogmatic technical competence they gave to the growing band of students which had realized that the war with France would lead to an unprecedented demand for physicians and surgeons. Students doubtless also apprehended that the College of Surgeons of Edinburgh kept the University medical school on its toes by providing competition, particularly in the few areas where the University lacked expertise.[35] In short, before the rise of the Paris clinical school in the mid-1790s, Edinburgh's medical school could claim to be the best in Europe.

Though students were often compelled to rely on their own initiative in an academic marketplace, they could take refuge in the many student societies. During the 1790s, for example, potential scientists and medicals, at that time barely separable, could choose from the Royal Medical and Royal Physical societies (which were so well established that they owned their premises), the Agricultural Society of Edinburgh, the American Physical Society, the Chirurgo-Physical Society, the Hibernian Medical Society, the Natural History Society of Edinburgh, an ephemeral Chemical Society, and not least the Academy of Physics.[36] As many of these societies were nurtured by the professoriate, they mitigated to some extent the impersonality inherent in big lectures. The range of their activity was impressively varied: it encompassed the attack on Hutton's theory of the earth delivered at the Royal Medical Society in 1796 by the young Robert Jameson (professor of natural history, 1804–1854) and Henry Brougham's exploration of the problems of inductive science at the Academy of Physics between 1797 and 1800.[37]

IV

The system of academic *laissez-faire* operating at the University of Edinburgh in the late eighteenth century stood in decided contrast to that at Oxford and Cambridge. Given the prerequisite that the Town Council in particular had made at this time a remarkable number of good appointments to scientific and medical chairs, sometimes by successfully wooing professors from the University of Glasgow, which acted as its chief Scottish rival, their incumbents were generally encouraged by the class fee

[33] Cockburn, *Memorials*, p. 46. Henry Brougham, later British Chancellor, thought Black the equal of Pitt or Fox as an orator: Brougham, *Lives of Philosophers of the Time of George III* (London: Griffin, 1866), pp. 19–21.

[34] Erwin H. Ackernecht, *Medicine at the Paris Hospital 1794–1848* (Baltimore: Johns Hopkins Press, 1967), p. 27.

[35] It is significant that the Scottish Universities Commission (1826–1830) collected much more evidence from the Edinburgh College of Surgeons than from the Edinburgh College of Physicians.

[36] C. P. Finlayson, "Records of Scientific and Medical Societies preserved in the University Library, Edinburgh," *The Bibliotheck: A Journal of Bibliographical Notes and Queries mainly of Scottish Interest*, 1958, *1*: 14–19.

[37] J. M. Sweet and C. D. Waterston, "Robert Jameson's Approach to the Wernerian Theory of the Earth, 1796," *Annals of Science*, 1967, *23*: 81–95 (p. 84); John Clive, *Scotch Reviewers: The Edinburgh Review, 1802–1815* (Cambridge, Mass.: Harvard Univ. Press, 1957), p. 21.

arrangement to increase their exertions, especially in teaching and publication.[38] Correspondingly, the students who had frequently chosen quite deliberately to study under the savants of the University and to partake of the wide range of cheap, philosophical, scientific, and medical instruction which it offered, enjoyed both the flexibility and responsibility of *lernfreiheit*. Toward the end of the century, however, the weaknesses of stimulating professors to speculate in an academic marketplace gradually appeared: the very success of some professors in gaining or maintaining large, heterogeneous classes created problems of pedagogy and of size; and the concern for remunerative professorial monopoly not only hindered the recognition of new subjects for graduation but also inhibited the impoverished University from recommending the creation of new chairs. Perhaps it was not accidental that the University's scientific reputation reached its maximum halfway between the abolition of regenting in 1708 and the incipient anglicization of the Universities (Scotland) Act of 1858. But certainly the concern for teaching and scholarship, so intimately associated with the University's internal organization, gave to it the enviable distinction of being the first modern British university.[39]

[38] The greater status, opportunities, and remuneration to be enjoyed at Edinburgh attracted Cullen, Black, Robison, and Thomas Charles Hope from Glasgow.

[39] The continuing importance of the University of Edinburgh in British science is stressed in my paper "Individualism and the Structure of British Science in 1830," to appear in *Historical Studies in the Physical Sciences*, 3.

IV

PROFESSORS ROBISON AND PLAYFAIR, AND THE *THEOPHOBIA GALLICA*: NATURAL PHILOSOPHY, RELIGION AND POLITICS IN EDINBURGH, 1789–1815.

FOR obvious reasons the political and social effects of the French Revolution on Britain remain perpetually fascinating to political and social historians. Yet with the exception of the radical minister and natural philosopher Joseph Priestley, its influence on British scientists and institutions devoted to science has not received the attention it deserves. The reason for this neglect is clear: as long as the science of the past is interpreted as being nothing more than ideas and knowledge about the external world of nature then its social and institutional aspects will continue to be disregarded. If, however, past science is viewed as an activity which was socially organized and countenanced, we may expect it to have shown sensitivity in various degrees to some of the diverse elements in its social environment. This claim should receive particular justification from the study of the scientific activity of individuals who were associated with institutions in which sciences were taught, especially during a time of persistent stress and repeated crisis. Britain endured such a period between 1789 and 1815 when France was convulsed by the Revolution and its Napoleonic sequel. In those years among her few institutions largely if not exclusively devoted to teaching, research, and publication in scientific fields, the University of Edinburgh was pre-eminent. It deservedly maintained its reputation of being for science the outstanding university in Europe and the English speaking world; its medical school acted as the chief magnet for hundreds of students who flocked to it from Scotland, England, Ireland and the colonies (1). In those years natural philosophy was taught in the Arts faculty by two gifted professors: John Robison (professor of natural philosophy 1774–1805) and John Playfair (professor of mathematics 1785–1805, professor of natural philosophy 1805–1819, F.R.S. 1807). My aim in this paper is to explore some of the relations which existed between natural philosophy, religion and politics in Edinburgh and its University during the French Revolution. To this end my discussion will be focussed on the contrasting political activities, philosophical attitudes and religious positions of Robison and Playfair wh successively occupied one of the most important positions then available i British science.

I

In the two decades during which Britain and France waged almost contin uous war most things in Scotland and elsewhere in Britain were soaked in th wash of the French Revolution (2). After the execution of Louis XVI in 179 British suspicion of French changes hardened and the glories of the nativ constitution were increasingly sung. Few serious revolutionaries existed i Britain in the 1790s, but mild reformers of various kinds could be conven iently labelled and disabled as Jacobins. In Scotland suspicion of republica zeal was exacerbated by the Scottish Tories whose operations revealed onl too clearly their self-interest which was scarcely disguised as an ideologica stance. Fearing the threat of mob violence to their property and prerogative they suspected institutions and attitudes based on popular support and feeling Hence the Scottish Tories, who possessed wealth, rank and political power frequently tainted those who felt and showed discontent with the politica *status quo* in Britain. Whether it was in any way inspired by French events o not, all innovation could be conveniently tarred with the hated label of Jacob inism.

During the late 1790s only a few Whigs were left in Scotland and Edin burgh, particularly after the deposition in 1796 of the Whig Henry Erskin from the Deanship of the Faculty of Advocates. Earlier in 1793 the fate o Thomas Muir gave a clear warning to supporters of reform: for arrangin and supporting the first meeting of the Friends of the People held in Edinburg in 1792, the distinguished radical advocate had been sentenced by Judge Brax field to fourteen years' transportation to Botany Bay. There is no doubt tha the Scottish judges, led by the coarse and domineering Braxfield, were mor attuned to the panic of the ruling classes and more partial than their Englis counterparts. Lacking political power the hard core of Scottish Whigs, wh were mainly concentrated in Edinburgh, could anticipate little improvemen in the immediate future. Their positive action was consequently restricted t sticking to their principles and defending them when challenged. In this Whi caucus the most important group was the lawyers who by the nature of thei profession still enjoyed some technique and room for manoeuvre. By contras the Church of Scotland, then dominated by the Moderate party, offered littl sanctuary. At that time 'Moderatism took on ugly features, being little mor than the Dundas interest at prayer, with nepotism and pluralism the main orde of service' (3). In the flourishing Edinburgh medical profession two private teachers, John Thomson and John Allen, stood out as sturdy Whigs. The last group of importance in the Whig caucus was formed by three University professors who were close friends: Playfair, Dugald Stewart (professor of moral philosophy 1785–1810) and Andrew Dalzel (professor of Greek 1772–1806). Of these three Playfair held a politically neutral chair. With his two friends it was different. Dalzel lectured on Greek liberty; and Stewart enunciated the principles and uses of liberty in general. Both were suspected of being Jacobins. Henry Cockburn acknowledged that 'Stewart, in particular, though too spotless and too retired to be openly denounced, was an object of great secret alarm' (4). As late as January 1793 Stewart still privately approved of Tom Paine's *The rights of man*; but by 1794 he found it expedient to apologize in private to Judge Abercromby who urged him to publicly withdraw his praise of some of the allegedly subversive ideas promulgated by Condorcet (5).

Though the Whig Cockburn may have exaggerated the gloom which pervaded the 1790s and began to disperse in the 1800s, there is no doubt that at this time Henry Dundas, the greatest of Scotland's political managers, was its benevolent dictator, first as Home Secretary (1791–94) and then as Secretary of State for War (1794–1801). During the later phases of his reign, the bench, the pulpit, the press and the parliamentary electors suffered his dominion: assisted by his nephew Robert Dundas, Lord Advocate of Scotland (1789–1801), he enjoyed ample means of rewarding submission and disabling opposition. In this situation possible channels for reforming sentiments were virtually closed to the Whigs; and public opinion, as a means of initiating action or of curbing excess, hardly existed. The Whig caucus was therefore small, isolated, and sometimes suspected. Particularly after the Terror of 1793 popular opinion in Scotland increasingly supported the Scottish Tories in their denunciations of Whigs as potential traitors, as friends of France, and as enemies of their own country. P. A. Brown succinctly noted that 'Others besides Coleridge preferred the administration even of Goose and Goody to

> The coward whine and Frenchified
> Slaver and slang of the other side! (6)

Within the University this widespread suspicion of French democracy received copious expression. For instance in 1792 the University's loyal address to George III referred to the excellence of the British constitution established in 1688. Again in that year Senate promised to labour with assiduity to instil into the students 'just sentiments with respect to the nature of Society' (7). By 1799 David Hume (nephew of the philosopher and professor of Scots law

1786–1822) was complaining in the Senate about the blasphemous and seditious discourses which were being delivered at the Speculative Society, a studen debating-society and nest-bed of the irrepressible young Whig reformers wh *inter alia* founded the *Edinburgh Review* (8). In the following year Stewart bega his famous lectures on political economy, 'and not a few hoped to catch Stewar in dangerous propositions' (9). The longest and fiercest expression of 'anti Jacobinism' within the University came, however, from Robinson. In Autum 1797 he published his *Proofs of a conspiracy against all the religions and governments of Europe, carried on in the secret meetings of free masons, illuminati, and readin societies* which was so popular that it went through four editions in slightl more than a year.

II

Robison, it should be emphasized, was a much travelled though reserve scholar of wide experience. Through the patronage of Admiral Sir Charle Knowles (d. 1777) he witnessed the fall of Quebec in 1759, observed the aftermath of the Lisbon earthquake in 1760, and tested John Harrison's chronomete for the Board of Longitude in its trial voyage to Jamaica in 1760–1761. Thoug his forte was applied mechanics, another patron Joseph Black (professor o chemistry at the University of Edinburgh 1766–1799) gained for him th lectureship in chemistry at the University of Glasgow in 1766. Four years late at the invitation of Queen Catherine the Great, Robison and Knowles joine the small group of British expatriates in her Court to work on applied nava mechanics. The Empress was so impressed by his performance that in 1771 sh approved the invitation he extended to James Watt to come to St Petersbur as Master Founder of Iron Ordnance (11). By 1772 she had appointed him a Professor of Mathematics at Cronstadt where he taught the Imperial Sea Cade Corps of Nobles. In 1774, however, Robison was successfully induced b Black and by Principal William Robertson to assume the vacant chair o natural philosophy at the University of Edinburgh at a pecuniary loss in spit of having drawn a better offer from Queen Catherine. Once ensconced in hi chair he set intellectually rigorous standards in his lectures and continued hi varied activities as a technical consultant for government departments an private industry. No wonder that after his death James Watt recalled that 'H had the quickest and clearest comprehension of every question in science o any person I ever knew . . . . ' (12).

In spite of its palpable absurdities, Robison's *Proofs of a conspiracy* appealed to the pervasive prejudice, intolerance and uneasiness of the times. Coming from such a respected professor and natural philosopher, who was Secretary t he Royal Society of Edinburgh from its inception in 1783 until his resignation n 1798, it rapidly achieved wide circulation not only in Britain but also in the Jnited States of America (13). Robison claimed that in France and Germany nasonic lodges had been taken over by *illuminati* in religion and politics who nad been particularly active in the French Revolution. He warned the nervous 3ritish public that British lodges were potentially subversive. In company vith the Abbé Barruel, whose *Memoires pour servir a l'histoire du Jacobinisme* ilso published in 1797 attained equally wide circulation, he denounced Voltaire, Condorcet, Turgot, d'Holbach, d'Alembert and Diderot as venal atheists and omenting revolutionaries. Like Edmund Burke's *Letters on a regicide peace* oublished in 1796, it combined outraged horror and extravagant invective. Robison, who regarded the British constitution as exemplary (14), genuinely eared the erosive powers of 'Jacobinism'. As he confessed to James Watt, 'We ire posting as hard as we can to brutality and barbarism, and must, I think, oon shake hands with confusion and calamity . . . .' (15). Quite approp- iately Robison dedicated his book to William Wyndham, British Secretary or War (1794–1801), whose fixed antipathy to any reforming constitutional hange had been conspicuously reflected in his successful advocacy of the sus- oension of the Habeas Corpus Act in May 1794.

The chief British victim of Robison's attack was Joseph Priestley (F.R.S. 766), the radical Unitarian minister and natural philosopher, whose house ind laboratory in Birmingham had been destroyed during the riots of 14–16 uly 1791. At least retrospectively, the British government condoned the listurbances; and though George III deplored the means employed he told Henry Dundas: 'I cannot but feel better pleased that Priestley is the sufferer for he doctrines he and his party have instilled' (16). No doubt Robison agreed vith his former colleague Hugh Blair (professor of rhetoric 1762–1784) that 'Dr Priestley and his gang brought them [the riots] on their own head; and there is io harm in their having some taste of that *Majesty of the People* they are so fond of' (17). Six years later Robison capitalized on Priestley's unpopularity in Church and State circles by attacking his views on politics, religion and natural ohilosophy as a related body of allegedly 'illuminist' ideas. Robison had little ympathy with Priestley's utilitarianism and his unqualified belief in the per- ectibility of man. But his chief opposition to Priestley stemmed from the atter's vigorous support of the indefeasible rights of man. In Robison's opinion he unbridled expression of personal rights would lead to perpetual social urbulence. With a censorious glance at Paine and Priestley, he deplored their nfluence: 'that accursed maxim, which now fills every mind, of thinking continually of our rights, and anxiously demanding them from every quarter is the greatest bane of life – filling the mind with discontent, and causing it t rankle at every thought of obligation – The dreadful situation of Europe a this day shows how hostile this maxim is to peace and order' (18). Nor ha Robison much sympathy with Priestley's materialism as it had been manifeste in his physical explanation of David Hartley's associationist theory of min (19). Priestley's assumption of a refined undulating aether to explain ment processes was in Robison's opinion criminal in at least two respects. It wa simply at odds with rational mechanics; and, more importantly, Priestley ha unjustifiably and dogmatically improvised on the hypothesis of the aethe which Newton had cautiously suggested to explain natural processes. Robiso consistently and fiercely opposed the assumption, whether speculative or dog matic, that intervening fluids caused field-phenomena: for him the properti of these fluids were unknowable or unknown so that their gratuitous use wa totally redundant; and, in any event, their introduction merely multiplied ol difficulties such as the problem of action at a distance. No wonder then tha when he attacked Priestley's advocacy of a refined undulating aether to explai mental processes, he pungently pointed out: 'Newton's aether is assumed as *fac totum* by every precipitate sciolist, who in despite of logic, and in contra diction to all the principles of mechanics, gives us theories of muscular motio of animal sensation, and even of intelligence and volition by the undulation c aetherial fluids' (20).

Even more dangerous for Robison was that the Unitarian minister by h adoption of fluid theories encouraged atheism by blandly reducing God t nothing but the most extensive and refined undulation, and his own ment processes to 'the quiverings of some fiery marsh *miasma*' (21). Robison clearl saw himself as a disciple of Newton's theology and not like Priestley as a dev iator from it. Keen to involve God in His created universe and to keep Hi active there, Robison significantly appealed to the authority of the Gener Scholium which Newton had added to the second edition of his *Princip Mathematica*. In quoting verbatim and at length Newton's views on the contin ing superintendence and dominion by God of His universe from moment t moment, Robison put himself quite explicitly in the Newtonian voluntari theological tradition from which in his opinion Priestley had grievousl strayed (22).

The message of Robison's book was unconcealed. Suspicious of circulatin libraries as 'Nurseries of Sedition and Impiety', he urged the banning of publi meetings, the proscription of irreligion, and the maintenance of unreforme government in its vital aspects such as continuing corruption and limitatio on suffrage (23). Indeed Robison's warnings were fully attuned to the repre ive activities of Pitt's government not only in England and Scotland but also n 1798 in Ireland. It seems that the friends of government, particularly the ,ord Advocate of Scotland, approved Robison's attempt to inform his country- nen of the plots being laid against order and peace (24). Certainly the coercive neasures which Pitt's government introduced in 1798 and 1799, such as ban- ing secret associations and censoring printing presses to exclude dangerous oreign material, fulfilled Robison's desiderata.

It must not be supposed that his *Proofs of a conspiracy* was Robison's solitary enture at that time into the area of politics – religion – natural philosophy. rom 1797 until 1800 he acted as the senior scientific contributor to the *Supple- ent to the third edition of the Encyclopaedia Britannica* which was edited and argely written by George Gleig who had previously edited the last six volumes f the third edition to which Robison had contributed. Gleig, later the Bishop f Brechin (1808–40), fully shared Robison's abhorrence of political, religious nd moral innovations (25). Again like Robison he deplored the atheism of rench determinists such as La Place and feared the results of setting the rabble ree from the restraints of religion. Not surprisingly the *Supplement* was per- asively and explicitly 'anti-Jacobin' in attitude, and more emphatic in this espect than Gleig's last volumes of the third edition had been. Every oppor- unity was taken by Gleig and Robison to support and diffuse the positions dopted by Robison in his 1797 book. A few examples, mainly culled from he opening pages of the *Supplement*, must suffice to show the frequency and ntensity of its characteristic bias and flavour.

The work's chief aim was boldly and proudly set out by Gleig in his dedi- ation to George III whom he regarded as the guardian of European law, eligion, morality and social order: it was to combat the anarchy and atheism vhich in his opinion the French encyclopaedists had deliberately laboured to pread (26). Accordingly by its third page Gleig in his article 'Action' was varmly deploring the dreadful consequences which resulted in France 'from hat pretended philosophy which excludes the agency of mind from the uni- erse . . . . ' (27). Robison, too, unable to bend his first article 'Arch' to pol- mical purposes, eagerly exploited the opportunities which his second article Astronomy' afforded him. His fiercest thrusts were naturally reserved for the rench determinists and atheists. For instance, in reference to the eternal dur- bility of the solar system which oscillates periodically about a mean state, Robison characteristically affirmed that it 'strikes the mind of a Newton, and ndeed any heart possessed of sensibility to moral or intellectual excellence, as mark of wisdom prompted by benevolence. But De La Place and others, nfected with the *Theophobia Gallica* engendered by our licentious desires, are eager to point it out as a mark of fatalism' (28). In subsequent articles Burke was praised for alerting the supporters of order and religion; and Bailly Brissot, Condorcet, Voltaire, Rousseau, D'Alembert and Diderot were denounced as fomenters of revolution and atheism (29). Needless to say the long exposure of Illuminism was based on the books by Robison and Barruel (30) The necessity of social, religious and political stability was avidly supported throughout the *Supplement*: quite typically the career of Robert Burns, who had held 'Jacobin' sentiments and had succumbed to the hard-drinking of the Dumfries gentry, was adduced as 'a melancholy proof of the danger of *suddenly* elevating even the greatest mind above its original level' (31). In many respect therefore, the *Supplement* can be seen as a substantiation and amplification o the views on politics, religion, and natural philosophy, which Robison had set out in his book.

III

Not content with two displays of British xenophobia and suspicion o Gallic innovation, Robison provided a third exhibition in 1803 when his edition of Joseph Black's Lectures appeared (32). Black had died in 1799, leaving behind very few publications and a mass of imperfect lecture notes. Though he had laid the basis of pneumatic chemistry and discovered the principle of latent heat, most of his professorial energy had been devoted to simple and elegant lecturing and very little to research. In deference to his patron Robison was keen to prevent literal publication of Black's scrappy lecture notes and to claim for him priority and originality. Moreover Robison's disappointment was deepened when he realized from studying Black's notes that they showed merely piecemeal accommodation of Lavoisier's ideas. Robison apprehended only too clearly that in the 1780s Lavoisier and his school had successfully challenged Black for the leadership of European chemistry. Loath to publish a work in which Black would have appeared as a humble pupil of Lavoisier and as a dull lecturer, Robison edited the lecture notes accordingly.

Robison's vindication of the reputation, originality and priority due to his friend, patron and colleague was set in a double context. Firstly, he was intellectually committed to the phlogiston theory of combustion: for him any satisfactory theory of that process had to explain all aspects of combustion including the production of heat and light; Lavoisier's exclusive insistence on mere weight relations in chemical reactions was too simplifying. Secondly Robison suspected and hated French innovations in science to such an extent that he erroneously believed that the new calendar, the new metric system o weights and measures, and the new nomenclature in chemistry were the sectarian works of Jacobins tainted by their intimacy with Robespierre (33). He interpreted the new nomenclature as an effort of Lavoisier's junto to obliterate non-French contributions to chemistry such as Black's researches. He even alleged that Madame Lavoisier, dressed as a priestess, had ceremonially burned on an altar to the accompaniment of a solemn requiem a copy of Stahl's *Chemiae dogmaticae*, a work which elaborated the phlogiston theory (34). Yet Robison was sensitive to one aspect of the national context of French science: the new French chemistry led by Lavoisier, Fourcroy, Monge and Morveau had been 'propagated as a public concern; and even propagated in the way in which that nation always chooses to act – by address, and with authority' (35). It is clear that Robison's detestation of 'Jacobinism' was exacerbated by his suspicions of the Lavoisier school which he alleged had scandalously neglected Black's claims for recognition. Though Robison's colleague Dalzel believed that his mind was sadly disrupted by the opium he took to ease severe abdominal pains, Robison's xenophobic 'anti-Jacobin' forays were not merely the productions of a disordered imagination (36). To the end of his life he consistently attacked fluid theories of phenomena such as electricity on the same grounds as those on which he had condemned Priestley's hypothesis of a ubiquitous undulating aether (37). Nor did he ever spare French atheists. Having attacked La Place's *Système du monde* merely *en passant* in his *Proofs of a conspiracy*, Robison exposed the French deviator from Newton's theology at greater length seven years later in his incomplete and highly competent textbook (38). He deplored the pointed contrast between Newton's Christianity and La Place's scepticism: in his concluding passage, a parody of Newton's General Scholium, La Place had studiously avoided all references to God as contriver, creator and governor. As Robison sadly acknowledged, 'Newton, one of the most pious of mankind, was set at the head of the atheistical sect' (39). That was anathema to him. Like Newton and unlike La Place, Robison's pursuit of natural knowledge was inseparable from his theological beliefs. Only a year before his death he told Henry Brougham about the importance he had always attached to natural theology. He was anxious that 'his students should not only learn the Laws of Nature, but that they should also perceive that these Laws were beautiful Marks of Wisdom, prompted by Beneficence. Such a view was, at all times, proper, and, in the present day cannot be too much kept in sight, when our Neighbours on the Continent are doing everything in their power, by their Colleges of Natural History, to banish the thought of an Artist, the Author and Preserver of this fair World' (40).

IV

Robison's successor in 1805 as professor of natural philosophy was the Reverend John Playfair who had occupied the chair of mathematics for twenty years (41). Playfair and his close friend Stewart shared the enviable reputatior of being regarded as the two great non-medical teachers at the University oi Edinburgh around 1800 (42). His published works in both mathematics anc geology had revealed rare perspicuity combined with wide information. Ir his *Illustrations of the Huttonian theory of the earth*, he had brilliantly expoundec and developed the geological views of his deceased agnostic friend James Hutton who was suspected of atheism; and had defended them as supporting and not subverting natural and indeed revealed theology. He stoutly uphel the timelessness implicit in Hutton's theory by deliberately comparing it wit La Place's demonstration of the periodic and self-correcting disturbances in th planetary system (43). Perhaps characteristically he derived support from Franci Bacon for his views that natural philosophy and divine philosophy were separ- ate though not incompatible activities and that truths about nature were no to be found in Genesis (44). Playfair again showed his patriotism by turning also to Newton but not for any theological views. In stressing that Hutton' theory was teleologically acceptable and in asserting that for Hutton the mos valuable part of his work lay in the evidence it provided of wise and beneficen design, Playfair did not once invoke Newton's authority (45). Instead it wa chiefly in defending Hutton's views on the existence and effects of subterranea compressed heat, the real novelty of the theory, that Playfair appealed to New ton for sanction. Twice he quoted from Query 11 of the *Opticks*, firstly to stres that the effects ascribed by Hutton to compressed heat closely resembled thos postulated by Newton to exist in the Sun and the fixed stars, and secondly t suggest that heat could exist without fuel (46). As a major aim of his *Illustration* was to preserve and expand the independence of geological enquiry by arguin *inter alia* that geologists should concern themselves with proximate and nc final causes, Playfair coolly avoided extensive discussion of theological issue such as God's continuing superintendence of His world. His passing reference to an omniscient and benevolent deity differed sharply from Robison's insist- ence on God's omnipotence.

Within Edinburgh society at large Playfair, Stewart, Henry Mackenzie an Sir James Hall were the City's 'senior literati' in 1803 according to Franc Jeffrey (47). Unlike Robison, Playfair was sociable and indeed the soul of th literary Friday Club which arose in 1803 (48). His reputation for benevoler nobility was firmly established by this time and subsequently it even cowe the aggressive James Mill into rare humility (49). Certainly he moved easily and successfully in both the learned and fashionable worlds to the benefit of both. Particularly in old age he made his social mark: as Sydney Smith confessed to Jeffrey, 'Mrs. Apreece and the Miss Berries say that upon the whole he is the only man who can be called irresistible' (50). For Henry Cockburn and his friends Playfair realized their 'ideas of an amiable philosopher' (51). Even that arch Tory John Gibson Lockhart, the biographer of Sir Walter Scott, referred enthusiastically to Playfair as 'this fine old Archimedes' (52).

Playfair's high reputation in the City of Edinburgh was equalled by his standing as a professor within the University: his gift of lucid exposition was particularly admired. As a staunch Whig he used his professorial opportunities unostentatiously though firmly to spread his beliefs. Even during the difficult 1790s he encouraged free and wide discussion in the Academical Society, one of the university's many student societies, which was formed in 1796 and met in his class-room. It was no accident that liberally minded students, such as Henry Brougham, the third Earl Radnor, Francis Horner, and Leonard Horner, eagerly attended the lectures delivered by Stewart and the more accessible Playfair. Furthermore their houses were open to affluent boarders at about £300 per annum. Lord John Russell, a future leader of the Whigs and British Prime Minister, was only one of many students who enjoyed the pleasures of Playfair's intellect, his zealous love of liberty, and not least his gracious table (53).

Playfair's mettle was seriously tested as soon as he assumed his new chair in 1805 when the Leslie controversy erupted (54). When Playfair had been moved on 6 February from the mathematics Chair to that of natural philosophy, one of the first candidates for the vacant post was the Reverend Thomas Macknight who had indicated his willingness to resign his parochial charge if he should be elected to the Chair by the Town Council, then its patrons. However, the Moderate party of the Edinburgh clergy, keen to multiply clerical Chairs, expressed their determination to support Macknight only if he retained his parish and thereby became a potential pluralist. On discovering this policy, Stewart and Playfair protested vigorously to the Lord Provost of Edinburgh, drawing his attention to the danger of uniting academic and clerical posts and also alleging that the Moderates were trying to subvert the precious intellectual independence of the University. In retaliation against the Moderates they began to canvass on behalf of John Leslie, the outstanding candidate for the Chair. Playfair in particular had a strong personal reason for supporting his friend and protégé Leslie (F.R.S. 1807): both men were extensively patronized by two wealthy and determined Whigs, the Ferguson brothers of Raith (55).

By mid-February 1805 rumours were spread that Leslie's famous book *An experimental inquiry into the nature and propagation of heat* contained heretica remarks. In note xvi Leslie had indeed written favourably of the sceptical Davi Hume's doctrines that causation did not imply the necessary connexion o cause and effect and was nothing but an observed constant and invariabl sequence of events (56). It was alleged *contra* Leslie that his espousal of Hume' views, if extended to natural theology, would inevitably destroy its chief basi i.e., the argument from design. Indeed the Edinburgh ministers increased thei pressure on the Town Council and Senate by threatening to exercise thei ancient right of advising the Town Council about appointments to chair Meanwhile in late February Leslie had wisely taken the precaution of informin the Town Council that he was entirely orthodox and that he dissociated himse from Hume's doctrine of causation as far as it related to religion. The Tow Council was impressed by Leslie who enjoyed the support of savants such a Sir Joseph Banks and the status which the Royal Society of London had give him in early 1805 by the award of the Rumford medal for his work on heat it also resented the challenge to its authority issued by the Moderates. Accord ingly it elected Leslie to the chair in mid-March while the Edinburgh ministe were still plotting. Faced by this *fait accompli* the Edinburgh ministers split generally the Evangelical group favoured acquiescence; the Moderates, how ever, determined to continue the fight. They succeeded in pushing the matte through the Presbytery and Synod levels up to the chief forum of debate an decision in the Church of Scotland, i.e., the General Assembly which met i late May 1805. Even by the standards of Scottish ecclesiastical warfare th debate was unparalleled in its angry bitterness. After two days' contention t which Stewart as the University's representative made a telling contributio the General Assembly decided by the narrow majority of 96 to 84 that th Leslie matter should be dropped. The Evangelicals within the Church of Sco land had at last disturbed the dominance which the Moderates had enjoye for several decades.

The issues involved in the Leslie affair were many and in one respect para doxical. Firstly, the conflict about the location of ecclesiastical power betwee the Moderates and Evangelicals was paralleled by the dispute about academi power fought by the Town Council and Senate against the Moderate group i the Edinburgh clergy. As a result of this contention the right of clergy t supervise university appointments was successfully challenged, the propriet of pluralism questioned, and one important implication of Hume's philosoph was re-ventilated. In the debate on the relation between natural and reveale religion, the Moderates not unexpectedly emphasized the former and th Evangelicals the latter. Yet the Evangelicals, in supporting Leslie, paradoxicall embraced the views on causation held by the atheist Hume. They realized that Hume's doctrine demolished the chief foundation of the Moderates' cherished natural theology, leaving a *tabula rasa* on which only revealed religion could be built.

The University's dominant voices and polemicists in the Leslie affair were Stewart and Playfair. Indeed this was the only occasion on which either of them decided to indulge in overt political action and ideological commitment. Stewart published *A short statement of some important facts, relative to the late election of a Mathematical Professor in the University of Edinburgh* in which he exposed the machinations of the Moderates and attempted to demonstrate that philosophic necessitarianism tends to exclude God from His universe. Playfair distinguished himself with a *Letter to the Lord Provost*, and a *Letter to the author of the examination of Professor Stewart's short statement of facts* which Cockburn thought one of the best controversial pamphlets in English. His credentials were impeccable: though he had qualified and practised as a clergyman, he had resigned his living in 1782 to act as a private tutor and had not reverted of it. His own career demonstrated his basic point that the Edinburgh chair to mathematics was a full-time job if the high standards of research and teaching attained for it by the Gregorys and Maclaurin were to be maintained (57). The inseparable Playfair and Stewart formed an effective pair, though in a bitter pamphleteering war even Playfair's previous priesthood did not render him immune from obloquy. It was not accidental that in a skilful polemic the Reverend John Inglis, a leading Edinburgh Moderate, referred to Robison's exposure in his *Proofs of a conspiracy* of the Continental *illuminati* and revolutionaries, one of whose main aims was allegedly to seize the universities and to exclude clergymen from them. Though he disavowed the suspicions he knew he would raise, Inglis warned his readers that Stewart and Playfair shared the illuminatist aims of separating the interests of religion and literate culture and of secularizing the universities (58).

Their support of Leslie in 1805 was however not new. Trouble with respect to Leslie had arisen previously at the University of St Andrews in 1795 and 1804 when he had twice failed to gain the chair of natural philosophy. On the first occasion Stewart's refusal to write a testimonial for the Moderate candidate John Rotherham had irritated John Hill, step-brother of the Reverend George Hill, leader of the Moderates in the Church of Scotland and Principal of St Mary's College at St Andrews, as he confessed to the Lord Provost of Edinburgh: 'This shows a keenness that I do not like & Leslie whom Stuart [*sic*] supports is as a philosopher sceptical and in political matters what no good man shou'd be. I cannot bear the thought of such a man getting to St. And. & am astonished at Stuart & Playfair who always go together giving him their Countenance.' On the second occasion Hill himself reported to Henry Dundas that Leslie was 'a professed atheist, and was a democratical leader in the times of trouble' (59). Hill was probably correct on one point: though he was hardly an active republican but a Whig, Leslie was with little doubt an atheist (60). It is clear that his partly deserved reputation for atheism and 'Jacobinism' crucially hindered the attempts he made in 1795 and 1804 to gain a Chair at St Andrews. As a result of these two failures, Leslie's scorn of the Hill family and their monopolizing spirit increased just as much as his hatred of 'the pestilential air of monkery' (61). When the Leslie controversy erupted it is not surprising that in particular Stewart, who had old if obscure scores to settle with the Moderates, strongly supported Leslie who had also suffered from the exertion of the Hills' power. Nor is it surprising that in their support of Leslie in 1805 for a chair at the University of which they were distinguished professors Stewart and Playfair once more joined forces, this time publicly, to prevent yet another triumph of the Hillite Tories and the Edinburgh Moderates. Their immediate campaign for Leslie and their exposition of the issues involved resulted not only from their concern with the intellectual independence of the University but also from their desire to bring those two rabid groups to heel. The defeat of the Moderates in the Leslie affair has been customarily interpreted as a crucial sign indicating the emergence of the Evangelicals as a powerful group within the Church of Scotland. Though much remains to be discovered perhaps it could also be regarded as one of the first successes of nineteenth-century Scottish Whiggery, an achievement engineered by Playfair and Stewart.

V

As Professor of natural philosophy Playfair published little specialized research Instead he revelled in his role as the first British natural philosopher to make extensive contributions to that new and characteristic genre, the nineteenth-century periodical. Reviews were Playfair's forte. Accordingly in fifteen years beginning in 1804 he published anonymously about sixty articles in the Whig *Edinburgh Review* (62). Though his pupil the coruscating Henry Brougham (F.R.S. 1803) and his friend John Thomson covered special areas within science, the main contributor in the field of theoretical and practical science was Playfair. It is a common-place that Francis Jeffrey and his cohorts introduced the novelty of articles on political economy; yet it was equally important that through Playfair's efforts the importance of science in general literate culture was demonstrated (63). The *Review* suited Playfair well. No doubt he welcomed the contributors' independence of booksellers, the handsome fees paid by Archibald Constable, and the wide range of books he reviewed. Its political stance, too, was attractive: like most of the Edinburgh reviewers who were convinced that silent acceptance of the political *status quo* would bring disaster, he advocated moderate non-violent reform, a position half-way between obstructive conservatism and utopian radicalism.

Two aspects of Playfair's work in the *Edinburgh Review* are striking. Firstly, like other contributors, he used his reviews as a means of ventilating his own concerns. Secondly, at a time when British xenophobia was still rife he urged and demonstrated an urbane catholicity and intellectual largesse which did not exclude the political enemy France. In scientific matters he opposed the narrow British insularity which the wars and Robison had encouraged. Indeed his early articles in the *Review* demonstrate both these points. Quite characteristically Playfair used his review of a mathematical work by a woman as a vehicle for his well-known feminist sentiments (64). He exploited Horsley's *Euclid* to urge the cause of algebra as the equal of geometry in proving propositions and its superiority for discovering them, and to compare Continental progress with British stagnation in mathematics (65). Naturally he concluded his review of Small's *Kepler* with a homily on inductive investigation and the legitimate uses of hypothesis and of theory (66). Not surprisingly, he introduced a review of an Italian work on plant physiology with some remarks on the distinctively Italian style of science and the seven most important Italian scientific societies (67).

This catholicity was most conspicuously displayed in his views on French innovations in science. Before Playfair began to write for the *Review* Brougham had used its columns to denounce the authoritarian Lavoisier junto in his review of Robison's edition of *Black's lectures*. Yet Brougham argued that the new chemical nomenclature was not derived from the 'innovating phrenzy, and puerile vanity, which produced the new calendar and metrology' (68). Unlike them, the new nomenclature was not merely destructive: according to Brougham it had followed positively beneficial changes in chemical knowledge. Four years later in reviewing Mechain and Delambre's famous work on the length of the arc of the Earth's meridian, Playfair struck out boldly in dissenting from the views expressed by Robison and Brougham. In welcoming the metric system of weights and measures, Playfair criticized the metrological reformers for having been cautious in their innovations: they should have adopted the duodecimal and not the decimal system of numbers (69). His peroration urged Britain to copy France by adopting the metric system almost *in toto* and it succinctly encapsulated one of his characteristic attitudes:

> . . . this cannot be done, especially in our own case, without a certain sacrifice of national vanity; and the times do not give much encouragement to hope that such a sacrifice will be made. The calamities which the power and ambition of the French government have brought on Europe, induce us to look with jealousy and suspicion on their most innocent and laudable exertions. We ought not, however, to yield to such prejudices, where good sense and argument are so obviously against them. In a matter that concerns the arts and sciences only, the maxim may be safely admitted, *Fas est et ab hoste doceri* (70).

Playfair's subsequent articles in the *Review* on French science are not unexpectedly descants on this theme. In his thirty-five page eulogy of La Place's *Traité de méchanique céleste*, Playfair delicately devoted just one page to the question of whether the stability and permanence of the solar system are contingent or necessary. Having gently chided La Place for ignoring the way in which his discoveries 'lead to a very beautiful extension of the doctrine of *final causes*,' Playfair devoted more space to British neglect of higher mathematics, to the regrettable dominance in Britain of synthetic geometry, and to an attack on the mathematics teaching dispensed at the University of Cambridge (71). A year later in his commendation of the *Compte rendu par l'Institut de France*, he impartially acknowledged French dominance in physical and mathematical sciences. Furthermore he made a crucial distinction between the French people, in his view the most enlightened European nation, and the war-mongering Emperor Napoleon (72). By 1810 in a second eulogy of La Place's work, this time his *System of the world*, Playfair totally ignored the implicit scepticism and determinism which had so outraged Robison; indeed he made only two passing references to his own belief that La Place's demonstration of the periodical nature of astronomical irregularities confirmed God's wisdom and benificence (73). His policy was clearly to either smoothly ignore or genially minimize the religious problems associated with natural philosophy. By 1814 Playfair felt sufficiently confident to use the concluding paragraph of his well-known text-book to bracket together, without apology or qualification, Newton and La Place, a conjunction which Robison would have abhorred (74). Again in contrast with Robison, Playfair felt that the discovery of more physical mechanical causes and agents did not exclude God's governance from nature and thereby encourage atheism: on the contrary, whether explained or not, the *de facto* contingent regularities observed in nature were for him sufficient indication of God's dominion (75). In short in his early *Edinburgh Review* articles Playfair blandly supported though he did not justify in detail three unpopular courses of action with regard to natural philosophy: 'to leave the matter open to inquiry; to abstain from dogmatising; and to avoid whatever can narrow the field of philosophical investigation' (76).

VI

An apposite coda was provided by Playfair himself in 1815 when he at last delivered and published his biography of Robison, his predecessor as professor of natural philosophy in the University and as Secretary of the Royal Society of Edinburgh (77). In this memoir Playfair generously explained Robison's credulity by showing how it was fostered by the indiscriminating suspicion and alarm so pervasive in the 1790s. He calmly evaluated Lavoisier's behaviour to Black, the new chemical nomenclature, the metric system, and the new calendar against all of which Robison had inveighed. Quite characteristically with the exception of the calendar Playfair defended what had been anathematic to Robison (78). He gave short shrift, too, to Robison's conspiracy theory of the French Revolution. For Playfair the visions of German *illuminati* or the activities of French free-masons were by themselves inadequate agents of such a great change. Showing his debt to the conjectural and cultural historians of eighteenth century Scotland, Playfair argued that political upheavals occur as the result of 'an impulse communicated to the whole, not in consequence of a force that can act only on a few' (79). He insisted that in France the nation's political maturity far exceeded the degree of liberty it enjoyed so that in a crisis total revolution had occurred. The chief political implication of the French Revolution for Britain was made abundantly clear by Playfair to the Fellows of the Royal Society of Edinburgh and to the readers of its *Transactions*:

> It will be happy for mankind, if they learn from these disasters, the great lessons which they seem so much calculated to enforce, and if, while the people reflect on the danger of sudden innovation, their rulers consider, that it is only by a gradual reformation of abuses, and by extending, rather than abridging, the liberties of the people, that a remedy can be provided against similar convulsions (80).

Acknowledgments

I am grateful to the University of Pennsylvania for the tenure of a visiting professorship in Spring 1970 when the first draft of this paper was written. For help and encouragement I am indebted to the faculty and students of its

Department of History and Philosophy of Science, particularly Dr A. W. Thackray, and to Dr A. C. Chitnis of the University of Stirling. For granting permission to refer to manuscripts and to quote from them I am grateful to: the Trustees of the National Library of Scotland; the Keeper of Manuscripts of Edinburgh University Library; the Librarian of University College London; and the Curator of the E. F. Smith Collection in the Library of the University of Pennsylvania.

NOTES

(1) A. Grant, *The story of the University of Edinburgh* (London, 1884), *passim*; D. B. Horn, *A short history of the University of Edinburgh*, 1556–1889 (Edinburgh, 1967), pp. 36–94. The importance of the University of Edinburgh in British science during the industrial revolution is stressed by J. B. Morrell, 'Individualism and the structure of British science in 1830', *Historical studies in the physical sciences* (in the press); *idem*, 'The University of Edinburgh in the late eighteenth century: its scientific eminence and academic structure', *Isis* (in the press); *idem*, 'Practical chemistry in the University of Edinburgh, 1799–1843', *Ambix* **16**, 66–80 (1969).

(2) The paragraphs which deal with Scottish anti-Jacobinism are based on: P. A. Brown, *The French Revolution in English History* (London, 1918); H. W. Meikle, *Scotland and the French Revolution* (Glasgow, 1912); T. C. Smout, *A history of the Scottish people* 1560–1830 (London, 1969); W. Ferguson, *Scotland* 1689 *to the present* (Edinburgh, 1968).

(3) Ferguson, *op. cit.* (2), p. 227.

(4) H. Cockburn, *Memorials of his time* (Edinburgh and London, 1910), p. 78.

(5) J. Veitch, 'Memoir of Dugald Stewart', *The collected works of Dugald Stewart*, ed. W. Hamilton (Edinburgh, 1854–1860), **10**, pp. lxxi–lxxiv.

(6) Brown, *op. cit.* (2), p. 174.

(7) Horn, *op. cit.* (1), p. 40.

(8) G. C. H. Paton, 'A biography of Baron Hume,' *Baron David Hume's lectures* 1786–1822 (Edinburgh, 1958), **6**, pp. 344–348.

(9) Cockburn, *op. cit.* (4), p. 169.

(10) The basic biography is J. Playfair, 'Biographical account of John Robison,' *The works of John Playfair* (Edinburgh, 1822), **4**, pp. 121–178. This was corrected in parts by T. Young, 'Life of Robison', *Miscellaneous works of the late Thomas Young*, ed. G. Peacock (London, 1855), **2**, pp. 505–517.

(11) Robison to Watt, 22 April 1771, *Partners in science: letters of James Watt and Joseph Black*, ed. E. Robinson & D. McKie (London, 1970), p. 24.

(12) J. P. Muirhead, *The origin and progress of the mechanical inventions of James Watt* (London, 1854), **2**, p. 298.

(13) *Monthly Magazine*, **4**, 503 (1797); *Monthly Review*, **25**, 303–315 (1798); *Analytical Review*, **26**, 401–407 (1797); Cornelius, *Extracts from Professor Robison's 'Proofs of a Conspiracy,' etc.* (Boston, Mass., 1799). The deep impression made in the United States of America may be judged from the letter of 20 March 1805 from Timothy Dwight, President of Yale, to Robison: 'Multitudes of my countrymen, and among them the wisest and best, feel deeply indebted to you for your efforts in the cause of truth and righteousness —efforts, in their opinion, able, upright, and indispensably demanded by the time

... beyond all doubt, you have contributed largely and effectually to the erection of an immovable standard against the miserable scheme of profligacy formed by Weishaupt, and then spreading through this country as well as through Europe'. See *Life of Benjamin Silliman*, ed. G. P. Fisher (Philadelphia, 1866), **1**, p. 157.

(14) J. Robison, *Proofs of a conspiracy against all the religions and governments of Europe, carried on in the secret meetings of free masons, illuminati, and reading societies*, 4th edn. plus postscript (New York, 1798), p. 340.

(15) Robison to Watt, 11 December 1799, Robinson and McKie, *op. cit.* (11), p. 318.

(16) J. A. Langford, *Century of Birmingham Life* (Birmingham, 1868), **1**, p. 477.

(17) Blair to Lady Miller, 20 August 1791, E. F. Smith Collection, University of Pennsylvania Library.

(18) John Robison to John Lee, 5 January 1799, National Library of Scotland, MS. 3431, f. 279.

(19) J. Priestley, *Hartley's theory of the human mind on the principle of the association of ideas* (London, 1775), *passim.*

(20) Robison, *op. cit.* (14), p. 369.

(21) *Ibid.*, p. 329.

(22) *Ibid.*, pp. 181–182. The voluntarist tradition's stress on God's omnipotence and not omniscience is incisively analysed by J. E. McGuire, 'Force, active principles, and Newton's invisible realm,' *Ambix*, **15**, 154–208 (1968).

(23) *Ibid.*, pp. 273, 370, 389.

(24) George Gleig to Robison, 23 January 1798, National Library of Scotland, MS. 3869, f. 52; and Robison to Robert Dundas, 31 January 1798, Edinburgh University Library, MS. La. II. 500.

(25) George Gleig to John Robison, 24 May 1797, National Library of Scotland, MS. 3869, ff. 11–13.

(26) *Supplement to the third edition of the Encyclopaedia Britannica*, 2nd edn. (Edinburgh, 1803), **1**, pp. iii–iv.

(27) *Ibid.*, p. 3.

(28) *Ibid.*, p. 53.

(29) *Ibid.*, pp. 62–63, 118–120, 139–141, 193, 453–454.

(30) *Ibid.*, p. 781.

(31) *Ibid.*, p. 147.

(32) This paragraph is based on: *Lectures on the elements of chemistry, delivered in the University of Edinburgh; by the late Joseph Black*, ed. J. Robison (Philadelphia, 1806), **1**, pp. iv–xii; Robinson and McKie, *op. cit.* (11), pp. 322–386; Robison to James Black, 21 April 1802, D. McKie and D. Kennedy, 'On some letters of Joseph Black and others,' *Ann. Sci.*, **16**, 161–170 (1960).

(33) *Black's lectures*, **2**, p. 355; McKie and Kennedy, *op. cit.* (32), p. 168.

(34) *Black's Lectures*, **2**, p. 358.

(35) *Ibid.*, **2**, p. 354.

(36) C. Innes, 'Memoir of Professor Dalzel,' A. Dalzel, *History of the University of Edinburgh from its foundation* (Edinburgh, 1862), **1**, 154-155.

(37) J. Robison, *A system of mechanical philosophy*, ed. D. Brewster (Edinburgh, 1822), **2**, pp. 178–198 shows his opposition to fluid theories of electricity.

(38) Robison, *Proofs of a conspiracy*, pp. 182–183; J. Robison, *Elements of mechanical philosophy, being the substance of a course of lectures on that science* (Edinburgh, 1804), pp. 682–695.

(39) Robison, *Elements of mechanical philosophy*, p. 694.
(40) John Robison to Henry Brougham, 3 April 1804, Edinburgh University Library, La. II 583/11.
(41) The basic biography is James Playfair, 'Biographical account of the late Professor Playfair, *The works of John Playfair* (Edinburgh, 1822), **1**, pp. xi–lxxvi.
(42) *The life and times of Henry Lord Brougham written by himself*, 3rd edn. (Edinburgh, 1872), p. 66.
(43) J. Playfair, *Illustrations of the Huttonian theory of the earth* (Edinburgh, 1802), pp. 437–440.
(44) *Ibid.*, pp. 125–128, 137, and especially 477–478.
(45) For example, *ibid.*, pp. 119–122.
(46) *Ibid.*, pp. 181–182 and 187.
(47) H. Cockburn, *Life of Lord Jeffrey* (Philadelphia, 1856), **1**, p. 121.
(48) H. A. Cockburn, 'An account of the Friday Club, written by Lord Cockburn, together with notes on certain other social clubs in Edinburgh,' *The Book of the Old Edinburgh Club*, **3**, 116 (1910).
(49) James Mill to Macvey Napier, 30 April 1818, *Selections from the correspondence of the late Macvey Napier*, ed. M. Napier (London, 1877), pp. 18–19.
(50) Sydney Smith to Francis Jeffrey, 22 June 1811, *The letters of Sydney Smith*, ed. N. C. Smith (Oxford, 1953), p. 209. The following year Mrs Apreece found Humphry Davy even more irresistible and married him.
(51) Cockburn, *Memorials*, pp. 338–339.
(52) [J. G. Lockhart], *Peter's letters to his kinsfolk*, 2nd edn. (New York, 1820), p. 103.
(53) John Playfair to Henry Brougham, 18 March 1810, Brougham MSS., University College Library, London. In a letter of 17 April 1811 to Mary Berry, Playfair expressed approval of young Russell who was then lodging with him: *Extracts of the journals and correspondence of Miss Berry*, ed. T. Lewis (London, 1865), **2**, p. 474.
(54) My account of the Leslie controversy is based on: *Tracts historical and philosophical, relative to . . . the election of Mr Leslie to the Professorship of Mathematics in that University* (Edinburgh, 1806); Cockburn, *Memorials*, pp. 186–195; F. Horner, 'Professor Stewart's statement of facts,' *Edinburgh Review*, **7**, 113–134 (1806); and the fundamental article by I. D. L. Clark, 'The Leslie controversy, 1805,' *Records of the Scottish Church History* Society, **14**, 179–197 (1963).
(55) M. Napier, *Memoir of John Leslie* (Edinburgh, 1836), p. 7.
(56) J. Leslie, *An experimental inquiry into the nature and propagation of heat* (London, 1804), p. 521.
(57) J. Playfair, 'Letter to the Lord Provost,' printed in *The works of Dugald Stewart* (Cambridge, 1829), **7**, pp. 303–310.
(58) J. Inglis, *An examination of Mr Dugald Stewart's pamphlet, relative to the late election of a mathematical professor in the University of Edinburgh* 2nd edn. (Edinburgh, 1806), pp. 54–55.
(59) Clark, *op. cit.*, (54), p. 188.
(60) With reference to the natural philosophy chair at the University of St Andrews, Leslie told James Brown in a letter of 19 November 1804: 'My politics and religion I believe would bear the ordeal; the former are much cooled, and I am always ready in the *externals* of devotion to comply with custom' (Edinburgh University Library, MS. Dc. 2. 57). By the mid-1820s it was common knowledge in Edinburgh that Leslie was an atheist. See National Library of Scotland, MS. 3456 (John Lee papers), f. 7.

(61) John Leslie to James Brown, no date, Edinburgh University Library, MS. Dc. 2. 57. In 1804 and 1805 Leslie was particularly anxious to cast down the Hills to whom he gave the title 'The Mountain'. Again in reference to the St Andrews chair he confessed to James Brown in a letter of 16 November 1804: 'I am not anxious to have the place, and yet I should like to overthrow the domineering faction of the mountain . . . But always remember *Ecraser l'Infame*' (Edinburgh University Library, MS. Dc. 2. 57).

(62) *The Wellesley index to victorian periodicals*, ed. W. E. Houghton (Toronto, 1966), **1**, pp. 1049–1050.

(63) This aspect of the *Review's* significance is surprisingly neglected by J. Clive, *Scotch reviewers: the Edinburgh Review*, 1802–1815 (Cambridge, Mass., 1957).

(64) J. Playfair, 'Donna Agnesi's analytical institutions,' *Edinburgh Review* **3**, 410 (1804).

(65) J. Playfair, 'Bishop Horsley's edition of Euclid,' *Edinburgh Review* **4**, 261–262 (1804).

(66) J. Playfair, 'Dr Small's account of Kepler's discoveries,' *Edinburgh Review* **5**, 451 (1805).

(67) J. Playfair, 'San Martino, sopra il carbone nei pianti,' *Edinburgh Review* **6**, 171-174 (1805).

(68) H. Brougham, 'Dr Black's lectures,' *Edinburgh Review* **3**, 21-22 (1803).

(69) J. Playfair, 'Mechain and Delambre, mesure d'un arc du méridien,' *Edinburgh Review* **9**, 376 (1807).

(70) *Ibid.*, pp. 390–391.

(71) J. Playfair, 'La Place, traité de méchanique céleste,' *Edinburgh Review* **11**, 278–279 (1808).

(72) J. Playfair, 'Compte rendu par l'Institut de France,' *Edinburgh Review* **15**, 1 and 22–23 (1810).

(73) J. Playfair, 'La Place's system of the world,' *Edinburgh Review* **15**, 403 and 411–412 (1810).

(74) J. Playfair, *Outlines of natural philosophy, being heads of lectures delivered in the University of Edinburgh* (Edinburgh, 1812–1814), **2**, pp. 340–341.

(75) J. Playfair, 'Prevost, vie de G. L. Le Sage', *Edinburgh Review* **10**, 150 (1807).

(76) J. Playfair, 'Vince on gravitation,' *Edinburgh Review* **13**, 116 (1809).

(77) J. Playfair, 'Biographical account of John Robison,' *Trans. Roy. Soc. Edin.*, **7**, 495–539 (1815), reproduced in *The works of John Playfair* (Edinburgh, 1822), **4**, pp. 121–178.

(78) *Ibid.*, pp. 170–173.

(79) *Ibid.*, p. 166.

(80) *Ibid.*, p. 168.

V

The Leslie affair: careers, kirk and politics in Edinburgh in 1805*

In recent years there has been a renewed interest in the work of John Leslie (1766–1832), who was successively professor of mathematics and professor of natural philosophy at the university of Edinburgh.[1] Much of this scholarship concentrates on Leslie's contributions to natural philosophy, but the already well-known controversy surrounding his election to the mathematics chair in 1805 has not been ignored. It has been recently argued by Dr John Burke that the chief ingredients of that controversy were suspicion of Leslie's religious beliefs and the subsequent debate on the relation between cause and effect.[2] This argument can usefully be extended. The Leslie case has long been seen as a landmark in the continuing struggle between the Moderate and Evangelical parties within the Church of Scotland. Similarly the metaphysical debate on the relation between cause and effect has often been regarded as camouflage which covered more personal and certainly less metaphysical issues which were at stake. Leslie in any case had made several attempts before 1805 to obtain a Scottish university chair: the victory of 1805 was in fact the triumphant conclusion of a long-standing battle involving personal jealousies and feuds which had been exacerbated by political and ecclesiastical party differences.[3] Almost all previous accounts of the

* For permission to cite and to quote from manuscripts in their care the author is grateful to Messrs Josiah Wedgwood & Sons Ltd., Barlaston, and to the University of Keele Library, where the manuscripts are deposited. For valuable critical comment on an earlier version of this article he is indebted to Mr J. R. R. Christie, Mr R. S. Porter, Dr S. Shapin, Mr R. N. Smart and Mr D. J. Withrington.

1 G. N. Cantor, 'Henry Brougham and the Scottish methodological tradition', *Studies in the History and Philosophy of Science*, ii (1971), 69–89; J. B. Morrell, 'Science and Scottish university reform: Edinburgh in 1826', *British Journal for the History of Science*, vi (1972), 39–56; Richard G. Olson, 'Count Rumford, Sir John Leslie, and the study of the nature and propagation of heat at the beginning of the nineteenth century', *Annals of Science*, xxvi (1970), 273–304; Richard G. Olson, 'Scottish philosophy and mathematics: 1750–1830', *Journal of the History of Ideas*, xxxii (1971), 29–44; Richard G. Olson, 'The reception of Boscovitch's ideas in Scotland', *Isis*, lx (1969), 91–103; Robert E. Schofield, *Mechanism and Materialism: British Natural Philosophy in an Age of Reason* (Princeton, 1970), 282–8.

2 John G. Burke, 'Kirk and causality in Edinburgh, 1805', *Isis*, lxi (1970), 340–54.

3 An outline of my analysis appeared in J. B. Morrell, 'Professors Robison and Playfair, and the theophobia gallica: natural philosophy, religion and politics in Edinburgh, 1789–1815', *Notes and Records of the Royal Society of London*, xxvi (1971), 43–63 (esp. 53–56).

Leslie controversy have tried to place it in the context of Scottish ecclesiastical and political affairs.[1] This paper is totally compatible with these valuable interpretations even though its chief novelty is the attempt, by using Leslie's unpublished correspondence, to see the case primarily from Leslie's own point of view.

On 6 February 1805 John Playfair was moved from the chair of mathematics to that of natural philosophy in the university of Edinburgh, the patrons of both chairs being the town council. One of the first candidates to appear for the vacant chair of mathematics was the Reverend Thomas Macknight, who had agreed to resign his incumbency if he should be elected. However, the Moderate group within the Edinburgh clergy was determined to support Macknight, himself an Edinburgh Moderate, only if he kept his parish living. On discovering this prospective case of pluralism, Dugald Stewart, professor of moral philosophy, and Playfair drew the attention of the lord provost to its difficulties and dangers; and they began to canvass on behalf of Leslie, whose quality and range of publication made him a strong candidate. By mid-February doubts were being circulated by the Edinburgh Moderates about Leslie's religious orthodoxy, mainly on the basis of footnote xvi of his *An Experimental Enquiry into the Nature and Propogation of Heat*. In that note Leslie had written favourably about the sceptical David Hume's doctrine of causation by asserting that in natural philosophy causation was nothing but an observed, constant and invariable sequence of events.[2] Hume's attack on the necessary connection between cause and effect, when applied to physical matters, had been publicly supported in the university for twenty years by Professors Robison and Stewart without any objection being raised by the Edinburgh Moderates; yet with respect to Leslie's candidature the Edinburgh Moderate ministers threatened to revive their lapsed right of advising the town council about elections to chairs. Leslie wisely proclaimed his orthodoxy; and the town council, impressed by his scientific achievements and by the award of the Rumford medals of the Royal Society of London on 7 February, rejected the Moderates' pleas and elected Leslie to the mathematics chair on 13 March. Only at this stage was there a public split among the Edinburgh ministers: the Evangelicals accepted Leslie's protestations and his election; the Moderates, however, continued the fight by pushing the matter through the presbytery and synod to the general assembly which debated the case

1 The best account is Ian D. L. Clark, 'The Leslie controversy, 1805', *Records of the Scottish Church History Society*, xiv (1963), 179–97. Clark (188) was the first to state that difficulties with respect to Leslie had arisen at St Andrews in 1795 and 1804.

2 John Leslie, *An Experimental Enquiry into the Nature and Propogation of Heat* (London, 1804), 521, where Leslie used Hume's views on physical causation to deny the existence of unobservable etherial fluids.

on 22 and 23 May 1805. By the narrow majority of 96 to 84 the assembly decided to drop the matter. In that way Leslie was cleared of the imputation of atheism, and the conduct of the Edinburgh presbytery (*de facto* the Edinburgh Moderates) was publicly rebuffed.

The defeat of the Moderates in the Leslie affair has been customarily interpreted as an important sign indicating that the Evangelicals had emerged as a powerful force within the Church of Scotland. For instance, Cunningham ascribed to it the subsequent rancour of the Edinburgh Moderates. In explaining why the Moderates, previously advocates of intellectual liberty, and the Evangelicals, previously exponents of severe orthodoxy, had exchanged their customary attitudes, Cunningham pointed out that personalities often interfere with principles: quite simply the Moderates, who in the eighteenth century had defended David Hume and Lord Kames against persecution, were themselves persecuting Leslie in 1805 in order to procure the chair for one of themselves.[1] Similarly George Grub saw the Leslie controversy as primarily a contribution to the long-standing debate about pluralism, in this case the projected union of a parochial ministry and an academic post.[2] Mathieson strengthened and expanded Grub's interpretation but pointed out that in the Leslie case Moderatism jettisoned its former undogmatic, accommodating and indeed 'moderate' attitude when its leaders not only insinuated that men of letters per se were hostile to religion but also attempted to re-establish clerical control of education.[3] Dr Ian Clark confirmed this interpretation by arguing that what was involved in the Leslie controversy was nothing less than the survival of Moderatism as a theological and ecclesiological system; and accordingly he has claimed that it was the Leslie case, and not the Disruption in 1843, which effected a crucial shift in the fortunes of the Moderates.[4] In exploring the characteristics and ultimate weaknesses of the Moderate programme, he argued that initially the Moderates tried to harmonise the interests of church and state without falling into erastianism, but that when the French Revolution broke out they aligned themselves with the predominant political interest in the hope of maintaining their power. Just at this time Henry Dundas, first as home secretary (1791–4) and then as secretary for war

1 John Cunningham, *The Church History of Scotland, from the Commencement of the Christian Era to the Present Time* (2nd ed., Edinburgh, 1882), ii, 430–3.

2 George Grub, *The Ecclesiastical History of Scotland* (Edinburgh, 1861), iv, 154–5.

3 William Law Mathieson, *Church and Reform in Scotland: a History from 1797 to 1843* (Glasgow, 1916), 75–115 (esp. 90–100).

4 Clark, 'Leslie Controversy', 179; also his 'From protest to reaction: the Moderate regime in the Church of Scotland, 1752–1805', N. T. Phillipson and Rosalind Mitchison (eds), *Scotland in the Age of Improvement* (Edinburgh, 1970), 200–24.

(1794–1801), was consolidating the network of political and ecclesiastical patronage which made him the greatest of Scotland's 'managers'. Not unexpectedly during the troubled 1790s, when fear of internal subversion was at its height, the Moderates became almost totally dependent on Dundas's patronage. Such an alliance with Dundas spurred the Evangelicals to seek support from political opposition groups. This meant that the Evangelicals became aligned with the Foxite Whigs, led by Henry Erskine. Thus between 1790 and 1804 the Scottish Tories were scarcely distinguishable from the Moderates and the Scottish Whigs from the Evangelicals. In short, the Leslie affair was the culmination of a conflict within the Church of Scotland between the rival Moderate and Evangelical parties in which the Moderates suffered a severe defeat: it is indeed misleading to conclude that in 1805 'a more moderate spirit had penetrated Scottish Presbyterianism'.[1]

Too much importance has been attributed to the metaphysical component of the Leslie affair. Henry Cockburn put this trenchantly: metaphysics, he said, 'were the pretence; while a claim of clerical domination over seats of learning was the real subject'.[2] This view was expressed at the assembly of 1805 by no less than seven speakers of mainly Whig Evangelical persuasion who tried to expose the allegedly pure motives of the Edinburgh Moderates. Malcolm Laing, for example, asserted that the whole business had 'originated in a contest for the mathematical chair in this college, between the friends of literature in the university, and certain of the clergy, inflamed by *l'esprit du corps* for a monopoly in favour of their order'.[3] He then averred that after Leslie's appointment to the chair the Edinburgh Moderates 'immediately had recourse to that system of intrigue and misrepresentation, which they have too long and too successfully pursued, and by which they seem to have resolved to appropriate the enjoyment of academical honours and advantages exclusively to themselves'.[4] Henry Erskine, the lay leader of the Evangelicals, put

1 Burke, 'Kirk and causality', 348.

2 Henry Cockburn, *Memorials of His Time* (Edinburgh, 1856), 203. Similar views to Cockburn's are found in: [Henry Brougham], 'Leslie's inquiry into the nature of heat', *Edinburgh Review,* vii (1805), 63–91 (75); [Francis Horner], 'Professor Stewart's statement of facts', *Edinburgh Review,* vii (1805), 113–34 (131); David Welsh, *Account of the Life and Writings of Thomas Brown* (Edinburgh, 1825), 94–96; 'John Leslie' in Robert Chambers (ed.), *A Biographical Dictionary of Eminent Scotsmen* (Glasgow, 1854), iii, 416–26 (418–20); Mathieson, *Church and Reform*, 98; William Ferguson, *Scotland: 1689 to the present* (Edinburgh, 1968), 271–2; Clark, 'From protest to reaction', 201.

3 *Report of the Proceedings and Debate in the General Assembly of the Church of Scotland, respecting the Election of Mr Leslie to the Mathematical Chair in the University of Edinburgh* (2nd ed., Edinburgh, 1806), 145. See also the speeches by William Laurence Brown, James Fergusson, Henry Erskine, the earl of Lauderdale, Adam Gillies and Dugald Stewart, ibid., 93, 126, 159, 171, 174 and 180.

4 Ibid., 146.

the matter in equally indelicate personal terms: Leslie had sinned in not making 'a sufficiently respectful bow to Dr Finlayson and to Dr Inglis',[1] who were respectively the chief organiser and the leading spokesman of the Edinburgh Moderates. In the vigorous pamphleteering warfare associated with the Leslie case, David Brewster, Playfair, Stewart and Andrew Mitchell Thomson were united in judging that Leslie's scientific eminence had allowed him to frustrate the caballing ambition of the Tory Edinburgh Moderates.[2]

When Leslie was elected to the Edinburgh mathematics chair he was almost thirty-nine years old. It was by no means his first job: indeed for no less than seventeen years he had occupied a number of situations which he hoped would give him financial reward as well as sufficient leisure in which to pursue his research, and had stood as a candidate for appropriate Scottish university chairs when they became vacant. When he finally succeeded in March 1805, he had already been a candidate for four chairs: natural philosophy at St Andrews in 1795; natural philosophy at Glasgow in 1796; natural philosophy at St Andrews in late 1804; and natural philosophy at Edinburgh in early February 1805. Only at his fifth attempt, therefore, did Leslie succeed; and the type of opposition which, in Leslie's opinion, had checked his professorial ambitions before 1805 was still active against him in 1805. The public controversy which erupted in mid-February 1805 had been previously rehearsed in private: the issues raised then, and the nature if not the identity of the opposition, were distressingly familiar to Leslie and to his supporters.

As Leslie was born at Largo, Fife, it is not surprising that his early education and some of his later aspirations were focused on the university of St Andrews. By the end of 1779–80, his first session there, his outstanding mathematical ability had attracted the attention of the university's chancellor, the eighth Earl of Kinnoul, who then began to pay the cost of Leslie's education with the intention that he should enter the church.[3] In 1785 he went to Edinburgh, where he

1 Ibid., 159.

2 [David Brewster], *An Examination of the Letter addressed to Principal Hill, on the Case of Mr Leslie, in a Letter to its Anonymous Author . . . By a Calm Observer* (Edinburgh, 1806), 23–25, 69–70, 80–85; John Playfair, *A Letter to the Author of the Examination of Professor Stewart's Short Statement of Facts* (Edinburgh, 1806), 34, 57, 60, 74, 85, 112, 116; Dugald Stewart, *Postcript to Mr Stewart's Short Statement of Facts relative to the Election of Professor Leslie* (Edinburgh, 1805), 6–9, 47–48; Andrew Mitchell Thomson, *A Letter to the Reverend Dr. Inglis, Author of 'An Examination of Professor Stewart's Short Statement of Facts relative to the Election of Mr Leslie'* (Edinburgh 1806), 3–5, 11, 34, 68–71, 120, 173, 177, and Thomson's *A Letter to the Reverend Principal Hill on the Case of Mr John Leslie, Professor of Mathematics in the University of Edinburgh* (Edinburgh, 1805), 124–7.

3 Macvey Napier, 'Memoir of John Leslie' in John Leslie, *Treatises on Various Subjects of Natural and Chemical Philosophy* (Edinburgh, 1838), 5–7. From 1765 to his death in 1787, Kinnoul as chancellor of St Andrews took great interest in the

devoted his efforts to science though he was formally registered as a divinity student.[1] During the session 1787–8, Leslie's last at Edinburgh, the death of Kinnoul left him without a patron; but in compensation he unobtrusively relinquished a clerical career for which he had little enthusiasm. From 1788 to 1795 Leslie earned a living as a private tutor to the Randolphs in Virginia and to the Wedgwoods in Staffordshire, as a translator, and as a reviewer. On 5 October 1795, however, the chair of natural philosophy at the university of St Andrews became vacant when George Forrest died. This was really the first appropriate chair in a Scottish university for which Leslie could have applied; he was therefore fast off the mark in lobbying for support and 'interest'. Such alacrity is not surprising, because Leslie had contemplated that chair for several years. As early as 1789 he had asked James Brown to make secret enquiries about the possibility of his being Forrest's assistant, and of his purchasing the succession to the chair. Certainly by that time he entertained the vision of reviving or creating the study of natural philosophy at St Andrews, which was his *alma mater*.[2] Three years later Leslie was deploring the speed with which the university of St Andrews was declining under the insatiable ambition and oppressive monopoly of the Hill family, while simultaneously enquiring about Forrest's health and the patronage of Forrest's chair.[3] In 1794 Leslie was hoping once more to be appointed as Forrest's assistant, which would enable him in conjunction with Brown to kindle an ardour for science at St Andrews. At the same time Leslie urged Brown to represent to some of the professors there that they should resist the monopoly exerted by the Hill family junto.[4] There is therefore no doubt that by late 1795 Leslie nurtured an ambition to revive natural philosophy at St Andrews, where a drowsy torpor was in his opinion deliberately fostered by the Hill régime. As the most recent historian of St Andrews has remarked, this régime was dominated by the Reverend George Hill, principal of St Mary's College, St Andrews (1791–1819), who was leader of the Scottish Moderates after Robertson's withdrawal, politically conservative, closely associated with Henry Dundas, and inclined towards nepotism in appointments to chairs at St Andrews. No wonder that the first verse

---

university. Mr R. N. Smart has kindly pointed out that Leslie gained chancellor's prizes in five of his six years as a student at St Andrews, a feat unequalled during Kinnoul's chancellorship.

1 The system of *lernfreiheit* is described in J. B. Morrell, 'The university of Edinburgh in the late eighteenth century: its scientific eminence and academic structure', *Isis*, lxii (1971), 158–71.

2 E[dinburgh] U[niversity] L[ibrary], Dc. 2.57, fos. 168–9, Leslie to Brown, 11 Jan. 1789. From 1785 until 1796 Brown was assistant to Nicholas Vilant, professor of mathematics at the university of St Andrews.

3 EUL, Leslie to Brown, 12 May 1792, fos. 182–3.

4 EUL, Leslie to Brown, 24 Apr. 1794, f. 196.

of Psalm 121 was then popular: 'I will lift up mine eyes unto the hills, from whence cometh my help'.[1]

Though there is no evidence, one suspects that an important source of Leslie's opposition to the Hill junto was simply that they had not patronised him. Additionally, however, Leslie harboured a low view of the clergy in general. He saw them as vehicles of superstition, of bigotry, and of persecution. When in 1794 Joseph Priestley emigrated to America, Leslie attributed this to the persecution Priestley had suffered from a furious and bigoted priesthood.[2] In the same year he deplored the erastianism of many of the Scottish clergy, who, he alleged, were merely acting as trumpeters of the state.[3] In politics, too, Leslie and the Hills were diametrically opposed. Leslie's views on politics did fluctuate somewhat between 1789 and 1795, but their general tenor confirms the view that he repudiated Toryism along with Calvinism and Moderatism.[4] Leslie's ultra-Whiggism is displayed most palpably in the following extract written at the height of the Jacobin Terror:

> 'The French republic must eventually triumph over all opposition. Whatever opinions may be entertained with regard to the severities which they have exercised (& which admit of some apology), they must be allowed to possess, in an eminent degree, abilities, vigor, perseverance, and the most intrepid courage. It is the attachment to principles, not to persons, that binds and gives energy to the whole. Every thing gives way to the Majesty of the People, the most formidable engine ever put in action.'[5]

Not surprisingly Leslie was distressed by persecution and folly at home, by the submissive political atmosphere in Scotland achieved by either interest or compulsion, and by the flagrant tyranny of the state trial of Maurice Margarot, one of the leaders of the British Convention.[6]

Leslie must have known in October 1795 that his personal antipathy to the Hills, his scorn of the Scottish Moderates and his opposition to Toryism would not help him to gain the chair of natural philosophy at St Andrews. Yet he tried immediately to induce Sir Joseph Banks to sing his scientific merits to Joseph McCormick, principal of the United College, St Andrews, and to Henry Dundas, whom Leslie regarded as the decisive person in the election. Clearly

1 Ronald Gordon Cant, *The University of St Andrews: a Short History* (Edinburgh, 1970), 98–99. From 1788 until 1811 Henry Dundas was chancellor of the university of St Andrews.

2 W[edgwood] P[apers], no. 243, Leslie to Thomas Wedgwood, 8 Apr. 1794.

3 WP 242, Leslie to Wedgwood, 8 Feb. 1794.

4 William Hanna, *Memoirs of the Life and Writings of Thomas Chalmers* (Edinburgh, 1849), i, 10, 11, 14, 15.

5 WP 242, Leslie to Wedgwood, 8 Feb. 1794.

6 Ibid; EUL, Leslie to Brown, 9 Jan. 1794, fos. 190–1; and Henry W. Meikle, *Scotland and the French Revolution* (Glasgow, 1912), 67–160.

he hoped that, in the likely absence of nepotism, his scientific reputation might overcome his unacceptable politics. Though Banks felt it invidious to interfere in such a matter, Leslie continued his canvass in opposition to that of John Rotherham, whom he rightly regarded as his most formidable antagonist. Rotherham, like Leslie, was eager for a permanent post, having been disappointed in his hopes of succeeding Joseph Black as professor of chemistry at the university of Edinburgh.[1] Unfortunately for Leslie, Rotherham enjoyed the friendship and support of Sir James Stirling, then lord provost of Edinburgh, who had been knighted for his firm conduct during the 'reform' riots of 1792.[2] By late October Leslie was so concerned about the probability of Rotherham's success that he tried to acquire possibly dishonourable details about Rotherham's career to use discreetly against his opponent.[3] However, by early November Leslie had gained a crumb of comfort. Though the Hill party had by then countenanced Rotherham, Henry Dundas had told Leslie that he would refrain from political interference and leave the election to be decided on scientific merit. Leslie was jubilant at bringing the Hills into the dilemma of supporting Rotherham, whose testimonials he regarded as inferior and who lacked the support of Dundas. Yet precisely because the Hills were in that dilemma Leslie feared that they would indulge in unjustifiable measures to procure the compliant Rotherham. As he told Wedgwood:

> 'I have even some apprehensions that they will contrive to give me a secret stab. I trust my character would sustain the minutest scrutiny; but it is in their power to spread private surmises with regard to my sentiments. . . . Dr Rotherham's recommendations seem dictated from this place and chime perpetually on his social qualities and his regular attendance at church! I must therefore be prepared to meet him on the ground of domestic virtues.'[4]

On 23 November the seven professors of the United College, St Andrews, elected and admitted Rotherham to the chair of natural philosophy, Leslie and his friend James Brown being unsuccessful candidates.[5] Whereas Rotherham had appeared as a good sort of man, though vulgar, to the Hill party and was far from being a

1 N[ational] L[ibrary of] S[cotland], MS no. 9818, fos. 8–9, Leslie to Banks, 15 Oct. 1795. On 21 Oct. 1795 Thomas Charles Hope, on Black's recommendation, had been appointed to the chair of medicine and chemistry at Edinburgh: see Edinburgh Town Council Minutes, cxxiv (21 Oct. 1795), 319. Between 1793 and 1795 Rotherham had acted as Black's assistant.

2 Henry W. Meikle, 'The King's birthday riot in Edinburgh, June 1792', *ante*, vii (1910), 21–28.

3 Bodleian Library, Oxford, Add. MS. C 89, fos. 206–7, Leslie to Ralph Griffiths, 29 Oct. 1795.

4 WP 248, Leslie to Wedgwood, 4 Nov. 1795.

5 The dates of admission to chairs are given in James Maitland Anderson, *Matriculation Roll of the University of St Andrews, 1747–1897* (Edinburgh, 1905).

republican, both Leslie and Brown were personally and politically suspect.[1] It is definite that both the lord provost of Edinburgh and Robert Dundas, then lord advocate of Scotland, actively supported Rotherham[2]; and they may have lobbied against Leslie. Certainly John Hill, step-brother of George Hill, gave Lord Provost Stirling ammunition against Leslie:

> 'I have just now seen Dr Rotherham and find the Lord Advocate's writing to Barron becomes more and more necessary. Dugald Stewart has refused Mr Ramsay's request to write even an open testimony to Rotherham's merit. This shows a keenness that I do not like and Leslie whom Stuart supports is as a philosopher sceptical and in political matters what no good man shou'd be. I cannot bear the thought of such a man getting to St. And^{s} and I am astonished at Stuart and Playfair who always go together giving him their countenance. . . . Let my name not be heard in the matter.'[3]

Some of this ammunition seems to have been used against Leslie by the Hill party, who, in Leslie's view, had insinuated privately that his religious and political principles were not orthodox.[4] Leslie's general explanation of his failure was that the Hill party, acting unconstitutionally, had elected Rotherham for his personal pliability and his political acceptability; and in addition Rotherham had enjoyed the crucial support of Provost Stirling.[5] For Leslie the chief villains were the Hill family, whom he described in December 1795 as 'dark jesuitical characters', 'a corrupt faction', 'a clerical junto', 'hypocrites', 'corrupt family junto', 'jesuitical faction', 'corrupt jesuitical faction', and 'holy priests who led the junto'. Even allowing for the known extravagance of Leslie's style and the bitterness caused by his failure, the consistency with which he characterised the Hill party is significant: though professed Moderates they epitomised for him clerical factionalism and secret machination. In electing Rotherham the Hills had elected a known Tory; but they had avoided nepotism and chosen a stranger with a scientific reputation, some university teaching experience, and more personal independence than Leslie suspected. Nevertheless Leslie saw Rotherham's success as mainly a conspiracy against himself engineered by the

1 Hanna, *Chalmers*, i, 466; and EUL, Dc. 4.41, George Hill to Alexander Carlyle, 24 Nov. 1795.

2 NLS 7, f. 67, James Stirling to Robert Dundas, 4 Nov. 1795; NLS 7, fo. 65, Robert Dundas to Henry Dundas, 5 Nov. 1795; NLS 7, fo. 70, William Barron to Robert Dundas, 7 Nov. 1795. Stirling was a firm political ally of the Dundases.

3 NLS 7, fo. 68, John Hill to James Stirling [4 Nov. 1795].

4 WP 250, Leslie to Wedgwood, 25 Dec. 1795.

5 Bodleian C 89, fo. 208, Leslie to Griffiths, 2 Dec. 1795; B[anks] C[orrespondence], British Museum (Natural History), ix, fos. 324–325, Leslie to Banks, 7 Dec. 1795; WP 250, Leslie to Wedgwood, 25 Dec. 1795. The derogatory descriptions of the Hill party are taken from these three letters.

Hills: his own failure had confirmed his suspicious expectations about Tory clerical combinations.

By late December 1795 Leslie's hopes of another chair were rising: John Anderson, professor of natural philosophy at the university of Glasgow, was quite ill; and Stewart had suggested that Leslie should aim for that chair when vacant.[1] Within a week of Anderson's death on 13 January 1796 Leslie had begun his canvass, actively supported by Playfair. As always, Leslie nurtured ambitious plans, in this case to gain the Glasgow chair and eventually have Brown as his mathematical colleague there.[2] Ironically Brown began lobbying for the vacant Glasgow chair without telling Leslie, thus temporarily straining the relations between the two friends.[3] Leslie was careful in his canvass to stress that he had an equable temper and inoffensive disposition, unlike the deceased Anderson, who had been a troublesome, combustible man.[4] On 13 April 1796 Brown was elected to the Glasgow natural philosophy chair.[5] Though Brown was supported by such eminent figures as John Hunter and Lord Monboddo, it seems he owed his success to his being a compromise candidate supported by a coalition.[6] The reasons for Leslie's failure remain obscure. It seems that the Hills played no part in the election.[7] Perhaps Leslie gave the impression to the electors of being potentially another jolly jack phosphorus, as Anderson was known. Perhaps he did not conceal his view that the teaching of natural philosophy using showy apparatus was mere quackery. Quite definitely Leslie was not the sort of man to be chosen as a compromise candidate. It is regrettable that Leslie's letters give no explanation of his failure, except in one in which he denounced universities as caballing monkish institutions.[8]

Fortunately for Leslie in 1797 the private patronage of the Wedgwood family once more came to his aid when Thomas Wedgwood offered him an annuity of £150 per year.[9] This generous patronage, which began on 1 July 1797, was a boon for Leslie. It ended his financial worries; it gave him the entire command of his time; and it enabled him to acquire a more extensive collection of more adequate apparatus. Furthermore, he acquired an extra motive

1 WP 250, Leslie to Wedgwood, 25 Dec. 1795.
2 EUL, fos. 207–208, Leslie to Brown, 20 Jan. 1796.
3 EUL, fos. 209–10, Leslie to Brown [n.d., but clearly early Feb. 1796]; and EUL, fo. 211, 11 Feb. 1796.
4 WP 252, Leslie to Wedgwood, 2 Mar. 1796.
5 James Coutts, *A History of the University of Glasgow* (Glasgow, 1909), 321.
6 E. L. Cloyd, *James Burnett: Lord Monboddo* (Oxford, 1972), 158; Charles Roger, *History of St Andrews, with a Full Account of the Recent Improvements in the City* (Edinburgh, 1849), 157.
7 EUL, Dc. 4.41, George Hill to Alexander Carlyle, 12 Apr. 1796.
8 EUL, fo. 213, Leslie to Brown, 19 Apr. 1797.
9 R. B. Litchfield, *Tom Wedgwood the First Photographer* (London, 1903), 45–47.

for doing science in addition to those of rational curiosity, desire for reputation, obligation to society, and posthumous fame: his gratitude to Wedgwood, whose benevolent aims he wished to fulfil.[1] The advantages of the annuity to Leslie quickly became apparent. In 1797 his friend James Brown fell ill and recommended that Leslie would effectively teach the natural philosophy class at Glasgow for session 1797–8. Before the time of the annuity, Leslie would have eagerly accepted such a post. But in October 1797 he declined the offer of it, pointing out that the large annuity rendered it unnecessary and inexpedient for him to accept any temporary or conditional employment.[2]

For the next seven years Leslie used his financial independence so effectively that by 1804 he had published six papers and his famous book on heat.[3] During this septennium, however, he still flirted mildly with the idea of acquiring an academic post. In summer 1799, for instance, Brown had again suggested that Leslie could assist or replace him in his teaching at Glasgow. Though Leslie felt his chances of being appointed assistant or deputy to Brown were slim, he bothered to make exploratory enquiries via Playfair.[4] On the whole Leslie led a settled and comfortable life, pursuing his research, until autumn 1803, when he found himself suddenly pressed financially: not only was inflation eroding the value of his annuity, but he lost most of his capital because of the failure of his bank in Paris (Sir Robert Smyth and Company).[5] Leslie himself reckoned that he would lose at least £800.[6] No wonder that by 1804 he was once again casting about for employment. Yet again he looked to an academic post, this time enquiring from his old acquaintance Charles Hutton about a possible chair in natural philosophy or chemistry at Woolwich Academy, adding rather spuriously that for years he had wished to live near London.[7]

A further prospect, this time of an ambivalent kind, opened for Leslie in 1804 when Rotherham, professor of natural philosophy at

1 WP 260, Leslie to Wedgwood, 12 Sept. 1797.

2 Coutts, *University of Glasgow*, 321; and information from Senate Minutes of 12 and 19 Oct. 1797 kindly given to me by Mrs E. Simpson of Glasgow University Archives.

3 The papers were: 'On the resolution of indeterminate problems', *Transactions of the Royal Society of Edinburgh*, ii (1790), 193–212 (read by Playfair on 1 Dec. 1788); 'Description of an hygrometer and photometer', *Nicholson's Journal*, iii (1800), 461–7; 'On the absorbent powers of different earths', ibid., iv (1801), 196–200; 'Observations and experiments on light and heat, with some remarks on the enquiries of Dr Herschel, respecting those objects', ibid., iv (1801), 344–50; 'Further remarks on the inquiries of Dr. Herschel respecting light and heat', ibid., iv (1801), 416–21; 'On capillary action', *Philosophical Magazine*, xiv (1802), 193–205.

4 EUL, fo. 226, Leslie to Brown, 24 Oct. 1799.

5 WP 294, Leslie to Wedgwood, 30 Sept. 1803.

6 WP 298, Leslie to Wedgwood, 19 May 1804.

7 EUL, La II, 425/30, Leslie to Charles Hutton, 19 Sept. 1804.

St Andrews, died on 6 November. Leslie was still keen to revive the study of natural philosophy at St Andrews, but knew that for a second time he would be compelled to do battle with the Hill party, whom he hated violently. Though he had now an impressive book to his credit, he realised that his chances of succeeding were slim and he was therefore undecided about appearing publicly as a candidate. At the same time he relished the possibility of overthrowing the domineering faction of the mountain (as he called the Hill family)[1]; and he nurtured the hope that he would be acceptable to the anti-Hill party at St Andrews. As he told Brown:

> 'My politics and religion I believe would bear the ordeal; the former are much cooled & I am always ready in the *externals* of devotion to comply with custom.'[2]

Eager to cast down the Hills, Leslie did not neglect external influence including that of Sir William Erskine, MP for Fife, though he felt that public testimonials were in his case both idle and degrading.[3]

The election was important to the rather delicate balance of parties which then existed at St Andrews. Compared with the situation there in 1796, the anti-Hill party, led by James Playfair, principal of the United College, was stronger. No-one was more aware of this than George Hill, who on the day of Rotherham's death urged Henry Dundas to intimate to Playfair the desirability of Playfair's supporting James MacDonald, the Hills' candidate.[4] Shortly before the election, Hill stressed to Dundas that Rotherham had been recently a reliable member of the Hill party, and that unless his successor should be likewise the United College and possibly the whole university would fall into the hands of the anti-Hill party, who in Hill's view were Foxite Whigs or republicans.[5] Each party had its own candidate. MacDonald, a local clergyman, was the immediate nominee of the Hills, to whom he was closely related by marriage. Unlike that of Rotherham in 1795, MacDonald's candidature raised the familiar and contentious issues of pluralism and nepotism. He was also such an unqualified candidate that Dundas felt he should withdraw. Thomas Jackson, rector of Ayr Academy and probably a mild Whig, was the candidate of the

1 EUL, fo. 237, Leslie to Brown, 16 Nov. 1804. Later in this letter Leslie advised Brown to remember 'écraser l'infame'. It is significant that, in connection with the Hill party, Leslie used Voltaire's famous rallying-cry against clerical fanaticism and persecution.

2 EUL, item 166, Leslie to Brown, 19 Nov. 1804. In EUL, Dc. 2.57, folio numbers finish at 240 and are succeeded by item numbers beginning at 166.

3 EUL, fo. 93, Leslie to Brown [n.d. but on internal evidence late Nov. 1804].

4 St A[ndrews University], MS 4800, George Hill to Henry Dundas, 6 Nov. 1804.

5 St A. 4802, Hill to Dundas, 26 Nov. 1804.

Playfair party, which itself was not above nepotism.[1] The other candidates, such as Leslie, the young Thomas Chalmers, Thomas Duncan (rector of Dundee Academy) and the chemist Thomas Thomson, were also-rans because they lacked the support of the Playfair party.[2] Perhaps Leslie was not taken up by the anti-Hill party because they agreed with the Hills that his character and temper were inappropriate to the small corporation at St Andrews. Certainly Hill asserted to Dundas that Leslie, though a mathematical genius who had lately published a book on heat, was 'a professed atheist, and was a democratical leader in the times of trouble'.[3] The contest was fought therefore between Jackson and MacDonald, the nominees of the two contending parties. On 1 December 1804 MacDonald was elected; but Playfair, conceiving that he ought to have had a vote and also a casting vote in the case of equality of votes, unsuccessfully took the matter to the court of session. MacDonald was admitted as professor on 14 February 1805, but the litigation continued until on 26 May 1809 the house of lords declared that MacDonald had been illegally elected. Jackson was duly admitted to the chair on 29 June 1809.[4] The length and bitterness of the litigation associated with this election confirms the view that Leslie was not elected because he was not an appropriate vehicle for the intriguing scrambling of the two contending parties at St Andrews.[5]

A fourth opportunity for a Scottish university chair appeared for Leslie early in 1805 upon the death of John Robison, professor of natural philosophy at Edinburgh, on 30 January. Having had considerable experience of professorial elections, Leslie and his friends began canvassing immediately.[6] John Playfair, professor of

1 In 1799 MacDonald had married Jean Hill, sister of George Hill and of Henry David Hill (professor of Greek, United College, St Andrews, 1789–1820), and step-sister of John Hill (professor of humanity, Edinburgh University, 1775–1805): *Fasti Ecclesiae Scoticanae*, ed. Hew Scott (Edinburgh, 1925), v, 207, 235. James Hunter, son of John Hunter (professor of humanity), was admitted professor of logic on 15 May 1804. The elder Hunter was a leading member of the anti-Hill faction.

2 Hanna, *Chalmers*, i, 90; EUL, fos. 142–3, Leslie to Brown, 1804 [on internal evidence mid-Nov.].

3 St A. 4802, Hill to Dundas, 26 Nov. 1804.

4 The seven professors and possibly the principal of the United College, St Andrews, were the electors. Four professors voted for MacDonald and three for Jackson. The litigation concerned the voting rights of Principal James Playfair, a supporter of Jackson. If he had no ordinary vote, then the result was victory for MacDonald. If his ordinary vote counted, then the result was a tie. If additionally he had a casting vote in the event of a tie, then the result was four votes for MacDonald and five for Jackson.

5 The internecine warfare and nepotism at St Andrews during the Hill regime was criticized in connection with this election by the whiggish James Hall, *Travels in Scotland* (London, 1807), i, 151, 153.

6 BC, xv, fos. 262–3, Robert Ferguson to Banks, 31 Jan. 1805; NLS 9818, fos. 10–11, Leslie to Banks, 3 Feb. 1805; WP 304, Leslie to Josiah Wedgwood, 4 Feb. 1805.

mathematics at Edinburgh, was quickly brought forward by his colleagues; and Thomas Macknight, who had from time to time acted as a deputy professor of both Greek and natural philosophy, was supported by some of the town council. Leslie had reasonable hopes of success because the town council seemed determined to elect the most meritorious candidate. At the same time he felt that if Playfair were elected to the natural philosophy chair then an opening would be created for him in the chair of mathematics.[1] Indeed Playfair himself seems to have advised Leslie to stand for the natural philosophy chair in order to secure immediate public notice and not to lose ground.[2] Playfair was duly elected to the natural philosophy chair by the town council on 6 February, leaving his mathematics chair vacant.

For the fifth time Leslie became a candidate for a Scottish university chair. One accompaniment to his canvass was without doubt familiar to him. While standing for the natural philosophy chair Leslie had feared that prejudicial rumours might be circulated about his religion and politics.[3] By 15 February he was certain that the Edinburgh Moderates were plotting against him principally by scattering what he described as 'voces ambiguas'.[4] In compensation, however, Leslie had a new weapon. By mid-February he knew from Banks that on 7 February the council of the Royal Society of London had awarded to him the Rumford medals for his research on heat.[5] Leslie realised immediately that such public and national testimony would weigh heavily in his favour, particularly when shining before the town council. He also realised that 'the only formidable opponent is a clergyman [Macknight] here, who has private connexions with certain inferior members of the town council, & is farther supported by the high church party [Moderates], who wish to share all the professorships among them. However, it is a measure extremely unpopular & the public voice is clearly on my side.'[6]

Leslie's fears that, as on previous occasions, rumours might be circulated about his religious principles were quickly justified. On 20 February, in his Fast Day Sermon, James Finlayson insisted that it was dangerous and sinful to appoint men of suspicious principles to preside over the education of the young. Clearly he was referring

1 EUL, item 168, Leslie to Brown, 2 Feb. 1805. It appears that Macknight withdrew his candidature in favour of Playfair.
2 NLS 9818, fos. 12–13, Leslie to Banks, 15 Feb. 1805.
3 EUL item 169, Leslie to Brown, 6 Feb. 1805.
4 EUL fos. 115–16, Leslie to Brown, 15 Feb. [1805].
5 NLS 331, fo. 201, Banks to Leslie, 8 Feb. 1805. Though Banks felt it improper for him to give a written testimonial in support of Leslie, he was fully aware that the Rumford medals were an adequate substitute and was eager for Leslie to succeed.
6 NLS 9818, fos. 12–13, Leslie to Banks, 15 Feb. 1805.

to Leslie, to whom he felt strongly antipathetic.[1] Leslie had good cause to be worried and angered by Finlayson's innuendos. Finlayson was professor of logic in the university, he enjoyed the ear of Henry Dundas, and in his capacity as the adept manager of the Moderate interest in church politics he was known as the jesuit of the party.[2] Indeed, in a memorable vignette, Henry Cockburn stressed Finlayson's jesuitical aspect: 'He was a grim, firm-set, dark, clerical man . . . with a distressing pair of black, piercing, Jesuitical eyes, which moved slowly, and rested long on any one they were turned to, as if he intended to look him down, and knew that he could do so; a severe and formidable person.'[3] Faced with Finlayson's indelicate remarks, Leslie could have kept fairly quiet as he had done in 1796 when the St Andrews Moderates had tried in his opinion to smear his character. In 1805, however, having been traduced by the *eminence grise* of the Edinburgh Moderates, he retaliated by angry denial and apparently intended to threaten Finlayson with legal action. Even so, Finlayson's innuendos had some effect: Sir William Fettes, the lord provost of Edinburgh, though highly impressed by Leslie's scientific achievements, had his suspicions of Leslie's character. Fortunately for Leslie, Fettes placed great reliance on the opinions of Stewart and Playfair, who by late February were strongly espousing Leslie's cause.[4] Some of Leslie's testimonials strongly stressed his religious orthodoxy. For instance, the Reverend Thomas Laurie, Newburn, Fife, and the Reverend Spence Oliphant, Largo, Fife, who differed on church politics, both supported Leslie's character against the attacks made on it by the Edinburgh Moderates. Others stressed his scientific attainments, which were very superior to those of Macknight.[5] On previous occasions Leslie had never persistently expected success. This time, however, he told James Brown:

> 'My success is now *almost* certain. A very few days will decide it. I have fought a very hard battle with McK & the whole set of the soi-disant-moderates; & I begin to think much better of the wild

1 EUL fos. 52, 54, Thomas Chalmers to Brown, 24 and 28 Feb. 1805.
2 Clark, 'From protest to reaction', 214.
3 Cockburn, *Memorials*, 21.
4 EUL, fos. 52, 54, Chalmers to Brown, 24 and 28 Feb. 1805. Stewart's first letter to the lord provost was dated 12 Feb. 1805; the first one of Playfair, 23 Feb. 1805. See Edinburgh Town Council Minutes, cxlii, entry for 20 Mar. 1805.
5 In order to justify its election of Leslie, the Edinburgh town council unanimously supported the lord provost's highly unusual suggestion that testimonials and letters supporting Leslie should be recorded. They occupy Town Council Minutes, cxlii, 139–200, 20 Mar. 1805. Leslie's supporters were Charles Hutton, John Robison, Francis Maseres, Nevil Maskelyne, Reverend Thomas Laurie, Reverend Spence Oliphant, Sir William Erskine, Josiah Wedgwood jnr., Thomas Wedgwood, Playfair (2), Stewart (2) and George Dempster. Leslie had wisely ensured an effective mixture of prominent English scientists, eminent Edinburgh professors, and public men of Fife. The Robison letter [n.d. but on internal evidence probably 1795] was to Playfair and not Leslie.

V

> party than ever. When we meet I shall amuse you with the infamous manoeuvres of the high church party. Their engines have recoiled upon them, and they have sunk in the public opinion.'[1]

Besides hinting that the Evangelicals had begun to support Leslie, this letter confirms that in Leslie's opinion his opponents were the Edinburgh Moderates. After he had been unanimously elected to the mathematics chair on 13 March, Leslie consistently maintained and developed that opinion. It is significant that the terms he used to describe the Edinburgh Moderates in 1805 echo those he used to describe the St Andrews Moderates in 1795: 'junto of clergy', 'jesuitical faction', 'the jesuits' (thrice), 'the inquisitors' (twice), 'the junto' (twice), 'soi-disant moderes [*sic*]' and 'jesuitical clergy'.[2] Leslie identified Finlayson as the leading dark designer of the plot against him, just as years later Cockburn labelled Finlayson as 'the underground soul of the dark confederacy'.[3]

Leslie, too, consistently maintained that the chief motive of the Moderates was clerical domination of the university of Edinburgh on the pattern of St Andrews, and that the controversy about cause and effect was a mere cover of their real motive and object. On the day after his election, Leslie told Wedgwood that Macknight was:

> 'supported by a jesuitical faction of their [sic] brethren, who seek by every art, however diabolical, to increase the power of the church, that is, of themselves. Their conduct has shown that they would have cheerfully burnt alive either myself or my opponent, if it would have tended in the smallest degree to their own aggrandisement. Could you have imagined that my philological note on Causation was the *ostensible* ground on which they proceeded against me?'[4]

He expounded a similar view a month later to Sir Joseph Banks:

> 'The fact is, that all this clamour about orthodoxy is a *mere pretext*; the great object was to gain possession of the college. If they had succeeded at Edin^r, *as they have in other places*, the University would, in the course of years, have become a mere clerical corporation. My opponents affect to style themselves the moderate party, & are generally reckoned rather lax in their discipline. They attempted to drive their point *by fixing on* an obscure subject (causation), & sought to intimidate the magistrates'.[5]

1 EUL, fo. 157, Leslie to Brown, [n.d. but on internal evidence early Mar. 1805].

2 The letters in which Leslie used these terms were: NLS 9818, fos. 14–15, Leslie to Banks, 13 Mar. 1805; WP 305, Leslie to Wedgwood, 14 Mar. 1805; EUL, item 171, Leslie to Brown, 25 Mar. 1805; EUL, item 172, Leslie to Brown, 12 Apr. 1805; WP 306, Leslie to Wedgwood, 29 Apr. 1805.

3 EUL, items 171, 172, Leslie to Brown, 25 Mar. and 12 Apr. 1805; Cockburn, *Memorials*, 209.

4 WP 305, Leslie to Wedgwood, 14 Mar. 1805, The italics are mine.

5 BC, xv, fos. 367–9, Leslie to Banks, 28 Apr. 1805. The italics are mine.

There is, then, considerable evidence to confirm that the chief components of the Leslie affair were personal feuds, and differences of party and ecclesiastical politics. Accordingly the public debate on causation was not a primary issue but a mere pretence dragged out to cover the personal and party infighting in which Leslie, his supporters and his opponents alike indulged. It is, of course, difficult to discover whether the jealousies and feuds were in the first instance secondary to political and ecclesiastical differences. Certainly Leslie deplored the clerical ambition of the Hill family at St Andrews several years before he applied for a chair there. Presumably he realised that the appointment in 1788 of Henry Dundas as chancellor of St Andrews severely reduced his chances of advancing his own career there. There is no doubt that his personal hostility to the Hill party was reinforced in the 1790s by his vehement anti-clericalism, his virulent republicanism, and his related scorn of all incorporated juntos whether they were the Hill party at St Andrews or the Royal Society of Edinburgh.[1] In particular he despised erastian clergy, while respecting independent clergy such as John Playfair. For the Hill party in the 1790s Leslie was doubly disqualified: he certainly entertained strong republican views and probably leaned towards scepticism in his religious opinions. Even if he was more a republican sceptic than a democratic atheist, it is clear why the Hill party genuinely suspected his political and religious views. Nevertheless Leslie's attempts to acquire a chair at St Andrews in 1795 (and in 1804) had been baulked, in his opinion, by the monopolising and hypocritical St Andrews clerical and family junto which was one of the two leading groups of the erastian Moderates. Presumably John Playfair and Stewart shared Leslie's interpretation; and other prominent Whig/Independents and Whig/Evangelicals may have done so.

By 1805, however, there were both new and familiar components in the election to the Edinburgh mathematics chair and the associated public debate. Edinburgh was by that time the only Scottish university not effectively closed to him. Though the 1805 election was for Leslie a desperate last chance, the patronage of the chair was at least held by the town council and not by the sitting professoriate. Crucially for Leslie it was only during his fifth attempt for a chair that he could produce visible tokens of his national scientific reputation in the form of the Rumford medals. In politics Leslie's opinions had cooled: by 1805 he was a Whig. His religious views in 1805 remain obscure but certainly he did not flaunt his scepticism. Nevertheless the legacy of mistrust and hostility remained: for the

1 S. Shapin, 'Property, patronage, and the politics of science: the founding of the Royal Society of Edinburgh', *British Journal for the History of Science*, vii (1974), 1–41 (38).

Edinburgh Moderates in 1805 Leslie was still the democratic atheist; for Leslie, Stewart and Playfair the Edinburgh Moderates were providing in 1805 the same sort of opposition as the St Andrews Moderates had offered in 1795 and in 1804. By 1805, therefore, the Leslie party felt that the opposition was familiar in type if not in identity: once more a hypocritical and erastian clerical junto was intent on clerical domination of a university. Moreover before 1805 the resentment felt by Leslie and Stewart against Tory Moderatism in universities had been fed but not given public outlet. In 1805, however, the possibility existed of publicly reversing what they regarded as excessive clerical domination of the universities of St Andrews and Edinburgh. Their accumulated bitterness helped to spice the Leslie affair. Once Finlayson and Stewart had raised their respective banners the battle increasingly became polarised into one between largely Tory Moderates and Whig Evangelicals. Before 1805 the Evangelicals as a group had not apparently supported Leslie's attempts to gain a chair. In 1805, however, probably urged by Stewart, the Evangelicals began to support Leslie before the election, and more conspicuously after it, because they welcomed an opportunity of defeating their traditional Moderate opponents. At the same time they took the risk of 'arraying themselves on the side of irreligion, in order to secure the triumph of a political partisan, who was openly accused before the supreme judicature of the church of having uttered infidel opinions in his writings'.[1]

The interpretation of this paper is entirely in harmony with the fact that the university's chief polemicists on Leslie's behalf were Stewart and Playfair, who in 1805 disturbed themselves from their habitual reserve to be Leslie's warmest and steadiest champions. In many ways they were not only closely associated with Leslie but also hostile to his opponents. At the personal level, Leslie was a close friend of Playfair from at least the late 1780s and of Stewart from at least the mid-1790s. Both of them had been Leslie's chief supporters and advisers in all his previous four attempts to gain a chair. Playfair in particular had been a scientific mentor of Leslie in the late 1780s, and both men were later and extensively patronised by the Ferguson brothers of Raith, two wealthy and devoted Whigs.[2] At the political level, Leslie, Stewart and Playfair were Whigs during the 1790s, when the Scottish Whig caucus was small and powerless.[3] Ecclesiastically both Stewart and Playfair, it seems, had supported the Moderatism of William Robertson, to whom Playfair at least

1 *Edinburgh Weekly Journal*, 14 Nov. 1832, 365. I am grateful to Dr S. Shapin for this reference.

2 Napier, *Leslie*, 7. Leslie's first published paper was read in 1788 to the Royal Society of Edinburgh by Playfair.

3 Morrell, 'Robison and Playfair', 44–46.

was deeply indebted for patronage.[1] Certainly they deplored the Moderatism of the Hills and of Finlayson, which they regarded as alien to that of Robertson.[2] One suspects, too, that they despised the descent of the Moderates into erastianism once Robertson had resigned the leadership of the party in 1780. Both men were decidedly opposed to the union of clerical and academic posts, fearing that their own careers would be jeopardised in a university largely staffed and controlled by Moderate members of the Edinburgh presbytery. Indeed in the last election to an arts chair before 1805, that for the regius chair of rhetoric, Thomas Brown, a Whig protégé of Stewart, had been defeated by Andrew Brown, at that time minister of Old St Giles', Edinburgh. Thomas Brown's explanation of his failure was couched in terms familiar enough to Leslie:

> 'The truth of the matter is, that Finlayson and the governing churchmen have been able to persuade the Dundases that it is absolutely necessary to secure the interest of *moderation* by throwing out to the hopes of the party as many good things as possible, and that the interest of universities should at all times be sacrificed to that of the church.'[3]

No doubt Stewart was irritated by Finlayson's successful management of that election. Stewart's opposition to pluralism perhaps also stemmed from the realisation that through pluralism the Edinburgh Moderates could increase their power in the university senate without losing any in the Edinburgh presbytery.

In all these ways Stewart and Playfair had much in common with Leslie. Why then was their support of Leslie at last open and not covert in 1805? Firstly, the transfer by the town council of Playfair from the mathematics to the natural philosophy chair on 6 February 1805 showed that a known and prominent Whig, if of proved merit

1 NLS 3944, fo. 146, John Playfair to William Robertson, junior, 22 June 1793, averred that for twenty years Robertson, senior, had been his best and steadiest friend and adviser. The importance of Robertson's brand of Moderatism to the university is rightly stressed by Jeremy J. Cater, 'The making of Principal Robertson in 1762: politics and the university of Edinburgh in the second half of the eighteenth century', *ante*, xlix (1970), 60–84.

2 Four years before the Leslie affair, Stewart had quoted with approval extracts from assessments of Robertson by two high flyers, John Erskine and Henry Moncreiff Wellwood: Stewart, 'Account of the life and writings of William Robertson' in *Collected Works of Dugald Stewart*, ed. William Hamilton, x (Edinburgh, 1858), 99–242 (192–3, 235–7). Both Erskine and Wellwood stressed Robertson's political independence, his tolerance, and his lack of personal rancour. Stewart's deliberate publication of such views was surely an offence in the eyes of the erastian Moderate leaders of 1801.

3 Thomas Brown to Miss Brown, 10 June 1801, in Welsh, *Thomas Brown*, 165. Finlayson was, of course, hostile to Brown's whiggery. Henry W. Meikle, 'The chair of Rhetoric and Belles-Lettres in the university of Edinburgh', *University of Edinburgh Journal*, xiii (1944–45), 89–103 (96) points out that by 1800 Andrew Brown himself said he was almost the only Edinburgh minister without some kind of provision independent of his stipend.

as teacher and researcher, could be elected to an important chair. It seemed that this precedent indicated that in the election to the mathematics chair the town council would again act on grounds of public utility. Secondly, both Stewart and Playfair had the ear of Sir William Fettes, the lord provost of Edinburgh, and through him could expect for the first time to be influential in university appointments. Thirdly, Dundas had swayed the town council, although not without difficulty, from about 1782; but from 1802 his political power in Scotland was waning, and from late February 1805 his political activities were largely suspended in the months immediately preceding his impeachment.[1] Fourthly, one suspects that Stewart expected that the town council would resent and resist the attempts at interference made by the Edinburgh Moderates.[2] Again, both Stewart and Playfair surely knew that the Edinburgh ministers, particularly the Moderates, were on such bad terms with the town council that on the day of Leslie's election those ministers threatened legal action if the council continued to delay paying their stipends of £200 per minister.[3] Lastly, both Stewart and Playfair perhaps hoped to be able to exploit the growing split between the Edinburgh and St Andrews Moderates[4]; and they surely banked on the support of the Evangelicals, some of whose leaders had been close pupils of Stewart. The confluence of all these contingencies created a golden opportunity for Playfair and Stewart, free from effective retribution, not only to indulge in metaphysical debate for which they were eminently qualified but more basically to confirm the rise of the Evangelicals and the Whigs, to maintain the national reputation of the university, and not least to settle some old personal scores.

1 Holden Furber, *Henry Dundas: First Viscount Melville, 1742–1811* (London, 1931), 149, 197, 278. Burke, 'Kirk and causality', 342, states that Macknight's candidature was blessed by Dundas. The evidence he offers refers to the intentions expressed by Dundas's friends and relations in 1801; and not to what Dundas himself did in Feb. and Mar. 1805. The only positive statement I have discovered was Leslie's: 'Lord Melville very properly declined all interference'—see NLS 9818, fos. 14–15, Leslie to Banks, 13 Mar. 1805.

2 *Memorial for the Lord Provost, Magistrates, and Council of the City of Edinburgh against the Reverend Dr Henry Grieve, the Reverend Dr John Inglis, and the Reverend Mr David Ritchie, as a Committee of the Ministers of the Gospel in Edinburgh* (Edinburgh, 22 May 1805), 24, shows that the town council saw that if it had capitulated to the avisamentum offered by the Edinburgh Moderates or to the attack they made on Leslie's religious principles, then it would have become possible to exclude laymen from Edinburgh chairs for ever. In such circumstances, the power of the town council would have been severely limited; such a restriction was unacceptable to the town council.

3 Edinburgh Town Council Minutes, cxlii, 12 Mar. 1805.

4 George Cook, *Life of the late George Hill* (Edinburgh, 1820), 195–203, 206, shows how divided the Edinburgh and St Andrews leaders of the Moderates had become by 1808.

VI

THOMAS THOMSON: PROFESSOR OF CHEMISTRY AND UNIVERSITY REFORMER

THOMAS THOMSON (1773-1852) is primarily remembered as the author of the textbook *A System of Chemistry* which dominated the British field for about 30 years. In his chosen subject of chemistry his enthusiastic support of Daltonian chemical atomism and his zealous support of Prout's hypothesis have been recently recognized.[1] Yet his activities were not as restricted as received opinion suggests. When Thomson assumed in 1818 the newly created Regius Chair of Chemistry at the University of Glasgow, the prospects for him as teacher and researcher were apparently encouraging. But he met difficulties in his attempts to elevate the status of the Regius Professors at Glasgow and in his concurrent endeavours to develop chemistry as an autonomous science. The ensuing controversy, first private and then public, spanned more than 20 rancorous years. Only one of Thomson's obituarists, however, even briefly mentions this debate;[2] and recent writers on Thomson either ignore it completely or skim over it lightly.[3] The main purpose of this paper is therefore to redress the balance of previous work on Thomson by outlining the chief features of his professorial period, paying particular attention to his style of teaching and attitude to his subject. For Thomson the development of his discipline was inseparable from the question of his status as a Regius Professor. Accordingly I also try to show that he played an important role in the movement for reform of the Scottish Universities and I discuss the structure of power at the University of Glasgow. Such analysis is necessary for understanding Thomson's appraisal of his situation as Regius Professor of Chemistry. In order to put his professorial period into the context of his earlier work I introduce the main body of the article with a short reconsideration of the form and significance of his career before 1817, when he moved to Glasgow.

[1] See W. H. Brock and D. M. Knight, "The Atomic Debates", *Isis*, lvi (1965), 5-25 (8); and W. V. Farrar, "Nineteenth-Century Speculations on the Complexity of the Chemical Elements", *British Journal for the History of Science*, ii (1964-65), 297-323 (299-300).

[2] Anon., "Biographical Notice of the late Thomas Thomson", *The Glasgow Medical Journal*, v (1857), 69-80, 121-153 (145). The other primary obituarists are: R. D. Thomson, "Memoir of the late Dr. Thomas Thomson", *Edinburgh New Philosophical Journal*, liv (1852-1853), 86-98; and W. Crum, "Sketch of the Life and Labours of Dr. Thomas Thomson", *Proceedings of the Philosophical Society of Glasgow*, iii (1855), 250-264.

[3] H. S. Klickstein, "Thomas Thomson Pioneer Historian of Chemistry", *Chymia*, i (1948), 37-53; J. R. Partington, "Thomas Thomson, 1773-1852", *Annals of Science*, vi (1949), 115-126; A. Kent, "Thomas Thomson (1773-1852) Historian of Chemistry", *British Journal for the History of Science*, ii (1964-65), 59-63.

I.

Thomson's fervid support of Dalton's chemical atomism has never been systematically studied,[4] yet it is clear in broad terms that his role was important and maybe decisive. Though relations between Dalton and Thomson from 1804 to 1807 remain obscure, circumstantial evidence suggests that Dalton learned of Richter's work on equivalent weights in April 1807 when in Thomson's Edinburgh class-room he publicly expounded for the first time his *New System of Chemical Philosophy*.[5] Furthermore, in the third edition of his *System of Chemistry*, mostly written before Dalton's arrival in Edinburgh,[6] Thomson extended the latter's theory from gases to acids, bases, and salts;[7] and early in 1808 he was the first to submit an experimental illustration of the Law of Multiple Proportions[8] at least four months before the publication of Dalton's *New System*. This paper also established a method of determining empirical formulae.[9] After 1808 Thomson's enthusiasm for chemical atomism burgeoned: it is palpably displayed in the successive editions of his *System of Chemistry* and in the columns of the journal *Annals of Philosophy*, of which he was the editor.

Until 1817 Thomson earned his living mainly as a writer and as a teacher. While a medical student at the University of Edinburgh he exploited the interregnum in British chemistry[10] by assuming in 1796 the post of assistant editor of the *Supplement to the Third Edition of the Encyclopaedia Britannica*. Within four years he had drawn up the outline of his *System* which appeared in five parts in the *Supplement*.[11] From 1800 to 1811 Thomson capitalized on the popularity of chemistry in Edinburgh as a private teacher, giving both winter and summer classes to annual audiences of about 120.[12] For Thomson mere lecturing was pedagogically insufficient; accordingly he instituted practical laboratory classes about which tantalizingly little is known.[13]

While teaching at Edinburgh he collaborated with his brother James and his close friend James Mill (father of John Stuart Mill), in

4 Dalton's chemical atomic theory was used by Thomson *inter alia* for pedagogic and opportunist reasons.

5 A. W. Thackray, "The Origin of Dalton's Chemical Atomic Theory: Daltonian Doubts Resolved", *Isis*, lvii (1966), 35-55 (53); *idem.*, "Documents relating to the origins of Dalton's chemical atomic theory", *Memoirs and Proceedings of the Manchester Literary and Philosophical Society*, cviii (1965-1966), 1-22 (18-19).

6 See Thomson's letter of 8 March 1807 to Dalton reproduced in H. E. Roscoe and A. Harden, *A New View of the Origin of Dalton's Atomic Theory* (London, 1896), 141-142.

7 T. Thomson, *A System of Chemistry* (3rd edn., Edinburgh, 1807), iii, 424-628.

8 T. Thomson, "On oxalic acid", *Phil. Trans.*, xcviii (1808), 63-95 (read 14 January 1808). Cf. W. H. Wollaston, "On Super-acid and Sub-acid Salts", *ibid.*, 96-102 (read 28 January 1808).

9 F. Greenaway, *John Dalton and the Atom* (London, 1966), 149-150.

10 See T. Thomson, *The History of Chemistry* (London, 1830-1831), ii, 139-141.

11 "Chemistry", *Supplement to the Third Edition of the Encyclopaedia Britannica* (Edinburgh, 1801), i, 210 f.; "Mineralogy", *ibid.*, ii, 193 f.; "Vegetable and Animal Substances and Dyeing", *ibid.*, ii, 529 f.

12 Thomson's winter class in 1803-1804 numbered about eighty. See letter of 6 January 1804 by William Sligo (University of Edinburgh Library, no. Dc. 4.101-3).

13 The fullest source: anon., "Biographical Notice of the late Thomas Thomson", *The Glasgow Medical Journal*, v (1857), 123.

producing a postal literary periodical *The Literary Journal*[14] which in its early issues was dominated by Thomson's articles on science.[15] He withdrew from this first adventure in journalism[16] owing to the success of his textbook *A System of Chemistry* (first edition, 1802), which no doubt was published *inter alia* as a supplement to his own lectures. This popular work, which went through six editions in the next 18 years, was the first systematic British treatise of a non-elementary kind to break the French monopoly created and maintained by Macquer, Lavoisier, Fourcroy, Chaptal, etc. Thomson's Preface demonstrated explicit nationalism: the lack of British works had nurtured the myth that chemistry was essentially a French science.[17] He accepted this challenge so successfully that in 1807 and 1817 Berthollet acquired the pages of the third and fifth editions of the *System* as they were printed so that he could speedily supervise a French translation.[18] Clearly Thomson was by 1817 a textbook writer of European stature. In the field of scientific journalism, too, Thomson made his mark from 1813 as an aggressive and occasionally belligerent editor of the *Annals of Philosophy*. His abstracts of currently published research by Continental as well as British chemists and his annual reports on the progress of science constituted a deliberate move against insularity.

In addition to these activities, Thomson was employed by the British Government as a technical consultant. Along with Professors Hope and Coventry he investigated in 1805 the problem of the relative quantity of malt which could be made from English and Scottish barley.[19] During this enquiry he invented a direct-reading saccharometer which became known as Allen's saccharometer. This instrument was so much more accurate than others that it was illegally and exclusively used by the Scotch Excise Board from 1805 until 1816 when Parliament sanctioned its employment.[20]

[14] *The Literary Journal, A Review of Literature, Science, Manners and Politics*: first series, 1803-1805, 5 vols; second series, 1806, 2 vols.

[15] *The Prospectus* (1802) sets out some characteristic Thomsonian attitudes and ideals: the attribution of due credit to British discoverers; the rapid communication of new scientific discoveries; the application of sciences to agriculture and manufactures; and the history of sciences. Thomson's aims were not completely realized until he founded his own periodical, *Annals of Philosophy*, in 1813.

[16] Thomson resigned as a contributor in June 1803. See letter by William Sligo previously cited.

[17] T. Thomson, *A System of Chemistry* (Edinburgh, 1802), i, Preface, 8.

[18] See respectively: M. Crosland, *The Society of Arcueil* (London, 1967), 329-300; and Thomson's gloating letter to Robert Jameson of 30 December 1816 (Pollok-Morris MSS.):

> "I have been applied to by Berthollet, Vauquelin & Gay Lussac to send over the sheets to Paris as they are thrown off here so that they may have a translation out as soon as possible after the original . . . It will be of considerable importance to the continental chemists, as at present there is no work in existence which can give a correct idea of the present state of chemistry. Thenard's book is a poor thing & so badly arranged that you cannot tell where to look for anything."

Riffault's preface to this translation of the fifth British edition shows that Thomson complied with the request. See: *Système de Chimie* . . . (Paris, 1818), i, Preface, 8.

[19] *The Glasgow Medical Journal*, v (1857), 132. Thomson characteristically submitted a minority report in *Papers . . . relating to Experiments made by Order of the Commissioners of Excise for Scotland, to ascertain the relative qualities of malt made from Barley and Scotch Bigg* (1806), 109-116.

[20] W. H. Roberts, *The Scottish Ale Brewer* . . . (Edinburgh, 1837), 29-30.

The following year Thomson was once more working for the Government on an excise problem concerning the strength of ales and porter,[21] his eventual reward in 1820 being £200 for four months' work.[22]

This multifarious opportunism was sustained by a pugnacious personality. Thomson, a seventh child of humble origins who lacked private patronage, never suffered from "that carelessness about posthumous fame, and that regardlessness of reputation"[23] which afflicted his revered master Joseph Black. In addition he was blunt and "decidedly sparing of complimentary language".[24] When, for instance, an Edinburgh reviewer attacked the second edition of his *System*, Thomson's merely defensive response was to christen the periodical the "*Stinkpot* of literature", a title by which it was affectionately known for some time.[25] Thomson's thersitic tendencies[26] were, I think, buttressed by a view of history best set out in his account of Priestley.[27] Thomson recognized that knowledge advances but painfully and stoically confessed that nations progress and decay. He summarized the arch of history as:

> "Poverty, Liberty, Industry, Power, Wealth, Dissipation, Anarchy, Destruction. And when a nation has once run this career, it seems incapable of renovation: virtue once destroyed can never be renewed."[28]

But his pessimism was not total. Simultaneously Thomson felt that education could perpetuate liberty: limited improvement, if not perfection, was attainable by deliberate social measures. He clearly belonged to the liberal-Radical tradition. As a life-long friend of the Utilitarian James Mill,[29] with whom for two years he amicably shared a house,[30] Thomson could hardly have held any other political allegiance. They had much in common not only in their careers but also in their moral code. Both responded to the stern ideals of:

[21] Thomson's letter of 20 April 1817 to Macvey Napier (British Museum, Add. MSS. 43, 612, f. 72); and Thomson's letter of 30 May 1817 to Robert Jameson (Pollok-Morris MSS.) which show that Thomson expected the introduction of his saccharometer by the English Excise Board and a reward of at least £20,000.

[22] English Excise Board Minutes, 20 September 1820. Contrast Thomson's salary of £50 p.a. as Professor.

[23] T. Thomson, *op. cit.* (10), i, 328.

[24] W. Crum, *op. cit.* (2), 255.

[25] The critic was Andrew Duncan, jnr., *The Edinburgh Review*, iv (1804), 120-151. Thomson replied with a thick pamphlet, *Remarks on the Edinburgh Review of Dr. Thomson's System of Chemistry by the author of that Work* (Edinburgh, 1804). The whole episode is ignored by J. Clive, *Scotch Reviewers: The Edinburgh Review, 1802-15* (London, 1957).

[26] Sir Robert Christison regarded him as "a follower of Thersites": "the most glaring ingredient in his character . . . was an uncontrollable propensity to sneer—not behind-backs, but in presence of his subject". See *The Life of Sir R. Christison, Bart., edited by his Sons* (Edinburgh and London, 1885-86), i, 366-367.

[27] T. Thomson, "Biographical Account of Dr. Joseph Priestley", *Annals of Philosophy*, i (1813), 81-99.

[28] T. Thomson, *op. cit.* (27), 97.

[29] See: A. Bain, *James Mill, a Biography* (London, 1882), *passsim.*

[30] 1 Queen's Square, Westminster. See Thomson's letter of 27 June 1815 to Macvey Napier (British Museum Add. MSS. 34, 611, f. 236).

"justice, temperance . . ., veracity, perseverance, readiness to encounter pain and especially labour; regard for the public good; estimation of persons according to their merits . . ., a life of exertion in contradiction to one of self-indulgent ease and sloth."[31]

Above all Thomson was an ardent defender of civil liberty,[32] a position sanctioned by his religion. He commended and in the main observed a sparse Christianity, demonstrated not in words, forms, subtle doctrines, or ecclesiastical observances but in conscientious discharge of his duties to his fellow men. He rejected the supernatural trimmings of Christianity as ontological garbage. For him ignorance was not the mother of devotion: he fervently advocated unrestricted inquiry, free from ecclesiastical interference.[33]

Such was the Scotsman whose outstanding accomplishments were recognized in the autumn of 1817 when on 5 September he was unanimously elected to succeed Cleghorn as the lecturer in Chemistry at the University of Glasgow.[34] The Tory Chancellor of the University, James Graham, third Duke of Montrose, and the Tory majority in the University, put party interest on one side[35] in order to acquire Thomson, who was quite sanguine about his prospects. He had been assured that the lectureship would be made into a Regius Professorship and was agog "to erect a laboratory upon a proper scale to establish a real chemical school in Glasgow and to breed up a set of young practical chemists".[36] Montrose did use his influence:[37] on 17 March 1818 Thomson became the first Regius Professor of Chemistry at Glasgow.

[31] J. S. Mill, *Autobiography* (Oxford (World's Classics), 1952), 39-40. Both Thomson and Mill were Scottish "lads o' pairts", contemporaries at Edinburgh University, chief collaborators in *The Literary Journal*, contributors to the *Encyclopaedia Britannica*, and vigorous scholar-popularizers distinguished for hard-working competence rather than innate brilliance.

[32] See e.g.: T. Thomson, "Baking", *Supplement to the Fourth, Fifth, and Sixth Editions of the Encyclopaedia Britannica* (Edinburgh, 1824), ii, 37-45, which contains an attack on the Corn Laws, and T. Thomson, *Travels in Sweden, during the Autumn of 1812* (London, 1813), 114-132, in which he daringly argues for the necessity of the Swedish revolution of 1809.

[33] See: *Glasgow Medical Journal*, v (1857), 122 and 148-9; T. Thomson, *op. cit.* (10), ii, 17 and 198; Thomson's letter of 27 January 1837 to the Rev. John Lee, Principal of Edinburgh University (National Library of Scotland, MS. 3441, f. 226), which *inter alia* discusses the relations between Church, University, and the progress of science.

[34] *Glasgow Medical Journal*, v (1857), 140. James Couper, Professor of Astronomy at Glasgow, was impressed by the unanimity of the election. On 5 September 1817 he wrote to Robert Jameson (Pollok-Morris MSS.):

> "His character & reputation was completely victorious over every feeling of private friendship and attachment. I have never seen any election so harmonious—& in which everyone felt so much self complacency in giving his vote for a man of such acknowledged merit."

[35] *Glasgow Medical Journal*, v (1857), 141; and A. Bain, *op. cit.* (29), 167.

[36] Thomson's letter of 9 September 1817 to his friend Robert Jameson (Pollok-Morris MSS.):

> "You have heard by this time that I have been unanimously elected to the lectureship of Chemistry in the University of Glasgow . . . I hesitated for some time whether I should become a candidate. But I was assured that it would immediately be made a Regius Professorship & this induced me to offer myself. Indeed I had no reason to look for a better situation, as except Edin^r. it is the best, which the country affords."

[37] R. D. Thomson, *op. cit.* (2), 94.

II.

The lineage of Glasgow chemistry was distinguished:[38] Cullen and Black, both of whom were revered by Thomson, had established chemistry as an autonomous science at Glasgow.[39] Thomson's aims were quite clear: not only to revive the Glasgow chemical tradition, which his predecessor Cleghorn had allowed to lapse; but also to establish his own as the best of the six chemistry courses of university rank available during 1818 in Scotland.[40] Thomson's competitor in Glasgow at Anderson's University was the contentious Andrew Ure; from 1830 to 1837, it was the equally formidable Thomas Graham. At Edinburgh Hope led no research school and received no salary, but his lecturing gifts ensured big classes obtained from the large Medical School and elsewhere. Hope was keen to teach not only chemistry but also chemical pharmacy.[41] At St. Andrews the same combination of a science and a trade was taught by Robert Briggs, Professor of Medicine and Anatomy, using apparatus bought by his University in 1811 for £253 from the entrepreneur Thomson.[42] Further north at King's College, Aberdeen, chemistry along with natural history was taught as a compulsory part of the M.A. by Patrick Forbes, Professor of Humanity (Latin),[43] who ignored pharmacy and emphasized mineralogy.[44] At Marischal College, George French, a surgeon and apothecary for whom chemistry was a hobby, occupied the Chair of Chemistry. For his students chemistry was an optional extra.[45] It is clear then that chemistry was popular and most effectively taught in Edinburgh and Glasgow, where Hope and Ure would compete with Thomson.

His assumption of the Regius Chair at Glasgow provided competition of another kind. Given his personality and commitments, Thomson could hardly have chosen a worse University than Glasgow with regard to political structure. The post-Reformation University of Edinburgh was municipally controlled, a situation which was provoking its staff to shout for academic freedom in rebellion against the control and reforming zeal of the Corporation.[46] St. Andrews was small and impoverished, while in Aberdeen the two colleges waged internecine warfare. At Glasgow, easily

38 See: A. Kent (ed.), *An Eighteenth-Century Lectureship in Chemistry* (Glasgow, 1950).

39 See: T. Thomson, *op. cit.* (10), i, 303-304 and 318-327.

40 A useful short survey is: A. Kent, "The Place of Chemistry . . . in the Scottish Universities", *Proc. Chem. Soc.*, April 1959, 109-113.

41 *Commissioners appointed to visit the Universities and Colleges of Scotland, Report relative to the University of Edinburgh* (1830), 55 and 73. Hope had easily the highest income of any Scottish Professor in the 1820's, i.e. slightly above £2,200 p.a.

42 *Report relative to the Universities and Colleges of St. Andrews* (1830), 7 and 26; and *Evidence . . . received by the Commissioners . . . for visiting the Universities of Scotland*, iii (1837), 253.

43 A. Findlay, *The Teaching of Chemistry in the Universities of Aberdeen* (Aberdeen, 1935), 2, and 43-48.

44 *Report relative to the University and King's College of Aberdeen* (1830), 14.

45 A. Findlay, *op. cit.* (43), 8-13.

46 Thomson attributed the success in science of Edinburgh University to its being the only Scottish University which was not a "close corporation". See: Thomson's letter of 27 January 1837 to John Lee (National Library of Scotland, MS. 3441, f. 226).

the richest of the five, the situation contrasted piquantly with that at Edinburgh:[47] it seemed that in the former University an oligarchy had assumed power to such an extent that academic freedom was being abused. Glasgow therefore offered to Thomson the certainty of intra-mural skirmishing on important issues in a University whose Medical School was beginning to rival that of Edinburgh.[48]

The constitutional history of the oligarchy within the Glasgow professoriate is complex. For our immediate purposes, however, it is sufficient to state that by 1809 a basic distinction had been confirmed by the College Professors' successful litigation against the Crown apropos the appointment in 1807 of Lockhart Muirhead as the first Regius Professor of Natural History. After 1809 two professorial groups existed in the University: the College, defined as the Principal and the occupants of the thirteen chairs founded before 1807, a group which formed a majority in Senate; and the Regius Professor of Natural History whose privileges were limited.[49] When the Crown in 1815 established two new Chairs of Surgery and Midwifery, their incumbents were therefore similarly restricted: they were excluded from elections of Professors, from disposal of College funds (five times those of the University), and from examining candidates for degrees even in the Medical School. Three years later Thomson and Robert Graham were appointed to the Regius Chairs of Chemistry and Botany respectively. Thomson asserted to the Scottish Universities Commission that he was deceived when he accepted the chair because he was unaware of these restraints; that when he did discover their nature he had already given up his London literary activities; "and as they could not be again resumed, he was under the necessity of accepting the Chair, clogged as it was".[50] Thomson must have grown even angrier when in 1820 William Jackson Hooker succeeded Graham as Regius Professor of Botany, and was freed by the terms of his appointment from most of the usual restrictions.

Thomson and his Regius colleagues were in a difficult position: they felt the behaviour of the College to be harsh and oppressive. For instance, while Thomson was the College-sponsored lecturer he received £70 per year from it; on being elevated to the Regius Chair, he received nothing from the College and a mere £50 per year from the Crown. There is no

47 L. J. Saunders, *Scottish Democracy 1815-1840* (Edinburgh and London, 1950), 312.

48 The development of the Glasgow Medical School during Thomson's incumbency is described by: A. Duncan, *Memorials of the Faculty of Physicians and Surgeons of Glasgow, 1599-1850* (Glasgow, 1896), 162-186; and J. Coutts, *A History of the University of Glasgow* (Glasgow, 1909), 512-569.

49 Useful background is provided by J. D. Mackie, *The University of Glasgow 1451-1951* (Glasgow, 1954), 243-268.

50 See Document submitted to the Commission by Thomson on behalf of the Regius Professors, *Evidence . . . received by the Commissioners . . . for visiting the Universities of Scotland*, ii (1837), 205-211 (206). Subsequently this work will be described as "Glasgow Evidence".

doubt that the College acted as proprietors rather than trustees.[51] Even when it initiated limited reform the basic distinction between Regius and College Professors remained uneroded.[52] Until 1827 the Regius Professors had not laid their grievances before the public owing to loyalty to the University,[53] but events forced their hand. Throughout that year the Scottish University Commissioners were taking evidence in Glasgow. The Regius Professors exploited their opportunity by transmitting in March 1827 a memorial setting out their case.[54] In the same year Charles Badham, an undistinguished Englishman, was admitted by the College to the Chair of Medicine without the approval of the Regius Professors. This was the fourth election to a College chair since 1818 made without the concurrence of Thomson and his colleagues, but it was the first medical one.[55] As Thomson pointed out to the Principal, the Reverend Duncan Macfarlan, in a fiercely worded letter which he laid before the Commission, the Regius Professors had a vital interest in the competence of the new Professor of Medicine, yet only they were debarred from judging his qualifications for that office. Macfarlan remained unmoved by Thomson's demand. In a characteristically terse reply he announced his resolve to uphold the legal judgement of 1809. For good measure he deprecated Thomson's reforming zeal "as calculated only to excite and foster a spirit of jealousy and contention, injurious alike to the interests of the University and of its individual members".[56] This rebuff so stung Thomson that he laid before the Commissioners his own account of the history and ignominious state of the Regius Professoriate at Glasgow.[57] By autumn 1827 this dispute could no longer be confined within the University walls: neither Thomson nor Macfarlan was prepared to give any ground.

It must be stressed at this point that inherent organizational features made the Scottish Universities inimical to change. Each professor had a basic salary: at Glasgow, College Professors an average of £300, Regius ones £50. The greater part of a professor's income was often derived from class and examination fees which depended on the number of students. Clearly professors of recognized subjects enrolled large numbers of

[51] Self-patronage by the professoriate was widely recognized and condemned. See, e.g. Sir W. Hamilton, "Patronage of Universities", *The Edinburgh Review*, lix (1834), 196-227 (221-226).

[52] As an example, in 1818 the College agreed that all the medical professors should examine candidates in medicine; but it stipulated that the Regius Professors should examine gratuitously, while the College Professors of Anatomy and Medicine were each to receive four guineas per successful candidate. By 1826, when over thirty students graduated in medicine, the issue had become contentious, particularly as Burns, Professor of Surgery, had withdrawn in a huff, leaving the burden of examining to be shared between Thomson and Towers, Professor of Midwifery. See: *Glasgow Evidence* (1837), 209.

[53] *Ibid.*, 209.

[54] *Ibid.*, 537-539.

[55] The non-medical elections were: Gibb, Hebrew, 1820; Sandford, Greek, 1821; Buchanan, Logic, 1827.

[56] *Glasgow Evidence* (1837), 209-210

[57] *Ibid.*, 205-211.

students, and were well paid in comparison with those of fringe disciplines. Furthermore, professors could assert an intra-mural legal monopoly of their subjects, but they could lose income if a chair in an allied subject were created and new subjects accepted for graduation. Personal interests were frequently hostile to change and encouraged recognized teachers to form conservative groupings, keen to preserve their status and monopoly. A telling example was Glasgow, where the College Professors strenuously maintained their privileges against the attacks of the Regius Professors led by Thomson.

While this conflict was intensifying, Thomson was leading Scottish University chemistry in both research and laboratory instruction. During his first year at Glasgow the lack of a laboratory plagued him,[58] but by autumn 1818 he had obtained one[59] at the College's expense.[60] In the following summer he began a series of atomic weight determinations[61] using excellent apparatus provided by the College and himself.[62] The dominant motif behind his activities was the belief that chemistry was an autonomous science. He gave the Commissioners short shrift when they asked if he lectured on chemical pharmacy:

> "Why, Pharmacy is a trade, not a science . . . I might as well give a course on Shoemaking as a course on Pharmacy. I know a different opinion exists elsewhere."[63]

Thomson was clearly deprecating the chemical pharmacy willingly taught at Edinburgh and St. Andrews.

Accordingly his lecture course was based on his own *System*, and he ran a laboratory class for six to ten students who attended three to four hours a day, except Sunday, for ten months of the year. It is clear that he did not initiate his students into research methods as Liebig did: they merely learnt and applied the manuscript rules of mineralogical analysis which Thomson had devised.[64] They also analysed more than a quarter of the salts the composition of which was announced in Thomson's *First Principles*,[65] a curiously incompetent work which aroused Berzelius's scorn. Thomson had for a time tried a more heuristic approach with those students who had attempted independent research, "but it did not

[58] Thomson's letter of 18 March 1818 to Macvey Napier (British Museum, Add. MSS. 34, 612, f. 176).

[59] Thomson's letter of 13 August 1818 to Dalton, reproduced in H. E. Roscoe and A. Harden, *op. cit.* (6), 171-172.

[60] *Glasgow Evidence* (1837), 202-203.

[61] T. Thomson, *An Attempt to Establish the First Principles of Chemistry by Experiment* (London, 1825), i, 25.

[62] *Glasgow Evidence* (1837), 34 and 541. The College, and not the Crown, contributed to the departmental expenses of the Regius Professors: clearly it was troubled by this drain on its revenues.

[63] *Ibid.*, 151.

[64] *Ibid.*, 151 and 203.

[65] T. Thomson, "Reply to Berzelius' attack on his 'First Principles of Chemistry' ", *Phil. Mag.*, v (1829), 217-223 (217).

answer; they were not aware of what particular branches were the most important and they spent their time uselessly and foolishly".[66] Many of these students studied chemistry as a pure science; the promising ones, however, invariably became industrial chemists, perhaps being seduced by the Glasgow manufacturers who also attended.[67] Such laboratory training cost money: Thomson's annual salary of £50 failed to cover his unavoidable laboratory expenses, his object (unlike that of his predecessor) "being to teach the science, and to raise up a race of practical chemists".[68] His laboratory class in 1827 was unique in a British university;[69] and his dedication to original work in his first decade at Glasgow is specially notable.

His open hostility to the College spurred him to pester that body for better accommodation. In 1827 his class was so big (207) that extra space had to be created in the available room by partially dismantling it.[70] Two years later Thomson was compelled to divide his 222 students[71] into two groups to which he lectured at a separate hour.[72] In response to Thomson's loud and urgent remonstrances and threats to cease lecturing, this impossible situation was remedied by the College which perhaps hoped that munificence would embarrass Thomson into silence. Whatever the College's motives, the new building for chemistry, erected at a cost of £5,000 in Shuttle Street outside the College walls, was opened in 1831. Thomson's dignity was compromised in that his department was extramural; yet the accommodation, containing a large teaching laboratory, was allegedly unsurpassed in arrangement and convenience. Even Thomson's acumen was satisfied. It was in the Shuttle Street laboratory that Thomson developed the teaching of qualitative and quantitative analysis, as the influential books of his pupils demonstrate.[73] No doubt in late 1831 Thomson, whose *History of Chemistry* had just been published, was all agog for further triumph, hoping that the proposals for constitutional

[66] *Glasgow Evidence* (1837), 203.

[67] *Ibid.*, 204. See also Thomson's letter of 8 December 1826 to Dalton (reproduced in H. E. Roscoe and A. Harden, *op. cit.* (6), 183-184) in which he refers to "the vortex of manufacture and business, which is here all powerful". Some students migrated to Lancashire to develop the chemical industry there, as Thomas Andrews pointed out. See his *Studium Generale* (London, 1867), 88.

[68] *Glasgow Evidence* (1837), 205.

[69] Thomson was fully aware that his laboratory class was unparalleled at this time: see T. Thomson, "History and Present State of Chemical Science", *The Edinburgh Review*, l (1829), 256-276 (276).

[70] *Glasgow Report* (1830), 77; and Thomson's letter of 25 February 1828 to Nutall (Torrey MSS., Academy of Natural Sciences of Philadelphia, U.S.A.).

[71] *Report of the Glasgow University Commissioners* (1839), 71.

[72] See Thomson's letter of 24 March 1830 to Macvey Napier (British Museum, Add. MSS. 34, 614, f. 313).

[73] See: *A Memorial respecting the Present State of the College of Glasgow, by the Regius Professors of Chemistry and Materia Medica* (London, 1835), 22; *Remarks on a Pamphlet, Entitled, "A Memorial . . . by the Regius Professors of Chemistry & Materia Medica"* (Glasgow, 1835), 20 (this pamphlet was written by Duncan Macfarlan, Principal of Glasgow University); A. Kent, "The Shuttle Street Laboratories", *Glasgow University Gazette* (1956), no. 25; and D. Murray, *Memories of The Old College of Glasgow* (Glasgow, 1927), 254-255.

reform in the Commissioners' *Report* would be implemented. Parliament was, however, fully occupied with the Reform Bill and was about to embark upon an intense programme of social improvement. Compared with such issues as the abolition of slavery (1833), working conditions in factories (1833), and the amendment of the Poor Law (1834), reform of the Scottish Universities seemed merely local: accordingly the 1830 *Report*, which proposed that the distinction between College and Regius Professors at Glasgow be abolished, was shelved.

III.

This lack of legislative action was not to Thomson's liking; as old age overtook him he began to feel the effects of Thomas Graham's competition at Anderson's University; and the sizes of his classes and his income showed a slight decline after 1833.[74] In that same year one of Thomson's protégées, John Couper,[75] was created Regius Professor of Materia Medica, an honour which lost him the salary of £70 a year formerly paid by the College to his predecessor.[76] As the Crown, too, refused to pay any salary to its nominee, Couper's position was anomalous. I suspect that the implications of Couper's appointment preyed on Thomson's mind. Certainly in no other way can one account for the letter which he wrote on 24 January 1834 to Lord Brougham and sent via his old friend James Mill.[77] The contents are extraordinary in view of Thomson's persistent insistence on the autonomy of chemistry and its practitioners, and his determination not to follow the example of chemists such as his friends Wollaston and Prout who had reverted to medicine.

Glasgow 24 Jan 1834

My Lord

In addressing your Lordship about a matter entirely personal, I am conscious of using a liberty not warranted by my former slender acquaintance; which after an interval of nearly fourty years may possibly have slipt from your remembrance. I have been induced to take the step by the high opinions which I have always entertained of your Lordship's scientific knowledge & of the indefatigable exertions which you have so successfully made to improve the education and encrease the knowledge of the whole community.

I was appointed Professor of Chemistry in Glasgow in 1817 with a salary of £50 a year and a class in some measure to create. For my predecessor had neglected the science so long that he was obliged at last to resign because he was not acquainted with its present state.

The chair was literally nominal—I was not a member of faculty in which body the legal management of the College rests—I had no vote in chusing professors, appointing to bursaries, exhibitions, etc. This to me who considered

74 *Glasgow University Report* (1839), 70-71.

75 See Thomson's letter of 25 January 1833 to Lord Brougham (Brougham MSS., University College Library, London).

76 J. Coutts, *op. cit.* (48), 536-537.

77 See Mill's letter of 21 January 1834 and Thomson's letter of 24 January 1834 both addressed to Lord Brougham (Brougham MSS., University College Library, London).

my chair as one of the most important in the College was mortifying. My predecessors got over this degrading situation by getting another chair to which these priveleges were attached. Dr. Cullen was made Professor of the practice of Medicine, Dr. Black of Anatomy, Dr. Hope of the practice.

The chair of practical Astronomy in this University is filled by Dr. Couper who is in his 82^{d} year. Could I procure that chair when vacant it would put me on a footing with my colleagues. The Crown is patron, and I venture to solicite your Lordship's kind interference with Lord Melbourn in my behalf.—The salary is about £250, which with my own, would just put me on a footing with the other Professors, whose salaries in general are about £300.—Such an addition would make me easy in my circumstances and enable me to procure some indulgences, which at my time of life are becoming requisite. Perhaps the long and assiduous labours of my past life and the great addition to the celebrity of our medical school, which has taken place since my being a professor here may give me some small claim to some remuneration—or at any rate furnish your Lordship with a good reason for applying in my favour.

Begging pardon for an application which your Lordship may perhaps think intrusive, I am with the greatest respect

Your Lordship's
Most obedient Servant
Thomas Thomson

Three points here require comment. First, Thomson's unsuccessful plan to secure the Astronomy chair, a College one, was politically naïve and chiefly motivated by blatant self interest, but certainly the position was a sinecure. The occupant, James Couper, had not lectured since 1808 when no students enrolled for his class.[78] Secondly, Thomson's academic income of £616 for 1833-34 was clearly the largest received by any Regius Professor, though it did compare unfavourably with those acquired by nine out of the thirteen College Professors.[79] Thirdly, the letter confirms independently and unequivocally why Thomson felt humiliated and aggrieved.

With the return to power of the second Whig government in 1835, Thomson saw his opportunity to re-open the debate on the political structure of Glasgow University. Early in that year Glasgow had elected two stern advocates of liberal reform, Colin Dunlop and James Oswald, who with the Tennants (Charles and John) were leaders of the radical Crow Club formed in 1832.[80] Dunlop, head of the Clyde Iron Works,[81] and John Tennant of the famous St. Rollox chemical works, were means through which Thomson and Oswald could have met. Certainly by 1835 Tennant, a pupil of Thomson's, was a close friend of his teacher:[82] they travelled together from Glasgow to London in June 1835 to initiate

78 *Glasgow Evidence* (1837), 34 and 149.

79 *Glasgow University Report* (1839), 70 and 215. Between 1832 and 1836 James Couper's average salary was £272 per annum.

80 J. Strang, *Glasgow and Its Clubs* (London and Glasgow, 1857), 452.

81 J. Strang, *op. cit.* (80), 461.

82 Thomson's will nominated him as one of nine executors.

parliamentary action, a plan devised by Thomson and his sounding-board Couper. In London Thomson drew up a *Memorial*[83] stating the grievances of the Regius Professors, had it printed there, and distributed copies to M.P.s. Meanwhile on 22 June 1835 Bannerman, M.P. for Aberdeen, had introduced his Bill to unite the two Universities of Aberdeen under the control of a rectorial Court.[84] Thomson, Tennant and Oswald decided to await the result of this Bill's second reading on 6 July before introducing their own. Bannerman's Bill was duly read, so that on 9 July[85] Oswald introduced his Bill "to transfer the management of the funds of the College to a College Court and to equalize all the Professorships as far as powers and privileges are concerned".[86] Thomson was optimistic: Oswald's Bill after all attempted merely to implement the *Report* of 1830. Clearly he placed excessive faith in Lord Melbourne, Prime Minister, who was indifferent to both issues.[87] Sir Robert Peel, however, favoured Bannerman's Bill but felt that legislation would be dangerous unless local reaction had been adequately consulted. Accordingly on 20 July Bannerman agreed to withdraw his Bill until the following session. Oswald had no option but to follow suit when pressed by Lord Stanley.[88] In the meantime Macfarlan in Glasgow had discovered Thomson's plans and even had to apply to him for a copy of the *Memorial*. The Principal was indeed so lumbering that his petition against Oswald's Bill was received by the House of Commons as late as 3 August.[89]

The 1835 *Memorial* by Thomson and John Couper offered to the public tantalizing glimpses of the political situation in the University of

[83] *op. cit.* (73).

[84] *A Statement of the Proceedings of the University and King's College of Aberdeen respecting the Royal Grant . . . and the Bill, recently before Parliament . . .* (Aberdeen, 1835), 32.

[85] *The House of Commons Journal* (1835), 440.

[86] Thomson's role in this episode is made clear in his letter of Wednesday 1 July 1835 to William Jackson Hooker (Royal Botanic Gardens Library, Kew, *Hooker Correspondence, English Letters*, vi (1832-1835), no. 259):

"I had not an opportunity of seeing you before I left Glasgow to inform you that Dr Couper & myself had thought it better . . . to endeavour to cut the Gordian knot by getting an act of parliament to put all the professors on a footing—I went up to London for that purpose & Mr. Tennant went with me. I drew up a memorial stating our grievances which I got printed & which we have distributed among the members of the House of Commons . . . And Mr. Oswald is to bring in a bill to transfer the management of the funds of the College to a College Court & to equalize all the Professorships as far as powers & priveleges are concerned. Mr. Bannerman the Member for Aberdeen has brought in a bill to unite the two Universities of Aberdeen & to put their funds under the control of a rectorial court. It is to be read a second time on Monday & we wait to see the result of that bill before bringing in ours. If it pass as we think it will our bill merely putting in force the resolutions of the Royal Commissioners must pass also.

"I write you at present to make you aware of what we are doing. I could not write before because we are only now beginning to see our way clearly. You will of course take no notice of this letter, even if Dr Burns should question you. You must be aware that he is not with us. He had his eye fixed on the Anatomy chair & expects to get it by currying favour with the Principal & Faculty. He will be disappointed. But we must not trust him.

"The Principal, etc. have heard of our proceedings and have applied for a copy of my memorial & one has been sent to them . . ."

[87] See Melbourne's reply to Lord Aberdeen, reported in *The Times* (18 July 1835).

[88] Report in *The Times* (21 July 1835); and *Hansard* (20 July 1835), 735-737.

[89] *The House of Commons Journal* (1835), 507.

Glasgow, which were to be mainly confirmed when the *Evidence* submitted to the Commission was published in 1837. It explored the issues of organization and patronage which Thomson had raised before the Commissioners in 1827. In addition it uncovered the intrigue behind the distinction between College and Regius Professors. Thomson asserted what Macfarlan denied: namely that in 1807 Macfarlan, as Dean of the Faculties, voted with the Tories who succeeded with the connivance of the Tory Officers of the Crown in preventing Muirhead from assuming full professorial rights.[90] While setting out in considerable detail the "humiliating and unprecedented situation of the six Regius Professors", Thomson did not conceal his scorn of "the old monkish part of the establishment",[91] who he alleged were "almost beyond the age of discharging the duties of their station with efficiency".[92] He also saw the conflict in wider terms as his peroration shows:[93]

> "Can any adequate reason be alleged for placing the Regius Professors in this degraded and subordinate situation? Are the sciences which they teach of less importance to the country than those branches which belong to the Faculty Professors? . . . Will it be alleged that Latin, Greek, Logic, Moral and Natural Philosophy, are of more importance than Chemistry, Natural History, Botany, Surgery, Materia Medica and Midwifery?"

This *Memorial* was influential, as a *Times* editorial confessed in referring to "*two* discontented informers, whose mean and selfish treachery to their brother professors should have excited disgust rather than obtained confidence".[94]

Macfarlan's reply, printed on the University presses, simply and blandly denies most of Thomson's points; it also ignores the 1830 *Report*. But he effectively exploited the generosity of the College in spending £6,000 on accommodation for the Regius Professors. In addition, not only did he attack Thomson's *Memorial* as puerile sophistry, but also Thomson himself was assaulted as being unsystematic and rudely quarrelsome. The main weight, however, of Macfarlan's performance lay in his reliance on the unquestionable authority of the Court of Session decision of 1809 and on the rights and privileges of an independent corporation.[95] In a subsequent pamphlet[96] published in spring 1836 the College set out to refute the 1830 *Report*, using Macfarlan's reply to Thomson's *Memorial* as scaffolding. Almost five years had elapsed from the publication of the

90 *Memorial* (1835), 12; *Remarks* (1835), 7-9.
91 *Memorial* (1835), 37.
92 *Ibid.*, 39.
93 *Ibid.*, 38.
94 *The Times* (7 July 1836).
95 *Remarks* (1835), 1, 16, 18, 24-25, 45.
96 *Observations by the Principal and Professors of Glasgow College, on Schemes of Reform, Proposed for the University of Glasgow, in connexion with the Report of the Royal Commissioners of Visitation* (Glasgow, 1836).

Commission's *Report* to this first public vindication by the College of its behaviour. The excuse offered for this delay was that:

"many of the representations made in it would never obtain credit, and that the proposed alterations would not be adopted, at least without a fair opportunity of considering and discussing their merits".[97]

However specious this assertion seems, the College could nevertheless point to the presence in the 1830 *Report* of palpable misrepresentations and erroneous details, the cumulative effect of which was to create a prejudiced and unfavourable view of the University. It was even ready to accept inspection to prevent malversation and to improve tuition. But, of course, it was unable to accept that proposal of Oswald's Bill concerning the creation of a Court to which the whole patronage and property of the College would be transferred:[98] such a Court, it was alleged, would at least be irresponsible, indifferent, incompetent, unrestrained and pragmatic. Yet if one considers the sweeping powers allocated to the Court in Oswald's Bill,[99] the College may have been right in holding that it would possess "no security against the incessant and injurious interposition of a meddling and superficial superintendence".[100] As expected, the most poisonous barbs were reserved for Thomson and Couper, the spokesmen of the Regius Professors:[101]

"It will be difficult to find an instance of human perversity and effrontery to match the conduct of some of their number, in endeavouring to set aside the very terms of their own appointment, and violating alike the rules of courtesy and the laws of truth, in their eager appetance of *that which is their neighbours.*"

From this time there was no hope of a rapprochement between the College and Thomson, whose irritability was exacerbated by the sudden death of his wife in late 1834: the dispute had descended to the level of personal malevolence; and any amelioration of the status of the Regius Professors could now be achieved only by frontal attack on what we might call "academic freedom".

IV.

Assault on the autonomy of the Scottish Universities was indeed forthcoming in spring 1836 in the shape of a Bill[102] providing for new constitutions and for the creation of permanent Boards of Visitors to enforce them. But the Whig government handled the Bill in dilatory fashion: not only was its introduction postponed from 30 March 1836, but

[97] *Idem.*, 6 (footnote).
[98] *Idem.*, 26.
[99] See *Parliamentary Papers*, iv (1835), for full details of the Bill for the Regulation of the University of Glasgow.
[100] *Observations* (1836), 29
[101] *Idem.*, 36.
[102] Bill for appointing a Board of Royal Visitors for regulating the Universities of Scotland.

the secrecy surrounding its details aroused suspicion in England as well as Scotland.[103] Such vacillation did, however, allow representations to be made. Thomson was fast off the mark with a letter of 11 April 1836 to the liberal Lord Advocate for Scotland. He pleaded for strong powers to be given to the Board of Visitors, who he hoped would discipline "a set of illiberal and malignent men enraged to the uttermost and possessed of uncontrollable powers of annoyance in every possible way". The composition of the Board was, of course, crucial. Thomson recommended that its majority be Glasgow business men, "independent in their circumstances and in every way liberal minded". Rather naïvely he proposed his friends Oswald and Dunlop, Glasgow M.P.s, as possible Visitors.[104] Only one other Glasgow Professor wrote to the Lord Advocate (i.e. only these two letters have survived): John Pringle Nicol, newly appointed Professor of Astronomy, urged the necessity of having scientists on the Board.[105]

As the Bill was introduced, read, and amended throughout June, the Scottish opposition instigated by Macfarlan found a focus in the presbyteries, synods, and the General Assembly of the Church of Scotland.[106] Towards the end of July the supporters of the heavily amended Bill began to lose heart.[107] It was no surprise that on 2 August the lounging Melbourne withdrew the Bill, after Wellington and Scots peers such as Haddington and Aberdeen had urged the expediency of postponing legislation until Scottish intractability had declined.[108] The government's reforming impulse had weakened after the passing of the Municipal Reform Act of 1835; and it refused to force through a Bill which if passed would have undoubtedly led to litigation in the Scottish courts. The result of the failure of the Bill was that each of the five Universities preserved its independence, its characteristic organization and academic traditions. The climacteric of reform had passed.

The government, however, lapsed into the hope that the Universities, if stimulated rather than coerced, might indulge in self-reform. After 1836 this was clearly a delusion. Nevertheless further Commissions were appointed in late 1836 for Aberdeen and Glasgow, and in 1840 for St. Andrews.[109] In the main the *Report of the Glasgow Commissioners* (1839) merely ratified the recommendations of the 1830 *Report*, with two clear

[103] See editorial, *The Times* (2 April 1836).

[104] Thomson's letter of 11 April 1836 to John Archibald Murray (National Library of Scotland, MS. 2904, f. 52).

[105] See John Pringle Nicol's letter of 12 May 1836 to John Archibald Murray (National Library of Scotland, MS. 2904, f. 60).

[106] See the list of petitions, received 28 June, against the Bill in *The Journal of the House of Lords*, lxviii (1836), 922; and Thomson's letter of 10 July 1836 to Murray (National Library of Scotland, MS. 2904, f. 76).

[107] See letters of Monteith and Bannerman to Murray (National Library of Scotland, MS. 2904, f. 86 and 93).

[108] *Hansard* (2 August 1836), 756-758. The Bill seemed likely to fail after the Lords' debate of 28 June: see *Hansard* (1836), 989-998.

[109] H. M. Knox, *Two Hundred and Fifty Years of Scottish Education 1696-1946* (Edinburgh and London, 1953), 50.

exceptions: first, the Court's powers were to be far less extensive than previously envisaged;[110] secondly, an annuity of £800, which expired in May 1839, should be renewed and placed at the disposal of the Court rather than the College.[111] This *Report* was, of course, shelved: Melbourne's ministry was tottering; and its Tory successor under Peel was simply too busy with major reforms. In the meantime Thomson maintained his hostility to the College junta, as he termed it, on the additional grounds that the power of such oligarchies precluded the improvement of scientific institutions and instruction. He clearly felt that after about 1810 French and Prussian scientific organizations had improved to such an extent that British science was likely to sink into mediocrity and insignificance.[112] Thomson may have had in his mind the condition of the Glasgow Medical School, but he could hardly have expected the severe reduction in the number of his students. Between 1836 and 1838 Thomson's enrolment dropped from 138 through 86 to 75,[113] not through his incompetence as a teacher[114] but owing to the deficiencies of the two College Professors of Anatomy and Medicine. Both these men were so ill that they lectured by deputy.[115] The state of the two most important medical classes clearly affected the numbers of students attending the others. In session 1839-40 Thomson's class numbered only 50;[116] and a mere four students, including Stenhouse and J. H. Gilbert, worked in his laboratory.[117] Such a decline was associated with the general fall at that time in the number of students in Scottish University Medical Schools, and with the growing popularity of the teaching hospitals in London, Dublin and Paris. Thomson felt that his academic income of £200 was completely inadequate for a person of his rank, and he took the unprecedented step (for him) of demanding an increase of salary from his former pupil, Andrew Rutherfurd, who on 20 April 1839 had been appointed Lord Advocate of Scotland: "necessity has no law & while your Lordship is *considering* I am *starving*".[118] Rutherfurd's intercessions were fruitful: in 1840 the £800 annuity was divided

[110] This weakening of reforming resolve was deplored by Thomson in a letter of 19 March 1839 to John Lee (National Library of Scotland, MS. 3442, f. 217).

[111] J. Coutts, *op. cit.* (48), 423.

[112] See Thomson's letter of 27 January 1837 to John Lee (National Library of Scotland, MS. 3441, f. 226).

[113] *Glasgow University Report* (1839), 71; and Thomson's letter of 22 December 1838 to John Lee (National Library of Scotland, MS. 3442, f. 202).

[114] Liebig judged Thomson to be still the best middle-aged teacher of chemistry in Britain. See his letter of 23 November 1837 to Wohler, *Aus Justus Liebigs und Friedrich Wohlers Briefwechsel in den Jahren 1829-1873* (Brunswick, 1888), i, 113.

[115] Dr. Jeffray, Professor of Anatomy since 1790, was so enfeebled by age, deafness, and loss of voice that he lectured by deputy—his son. Dr. Badham, Professor of Medicine since 1827, had suffered infirmity for many years and a substitute had lectured on the theory of medicine since 1832. The picture of Glasgow College as being composed of tottering men is confirmed by "A return . . . of the Names of the Professors in the University of Glasgow, whose Duties are at present performed by Assistants or Substitutes", *Parliamentary Papers*, xxix (1840).

[116] Thomson's letter of 12 November 1839 to Andrew Rutherfurd (National Library of Scotland, Rutherfurd Papers not catalogued).

[117] J. H. Gilbert, *J. Chem. Soc.*, xliii (1883), 238.

[118] Thomson's letter to Rutherfurd cited in footnote 116.

between the Regius Professors by the Chancellor of the Exchequer, Thomson receiving £200 of it.[119]

Though he was now financially less insecure and near the end of his teaching career, Thomson's zeal for reform remained undiminished and was perhaps prompted by the unrestricted appointment of Pagan to the Chair of Midwifery in 1840. To the surprise of the College the Regius Professors applied through a memorial to the Lord Advocate for their case to be litigated on the grounds that the prerogative of the Crown was involved.[120] The College, of course, retaliated with a short and rather decorous memorial, grounding its case on the legal precedent of 1809 and on the subsequent observance of that precedent by the Crown.[121] It is, however, significant that the College was not unanimous, the Professors of Medicine and Mathematics (William and James Thomson respectively) dissenting from the majority view.[122] Peel's Home Secretary, Graham, was sufficiently concerned to consult the Law Officers of the Crown in Scotland who advised him not to take proceedings against the College.[123] Thomson meanwhile continued to endure his degradation only obliquely: from 1841 his nephew and son-in-law, R. D. Thomson, trained by his uncle and Liebig, lectured on organic chemistry and ran the practical class. After 1846 on Senate authority he discharged the whole duties of the chair until his uncle died in 1852. Thomson's influence, however, lingered on. After the Regius Professors had protested to the Treasury about the College's proposal to move the site of the University, Supreme Court proceedings against the College were initiated in 1854 by the Crown, the Pursuers admitting that in the first commissions to the Professors of Surgery, Midwifery and Chemistry, certain exemptions were mistakenly allowed by the then advisers of the Crown.[124] Abolition of the invidious distinction between College and Regius Professors followed quickly when the Scottish Universities Act of 1858 was passed.

V.

Thomson's experience at the University of Glasgow demonstrates that the institutionalization of an autonomous science in early nineteenth century Britain could be sharply modified by the exigencies of a local situation. It seems clear that the quality of Thomson's research and of his novel teaching methods was adversely affected by the abrasive intensity of the intra-mural conflict about the status of the Regius Professors. Certainly

119 *Memorial in Action of Declarator, The Officers of State for Scotland against ... the University and College of Glasgow* (1857), 103.

120 *The Memorial of the undersigned Regius Professors of the University of Glasgow.* I have not succeeded in locating and reading a copy of this document.

121 *Memorial for The Principal and Professors, constituting the Faculty of Glasgow College, to the Right Honourable Her Majesty's Principal Secretary of State for the Home Department* (Glasgow, 1841).

122 *Memorial in Action of Declarator* ... (1857), 131.

123 Public Record Office, HO/103/9, letters of 23 November and 13 December 1841, and 4 February 1842.

124 *Memorial in Action of Declarator* ... (1857), 132.

he acted as their chief and vehement spokesman: every document concerning their position either originated from him or opposed his claims. Though the question of University reform at a national level was hardly a party matter, there is no doubt that locally it was exacerbated by the political and theological differences displayed by Macfarlan and Thomson. After the 1832 Reform Act, the elimination of abuses, particularly in patronage, was no longer a pipe-dream. Hence issues concerning the control of appointments produced bitter strife during the mid-1830s within the Church of Scotland and the Scottish Universities, particularly in Glasgow, by that time a traditional radical centre.

The basic difficulty in Thomson's situation at Glasgow was that for him the development of chemistry was inseparable from the Regius Professor dispute. As far as the College was concerned, Thomson was one of a number of Regius Professors inconveniently and sometimes suddenly foisted on it by the Government which refused to pay them adequate salaries. The College received no financial assistance from the Treasury to cover the departmental expenses associated with the activities of the Regius Professors. This was a genuine source of the animus directed by the College against the Regius Professors and particularly the egregiously ambitious Thomson. Though the College remained adamant about the restricted rights and privileges of the Regius Professors, it was not in principle opposed to the development of chemistry. In no other way can one account for the considerable expense it incurred in erecting the Shuttle Street laboratory. Thomson's conduct after that special act of generosity seemed to the College to be spitefully ungrateful as well as unnecessarily perverse. To Thomson, however, the situation appeared differently. When he accepted the chair he was unaware of the restraints attached to it. Hence he felt morally justified in urging the claims of the Regius Professors against the intransigence of the College. As one of the few significant British chemists who occupied a university chair in the early nineteenth century, Thomson was eager to advance not only his own status but also the related standing of his subject. When it became clear that the former aim would be thwarted he acted with characteristic bellicosity against what he felt to be injustice and degradation. Neither he nor the College was prepared to accept a compromise with regard to the Regius Professor dispute: each party was so strongly convinced of the rectitude of its case that the consequent impasse could be broken only by external interference.

If one considers the state of chemical teaching and research in other British institutions and universities, especially in the 1820's, then Thomson's work at Glasgow was more than locally important. During his incumbency the Glasgow chair of chemistry was in reputation second only to that of Edinburgh within British Universities, and in some respects it was more desirable. It is not surprising that Thomson was strongly committed to its growth, particularly as opportunities for translation to possibly better chairs were inevitably limited for a chemist of his stature. At a time when, especially in Scotland, chemistry was popular but academically trained British chemists were few, Thomson tried to develop the practical teaching of his subject and also a research school working on atomic weight determinations under his direction. Such achievements were uncommon in Georgian Britain as three obvious comparisons will demonstrate. Daubeny's career at the University of Oxford merely provides a sadly apt contrast,[125] but Hope's at the University of Edinburgh an illuminating one. The latter's speciality was the lecture-demonstration. Unfortunately he did not encourage practical work by his students who met this deficiency by forming their own chemical societies, attending the laboratory classes of the flourishing private teachers of chemistry in Edinburgh, and by going abroad to study practical chemistry under teachers such as Robiquet. Even after the opening of the new chemistry laboratory in May 1823, the practical classes were conducted under Hope's nominal supervision by his assistants. Clearly Hope's indifference to the practical teaching of chemistry decisively inhibited the growth of a research school at Edinburgh.[126] At the progressive English establishment, University College, London, however, Edward Turner was keen to establish a practical class, but as late as 1829 in his third year as professor the proposal was still under discussion.[127] Such contrasts with Thomson's professorial activities at Glasgow patently emphasize that he played a crucial role in the incipient professionalization of British science particularly in the decade during which Liebig began his epoch-making work at the University of Giessen. We lack a detailed and synoptic knowledge of the structure of British science at the accession of William IV. Nevertheless it is already abundantly evident that the contribution of the Scottish Universities and especially Thomson's pioneering work at Glasgow will be fundamental elements in it.

Acknowledgements

For granting permission to consult and publish manuscripts in their possession I am grateful to: Mrs. Seton Dickson, Symington, Ayrshire, owner of the Pollok–Morris MSS.; the Librarians of University College, London, and Royal Botanic Gardens, Kew; the Keeper of Manuscripts, the University of Edinburgh; the Trustees of the British Museum and the National Library of Scotland; and the Academy of Natural Sciences of Philadelphia.

[125] See, for instance, Daubeny's lecture registers reproduced in R. T. Gunther, *A History of The Daubeny Laboratory Magdalen College Oxford* (London, 1904), 65-135 (65-83).

[126] The details and implications of Hope's apathy towards practical teaching will be given in my paper "Practical Chemistry in the University of Edinburgh, 1799-1843", *Ambix*, xvi (1969) (in press).

[127] H. Terrey, "Edward Turner, M.D., F.R.S. (1798-1837)", *Annals of Science*, ii (1937), 137-152 (147).

My thanks for help and encouragement are also due to: the Librarian of the University of Glasgow and his staff; Dr. H. W. Jones and Mr. D. Fraser of the University of Bradford; Dr. A. Kent of the University of Glasgow; Miss J. M. Sweet, of the Royal Scottish Museum, Edinburgh, who generously allowed me to examine the Pollok–Morris MSS.; Professors N. Campbell and D. B. Horn of the University of Edinburgh; and the members of the Northern Seminar in the History of Science to whom a preliminary version of this paper was read on 6 December 1967 at Manchester.

VII

SCIENCE AND SCOTTISH UNIVERSITY REFORM: EDINBURGH IN 1826

In the late eighteenth century, which was for Scotland in many ways an 'Age of Improvement', the University of Edinburgh enjoyed a golden age.[1] Under the enlightened principalship of the Reverend William Robertson, the University offered wide, flexible, and mainly secular courses of study which were taught by conspicuously able professors.[2] If we restrict ourselves to scientific chairs, a roll-call of their occupants is distinctly impressive: John Robison (natural philosophy, 1774–1805); John Playfair (mathematics, 1785–1805); John Walker (natural history, 1779–1804); Daniel Rutherford (botany, 1786–1819); James Gregory (theory of medicine, 1776–89); William Cullen (practice of medicine, 1773–90); Alexander Monro secundus (anatomy, 1758–98); and their doyen Joseph Black (chemistry and medicine, 1766–99), 'so pale, so gentle, so elegant, and so illustrious'.[3] The scientific eminence of the University at that time is, of course, widely acknowledged.

If we turn, however, to the state of science in the University during the 1820s, a few years after the end of the French wars, we find that other British institutions as well as continental ones energetically challenged its reputation in science.[4] Within Scotland the standing of the medical school of the University of Glasgow rose dramatically largely through the efforts made by Thomas Thomson (professor of chemistry, 1818–52) and William Jackson Hooker (professor of botany, 1820–41). South of the border, too, competition increased rapidly in the 1820s. For instance, the teaching in the London surgical schools improved, London University was founded in 1826 very much on Edinburgh lines, and at the University of Cambridge a vigorous group of research-orientated teachers had modernized the mathematics tripos and was rejuvenating botany and geology. Nor must we forget the rise of the Dublin medical school. All these revived or new British institutions challenged in different ways the science teaching offered at the University of Edinburgh. The effect of such competition was not, however, immediately felt. During the 25 years of the French wars the total number of students had doubled from about

[1] T. C. Smout, *A History of the Scottish People, 1560–1830* (London, 1969); N. T. Phillipson and R. Mitchison (eds.), *Scotland in the Age of Improvement* (Edinburgh, 1970); D. D. McElroy, *Scotland's Age of Improvement: A Survey of Eighteenth-Century Literary Clubs and Societies* (Pullman, Washington, U.S.A., 1969).

[2] D. B. Horn, *A Short History of the University of Edinburgh, 1556–1889* (Edinburgh, 1967), pp. 36–94.

[3] H. Cockburn, *Memorials of his Time, 1779–1830* (Edinburgh and London, 1910), p. 46.

[4] J. B. Morrell, 'Individualism and the structure of British science in 1830', *Historical Studies in the Physical Sciences*, iii (1971) 183-204.

1000 to about 2000. Generally in the mid 1820s this number did not drop, and some 2000 students thronged the University's over-crowded classrooms in which they were taught by only twenty-seven professors of whom merely two were sinecurists.[5] Of the scientific professoriate only Robert Jameson (natural history, 1804–54), John Leslie (natural philosophy, 1819–32), and Thomas Charles Hope (chemistry and medicine, 1799–1844) could justifiably boast of an international reputation. It has been asserted that the professors of the early nineteenth century were on average inferior to their eighteenth-century predecessors, yet this assertion needs qualification at least where Jameson, Leslie, and Hope are concerned. It is just as important to realize that compared with the late eighteenth century the competitive pressure experienced by the professoriate had increased. Hence problems and difficulties associated with the University's activities in science became more apparent and more sharply defined during the 1820s.

These problems and difficulties did not remain private and local because in July 1826 the Scottish Universities Commission was established by Robert Peel, then Home Secretary. It scrutinized the activities in all directions of the five Scottish Universities (Edinburgh, Glasgow, St. Andrews, King's College of Aberdeen, and Marischal College of Aberdeen). Its comprehensive Report was published in 1831.[6] The establishment of this Commission has been recently interpreted as the first assault launched by aristocratic Scottish anglicizers against 'the Scottish system of a basically philosophical education'.[7] There is, however, another way of looking at the matter. I want to suggest that, at the dawn of the so-called Age of Reform, the Scottish Universities in general and Edinburgh in particular were facing or evading dire problems concerning effective organization and administration. Certainly when Peel was approached in late autumn 1825 by Joseph Hume, radical M.P. for Aberdeen and Lord Rector of Marischal College in 1824 and 1825, it was precisely this sort of problem which was worrying Hume.[8] In particular Hume, a renowned instigator and packer of parliamentary select committees, drew Peel's attention to the bitter struggle for power being waged in the University of Edinburgh between the Senate and the Town Council of Edinburgh, the latter at that time being the patrons of the University who were responsible for

[5] *Evidence, Oral and Documentary, taken and received by the Commissioners for visiting the Universities of Scotland: the University of Edinburgh* (Parliamentary Papers, xxxv, 1837), pp. 128–9. In future references this indispensable volume will be called *Edinburgh Evidence*. See also Lord Provost of Edinburgh to Lord Liverpool, 1 July 1814, British Museum Add. MSS. 38258, f. 124.

[6] *Report of the Royal Commission of Inquiry into the State of the Universities of Scotland* (Parliamentary Papers, xii, 1831). In future references this volume will be called *Report*. It consists of a general report and separate reports on the five Scottish Universities. When I have used the *Report* I have always checked its findings against *Edinburgh Evidence*.

[7] G. E. Davie, *The Democratic Intellect. Scotland and her Universities in the Nineteenth Century* (2nd edn., Edinburgh, 1964), pp. 26–40 (26).

[8] Peel to Lord Advocate of Scotland (Sir William Rae), 5 December 1825, British Museum Add. MSS. 40339, ff. 258–62.

election to about two-thirds of the chairs and for the general supervision of the University. Hume also pointed out to Peel that the time was ripe for the union of the two Aberdeen colleges which though small and impoverished competed with each other. These untidy arrangements at Edinburgh and Aberdeen, I suspect, did not satisfy Peel who revered administrative efficiency particularly if it was informed by a strong sense of public duty and accountability. In any event the question of the public value of the medical degrees granted by some of the Scottish Universities was already in Peel's mind. Quite characteristically Peel believed that any British medical degree should be a licence to practise in a technically competent way. No doubt, too, from spring 1825, he was aware of the difficulties raised for the Universities of Edinburgh and Glasgow, and their medical graduates, by the Apothecaries Act (1815) and proposed amendments to it.[9] Nor must we forget that as Home Secretary he held the patronage of the Regius chairs in the Scottish Universities; and that in this capacity he had insisted that the candidate with the best academic qualifications be appointed and not necessarily the most loyal Tory.[10] By autumn 1822 Peel's suspicions about the value of public testimonials for chairs were aroused, and he had already concluded that the Edinburgh Town Council was not competent to appoint professors in technical fields such as medicine. Nor was he unfamiliar with questions concerning the appointment of ministers to livings in the Church of Scotland.[11] In short, Peel was already brooding over some of the administrative inadequacies of the Scottish Universities when Hume approached him. But Hume was not alone in drawing Peel's attention to these deficiencies. In the previous month it was the Senate of the University of Edinburgh itself which on 1 November 1825 petitioned George IV and Peel to appoint commissioners to investigate the bitter dispute then raging between the Senate and the Town Council.[12] The immediate cause of this petition was simple. The Town Council supported the proposal made in 1824 by James Hamilton (professor of midwifery, 1800–39) that his subject be rendered compulsory for graduation in medicine. Without doubt Hamilton was keen to increase his share of the tuition and examination fees. The Senate, on the other hand, believed that it had, and ought to have, total control of all matters connected with graduation; and it therefore opposed Hamilton's proposal. As the relations between the Town Council and the Senate were complex, indefinite, and already hostile, the issue shifted to become one of sovereignty

[9] George Husband Baird, Principal of the University, raised these matters with Peel in a letter of 16 April 1825, British Museum Add. MSS. 40339, f. 221.

[10] Peel's views on testimonials and qualifications were given on 26 October 1822 to the second Viscount Melville, British Museum Add. MSS. 40317, f. 5.

[11] Letter of 28 October 1824 from Melville to Lord Elgin reproduced in W. Hanna, *Memoirs of the Life and Writings of Thomas Chalmers* (Edinburgh, 1851), iii. 497–8.

[12] L. J. Saunders, *Scottish Democracy, 1815–1840: the Social and Intellectual Background* (Edinburgh, 1950), 317–19; Senate Minutes, 1 November 1825. The University of Edinburgh traditionally dated its foundation as 1582 when royal sanction was granted by James VI to the Town Council to found a College.

and power. In late autumn 1825 Senate tried to break the impasse by petitioning Peel to set up a commission.

There seems little doubt that by late autumn 1825 Peel was familiar with some of the academic and administrative problems of the Scottish Universities in general and of the University of Edinburgh in particular. Not surprisingly he responded to the pleas made independently by Joseph Hume and by the Senate of the University of Edinburgh. With characteristic care and conscientiousness he consulted the Lord Advocate for Scotland, the senior Crown lawyer of Scotland, and indirectly the second Viscount Melville, then the political manager of Scotland[13] and its 'ministerial fount of crown patronage'.[14] As a prudent, conserving, non-coercive reformer, he quickly set up in summer 1826 the Commission for visiting the Universities and Colleges of Scotland. One of its duties reflected the concerns shared by Hume and Peel: the Commission was *inter alia* to inquire into and remedy 'certain irregularities, disputes, and deficiencies . . . in the Universities of Scotland, calculated to impair the utility of these establishments'.[15]

I

What was the academic structure of the University of Edinburgh in 1826 when the Royal Commission was appointed and began its work? The quick answer is that to a considerable extent it was pre-bureaucratic.[16] This was shown in several ways: the importance of personal connexions and personal whims, as opposed to qualifications and rules of procedure, produced unexpected and unpredictable behaviour; professors were at least as loyal to their clients as to the University; and the location and extent of various sorts of authority were not sharply defined. In order to elicit the pre-bureaucratic structure of the University of Edinburgh at that time I want to discuss two particular illustrations of it. The first is the mode of electing professors; the second is what may be called professorial *laissez-faire*.

About two-thirds of the chairs at the University of Edinburgh were under the patronage of the Town Council, which was also responsible for the general supervision of the University. During the 1820s the Town Council was enjoying its last decade of self-perpetuating power before reform of burghs and municipalities took place in the 1830s.[17] Its members were 'omnipotent, corrupt, impenetrable . . . Silent, powerful, submissive, mysterious, and irresponsible, they might have been sitting in Venice.'[18]

[13] Peel to Lord Advocate, 5 December 1825, British Museum Add. MSS. 40339, ff. 258–62.

[14] *The Life of Sir Robert Christison, Bart., edited by his Sons* (Edinburgh and London, 1885–6), i. 279.

[15] *Report*, p. 1.

[16] F. Musgrove, *Patterns of Power and Authority in English Education* (London, 1971), p. 88.

[17] A. J. Youngson, *The Making of Classical Edinburgh, 1750–1840* (Edinburgh, 1966), pp. 46–50.

[18] Cockburn, *Memorials*, p. 87.

For these thirty-three men, mainly merchants and craftsmen, university patronage was merely one of many activities: they were open to corruption, particularly when they were intellectually incapable of judging the academic worth of candidates; and they enjoyed many opportunities for satisfying their personal and political interests. Yet between about 1770 and 1815 these patrons secured for the University a galaxy of very able professors, though some concessions were made to the nepotistic claims pressed by academic dynasties. Indeed, up to the end of the French wars some of the most eminent professors, such as Stewart, Playfair, and Leslie, were zealous Whigs who had been appointed to their chairs by the dominantly Tory Town Council. This exception to the universal influence of party feeling and jobbing in Edinburgh may be explained, I think, if we remember that the financial interests of the City were directly connected with the ability of professors to attract students to its University.[19] By about 1820, however, the post-war revival of political interest and agitation apparently disturbed the Town Council which made political appointments to chairs in both 1820 and 1821.[20] In 1820, when the chair of moral philosophy became vacant, it was first offered by the Town Council to Sir James Mackintosh. Once he had declined to accept, the contest became a political one between the Whig William Hamilton and the Tory John Wilson who was vehemently attacked in the Whig columns of *The Scotsman*.[21] It appears that the Town Council succumbed to the pressure exerted by the Tory Government and by one of its Scottish agents Sir Walter Scott: Wilson was elected by 21 votes to 9. The bitterness of the political fighting in this election was, of course, yet another indication of the rising fortunes of the Edinburgh Whigs: Scott himself thought at the time that the Whigs showed more vigour in canvassing the Town Council than they had ever shown in any previous political contest in Scotland.[22] Party feeling ran riot on both sides, and even women were contaminated. Wilson's wife, for instance, was jubilant about her husband's success: 'the Tories have been triumphant, and I care not a straw for the impotent attempts of the scum of the defeated Whigs. I must say I chuckle at the downfall of the Whigs, whose meanness and wickedness I could not give you any idea of were I to write a ream of paper in the cause.'[23] The following year, a positively unsuccessful appointment was made when James Home, then 63 years old and professor of materia medica, was made

[19] This point was strongly made by anon. to Mrs Ricketts [1812], British Museum Add. MSS. 30009, f. 165.

[20] Early nineteenth-century Scottish politics are covered in W. Ferguson, *Scotland 1689 to the Present* (Edinburgh, 1968), pp. 266–90.

[21] A. Grant, *The Story of the University of Edinburgh during its first three hundred years* (London, 1884), ii. 347. The battle for the moral philosophy chair in 1820 is described in detail in E. Swann, *Christopher North: John Wilson* (Edinburgh and London, 1934), pp. 127–46, and M. Gordon, *Christopher North: A Memoir of John Wilson* (Edinburgh, 1862), i. 301–18.

[22] Gordon, *Wilson*, i. 308.

[23] Mrs Wilson to Mary(?), 27 July 1820, quoted in Gordon, *Wilson*, i. 317.

professor of the practice of medicine by the Town Council.[24] As one of his two opponents was John Thomson, then professor of military surgery and a redoubtable Whig, the contest degenerated again into a political one in which the Tory Home was the victor. No wonder that by 1825 Robert Mudie claimed that the patronage of the Town Council was characterized by 'civil ignorance, political influence, and clerical intrigue.'[25]

We must also be aware that after Waterloo the Town Council met difficulties in tempting good applicants to stand for some chairs, and in some cases it was rebuffed. In 1819, for instance, the vacant mathematics chair attracted a small field of which only William Wallace (the victor) and Charles Babbage were distinguished in any way.[26] Significantly James Ivory, a renowned Scottish mathematician, refused to stand even though he had just resigned from his post at the Royal Military College, Marlow, Buckinghamshire, which he had found intolerable.[27] Later that year the remunerative botany chair fell vacant and the Edinburgh savants tried desperately to entice the celebrated Robert Brown, the Librarian of the Linnean Society, to be a candidate.[28] But Brown refused to sever his London connexions for even three months a year: and the chair was unanimously given on 5 January 1821 to Robert Graham, the Tory candidate of the Melville group in the Town Council, from a final field of only two. Certainly the retiring Brown was discouraged by the advice Patrick Neill gave to him on how to appear as an academic self-puffer and gladiator: 'those possessing the power (in the election) are in general so completely ignorant, that means must be taken to let them know your *status* in the scientific world. It may sound strange to your ears to be told that certificates or testimonials are necessary. They may not be so to the Scavans of Paris, Vienna, or Berlin; but to the Town Council of Edinburgh they are indispensable. A few letters from first rate characters will be enough. One or two from Paris could soon be got. Please do not overlook this matter . . . I know all this will be repulsive to your feelings; but it is necessary to prepare for contingencies.'[29] It was ironic that the equally celebrated Sir James Smith, President of the Linnean Society, offered himself to the Town Council as a candidate for the botany chair only a few days after Graham had been appointed.[30] When he failed to receive an acknowledgement of his application from the

[24] Grant, *University of Edinburgh*, ii. 413.

[25] R. Mudie, *The Modern Athens* (Edinburgh, 1825), p. 220.

[26] Grant, *University of Edinburgh*, ii. 304.

[27] Ivory was so disturbed, perplexed, and saddened by what he regarded as persecution of himself by the colonel in charge of the Royal Military College that he ultimately resigned in 1819. See Ivory to Napier, 8 April 1816, British Museum Add. MSS., 34611, f. 382; 29 August 1817, B.M. Add. MSS. 34611, f. 439; 29 July 1819, B.M. Add. MSS. 34612, f. 272.

[28] H. R. Fletcher and W. H. Brown, *The Royal Botanic Garden Edinburgh, 1670–1970* (Edinburgh, 1970), pp. 99–102.

[29] Fletcher and Brown, *Royal Botanic Garden Edinburgh*, p. 100.

[30] Smith to Napier, 6 January 1820, British Museum Add. MSS. 34612, ff. 319–20, asked Napier to vet his letter of application for the chair.

Lord Provost of Edinburgh, Smith was understandably piqued. He told Macvey Napier, editor of the Supplement of the sixth edition of the *Encyclopaedia Britannica*, what Graham's election meant: 'I see your University will go the way of all such bodies—and will soon be not worth trying to save. Its very being depends on a worthy and impartial choice of professors. The first false step was choosing Monro.'[31]

All the professorial elections to which I have referred aroused considerable public interest not only because the welfare of the University was involved but also because patronage in general was a contentious issue in Scotland during the 1820s. It is a just commonplace that in Scotland the problems of parliamentary and burgh reform, which were also problems of patronage, were more dire than they were in England. In the legal arena the extensive powers of patronage enjoyed by the Lord Advocate for Scotland came under heavy fire.[32] In kirk politics, too, questions of patronage aroused acrimonious controversy frequently in connexion with pluralism and with intrusion by the British government in Scottish ecclesiastical appointments. These ecclesiastical disputes sometimes spread into the Universities. For instance in 1823 the Crown, who had just appointed Duncan Macfarlan as Principal of the University of Glasgow, presented him to the High Church of Glasgow.[33] This projected pluralism, as well as the imposed patronage, was successfully opposed by the evangelicals or high-flyers in the Glasgow Presbytery which judged that MacFarlan was an unqualified presentee. Ultimately the matter was carried by appeal to the General Assembly of the Church of Scotland at which the decision of the Glasgow Presbytery was reversed. In the autumn of that same year 1824, the same battle about pluralism and intrusion was again fought between the Moderates and their opponents in the University and town of St Andrews.[34] The occasion of this dispute was that in autumn 1824 Francis Nicoll, Principal of the United College of St Andrews, resigned the living of St Leonards church in the town. Though Thomas Chalmers (professor of moral philosophy) and the Presbytery of St Andrews appealed against the move, James Hunter (professor of logic) was appointed primarily by Melville on behalf of the Crown to the living. In a variety of activities, then, the question of patronage was widely and hotly debated, and the problems concerning patronage of chairs in the University of Edinburgh were therefore not merely intramural in their nature and importance.

The second example of the University's pre-bureaucratic structure

[31] Smith to Napier, 13 October 1820, British Museum Add. MSS. 34612, f. 389. Smith was referring to the election of Alexander Monro tertius to the chair of anatomy in 1798. This was perhaps the most obvious example of the nepotism and inbreeding shown in some appointments to medical chairs in the late eighteenth and early nineteenth centuries.

[32] G. W. T. Omond, *The Lord Advocates of Scotland* (Edinburgh, 1883), ii. 256–98, describes the period 1819–30 when Sir William Rae held the office.

[33] Hanna, *Chalmers*, ii. 395–400; iii. 19–21.

[34] Hanna, *Chalmers*, iii. 105–9, 494–8.

to which I wish to draw attention is the system of professorial *laissez-faire*.[35] An Edinburgh professor in the 1820s enjoyed a legal monopoly of his subject. He alone decided what and how he taught. This tradition of professorial engrossment was reflected in the system of remuneration then adopted by the Scottish Universities in general and in an extreme form at Edinburgh. An Edinburgh professor derived his emolument, out of which he usually met the expenses of his class, mainly from class fees. His basic salary was inevitably low. Indeed in the 1820s five Edinburgh medical professors received no salary whatsoever. This testing system stressed payment by popularity with students. As professors were so dependent on student fees for their livelihood, their own classes were likely to be their chief interest. Therefore the total programme followed by the minority of students intent on graduation was often of merely secondary importance to the professors. No wonder then that no entrance qualifications for particular classes were required; every man and his fee were welcome. The absence of admission requirements of course allowed many professors to recruit classes sufficiently big to ensure adequate remuneration. It also allowed any person of any age and training to attend any of the classes held in the University in whatever number and order best suited his particular preferences and pocket. It is most important to realize that neither individual professors nor the Senate interfered with the courses of study which non-graduating students chose to adopt. Hence, except in the medical faculty, few students followed the full degree programme. It is clear that this system of unrestricted *Lernfreiheit*, enjoyed by the majority of non-graduating students, fragmented the full degree programme, so that these students extended their loyalty primarily to those professors whose classes they had paid to attend. Essentially, Edinburgh professors were free-lance independent teachers permitted by the Senate and the Town Council to teach in the University. Under this system, however, the interests of individual professors and of the University were quite compatible and could be mutually reinforcing. As Leslie asserted on behalf of his colleagues and of himself, 'In following out our own plans, we most effectually contribute to the prosperity of the aggregate body. The University of Edinburgh owes all its advantages to the unfettered exertions of individuals.'[36]

Given the constitutional formlessness of the University[37] and the

35 This system, which by 1826 was virtually unchanged, is described in J. B. Morrell, 'The University of Edinburgh in the late eighteenth century: its scientific eminence and academic structure', *Isis*, lxii (1971), 158–71.

36 Letter of Leslie to Baird, 28 October 1823, quoted in Senate Minutes for 31 October 1823.

37 This constitutional formlessness is well shown by the ignorance of Baird concerning the post of Rector of the University. On 10 November 1825 the Lord Provost as Rector of the University and the Town Council as its patron physically and formally visited the University. As late as 4 November 1825, Baird wrote to Napier, asking about the origin, object, powers, and duties of the Rectorship and wondering whether the Lord Provost was eligible (British Museum Add. MSS. 34613, f. 324).

system of professorial *laissez-faire*, it is not surprising that professors jealously guarded their classes against both external and internal competition and innovation: quite simply a professor could face loss of income if a chair in an allied subject were created or if new subjects were accepted for graduation. Thus from the 1770s onwards the medical professoriate was expanded against the resistance of the Senate only by private and government endowment of new chairs. And after the French wars proposals for separate chairs in comparative anatomy (1816), intellectual power (1823), and political economy (1825) were scrapped after much professorial and political strife.[38] This last proposal was not fought over merely in Edinburgh. Its sponsor was the Whig economist and inveterate enemy of Wilson, James Ramsay McCulloch, editor of *The Scotsman*, who in 1824 had delivered in London the first Ricardo memorial lectures on political economy.[39] Aided by the advice on strategy given by Huskisson (President of the Board of Trade), who was sympathetic to the economic doctrines of McCulloch and Ricardo, McCulloch organized a Memorial to Lord Liverpool (the Prime Minister) urging the establishment of a chair of political economy—for himself. Indeed he told Napier what to do: 'Get as many of the professors to sign it as you can and be sure and make them write Professor so and so after their name—Do not ask anyone for a signature who you think would refuse, and let the things be kept as quiet as possible—It is sufficiently understood that I am to be the first Professor . . . You must not fail to say, as Huskisson said to me today, *that it is a science perfectly distinct and separate from every other taught in the University* and requiring the individual time and talents of a separate Professor to do it justice.'[40] This Memorial, signed *inter alia* by twelve Professors, was, of course, opposed by John Wilson who argued to Huskisson that the proposed chair would infringe his rights and privileges as professor of moral philosophy.[41] After discussion between Huskisson and Canning (Foreign Secretary), Lord Liverpool referred the matter to the Senate of the University.[42] By that time, however, Huskisson's enthusiasm for the proposal was waning mainly because of the strong opposition stemming from Liverpool, Melville, John Hope (Solicitor General for Scotland), and not least Peel. It seems that Peel finally squashed the proposal so

[38] Grant, *University of Edinburgh*, i. 325; Horn, *Short History*, p. 96. The affair of the proposed chair of political economy is described from different points of view by Gordon, *North*, ii. 83–9; Swann, *North*, pp. 173–6; and D. P. O'Brien, *J. R. McCulloch: A Study in Classical Economics* (London, 1970), 57–60.

[39] É. Halévy, *The Liberal Awakening, 1815–1830* (London, 1961), p. 193. Huskisson, Canning, Peel, and Lord Liverpool all attended these lectures.

[40] McCulloch to Napier, 17 May 1825, British Museum Add. MSS. 34613, f. 304. The italics were McCulloch's.

[41] Memorial of the undersigned Inhabitants of the City of Edinburgh to Lord Liverpool, dated 23 May 1825, British Museum Add. MSS. 38746, ff. 219–22; Wilson to Huskisson, 8 June 1825, British Museum Add. MSS. 38746, ff. 233–4.

[42] Canning to Huskisson, 11 June 1825, British Museum Add. MSS. 38746, f. 236; draft of Huskisson's reply to [Canning?] [no date], B.M. Add. MSS. 38746, f. 239; Huskisson to Wilson, 15 June 1825, quoted in Gordon, *North*, ii. 85–6.

effectively that Senate did not discuss the matter. On this occasion Peel's motives were mixed: he acted partly from party loyalty to Wilson, and partly from respect for the vested rights and just privileges of Wilson's chair.[43]

In these ways, then, the University of Edinburgh in the 1820s was pre-bureaucratic and ripe for external inquiry. But one of these ways was, to my mind, of paramount importance: the class fee system of remuneration of professors. For much of their emolument most professors were mainly dependent on the fee of 3 or 4 guineas paid by each member of the class. They depended financially on their clients, and not on their institution. Hence their loyalty tended to be chiefly exerted towards themselves and their clients, and not to the University. It is not surprising then that internecine quarrels among the professors were bitter, frequent, and public. In 1826, for instance, the young Thomas Graham noted that 'The Professors here are all at logger-heads with each other. Leslie calls Hope in his classroom "the showman in the other corner", while Dr. Hamilton has just received £500 from Hope for defamation.'[44]

II

I want to turn now to a trio of professors of science active in the 1820s to try to argue that their style of teaching and their appraisal of their professorial functions were strongly influenced by the pre-bureaucratic academic *laissez-faire* in which they operated. My basic thesis is that the search by professors for students and their fees could both motivate and regulate academic practice and innovation in their classes. In other words I want to suggest that professors were likely to try to introduce innovations in the content and the style of their work if these were likely to maintain or increase the sizes of their classes; but that they tended to resist or discourage innovations which would have significantly reduced their popularity with their students or would have reduced their remuneration. Indeed in some cases the search made by professors for students and their fees was a stronger motive than the pursuit of so-called pedagogic ideals. When the former and the latter motive were compatible, no problems were likely to arise; but when they were not, tensions were likely to appear. The particular science professors I want to discuss are Jameson, Leslie, and Hope. I have chosen these three men because they were deservedly the most eminent among the science professors; and their subjects were those in which Scots had been or were conspicuously active.

Let us look first at Jameson. As a prelude I want to say two things about him. Firstly he is sometimes portrayed as a whipping boy in history of geology because of his allegedly dogmatic advocacy of Wernerian

43 Gordon, *Wilson*, ii. 87, 89–90.
44 R. A. Smith, *The Life and Works of Thomas Graham* (Glasgow, 1884), p. 9.

geology.[45] Be that as it may, it is most important to realize that by the mid 1820s Jameson had produced a large number of distinguished students who received their first inspiration and instruction from him.[46] Now Jameson held two posts simultaneously: he was Regius professor of natural history, and also the Regius Keeper of the Natural History Museum, which by 1826 was so large that it threatened to fill the whole of the University.[47] Jameson was fortunate in that his subject was generally popular, but attendance at his class was not compulsory for graduation of any kind. Armed with a basic salary after 1812 of £100, Jameson was therefore thrown into the academic market-place. Though a feeble lecturer who lacked charisma, he had increased his class from about 50 to around 200 by 1826. Not unexpectedly the gown and the town, the young and the old, attended him: regular students, surveyors, civil engineers, army engineers, silversmiths, jewellers, and farmers all crowded into his classroom.[48] Now Jameson's success in attracting students was clearly due to the content and method of his teaching. He capitalized on the popularity of natural history by offering a synoptic yet detailed course which by 1821 covered 273 lecture topics. Jameson catered for every possible type of interest in his comprehensive lecture course, which spanned meteorology, hydrography, mineralogy, geology, botany, and zoology. Moreover, his students could anticipate demonstrations of specimens in the lectures, informal hour-long chats with him before lectures, and fields trips in which Jameson showed the students how to do his subject. These field trips were highly popular, whether they were to Salisbury Crags, to the Great Glen, or to the Western Isles. Perhaps most important of all was that only his students enjoyed free access to the Museum of Natural History of which he was Keeper. There he met students usually three times a week for exercises in the accurate description of the objects it contained; and in any event, Jameson was usually available most weekdays in his Museum if students wanted to meet him. By supplementing his lectures in these attractive ways and by giving useful privileges to his students, Jameson had in twenty years increased the size of his class and of its fees fourfold.

Now the Museum was a pedagogic device used by Jameson for keeping himself in business as a teacher, but it was more than that.[49] By 1826 the Museum, which Jameson had begun from scratch in 1804, had deservedly

[45] C. C. Gillispie, *Genesis and Geology* (New York, 1959), pp. 66–9.

[46] This has been conclusively shown in A. C. Chitnis, 'The Edinburgh professoriate 1790–1826, and the University's contribution to nineteenth century British society', University of Edinburgh Ph.D. thesis, 1968, Chapter IV; and L. Jameson, 'Biographical memoir of the late Professor Jameson', *Edinburgh New Philosophical Journal*, lvii (1854), 1–49 (2–3, 31–2).

[47] My account of Jameson as professor draws on *Report*, pp. 137–8; *Edinburgh Evidence*, pp. 141–8.

[48] *Evidence*, p. 142.

[49] My account of the Museum draws on *Report*, pp. 78–81, 176–9; and *Edinburgh Evidence*, pp. 142–6, 167–9, 178–84, 491–4, 558–9, 571, 619–23, 626–9.

acquired a distinguished reputation, both at home and abroad, for which he was largely responsible. Yet some of the arrangements associated with the Museum were vague, haphazard, and confused. For instance, by 1826 the question of ownership of the contents of the Museum had become embarrassing. In its early years Jameson alone had expanded the collection but subsequently both the University and the British government had donated specimens. By 1826, therefore, Jameson, the University, and the Government all claimed ownership of at least parts of the collection. The function of the Museum was equally confused. Was it an appendage of Jameson's class? Was it an enviable facility of the whole University? Or was it a public and national institution owned by the Crown? Its financing, too, was consequently *ad hoc*. From 1820 the Museum had been financed from three sources: about £650 p.a. from the public who usually paid 2s. 6d. per head for admission; £100 p.a. from the Crown as an annual grant; and about £150 p.a. from Jameson himself, even though as Regius Keeper of the Museum he received no salary from the Crown. It was, of course, possible to take different views of these three related problems concerning the ownership, the function, and the financing of the Museum. At one extreme, the Scottish Universities Commissioners argued in their Report that the Museum was 'the property of the Crown, but secured for the University.'[50] At the other extreme, Jameson clearly regarded himself as much the proprietor of the Museum as its trustee. He had therefore exploited for his own pedagogic purposes the confusions to which I have just referred. For instance, from 1820, without consultation he had implemented a differential scale of admission fees: members of his present class were admitted gratis to the Museum, whereas all other students and the general public had to pay an admission fee of at least 2s. 6d. a visit or of a guinea a year. Clearly Jameson's students enjoyed a useful perk in having free access to the Museum.

Jameson had, of course, another motive besides that of attracting students. It has been stressed recently that Jameson, the leading British exponent of Wernerian geology, used the Museum as a weapon in his warfare with the Huttonians.[51] Quite simply only Wernerian disciples and apostles were admitted without obstacle to the Museum; and, as Keeper, Jameson restricted the display of specimens to those which illustrated Werner's views. Not only did he keep at bay potential and active Huttonians. He even succeeded in hiding some parts of the Museum's contents which had been donated quite explicitly to the University and not to him. No doubt he revelled in his sequestration of James Hutton's mineral collection which the Royal Society of Edinburgh had given to the University in 1808. When the Scottish University Commissioners asked to see

[50] *Report*, p. 78.

[51] A. C. Chitnis, 'The University of Edinburgh's Natural History Museum and the Huttonian-Wernerian debate', *Annals of Science*, xxvi (1970), 85–94.

Hutton's collection it was shown to them in boxes which Jameson had never opened.[52] As an ardent Wernerian he preferred, quite naturally, to preserve himself from Plutonic plague and Huttonian heresy. By exploiting with admirable acumen the ambiguities and confusions associated with his position as both professor and Keeper, Jameson had made the latter serve the former.

Let us look now at our second professor John Leslie, who at the age of 53 was translated in 1819 by the Town Council from the chair of mathematics to the more prestigious one of natural philosophy. Clearly Leslie was by that time past his best as a researcher, yet he was still sufficiently alive to be concerned with academic standards. Nevertheless, as his friend and obituarist Macvey Napier reluctantly confessed, Leslie paid 'attention to his own interest' in that 'his care of his fortune went somewhat beyond what is seemly in a philosopher'.[53] This tension between Leslie's concern for intellectual attainments and his love of financial reward was manifest before 1819. For instance when Leslie visited Arcueil near Paris in 1814 he was delighted that the leading French savants flatteringly regarded Edinburgh as a 'centre des sciences exactes'; yet he clearly envied their social status and boggled at the annual incomes of £5000–£6000 received by Laplace and Bethollet.[54] This tension did not disappear in 1819 when Leslie assumed his second chair: on the contrary it was exacerbated because when he moved from the chair of mathematics his fixed annual salary dropped from £148 to £52. Consequently he became more dependent on being successful in the academic market-place. I think that he was quite aware of his predicament as professor of natural philosophy. That is why he told the Scottish University Commissioners: 'Let each Professor have a salary of £300 . . . Such a salary would bribe no man to indolence, while it would remove the temptation to descend from the dignity of academical instruction to cater after popularity.'[55] Perhaps, therefore, it was not accidental that between 1819 and 1826 the size of Leslie's class remained constant at about 150.

In two important respects Leslie increased the academic significance of his course and simultaneously rendered it more attractive to students. Firstly, he offered a course that was much wider than that given by his predecessor, Playfair.[56] He spanned general properties of bodies, statics, the laws of motion, physical astronomy, mechanics, hydrostatics, hydrodynamics, pneumatics, light, heat, magnetism, and electricity. Indeed this syllabus was so synoptic that Leslie had difficulty in covering it in his single year's course of about 120 lectures. The compromise he reached

[52] *Edinburgh Evidence*,, p. 619.

[53] M. Napier, 'Memoir of John Leslie', in J. Leslie, *Treatises on Various Subjects of Natural and Chemical Philosophy* (Edinburgh, 1838), pp. 1–46 (45).

[54] Leslie to Napier, August 1814, British Museum Add. MSS. 34611, ff. 99–100.

[55] *Edinburgh Evidence*, p. 159.

[56] *Report*, pp. 133–4.

was to treat some of its parts cursorily and to dwell chiefly on those which he regarded as fundamental, and which the students could comprehend the most readily. More significantly, Leslie again went far beyond the practise of his predecessor by using about 1000 lecture-experiments per session to illustrate and confirm physical principles and facts; and he built up a good collection of apparatus which by 1826 had cost £1600, of which £900 came from Leslie's pocket and £700 largely from the Town Council.[57] Leslie had put the matter clearly to Thomas Young in 1819 when asking for his help in providing apparatus.

> You know how miserable it has been; but I expect large funds to enable me to restore it to some degree of splendour. I wish to render the course much more Experimental than formerly and the public appears to expect it.[58]

No wonder that in 1822, when George IV paid his celebrated visit to Edinburgh, Leslie was keen to display in the university a couple of his best experiments to the royal suite.[59] In emphasizing this aspect of his teaching Leslie catered for fashionable demand without sacrificing intellectual standards.

In one important respect, however, Leslie was constrained by the arrangements of open access to the University classes and of *Lernfreiheit* which the students enjoyed. Though ideally students were intended to take the junior and senior mathematics classes before attempting natural philosophy, many of them took it in the same year as the first mathematics class. This mathematical ignorance of many of his students compelled Leslie against his personal wishes to take 'a low flight' by avoiding the less simple quantitative aspects of his subject.[60] As Leslie pointed out to the Scottish University Commissioners, 'I am obliged, under the circumstances in which I am placed, to consult the feelings of the public.'[61] This difficulty was exacerbated by his indistinct pronunciation and by his general inability to adapt his exposition to the level of his audience.[62] With characteristic entrepreneurship, Leslie tried to solve this problem by proposing to split his teaching into two sorts: the specialized and mathematical; and the elementary, qualitative, and popular. In 1823 he proposed to form an extra class in Special Physics to supplement the traditional course of natural philosophy which catered for 'the taste and

[57] *Report*, p. 134; *Edinburgh Evidence*, pp. 126, 158. Leslie joyfully wrote to James Brown, 19 January 1823, Edinburgh University Library MS. Dc.2.57, item 207, about his new lecture-room: 'I have now a large splendid class room with many conveniences—with gas lights, water fountains, etc. and I have access thro' another large adjoining room containing the cases and apparatus by a stair to a platform on the roof'.

[58] Leslie to Young, 13 September 1819, British Museum Add. MSS. 34612, ff. 291–2.

[59] Leslie to Sir Walter Scott [summer 1822], transmitted to Peel, British Museum Add. MSS. 40350, f. 250. Leslie also offered to furnish the King every day with 6–8 lb. of ice made with his famous congelation apparatus.

[60] *Report*, p. 134. In *Edinburgh Evidence*, pp. 556 and 561, Brewster mercilessly exposed the mathematical weakness of most students in the natural philosophy class since about 1800.

[61] *Report*, p. 134.

[62] Napier, *Leslie*, p. 34.

acquirements of the bulk of the students.'[63] Leslie hoped to give this Special Physics course in two parts: the first surveying magnetism, electricity, pneumatics, and meteorology; and the more mathematical second part covering optics, astronomy, and physical geography. As he pointed out, his proposal would enable students to move steadily from the easy to the more difficult parts of his subject. Unfortunately for him Senate banned it because of alleged interference with other established Chairs.[64] At the elementary level, however, he was more successful. In the winter of 1826–7, for instance, he followed his rival Hope in giving popular lectures before a mixed audience. 'Unseemly results are said to have followed', and this diversification of Leslie's teaching was not repeated owing to pressure exerted jointly by the Senate and the Town Council against the mounting of popular lectures in general within the University precincts.[65] It is clear that Leslie never solved the problem created by the moderate mathematical attainments of many of his students: quite simply what he regarded as intellectually respectable teaching would have decimated his class, yet for financial reasons he wanted a large one. No wonder that Leslie as a committed academic looked longingly at the methods of selecting pupils for the École Polytechnique in Paris; that he advocated the financial support of able indigent students; and that he urged the exclusion of elementary teaching in science and classics from the Scottish Universities.[66] Yet the self-same Leslie, as an academic financial entrepreneur, supported a move to make natural philosophy a compulsory subject for medical students who intended to graduate because in that way he would have doubled the size of his class.[67]

Our third man, Hope, began his long career as professor of chemistry with two great advantages: first, his subject was widely popular, useful vocationally, and compulsory for graduating students; secondly, he succeeded Joseph Black, his patron and exemplar, who had supported lucid simple and elegant lectures with impeccably neat lecture demonstrations displayed in his prime to audiences of about 200. Hope's teaching career is largely the story of the way he capitalized on these advantages.[68] It should be stressed that he had no salary whatsoever, and that additionally he himself had to meet the capital and running expenses associated with his class. No wonder, then, that once settled into his chair, he virtually abandoned research and immediately devoted his energy to rendering his subject and his lectures as attractive and popular as possible. David Brewster may well have had Hope in mind when he argued in 1830 that

[63] Leslie to Baird, 31 May 1823, quoted in Senate Minutes, 16 June 1823.

[64] Grant, *University of Edinburgh*, ii. 354; Senate Minutes, 22 November 1823.

[65] Ibid., ii. 354; Senate Minutes, 16 December 1826, and 14 February 1829.

[66] *Edinburgh Evidence*, pp. 125, 159.

[67] Horn, *Short History*, pp. 106–7; Leslie to Brown, 4 December 1820, Edinburgh University Library MSS. Dc.2.57, item 205.

[68] My account of Hope draws heavily on J. B. Morrell, 'Practical chemistry in the University of Edinburgh 1799–1843', *Ambix*, xvi (1969), 66–80.

such an unsalaried professor 'is forced to become a commercial speculator and under the dead weight of its degrading influence, his original researches are either neglected or abandoned.'[69] Yet Hope did succeed financially in the academic market-place. His spectacular and punctiliously organized lecture-demonstrations, using large apparatus specially designed for the purpose, were invariably successful. This is just one example of the way in which all Hope's efforts were expended on his class: no research papers poured from his pen; and unlike many of his colleagues such as Jameson and Leslie, he never felt the need to gain reputation and reward by writing textbooks. Though he lacked the eloquence and finesse of his predecessor, his clear if pompous exposition supported by his renowned lecture-demonstrations regularly gained for him in the 1820s audiences of over 500, easily the largest class in the University. Without feeling any compunctious visitings of academic conscience, Hope simplified and popularized his subject. As he avoided demanding and quantitative subject matter, his class varied enormously in age, training, and ambition. Such was his popularity that during the early 1820s 1 person in 300 in Edinburgh attended his lectures: Leonard Horner perceptively remarked in 1820 that 'Tommy Hope is gathering guineas not laurels—getting up his chemical drama in a new theatre, with great *eclat*'.[70] Yet Hope satisfied many students who thought his class was one of the best in the University. For instance, the Polish prince Adam Constantine Czartoryski, who attended the classes of Jameson, Leslie, and Hope between 1820 and 1823, rightly stressed that Hope had 'acquired quite a reputation for his method of teaching. He is just the opposite of Mr. Leslie. He is as inferior to him in point of genius, as he is superior to him in method, in the neatness of his demonstrations, in his skill in carrying out his experiments, and in his mode of expression which is elegant to the point of affectation.'[71]

There was, however, a deficiency in Hope's teaching arrangements, i.e. until 1823 he provided no opportunities for students to do practical work. Before that time enterprising students formed their own societies for doing experiments, attended the private classes of practical chemistry available in Edinburgh, or even migrated to London and Paris. Hope grudgingly acknowledged the desirability of practical chemistry by arranging in 1823 that his own part-time lecture assistant should run the practical class at his own responsibility and risk. Indeed Hope tolerated but did not positively encourage this practical class, which in his opinion was merely an optional extra unrelated to his lecture course. Clearly Hope saw practical chemistry as a potential challenge to his own lecture class;

[69] D. Brewster, 'Decline of science in England', *The Quarterly Review*, xliii (1830), 305–42 (326).

[70] L. Horner to Alexander Marcet, 8 November 1820, in K. M. Lyell (ed.), *Memoir of Leonard Horner* (London, 1890), i. 179.

[71] A. C. Czartoryski to A. G. Czartoryski, 27 January 1823, Edinburgh University Library MSS. Dc.2.78.

and in any event it did not promise to service his pecuniary interests. He wanted to preserve his monopoly of his subject at the expense of its development. Hence, though Hope was a popular lecturer, he trained very few competent practical chemists.

Perhaps by 1826 Hope had higher and indeed transcendental things on his mind. In the spring of that year he reached the zenith of his popularity as a demonstrator of amusing and brilliant experiments when he mounted in the University a new popular course to which women were admitted.[72] Fortunately Henry Cockburn has left us a delicious account of this highly lucrative enterprise:

> The fashionable place here now is the College; where Dr. Thomas Charles Hope lectures to ladies on Chemistry. He receives 300 of them by a back window, which he has converted into a door. Each of them brings a beau, and the ladies declare that there never was anything so delightful as these chemical flirtations. The Doctor is in absolute extacy with his audience of veils and feathers, and can't leave the Affinities. The only thing that inwardly corrodes him, is that in an evil moment, when he did not expect to draw £200, he published that he was to give the fees to found a Chemical prize, and that he can't now retract, though the said fees amount to about £700. Horrible ———. I wish some of his experiments would blow him up. Each female student would get a bit of him.[73]

III

My chief thesis in this paper is that the system of pre-bureaucratic *laissez-faire*, under which professors at the University of Edinburgh worked during the 1820s and before, not only permitted the administrative confusion which disturbed Peel but also presented these professors with stimuli and restraints. I have tried to argue that some aspects of the teaching of science, both in content and method, are rendered more comprehensible if we see the diverse activities of the professors as an entrepreneurial response to the opportunities and difficulties they faced. Jameson, Leslie, and Hope, the most distinguished of the scientific professoriate in the mid 1820s, all had to face two related problems, one financial and the other academic: firstly, to keep themselves in business as teachers by acquiring, maintaining, and if possible increasing the size of their class to ensure adequate remuneration; and secondly, to implement their intellectual ideals and pedagogic aims. I have tried to show that these three men solved these two inseparable problems in different ways. Jameson found no incompatibility between searching for students and pursuing his intellectual aims. Leslie, in contrast, was always aware of

[72] Hope apparently gave 22 lectures in all. His introductory lecture was described as 'more amusing than instructive—he showed very brilliant experiments but did not explain them at all' by Helen Mackenzie, wife of Lord Joshua Henry Mackenzie, in the note for 15 February 1826 in her diary, National Library of Scotland, MS. 6374, f. 2.

[73] *Letters chiefly connected with the Affairs of Scotland, from Henry Cockburn to Thomas Francis Kennedy* (London, 1874), pp. 137–8.

the tensions in being both a financial and an academic entrepreneur. In the case of Hope it seems that his very popularity with his students as a lecturer ultimately prompted him to put his own financial reward before the advancement of his subject. These three different responses to a common situation show clearly that institutional stimuli and restraints did not determine the content, level, and style of the teaching; nevertheless these stimuli and restraints tended to remind the professors ceaselessly that their chief source of income as teachers came from their students. In stressing the entrepreneurial aspect of the teaching done by Jameson, Leslie, and Hope, I have drawn attention on occasion to rather unflattering aspects of their work. Yet these men were active and dedicated teachers of science whose efforts were central to the life and attractions of their university: their courses were comprehensive, up to date, and intellectually competent. Indeed, the aggregate strength of the teaching done by this trio of professors is confirmed if we compare it with that done by their Oxford and Cambridge equivalents, i.e. Buckland, Cooke, Daubeny; Sedgwick, Farish, and Cumming. For example, the enterprising Buckland attracted a maximum of 100 students; Cooke enjoyed a sinecure as Sedley professor; and Daubeny was apparently a poor lecturer as well as a hopeless demonstrator of experiments.

The notion of Edinburgh science professors in the early nineteenth century as entrepreneurs may have a wider heuristic use if it is applied to the development and diffusion of science in other institutions. We must, of course, bear in mind that in the nineteenth century an entrepreneur could be not only a financial middleman between capital and labour, but also a person who produced entertainments and created an audience. This realization may help us to understand the ways in which during the nineteenth century the intellectual activity known as science was astonishingly transformed into a profession.

Acknowledgements

For permission to quote from manuscripts I am grateful to the Trustees of the British Museum, the Trustees of the National Library of Scotland, and the Keeper of Manuscripts in the Library of the University of Edinburgh. For help of various kinds I am indebted to Dr A. C. Chitnis (University of Stirling), Dr R. Fox (University of Lancaster), Dr D. Fraser (University of Bradford), Mr C. A. McLaren (Archivist of the University of Aberdeen), Mr R. Porter (Christ's College, Cambridge), and Professor T. C. Smout (University of Edinburgh).

VIII

THE CHEMIST BREEDERS: THE RESEARCH SCHOOLS OF LIEBIG AND THOMAS THOMSON

It is a just common-place that during the nineteenth century the activity known as science became professionalized.[1] Though this process took place in different countries at different times, its general characteristics are not elusive. One can point to the rapid growth of specialization and to the equally significant increase of self-consciousness among scientists. This shared awareness of their changing social and intellectual roles displayed itself most obviously in the formation of pressure groups and of specialized societies such as the British Association for the Advancement of Science (founded 1831) and the Chemical Society of London (founded 1841). Thirdly the extent of public recognition afforded to scientists and science was increased, through patronage dispensed, for instance, by government and by teaching institutions such as universities. Nor must we ignore the creation of more full-time jobs in science and of assured career structures which at their best were regularly expanding. Finally the first half of the nineteenth century saw the development of laboratory-based methods of teaching and the associated growth of research schools, some of which were institutionally financed. Clearly some of the main features of the professionalization of science were closely connected. There is no doubt, for instance, that the expansion of specialization and of good career prospects for trained and qualified specialists was associated with the growth of research schools centred on laboratories in which ambitious disciples devotedly served an apprenticeship and afterwards produced knowledge under the aegis of a revered master of research.

Few would dispute that Liebig's opening of his chemistry laboratory in 1824 at the University of Giessen was a crucial event in the history of nineteenth-century science. Yet Liebig's was by no means the first chemical laboratory in a European university or university-level teaching institution to which students were regularly admitted.[2] In Paris, for instance, the École Polytechnique offered laboratory instruction in chemistry from 1795. Even within the German universities, courses of practical chemistry had been made available from 1810 by Stromeyer at the University of Göttingen, from 1820

[1] Useful surveys are provided by: E. Ashby, *Technology and the Academics*, London, 1958; D. S. L. Cardwell, *The Organisation of Science in England: A Retrospect*, London, 1957; and E. Mendelsohn, "The Emergence of Science as a Profession in Nineteenth Century Europe", in K. Hill (ed.), *The Management of Scientists*, Boston, 1964.

[2] W. A. Smeaton, "The early history of laboratory instruction in chemistry at the École Polytechnique, Paris, and elsewhere", *Annals of Science*, **10**, 224–34, 1954.

by J. N. Fuchs at the University of Landshut in Bavaria, and again from 1820 by Döbereiner at the University of Jena. Further north in 1808 Berzelius had opened a teaching laboratory for a few students at the Collegium Medicum in Stockholm, though it was his own private laboratory, first situated in Hisinger's house and then in the Swedish Academy of Sciences, which his more famous pupils attended.[3]

Nevertheless Liebig's was the first institutional as opposed to private laboratory in which students experienced systematic preparation for chemical research, and in which they were deliberately groomed for membership of a highly effective research school. Though there are gaps in our understanding and knowledge of Liebig's career at Giessen, its broad shape and content are well known. Without denying that he made important contributions to chemical knowledge *per se*, such as his work on ethyl and benzoyl radicals, we should pay attention also to the ways in which he decisively created the new conditions in which such knowledge was produced. In particular one could profitably try to analyse the intellectual, institutional, technical, psychological and financial circumstances, whether necessary or desirable, out of which Liebig fashioned his famous school. Moreover at the present stage of development of history of science considered as a historical discipline, it may also be fruitful to attempt a tentative comparative study of Liebig's research school and of a similar though less effective one run by one of his immediate chemical predecessors and contemporaries. The outstanding British candidate for such a comparative study is Thomas Thomson who having been appointed in 1817 as lecturer in chemistry at the University of Glasgow was elevated the following year to the newly-created Regius chair which he held until his death in 1852. In contrast with his eminent British chemical contemporaries such as Humphry Davy, John Dalton and William Hyde Wollaston, Thomson occupied a university teaching post from which he tried to create a research school based on his teaching laboratory. Though Davy and Dalton were teachers and did produce a few distinguished pupils, they did not share one of Thomson's most cherished ambitions, i.e. "to erect a laboratory upon a proper scale to establish a real chemical school in Glasgow and to breed up a set of young practical chemists".[4] In contrast, too, with his fellow British chemistry professors active in the 1820s, he was ambitious not only to develop the practical teaching of his subject in the university laboratory he opened to students in 1818 but also to create a research school working in it under his direction. These ambitions were uncommon at that time. They stand in sharp contrast, for instance, to the indifference shown to the practical teaching of chemistry

[3] J. E. Jorpes, *Jac. Berzelius: His Life and Work*, Stockholm, 1966, 31–3.

[4] Thomson to Robert Jameson, professor of natural history at the University of Edinburgh (1804–54), 9 September 1817 (Pollok-Morris MSS).

by Thomas Charles Hope, Black's successor in the chemistry chair at the University of Edinburgh.[5] Such diverse authorities as Thomas Andrews and Ernst von Meyer rightly regard Thomson's as the first school of practical chemistry to be established in a British university.[6] For that reason *inter alia* this paper will try to give a tentative comparative analysis of two university schools of practical chemistry, each of which was the pioneer in its own country during the 1820s. In accord with that aim I shall divide the paper into two parts. Firstly I shall postulate a conjectural model of what may be called an ideal research school by drawing attention to the circumstances under which a research school could most successfully operate in the first half of the nineteenth century. Secondly I shall use these suggestions as a means of comparing the research schools which Liebig and Thomson ran. As my aim is deliberately restricted to examining just one very important aspect of their professorial work, I shall avoid giving a comprehensive account of their university careers. Liebig is a famous figure in history of science. I have relied, therefore, to a large extent on secondary sources for information about his career.[7] For the less known Thomson I have relied more on primary sources and on some previously unexploited manuscript material.[8]

I

In trying to postulate and analyse the most propitious conditions under which a laboratory-based research school could flourish in the first half of the nineteenth century, we must clearly take account of the chief elements of such an on-going enterprise whether they were intellectual, institutional, technical, psychological, or financial. Only if we do this can we fully understand what was at the time very much an entrepreneurial activity.

Clearly the most important person in a research school was its director. His intellectual function was to offer and supervise a programme of work, too large for he himself to accomplish unaided, which his students implemented.

[5] J. B. Morrell, "Practical chemistry in the University of Edinburgh, 1799–1843", *Ambix*, **16**, 66–80, 1969.

[6] P. G. Tait and A. Crum Brown (eds.), *The Scientific Papers of Thomas Andrews*, London, 1889, 394; E. von Meyer, *A History of Chemistry* (tr. G. McGowan), London, 1898, 194, 592.

[7] The basic source remains J. Volhard, *Justus von Liebig*, 2 vols., Leipzig, 1909, of which a reprint is badly needed. A useful guide is C. Paolini, *Justus von Liebig: Eine Bibliographie sämtlicher Veroffentlichungen, mit biographischen Anmerkungen*, Heidelberg, 1968.

[8] For the time being the basic accounts of Thomson are Anon. (R. D. Thomson), "Biographical Notice of the late Thomas Thomson", *The Glasgow Medical Journal*, **5**, 69–80 and 121–53, 1857; W. Crum, "Sketch of the Life and Labours of Dr. Thomas Thomson", *Proceedings of the Philosophical Society of Glasgow*, **3**, 250–64, 1855.

This programme was frequently related not only to the frustrations he suffered and the inspirations he enjoyed during his early career, but also to the state and status of his subject and of its various branches. Almost invariably the programme was more easily and more effectively initiated if the director had acquired in his subject a growing or established reputation which was consonant with his ambitions. If, however, he lacked the reputation to sustain his school then problems concerning his credibility and indeed competence inevitably arose. It is obvious that publication was closely related to his reputation. Some publication was necessary if a merely local reputation were to be converted into a national or better still an international one. Yet publication could have its dangers. For instance, if the director of a promising school published research which aroused hostile criticism from acknowledged leaders in his subject, then the feasibility of his ambitions could be questioned. If at the worst both his competence and character were effectively attacked, his reputation was virtually destroyed. Generally speaking the most favourable situation was one in which the director's reputation in his subject advanced neither in front of nor behind his ambitions for his school.

Manpower, too, was important for the creation, maintainance and expansion of a research group. Quite simply there had to be a regular supply of motivated students who were keen to apprentice themselves to a recognized or emerging master of his subject. With respect to the steady availability of students the university teacher was better placed than his contemporaries who were employed in non-teaching institutions or as merely occasional teachers. The motives of these student-acolytes were, of course, very varied. Some wanted to acquire intellectual and practical command of their subject through close contact with a master, particularly if he offered a unique and superior type of training at a very competitive financial rate. No doubt all the students expected that even a tenuous connection with an established teacher would further their careers. No doubt, too, the more successful students anticipated that through their master's reputation and contacts they would more easily penetrate the upper echelons of the prestigious scientific networks of which they wished to be members. The most ambitious ones perhaps saw themselves first as disciples of their master and later as apostles who would diffuse his work and methods by establishing their own schools modelled on his. A last motive that must not be forgotten was the award of a reputable and useful qualification, though in some institutions such a public label of competence in scientific research was not available for much of the nineteenth century. At best a qualification could increase the career prospects of a student, and for the master it was a singularly impeccable way of increasing the public recognition afforded to him and his institution. Of course the value of a research qualification such as the Ph.D. varied widely: in pre-bureaucratic institutions it depended largely on the reputation of the master. If his standing in his subject were low, the label he dispensed was relatively worthless; if, however, it were high, that label was a precious acquisition which could act as an "open sesame" to more attractive jobs.

The nature of the area of enquiry cultivated by the school and the character of the techniques it employed to explore that area could be vital to its success or failure. Generally it would appear that success was most likely to be achieved if a set of relatively simple, fast and reliable experimental techniques could be steadily applied by both brilliant and ordinary students to the solution of significant problems in a new or growing field of enquiry. The application of such techniques allowed the systematic intellectual occupation and colonization of certain areas of research which sometimes become the "property" of the school. If these techniques were successfully applied to a body of related problems then the specific identity and reputation of the school were consolidated; so, too, was its *esprit de corps*. Perhaps most important of all, the use of a set of relatively simple, fast, and reliable experimental methods allowed those students who were less than brilliant to do and to publish competent work. When these techniques were deployed on a large scale a knowledge factory was the likely result. This was characterized by the steady and systematic production of reliable experimental results by ordinary students whose scientific mediocrity had been converted into scientific competence by the acquisition and use of these very techniques. In this way a large research school could realize Francis Bacon's dream of levelling up men's wits.[9] If, however, the director of research lacked such techniques or if he intended to enter a developed field of enquiry where strong competition was to be met, then clearly the chances of dominant success were diminished. When deficiencies of field of enquiry and of technique existed together in a particular research school, the resulting work was likely to be sporadic in both quality and quantity.

If a school wanted a more than local reputation it had to publish its work. Thus relatively easy access to publication opportunities, or best of all control of them, enabled a school to convert private work into public knowledge and fame. Publication was vital to the success of any ambitious research school. Otherwise its reputation remained restricted and its students lacked the spur of seeing their names in print. It was sufficient if the director had access, for instance, to journals published by learned societies of which he was an influential member or to proprietary journals published by colleagues or friends. However the most desirable situation clearly occurred when the director controlled and published his own journal. In that case he himself, his friends, and his better

[9] F. Bacon, *Novum Organon*, aphorism 122 in J. M. Robertson (ed.), *The Philosophical Works of Francis Bacon*, London, 1905, 297.

students published without obstacle in a journal which created and consolidated the status of his school, and publicised its specific field and style of work. In short, an ambitious research school had to take the full measure of Faraday's famous maxim: "work, finish, publish".[10]

I have restricted discussion so far to the importance of the director's programme, the students, the field of study, the techniques employed and publication. Yet for a potentially valid intellectual programme to be implemented, power was necessary. Quite simply the director had to possess or be rapidly gaining sufficient power within his institution to realize his ambitions. Such power allowed or produced effective control by him of his research enterprise: it was particularly vital when problems concerning innovation or expansion arose. If the director's power were insufficient, he was forced to expend time and effort in increasing it and in coping with the difficulties its shortage produced. These deficiencies of personal power and self-determination within his institution could seriously deflect him from running his school which he regarded as his chief responsibility and ambition. They could, of course, take many forms. For instance, a large load of low-level teaching students for whom his subject was subsidiary in importance, or of administration, sapped time and energy. Less obviously, but just as insidiously, problems concerning status would be demoralizing. If the director had to concern himself with the status of his students, if his subject were generally regarded as being subsidiary or peripheral to the chief aims of his institution, or if he himself had to fight incessant battles to maintain or increase his own institutional status, then his confidence and that of his students in his ability to run a school could be seriously eroded.

The creation, maintainance and growth of the school's loyalty, cohesion and confidence depended, too, on the director's charismatic powers, which at best reinforced his institutional power. Though the notion of "charisma" has been subjected to criticism, the term is useful if it conveys the idea of extraordinarily effective, indeed messianic, leadership.[11] Such charisma, which was most effectively exerted in informal pre-bureaucratic contexts, helped to draw students in sufficient numbers to make the school viable. It enforced the standards and styles of work adopted by the school. It exacted from the students an unflagging almost fanatical devotion to research, particularly at times of intellectual failure and disappointment, and on occasion it also imposed fervent specialization. It contributed strongly to the school's sense of its own novel and distinctive identity and importance. And it compelled unquestioning and unswerving loyalty to the master and his school. Though a research school existed primarily to advance knowledge, its atmosphere could be highly evan-

[10] S. P. Thompson, *Michael Faraday, his Life and Work*, London, 1898, 267.

[11] H. Wolpe, "A critical analysis of some aspects of charisma", *The Sociological Review*, **16**, 305–18, 1968.

gelical as the prophet broke through accepted conventions and led his devoted followers into unexplored and promising lands of enquiry. No wonder, then, that disciple-fetishism arose once research schools produced these new conditions in which knowledge was created.[12] Indeed the extent to which students wished to be known as the pupils of a certain director indicates the strength of his charisma.

Lastly, institutional support was desirable to allow the director to run his school on a regular and permanent basis. Provided he had sufficient money from fees, his salary, and his own pocket, to equip and maintain a laboratory, it was of course possible for an ambitious man to build up a relatively small research school. Unless he was rich, or charged a "realistic" fee, a financial crisis almost invariably occurred when the financial loss he incurred in meeting the necessary costs of running his laboratory became intolerable. At that point of crisis he could either increase his fee, an act which was likely to reduce the number of his students, or he could appeal to his institution for a form of financial support which would at least not penalize him for being successful with his laboratory students. If his institution reacted generously to his pleas and his threats by, for instance, increasing his salary and by paying his necessary expenses such as capital outlay, materials, apparatus, and assistance, then financial restraints were removed. The director would thereby be enabled at least to maintain the "crisis" number of students without penalizing himself financially and without sacrificing his intellectual independence. In the most favourable financial circumstances created by institutional support he could reduce his laboratory fee, thus undercutting his rivals and encouraging even more students to work under him. If, however, his institution or the patron of his post responded with only marginal improvements or negatively, and if he was unwilling to raise his laboratory fee, then the future was inevitably one of stagnation or decline of the number of students in his school. In that depressing situation the director could try to move elsewhere for better institutional support. If movement was not possible, his fate was the stoical or resentful acceptance of institutional indifference or rejection. At the worst a combination of lack of institutional support and decreasing annual remuneration of the director could lead to the virtual extinction of a once flourishing school.

II

In discussing the research schools based on the university laboratories which Liebig and Thomson ran, I shall apply to them the chief features of the conjectural model in the order in which these were proposed in the first section of this paper. Accordingly let us turn first to the programme of research the

[12] The emergence of disciple-fetishism is stressed by Ashby (1), 26.

director envisaged or implemented and to the related question of his reputatio in the subject.

It would appear that the basis of Liebig's programme of research was th development of reliable experimental methods of analysing organic compounds an ambition he realized between 1823 and 1830.[13] Once he was armed wit such a weapon, he successfully created and invaded what came to be known a organic chemistry. His achievement in this field, such as the isolation, analysi and synthesis of new compounds, his work on radical theory, on the hydroge theory of acids and on agricultural chemistry, stands as a perpetual reminde that he was largely responsible for the metamorphosis of animal and vegetabl chemistry into organic chemistry and biochemistry. This experimentall based programme and accomplishment in organic chemistry was related to th frustrations he endured as a young man. These disappointments had th positive function of pushing him into actions he might otherwise not hav contemplated. His youthful ambition to be a chemist was hardly encourage by the formal teaching he received before October 1822 when he arrived i Paris. At his local Gymnasium his hunger for chemistry was not satisfied by th largely classical curriculum. Nor was his experimental work on fulminate appreciated by the apothecary at Heppenheim to whom he was apprenticed fo ten months in the winter of 1819–20. When he attended in 1820–21 the lecture on chemistry delivered at the new University of Bonn by Karl Wilhelm Kastner Liebig was unimpressed; and, in the following session when he followed Kastne to the University of Erlangen, he discovered that Kastner's practical chemica competence was so limited that he was unfamiliar with methods of minera analysis. In desperation, Liebig turned for intellectual succour to the lecture on philosophy delivered that same session by the famous Schelling. The resul was even greater disillusion: Kastner was merely incompetent; but Schellin was a fraud because his philosophy lacked a basis of real positive knowledge It is clear that after his experience of Schelling's Naturphilosophie Liebig ha little patience for some time with extravagantly speculative and confidentl deductive types of science.[14]

The more encouraging aspects of Liebig's early career were focused on th Grand Duke of Hesse, Gay-Lussac and Alexander von Humboldt. Liebig wa highly indebted to the Duke's patronage not only for the free borrowing o books from the ducal library at Darmstadt but also for two grants of money one to enable him to go to Bonn in 1820 and the second to permit him to go t

[13] Liebig, "Uber einen neuen Apparat zur Analyse organischer Korper", *Annalen de Physik und Chemie*, **21**, 1–42, 1830; H. E. Roscoe, "Justus Liebig", *Nature*, **8**, 27–8, 1873.

[14] For the early disappointments of Liebig's career, see Volhard (7), i, 13–23; and Justu von Liebig, "An Autobiographical Sketch" in J. Campbell Brown, *Essays and Addresse* London, 1914, 27–43 (31–4).

Paris in 1822. It was then for the first time during his irregular education that Liebig enjoyed positive inspiration. The lectures he heard in Paris during 1822–23 by Gay Lussac, Thenard and Dulong were refreshingly different from Kastner's and Schelling's: their unpretentious empirical approach, reinforced where possible by quantitative methods, focused attention on phenomena. The following winter, as is well known, Liebig enjoyed the rare privilege of working in the laboratory of Gay-Lussac whose situation did not allow him to take more than the occasional student. From Gay-Lussac he learned practical techniques of exact analytical chemistry and the less tangible arts of scientific research. It was in Gay-Lussac's laboratory, too, that Liebig conceived the ambition of founding in Germany on a permanent and not on an occasional footing a teaching laboratory where he would be to his students what Gay-Lussac had been to him.[15] In addition the publication of a joint paper with Gay-Lussac on silver fulminate confirmed his belief that organic chemistry in general and isomerism in particular were fruitful fields of enquiry.[16] His problem at this stage of his career was to find a post, a difficulty solved primarily by Humboldt. Through the very strong pressure Humboldt imposed on the Grand Duke, Liebig was appointed, without the professoriate being consulted, as extraordinary professor of chemistry at the University of Giessen on 26 May 1824. Once at Giessen he brooked no delay, rapidly established a small teaching laboratory, and inspired by Gay-Lussac he began his work on improving the methods of analysing organic compounds. In the mid 1820s very few professors of chemistry in German universities possessed a laboratory to which they regularly admitted students. Liebig's was therefore one of the earliest in those universities in which systematic instruction in practical chemistry was given. His entrepreneurial insight was also shown in his choice of organic chemistry as his field of activity. When Liebig assumed his chair, inorganic chemistry was attracting the attention of the more active professors of chemistry in German universities. In particular, Christian Gottlob Gmelin at Tübingen, Heinrich Rose and Mitscherlich at Berlin, all of whom had been pupils of Berzelius, and Stromeyer specialized in inorganic

[15] Liebig's positive inspirations are described by Volhard (7), i, 8–9, 32–52; Liebig (14), 36–7; A. W. Hofmann, *The Life-Work of Liebig*, London, 1876, 51–5; M. P. Crosland, *The Society of Arcueil*, London, 1967, 433–6 and 439–41. It should be stressed that the Grand Duke of Hesse responded to the pressure exerted on him by Kastner and by Schleiermacher (the Duke's secretary) by granting in 1822 and 1823 a total of 1680 fl. (£145) to Liebig to enable him to study in Paris; this was more than the 1213 fl. (£104) paid out by Liebig's father. Supported financially by his state and his father, Liebig made a flying start to his career.

[16] Gay-Lussac and Liebig, "Analyse du fulminate d'argent", *Annales de Chimie et de Physique*, **25**, 285–311, 1824. This paper was rapidly available in English in *Annals of Philosophy*, **7**, 413–26, 1824.

chemistry.[17] In the newly emerging field of organic chemistry, however, only one German university professor, Döbereiner, had made a significant contribution.[18] Liebig undoubtedly realized that Berzelius and Klaproth had brought to near perfection quantitative methods of analysing inorganic substances such as minerals.[19] He therefore decided to pin his future on his ability to develop simple and reliable methods of organic analysis without which progress in organic chemistry was impossible. His acute premonition led him to commit himself in the mid 1820s to a relatively unexplored new branch of chemistry into which Dumas and Berzelius were also moving, and not to a developed or exhausted one.

At all times in Liebig's career his publications were recognized by the doyens of his subject. Indeed the publication in 1824 of his joint paper with Gay-Lussac fully confirmed his reputation with the leading French chemists, particularly as Gay-Lussac rarely collaborated in this way with students. During his first ten years at Giessen his published work continued to extend his reputation in his subject, especially after he had perfected his methods of analysing organic compounds. Berzelius, for instance, regularly praised his work in his *Jahres-Bericht*. It is true that from the early 1830s he indulged in many bitter chemical quarrels with ferocious energy. Yet even when he was compelled to admit his mistakes, the basis of his reputation remained unimpugned: as Partington pointed out, "he was unquestionably the greatest chemist of his time . . .".[20] At no time did his fellow chemists suspect that he was not an asset to his subject.

When we turn to Thomson's programme of research we find it was in the well-established fields of inorganic and mineralogical quantitative analysis. In particular he tried desperately to determine atomic weights accurately and to provide experimental justification for Prout's hypothesis. He fervently believed that the "atomic labours", which occupied his opening five or six years at Glasgow, would reveal those elusive quantitative laws of chemical affinity for which chemists had hitherto sought so vainly;[21] and he hoped that his related work on mineralogy, done between 1825 and 1835, would elevate it to a chemical science. This research programme was most ambitiously and abundantly revealed in two books: *An Attempt to Establish the First Principles of*

[17] J. R. Partington, *A History of Chemistry*, London, 1964, iv, 180, 185–90, 205–11; *ibid.*, London, 1962, iii, 659–60.

[18] Partington (17), iv, 178–80.

[19] Liebig (14), 38–9.

[20] Partington (17), iv, 300.

[21] W. H. Brock, "Dalton versus Prout: The Problem of Prout's Hypotheses" in D. S. L. Cardwell (ed.), *John Dalton and the Progress of Science*, Manchester, 1968, 240–58; and Thomson to Dalton, 14 April 1823, in H. E. Roscoe and A. Harden, *A New View of the Origin of Dalton's Atomic Theory*, London, 1896, 177–8.

Chemistry by Experiment (1825), which he thought had raised chemistry to the rank of a mathematical science;[22] and his *Outlines of Mineralogy, Geology, and Mineral Analysis* (1836), in which he arranged minerals on the basis of their experimentally determined chemical composition and not of their physical properties. Thomson did not pursue these enquiries alone. Between about 1819 and 1824 his students contributed to his published research by determining in his laboratory the composition of more than a quarter of the salts in which he was interested.[23] Again, between 1825 and 1835, his laboratory students analysed slightly more minerals than Thomson did;[24] and 45 of these analyses done by students were published in 1836. It appears then that between 1819 and 1835 Thomson ran a research school focused on three related aims: to put Dalton's atomic theory on a wider and firmer experimental basis; to provide conclusive experimental evidence to substantiate Prout's hypothesis that the atomic weights of elements were whole-number multiples of that of hydrogen; and to determine the chemical composition and formulae of all known minerals, particularly those containing aluminium.

The origins of these connected programmes are quite clear. In the third edition of his best-selling *A System of Chemistry*, Thomson gave the first printed version of Dalton's atomic theory and applied it to acids, bases and salts.[25] Again before the publication of the first part of Dalton's *New System of Chemical Philosophy* Thomson had submitted in early 1808 the first experimental illustration of the Law of Multiple Proportions.[26] Thereafter Thomson acted as Dalton's bull-dog as decades later Huxley fought for Darwin. Thomson was again fast off the mark in espousing a new quantitative chemical cause when in 1815 he published Prout's anonymous paper on specific gravities of gases in his own journal *Annals of Philosophy*.[27] No wonder, then, that when he acquired his laboratory at Glasgow he immediately set to work to establish by experiment a coherent set of atomic weights which would confirm Prout's hypothesis. This investigation of the composition and formulae of salts was extended subsequently to encompass those of minerals. In replacing artificial external features by the natural one of chemical composition as the basis of classification of minerals, he realized his long-cherished ambition of elevating

[22] Thomson to Dalton, 19 April 1825, in Roscoe and Harden (21), 178–9.

[23] Thomson, *An Attempt to establish the First Principles of Chemistry by Experiment*, London, 1825, i, 25; Thomson, "Reply to Berzelius's attack on his 'First Principles of Chemistry'", *Philosophical Magazine*, **5**, 217–23 (217), 1829.

[24] Thomson, *Outlines of Mineralogy, Geology, and Mineral Analysis*, London, 1836, i, iii.

[25] Thomson, *A System of Chemistry* (3rd ed.), Edinburgh, 1807, iii, 424–628.

[26] Thomson, "On oxalic acid", *Philosophical Transactions of the Royal Society of London*, **98**, 63–95, 1808.

[27] Anon. (W. Prout), "On the Relation between the Specific Gravities of Bodies in their Gaseous State and the Weights of their Atoms" *Annals of Philosophy*, **6**,321–30, 1815.

mineralogy to a full science.[28] No doubt his private ambitions were to displace Berzelius from his position as the European doyen of quantitative inorganic analysis, to increase Britain's thin reputation in analytical chemistry, and of course to add to his own.

Unlike Liebig Thomson had not enjoyed the benefits of working as a student in the laboratory of a master chemist. He began his publishing career as an assistant editor of the *Supplement to the Third Edition of the Encyclopaedia Britannica* between 1796 and 1800. Indeed his long articles on chemistry and mineralogy in that *Supplement* were published before his first research paper.[29] In sharp contrast with Liebig he made his debut in print as an informed encyclopaedic compiler and arranger of other chemists' work: he began his chemical career at the writing desk. Once the *Supplement* was published Thomson exploited the popularity of chemistry in Edinburgh by making his living there from 1800 to 1811 as a private teacher and as a textbook writer. From the start his ambitions were high, though as a practical chemist he was self-taught.[30] Accordingly he seems to have introduced lecture demonstrations into his teaching in autumn 1803, and by January 1807 he had opened a class in practical chemistry for about a dozen pupils restricted to those who attended his lecture course.[31] The capital cost of mounting this practical class must have been considerable. Presumably he used part of the £600 he received in late 1806 from the Scottish Excise Board for the work he had done in 1805 with Professors Hope and Coventry on the relative quantities of malt which could be made from English and Scottish barley.[32] The reasons which prompted Thomson to create these opportunities for students to do practical chemistry under his direction were probably pedagogic and entrepreneurial. He felt no doubt on the basis of personal experience that mere lecturing was inadequate to produce competent practical chemists. Perhaps, too, Thomson realized that with the advent of Dalton's atomic theory, practical skill in analytical work had assumed even greater importance. More basically, between 1807

[28] See "Mineralogy", *Supplement to the Third Edition of the Encyclopaedia Britannica* (2nd ed.), Edinburgh, 1803, ii, 192–261 (193, 199–200). The first edition of the *Supplement* was published in 1800.

[29] Thomson, "Experiments to determine whether or not fluids be conductors of caloric", *Nicholson's Journal*, **4**, 529–45, 1801.

[30] He had been won to chemistry when he attended Professor Joseph Black's course of lectures delivered in 1795–6 at the University of Edinburgh. Though Black was a master of elegant lecture-demonstrations, he had no laboratory in which students could work.

[31] Advertisements in the *Edinburgh Evening Courant*, 13 October 1803, 25 October 1806, 22 October 1807.

[32] Scottish Excise Board Minutes, 24 November 1806, Scottish Record Office, Edinburgh. Hope and Coventry (professor of agriculture, University of Edinburgh, 1790–1831) also received £600 each for six months' work.

and 1811 his was the only course of practical chemistry available in Edinburgh. As such it helped him in attracting students to both his classes. The competition between chemistry teachers in 1806–7 in Edinburgh, though less than at the turn of the century, was still sharp.[33] Thomas Charles Hope, Black's successor in the unsalaried chair of chemistry at the University, attracted 317 students who revelled in his punctiliously organised and spectacular lecture-demonstrations.[34] In the private arena, the well-established John Murray was the most formidable rival.[35] But neither Hope nor Murray ran a practical class. Thomson's initiative in this respect no doubt helped him in the struggle to gain and keep students. It must not be forgotten that, as long as students paid a class-fee to individual teachers and not a sessional fee to an institution, a teacher in a competitive situation was often stimulated to advertise and introduce new practices in order to maintain and possibly to increase the size of his class and of his remuneration.[36]

Though little is known about Thomson's Edinburgh practical class, one point does seem clear. Around summer 1807 Thomson began work on the quantitative analysis of minerals, this research being published in the *Memoirs of the Wernerian Natural History Society* of which Thomson was a founder-member.[37] That same year Thomson acted as Sir James Hall's chief adversary in a number of debates between the Wernerians and the Huttonians in the Royal Society of Edinburgh. In these discussions, Thomson acted as the vehement spokesman for his friend Professor Robert Jameson, a leading exponent in print of Werner's views.[38] It seems likely therefore that his

[33] In Autumn 1800 chemistry courses were delivered in Edinburgh by no less than six lecturers: Professor Hope, Thomas Thomson, John Murray, Dr. Briggs, John Thomson and Henry Moyes. See advertisements in the *Edinburgh Evening Courant*, 18 October 1800, 30 October 1800 and 17 November 1800.

[34] Morrell (5), 67–8.

[35] Perhaps it was not accidental that in the three sessions beginning in autumn 1800, 1801 and 1802 Thomson and Murray fought for the same audience by lecturing at the same hour of the same day. Murray moved his hour in autumn 1803. See the *Edinburgh Evening Courant*, 9 & 18 October 1800, 23 October 1802, 29 October 1803. Both men were textbook writers and both published *A System of Chemistry* (Thomson 1802, Murray 1806).

[36] D. J. Withrington, "Education and Society in the Eighteenth Century" in N. T. Phillipson and R. Mitchison (eds.), *Scotland in the Age of Improvement*, Edinburgh, 1970, 169–99. He rightly concludes (192) that "in both schools and universities, throughout the century, the elemental challenge of their teachers' declining incomes was the greatest stimulus of all to a rethinking of their educational aims and practice".

[37] Thomson, "An Analysis of Fluor-spar", *Memoirs of the Wernerian Natural History Society*, **1**, 8–11, 1811.

[38] On 5 April 1807 Thomson read a paper on the geognosy of Werner at the Royal Society of Edinburgh. Within a month on 4 May 1807 he replied to certain objections raised by Sir James Hall against Werner's geognosy. Controversy again intensified in

commitment to Werner's mineralogy at this time directed his research into the field of mineralogical analysis. It would also appear that Thomson was teaching mineralogical analysis in his laboratory and maybe encouraging his better pupils to do research. None of the pupils named in the solitary suriviving laboratory class list became well-known chemists.[39] Yet one of them, Charles Mackenzie, published in 1811 an analysis of compact felspar which he had made in Thomson's laboratory in 1807.[40] Two other members of this laboratory class, James Ogilby and Stewart Murray Fullerton, were active and committed Wernerians.[41] All this leads to the conjecture that in his Edinburgh laboratory Thomson had created a very small embryonic research school working on mineralogical analysis in a Wernerian framework. This laboratory enterprise may have lasted from January 1807 to spring 1811 when Thomson finished teaching in Edinburgh, though no separate newspaper advertisements for it were apparently published after session 1807–8.

From 1811 to 1817 Thomson worked not as a regular teacher but as an unofficial historian of the Royal Society of London and chiefly as the London-based editor of his own scientific periodical *Annals of Philosophy*. Not unexpectedly chemistry was the journal's dominant subject and its columns a vehicle for Dalton's atomism and Prout's hypothesis. It was during this London period, too, that Thomson set himself up as an authoritative judge of European chemistry in his annual reports on the progress of science. No wonder, then, that when in 1818 he was promoted to the chair of chemistry at the University of Glasgow, he capitalized on his previous experience as a teacher and on his chief intellectual commitments by trying to create a research school working in his laboratory on inorganic and mineralogical chemistry in support of Dalton's atomic theory and Prout's multiples hypothesis. At that time his reputation was sufficient to carry such an ambitious programme:

---

early 1809 when on 6 February Sir James Hall read a paper in which he put some basic geological questions to Thomson. See the entries for these dates in the Minute-Book of the Royal Society of Edinburgh. Not one of these papers was published.

[39] The nine pupils who attended his laboratory were Stewart Murray Fullerton, James Ogilby, Charles Mackenzie, Patrick Mackenzie, Robert Chisholm, John Smith, Huggins, Benjamin Travers and George Rees. See: R. D. Thomson (8), 123. Of these nine students only Travers, later an eye-surgeon, became a nationally known figure.

[40] C. Mackenzie, "Analysis of Compact Felspar from the Pentland Hills", *Memoirs of the Wernerian Natural History Society*, **1**, 616–19, 1811.

[41] Fullerton was a founder-member of the Wernerian Natural History Society (f. 1808). Ogilby was an early member and contributor: Ogilby, "On the transition greenstone of Fassney", *Memoirs of the Wernerian Natural History Society*, **1**, 126–30, 1811; Ogilby, "On the veins that occur in the newest Floetz-trap formation of East Lothian", *ibid.*, 469–78. A general survey is given by J. M. Sweet, "The Wernerian Natural History Society in Edinburgh", in *Frieberger Forschungshefte, Abraham Gottleb Werner*, Leipzig, 1967, 205–18.

though his career before 1818 had been scarred by occasional belligerence and polemics, he was a textbook writer of European stature and a highly regarded systematic editor.[42] By 1825, however, Thomson's reputation was about to totter. He had distilled the results of ten years work done by himself and about five by his pupils into his *Attempt to Establish the First Principles of Chemistry by Experiment.* Doubtless Thomson felt that this book was the acme of a long career. Certainly his confidence in its value was high. As he explained in its Preface, his book "contains the result of many thousand experiments, conducted with as much care and precision as it was in my power to employ. They have occupied the whole of my time (except what was necessarily devoted to the duties of my situation) for the last five years. All those experiments which I considered as fundamental, were repeated so often, and varied in so many ways, that I repose the most perfect confidence in their accuracy".[43] In private, too, his confidence was unbounded: he was entranced by the accuracy and beauty of his results.[44] Unfortunately for Thomson the value of his work was seriously assailed on two fronts. In 1825 Thomson's friend Rainy showed that his specific gravity measurements, of which he was proud, were inaccurate.[45] Worse still two years later the reliability of his gravimetric analyses was assailed in the severest terms by Berzelius, then the "Grand Cham of chemistry".[46] He drew attention to the unacceptable scantiness of necessary detail in the book and concluded that many of Thomson's fundamental experiments were made at the writing desk. In an unusually dignified reply Thomson denied the charge that he had deliberately falsified results, but his reputation as a competent analytical chemist was badly tarnished.[47] Though his atomic weights were widely accepted in Britain and in America for about ten years, European chemists were not so tolerant and supported the implacable Berzelius. The whole episode shows that the egregiously ambitious Thomson, then a mature chemist aged fifty-two, had over-stretched his capacities. His first major publication as a professor had led to an attack on both his competence and his character from Europe's leading inorganic analytical chemist. Thomson was accustomed to dealing

[42] J. B. Morrell, "Thomas Thomson: Professor of Chemistry and University Reformer", *The British Journal for the History of Science*, **4**, 245–65 (247), 1969.

[43] Thomson (23), xiv.

[44] Thomson to Dalton, 19 April 1825, in Roscoe and Harden (21), 178–9.

[45] Brock (21), 250–3; Thomson (23), 50.

[46] W. V. Farrar, "Nineteenth-century speculations on the complexity of the chemical elements", *The British Journal for the History of Science*, **2**, 297–323 (299–301), 1965. For the importance of Berzelius as an analytical chemist, see F. Szabadváry, *History of Analytical Chemistry*, Oxford, 1966, 114–60.

[47] Thomson, "Reply to Berzelius's attack" (23); Crum (8), 261–3, unambiguously acknowledged the defects of Thomson's *First Principles*.

contumaciously with the envious sallies which Ure regularly launched against him, but attacks from Berzelius were far more wounding.[48] Subsequent work on atomic weights by Turner and Penny in the late 1820s and the 1830s confirmed the unreliability of Thomson's results and did nothing to enhance his reputation.[49]

To some extent Thomson did revive his standing when he published in 1836 the analyses made by his students and himself on hundreds of minerals including about fifty new species. On this occasion he took care to disable prospective critics by confessing that it was impossible to distinguish by experiment between the essential and the incidental constituents of minerals, and by giving practical details of the analytical techniques he had used.[50] Yet in contrast with the *First Principles* this work seems to have aroused little controversy or notice. The reasons for its apparent lack of effect are clear enough. Thomson discovered no new elements. His proposed formulae were sometimes not enlightening.[51] In any case by the mid 1830s the field of mineralogical analysis was well developed and for the time being did not lead to new research pastures. In that sense Thomson merely added a coping-stone to a building which had been almost completed by a galaxy of talented analysts: his work was lost among that of Stromeyer, Berzelius, H. and G. Rose, Mitscherlich, C. G. Gmelin, Bonsdorf, Berthier, Richard Phillips and Turner.[52] Between 1825 and 1835 Thomson was working not in a newly emerging field such as organic chemistry but a well developed one, and accordingly the competition he faced was severe. Indeed Thomson's two research programmes stand in sharp contrast with Liebig's major one. In 1825 Liebig was perfecting the

[48] The Brande-Ure axis attacked Thomson in "A Review of Dr. Thomson's System of Chemistry", *The Journal of Science and the Arts*, **4**, 299–321, 1818; "Thomson's System of Chemistry", *Quarterly Journal of Science and the Arts*, **11**, 119–71, 1821; "Dr. Thomas Thomson—and his 'Answer' ", *ibid.*, **13**, 333–53, 1822; "Review of Dr. Thomson on the Atomic Theory", *ibid.*, **20**, 113–41, 1826. Thomson replied in "Answer to the review of the sixth edition of my 'System of Chemistry' . . .", *Annals of Philosophy*, **3**, 241–73, 1822; and "Dr. Thomson's Answer to Dr. Ure's Review", *ibid.*, **11**, 1–14, 1826. Ure sometimes anticipated Berzelius' criticisms of Thomson's atomic weight determinations: in 1821, for instance, he had accused Thomson of "incessant twisting, stretching, and curtailing, of experimental results, to suit some fantastic atomic dress". See Ure's second attack on Thomson, *Quarterly Journal of Science and the Arts*, **11**, 171, 1821.

[49] Partington (17), iv, 225–32.

[50] Thomson (24), i, iii–iv, 355–553.

[51] Thomson's proposed formula for pyrope was: $10AlS + 5\,(\frac{10}{23}\,Mg + \frac{8}{23}\,Cal + \frac{5}{23}\,Chr)\,S + 3\,(\frac{3}{4}\,f + \frac{1}{4}\,mn)\,S^2$. See Thomson (24), i, 269. The modern formula is $Mg_3Al_2(SiO_4)_3$. In Thomson's, Al was alumina, S silica, Mg magnesia, Cal lime, Chr chromium oxide, *f* iron protoxide, and *mn* manganese protoxide.

[52] Thomson himself acknowledged the value of the work done by these analysts in Thomson (24), ii, 251–3.

technique on which his programme was to be based, whereas Thomson's slapdash practical techniques were about to confer on him a dubious reputation which was singularly incommensurate with his ambitions for his school and himself. Eleven years later Liebig's fame as a pioneer organic chemist was almost at its height, whereas Thomson's labours in the well worked and highly competitive field of mineralogical analysis only marginally elevated his reputation.

III

As university teachers both Liebig and Thomson had access to a regular supply of students for their laboratories. In Liebig's case, however, it seems likely that even before 1835 the majority of his laboratory students were not properly matriculated university students who had attended a gymnasium and had passed the leaving certificate which officially was indispensable for admission to a university. Most of his students simply went straight into his laboratory and orbit. Many of these were pharmacy students who no doubt appreciated that Liebig was a licensing examiner for prospective Hessian apothecaries. A minority of the students who worked in his laboratory before 1835 was recruited from those who attended his lectures; they were the survivors of the rigorous optional oral tests that Liebig gave.[53] After 1835, however, Liebig's fame was such that he admitted to his laboratory any student whose potential or accomplishment intrigued him. Up to about 1835 his laboratory students were mainly German and European, but from then on other foreigners in increasing numbers began to make the long pilgrimage to the Giessen laboratory and to render its membership agreeably cosmopolitan. Some of these registered as students, others did not. This means that accounts of Liebig's students which are derived solely from official class lists are necessarily partial and incomplete.[54] But certainly from the mid 1830s Liebig increasingly attracted students of increasing competence in research. One basic source of this magnetism was that students were put through a systematic course of practical chemistry in which training was imperceptibly transformed into research. Generally it appears that after an initial course of qualitative and quantitative analysis using known compounds each student was required to

[53] H. G. Good, "On the early history of Liebig's laboratory", *Journal of Chemical Education*, **13**, 557–62 (562), 1936.

[54] This reservation applies to A. Wankmüller, "Ausländische Studierende der Pharmacie und Chemie bei Liebig in Giessen", Tübinger Apothekengeschichtliche Abhandlungen, Heft 15, Deutscher Apotheker Verlag, Stuttgart, 1967; available also in *Deutsche Apotheker-Zeitung*, **107**, 463–6, 1967. I am grateful to Dr. W. H. Brock for drawing my attention to this paper; and for stressing that Wankmüller's list is based on the university's printed sessional lists of students, and not on the sometimes conflicting manuscript class lists.

produce pure substances in good yield from raw materials. This was a part of Liebig's training on which he laid great stress. Once this preliminary training had been satisfactorily completed, the student was allowed to pursue original research and compelled to work on his own under Liebig's general supervision.[55] The rarity of such systematic practical training more than compensated for the inadequate physical conditions which obtained until 1835. After 1839, too, this training became available at the absurdly cheap rate of 78 florins (£6 14s. od.) for a course which ran for six full days per week for eight to nine months.[56] No wonder that from 1839 students flocked to Giessen in greater numbers: the combination of the most rigorous practical training and the incredibly low cost (in comparison with Paris, London and Edinburgh) was irresistible. Moreover, successful students of Liebig's laboratory by their association with him furthered their own career prospects. The majority of his better students became teachers, and he often obtained posts for these protégés who modelled their work with apostolic fervour on his. For instance, in 1845 Liebig not only suggested Will, Fresenius and Hofmann, all of whom had been his laboratory assistants, for the chair of chemistry at the newly founded College of Chemistry in London, but he even accepted the conditions of appointment on Hofmann's behalf.[57] It is hardly surprising that Hoffmann ran his school at the College very much on Giessen lines. Those students of Liebig's who wanted a qualification to give them better career prospects could gain a Ph.D. at Giessen on the basis of one to three years' work depending on the speed of their research and the extent of their previous accomplishment. Honorary Ph.D.s were also

[55] Liebig (14), 37–8.

[56] W. Gregory, *Letter to the Right Honourable George Earl of Aberdeen on the state of the schools of chemistry in the United Kingdom*, London, 1842, 22, where 78 florins were stated to equal £6 14s. od. (i.e. £6.70). Gregory seems a reliable source: his figure of 1500 florins for the annual laboratory expenses of 1841 agrees with that given subsequently and independently by Volhard (7), i, 81; and he consistently assumed that 11.6 florins = £1. The standard I use throughout this paper for conversions is £1 sterling in the early 1840s. Liebig was not alone in Germany during the 1840s in offering very cheap courses of training in practical chemistry: at the nearby University of Marburg, tuition in practical chemistry under Bunsen and lodgings could be enjoyed for as little as £6 5s. od. per semester. It should be noted that in 1845 tuition alone, exclusive of chemicals and apparatus, at the Royal College of Chemistry in London cost £25. The financial attractiveness of some of the best German practical chemical courses is stressed by W. H. Brock, "Prologue to Heurism", in History of Education Society, *The Changing Curriculum*, London, 1970, 71–85 (76).

[57] J. Bentley, "The Chemical Department of the Royal School of Mines. Its origins and development under A. W. Hofmann," *Ambix*, **17**, 153–81 (163), 1970. Roscoe (13), 27, saw clearly that Liebig's great and personal achievement was to create a proper teaching laboratory from which "the flame of original research was carried throughout all lands by ardent disciples who more or less successfully continued, both as regards tuition and investigation, their master's work".

available to those who had already acquired scientific distinction. Clearly a Ph.D. was necessary for those who hoped to become German university teachers, but for others it could be irrelevant to their purposes. The important point, however, is that the few who for any reason needed a doctoral qualification could gain it by working in Liebig's laboratory. All these characteristics drew students to work in the Giessen laboratory. British students, in particular, began their trek to Giessen in the mid 1830's. The attractiveness of the laboratory there may be judged from the following list of subsequently well-known British students who worked in it:

Thomas Anderson
Albert James Bernays
John Blyth
Benjamin Collins Brodie, Jr.
John Lloyd Bullock
Walter Crum
George Fownes
William Francis
Edward Frankland
John Gardner
John Henry Gilbert
John Hall Gladstone
William Gregory
William Charles Henry
Henry Bence Jones
Robert John Kane
Augustus Matthiessen
William Allen Miller
James Sheridan Muspratt
Henry Minchin Noad
Lyon Playfair
Thomas Richardson
Edmund Ronalds
Henry Edward Schunk
Robert Angus Smith
John Stenhouse
Robert Dundas Thomson
Thomas Thomson, Jr.
Thomas George Tilley
Alexander William Williamson[58]

One point in connection with this impressive list needs to be stressed. Many of these British pupils of Liebig eventually held teaching posts. If we confine our attention to those who occupied university chairs or posts it is clear that by the 1850s the Liebig clan had assumed most of the "plums" available in British university chemistry:

Anderson, professor, University of Glasgow, 1852–74
Blyth, professor, Queen's College, Cork, 1849–72
Brodie, professor, University of Oxford, 1855–73
Frankland, professor, Owens College, Manchester, 1851–57
Gregory, professor, University of Edinburgh, 1844–58
Kane, president, Queen's College, Cork, 1845–73
Miller, professor, King's College, London, 1845–70
Playfair, professor, University of Edinburgh, 1858–69
Richardson, lecturer, University of Durham, 1856–67
Ronalds, professor, Queen's College, Galway, 1849–56
Williamson, professor, University College, London, 1849–87

Thomson was in one respect more favourably placed than Liebig. The size of his lecture class was larger than Liebig's. From it Thomson could draw

[58] Volhard (7) 85, 141; Wankmüller (54), 11–16; and *D.N.B.* I am grateful to Mr. K. Boughey for drawing Tilley to my attention.

medical students in order to convert them to chemists. As chemistry was an obligatory part of the pre-clinical medical course at Glasgow, this meant that as long as the medical school sustained its reputation there would be a regular supply of students on which Thomson could draw. However it was also possible for any keen student to attend Thomson's lecture and laboratory classes even if he were not a regular medical student; and the majority of his pupils who subsequently attained chemical eminence seem to have worked in his laboratory as private students. Thomson's laboratory class was necessarily run on a small scale until 1831 when the new larger laboratory in Shuttle Street was opened: he was compelled to restrict the size of his laboratory class to ten students who had access to the laboratory three to four hours a day except Sunday for ten months of the year.[59] Their chief concern at first was patently the analysis of minerals, as Thomson's pugnacious 1827 account of his experimental class shows: "The object of the class is to teach all those who wish to become practical chemists. I have a set of rules, which are in manuscript, in the laboratory; they make themselves quite masters of these rules, and I give them different minerals to analyse; they continue in the laboratory, such of them as are interested in the thing, till they become expert chemists, and there are five or six that have gone out of my laboratory that I think are as good chemists as any men in existence".[60] During this sort of training Thomson kept tight reins on his students, at least in the 1820s: he always prescribed work for his students to do. In the early 1820s he had apparently allowed some students to attempt independent research, but as they were not sufficiently *au fait* with the various branches of chemistry their progress in his opinion was irritatingly slow or non-existent.[61] Unlike Liebig, Thomson had not devised an easy transition for his laboratory students from learning to research. By the late thirties, the emphasis was still on mineralogical analysis, though under a less authoritarian regime. For instance, in session 1838–39 there were in Thomson's laboratory class only four students, including John Henry Gilbert. In later life he recalled that "after a little instruction in the use of the balance, I was at once set to analyse the minerals, Prehnite and Stilbite, and was referred to books for method. The Professor was, however, always ready to give kind attention and assistance to the student when required."[62]

There are unfortunately no surviving lists of Thomson's laboratory pupils, yet a few generalizations can be made on the basis of secondary or indirect

[59] *Evidence, Oral and Documentary, taken before the Commissioners for visiting the Universities of Scotland. The University of Glasgow.* Parliamentary Papers, **36**, (1837), 151 and 203. In future references this work will be called *Glasgow Evidence*.

[60] *Glasgow Evidence*, 203. This was taken in 1827 and published ten years later.

[61] *Ibid.*, 203.

[62] J. H. Gilbert, "Presidential Address", *Journal of the Chemical Society*, **43**, 224–63 (238), 1883.

evidence. It seems that Thomson's catchment area for both his lecture and laboratory classes was primarily the Glasgow region. An analysis of the published and unpublished lists of pupils who won prizes in Thomson's lecture class between 1823 and 1841 shows that almost half of them came from the Glasgow area, about a quarter from Scotland, about a sixth from England, and the rest in equal number from Jamaica, Canada, Siberia, Ireland and the Isle of Man.[63] It is important to realize that of these prizewinners only Robert Dundas Thomson, Thomas Richardson and James Finlay Weir Johnston subsequently became well-known chemists. It also seems that the laboratory fee for tuition of three to four hours a day for six days a week for ten months was about £1 per month, a charge which was of course totally under Thomson's control and discretion. Compared with equivalent laboratory courses elsewhere in Britain in the 1820s and 1830s Thomson's was cheap: it cost far less, for instance, than the courses available in Edinburgh which generally cost £3 3s. 0d. for tuition one hour a day for five days a week for three months.[64] Those who took advantage of the laboratory training he offered became academic and industrial chemists: a list of his less obscure pupils who became, or at some time intended, to be chemists is set out below. Most of these, but not all, were pupils in his laboratory.[65]

Academics	*Industrial Chemists*
Thomas Andrews	William Blythe
Thomas Clark	Hugh Colquhoun
Thomas Graham	Walter Crum
James Finlay Weir Johnston	Joseph Henry Gilbert
Charles Lehunt	Andrew Halliday
Thomas Richardson	Alexander Harvey
Andrew Steel	John Tennant
John Stenhouse	John Tennent
Robert Dundas Thomson	
Thomas Thomson, junior	

Though the above classification is arbitrary, Crum being a case in point, it does seem that in Thomson's opening years at Glasgow industrial chemists, both actual and prospective, found his lectures and laboratory attractive. For instance in session 1818–19, Thomson's first as professor, his friend Charles Macintosh, the Glasgow chemical manufacturer, became a student once more

[63] For 1823–33 see W. Innes Addison, *Prize Lists of the University of Glasgow, 1778–1833*, Glasgow, 1902; for 1835 to 1841 I am indebted to information kindly given to me by Miss E. Jack, Reference Librarian, University of Glasgow.

[64] Morrell (5), 79.

[65] R. D. Thomson, "Memoir of the late Dr. Thomas Thomson", *Edinburgh New Philosophical Journal*, **54**, 86–98 (95–6), 1852–3. Details about most of Thomson's pupils may be found in Partington (17), iv and *D.N.B.*

and regularly attended Thomson's lectures.[66] In the laboratory that session were to be found: one of the Dunlops of the Clyde Iron Works and St. Rollox; Angus, a sugar refiner from Greenock; John Tennant of the famous St. Rollox Chemical Works, Glasgow, who became a partner in 1820 and shortly afterwards Managing Director; Walter Crum, subsequently head of the well-known calico-printing firm at Thornliebank near Glasgow and close friend of Graham and Liebig; and Alexander Harvey.[67] The last-named may well illustrate the complaint Thomson made in 1826 to Dalton that his promising pupils had usually been absorbed "in the vortex of manufacture and business, which is here all powerful".[68] After four years as Thomson's laboratory assistant-cum-pupil, probably between 1818 and 1822, Harvey became chemical manager first of the St. Rollox works and then of Henry Menteith's turkey-red dyeing and calico-printing factory. From 1838 to his death he ran his own firm of dyers. In late life he attributed his success to his early training under Thomson: "my early knowledge of chemistry has had a tendency to carry me through all those different branches (of my career)".[69] A later pupil, John Tennent enjoyed an equally distinguished industrial and commercial career. After working for three years between 1834 and 1837 in Thomson's laboratory as a student, his fortunes steadily prospered: between 1837 and 1839, he was working for Charles Mackintosh on the artificial production of ultramarine; between 1839 and 1845, he was manager of Mackintosh's alum works at Campsie near Glasgow; from 1845 to 1847 he managed White's chrome works at Shawfield; from 1847 to 1853 he managed the chemical works at Bonnington near Edinburgh which used as raw materials the gas tar and ammoniacal liquor produced by the Edinburgh and the Edinburgh and Leith gas works; finally from 1853 until his death, he was a member of the Tennant firm, chemical manager of the St. Rollox works, and the planner and erector in 1863 of the chemical works at Hebburn-on-Tyne. Though Tennent published no papers his obituarist rightly pointed out that he was very successful in "the application of chemical and physical science to the manufacture of the most largely used chemical products, in the purest mercantile form, and upon the largest practicable scale . . .".[70]

[66] G. Macintosh, *Biographical Memoir of the late Charles Macintosh*, Glasgow, 1857, 111.

[67] F. H. Thomson, "Presidential Address for 1867", *Proceedings of the Philosophical Society of Glasgow*, **6**, 233–6, 1865–8.

[68] Thomson to Dalton, 8 December 1826, in Roscoe and Harden (21), 183–4. A year later it was noted that "his labours were incessant, both in instructing the ordinary University students, and also in training young chemists practically for the manufactures". See R. Christison, *The Life of Sir Robert Christison, Bart., ed. by his sons*, Edinburgh and London, 1885, i, 366.

[69] *Royal Commission on Scientific Instruction and the Advancement of Science:* Parliamentary Papers, **22**, (1874), 158.

[70] Obituary in *Journal of the Chemical Society*, **21**, xxix–xxxi, 1868.

Another pupil of Thomson's, his grand nephew Hugh Colquhoun, was engaged in 1825 by Charles Mackintosh "to superintend, during his temporary absence, a series of experiments intended to ascertain the best details of practice and apparatus for his most ingenious process of the conversion of iron to steel".[71] If pupils such as Crum, Tennant, Harvey, Tennent and Colquhoun are representative, it seems likely that many chemical works in the Glasgow area could draw on men who had learned basic practical skills in Thomson's laboratory. That is why Liebig, in his criticism of the state of chemistry teaching in Austria, pointedly ascribed the unique growth of the chemical industry in Glasgow to the training given there by Thomson and Graham: "Ich habe die Umgegend von Glasgow mit chemischen Fabriken jeder Art bedeckt gesehen, es ist das Centrum, es ist eins der wichtigsten Räder in der ungeheuren Maschine der englischen Industrie. Thomson, den ihr so gering achtet, Graham ist daran Schuld; überall sonst in diesem so gerühmten Lande findet ihr nichts der Art, wie in Glasgow".[72]

Thomson's academic pupils rarely received all their practical training under his aegis. For instance, before moving to work under Thomson, Stenhouse was a pupil in the laboratory at Anderson's University, Glasgow, which was run by Thomas Graham while he was professor of chemistry there between 1830 and 1837.[73] More importantly, a number of Thomson's pupils began their training with him and then completed it elsewhere: Andrews left Thomson to study under Dumas; and Johnston went to work in Berzelius' laboratory.[74]

[71] H. Colquhoun, "A New Form of Carbon", *Annals of Philosophy*, **12**, 1–13 (2), 1826.

[72] Liebig, "Der Zustand der Chemie in Oestreich", *Annalen der Pharmacie*, **25**, 339–47 (346), 1838. On the Glasgow chemical industry see A. and N. Clow, *The Chemical Revolution*, London, 1952. On the Tennant chemical works at St. Rollox, see E. W. D. Tennant, "The Early History of the St. Rollox Chemical Works", *Chemistry and Industry*, **66**, 666–73, 1947. A few of Thomson's students were active in the chemical industry in Lancashire. For instance Thomson's nephew William Blythe (1813–1879), an original member of the Chemical Society, eventually founded his own chemical works at Church, near Accrington, in 1845. Like so many of Thomson's students, he specialized in the dyeing and printing of fabrics, alkalis and sulphuric acid. See: R. S. Crossley, *Accrington Captains of Industry*, Accrington, 1930, 202–203 to which the Borough Librarian, Accrington, kindly drew my attention. Halliday operated a works devoted to mordants, gums and starches in Salford during the 1840s. For this information I am grateful to the Reference Librarian of Manchester Public Libraries.

[73] R. A. Smith, *The Life and Works of Thomas Graham*, 1884, 66, lists Stenhouse, Lyon Playfair, Gilbert, J. J. Griffin, Crum and Harvey *inter alia* as laboratory pupils of Graham between 1830 and 1837 at Anderson's University. Smith is unreliable, and I suspect that at least Gilbert, Crum and Harvey were never pupils of Graham.

[74] Having gone to the University of Glasgow in 1828–1829 in order "to study chemistry profoundly", Andrews worked in Dumas' laboratory in late 1830. See Andrews (6), x–xi. Having worked in Thomson's laboratory in 1826, Johnston was so impressed by Berzelius' laboratory when he visited it in 1829 that three years later he worked there. See Partington (17), iv, 148.

The majority of migrant pupils, however, went to Liebig partly for the better training and partly for a research qualification in physical science which was not then available at Glasgow: at least Gilbert, Richardson, Stenhouse, R. D. Thomson, T. Thomson junior, and Crum all made the pilgrimage to Giessen.[75] As Thomson's son, his nephew, and Richardson were among the first British students who worked in Liebig's laboratory to which they were sent by Thomson, it seems that Thomson was aware of the incompleteness of the training he gave in his laboratory. As the case of Richardson shows, these pupils learnt inorganic mineral analysis under him, after which they migrated to Giessen for organic techniques.[76] Nor was Thomson bitter about Liebig's success.[77] Indeed the Thomsons were on good terms with Liebig by 1837 when he paid his first visit to Britain: Thomson junior, regarded by Liebig as one of his most promising pupils, met Liebig at Hull in his capacity as "Reisebegleiter"; and Thomson himself acted as Glasgow's senior host to him.[78] It seems, then, that by the mid 1830s Thomson was prepared and even keen to relinquish his better laboratory pupils to more eminent chemists such as Liebig, as the following letter of 1838 from Thomson to Liebig conclusively shows:

> This letter will be given you by Mr. William McFarlane, the son of a calico-printer in this neighbourhood [Glasgow], who has been for two

[75] Thomson, junior, (1817–1878), worked in Liebig's laboratory in 1837. His father wanted his elder son to follow him by being a chemist. As J. D. Hooker pointed out in his obituary of Thomson, junior, *Proceedings of the Royal Geographical Society*, **22**, 309–15 (309–10), 1878, "for many years [before 1837] he worked a little daily at the University laboratory, finally spending a winter at Giessen under Liebig, who regarded him as one of his most promising pupils, and under whom he discovered pectic acid in carrots". Thomson's aims were ironically thwarted because in the late 1830s his son returned to botany, his first love, as a result of the encouragement given to him by Sir William Jackson Hooker, professor of botany at the University of Glasgow (1820–1841) and his son J. D. Hooker. Thereafter Thomson primed his nephew R. D. Thomson as his successor.

[76] During 1834–5 at least, Richardson who was a close friend of Thomson's son was hard at work in Thomson's laboratory analysing minerals. In 1836–7 he was a pupil of Liebig under whom he published on organic chemistry and graduated Ph.D. Then he went to Paris with Thomson, and completed his chemical apprenticeship under Liebig's close friend and collaborator, Pelouze, with whom he published jointly again on organic chemistry. See: Richardson, "Zusammensetzung des Cyanmethylen-Aethers", *Annalen der Pharmacie*, **23**, 138–40, 1837; Richardson and J. Pelouze, "Decomposition du cyanogène dans l'eau", *Comptes Rendus*, **6**, 187–9, 1838; *D.N.B.*, which seems the fullest source.

[77] *Testimonials in favour of William Gregory . . . as a Candidate for the vacant chair of chemistry in the University of Edinburgh*, Edinburgh, 1843, 18, in which Thomson asserted that Gregory "has had an excellent chemical education, having been a practical pupil for some time in Professor Liebig's laboratory at Giessen". Gregory had studied in Liebig's laboratory in autumn 1836 and summer 1841 specifically to learn the new methods of organic analysis (Gregory, *Testimonials*, 4, 5).

[78] Volhard (7), i, 133, 139–41.

> years a practical student of chemistry in my laboratory and has acquired a good deal of skill in the mode of analysing minerals, metals, etc. He is a young man of good abilities, excellent principles and great industry and goes to Giessen in order to get some knowledge of the mode of preparing and analysing vegetable bodies. He dined with us one day while you were in Glasgow; but perhaps you did not pay much attention to him.
>
> My son writes you by Mr. McFarlane. He intended to have spent the ensuing Summer at Giessen.[79]

Consequently, Thomson's pupils did not regard themselves as his disciples and apostles; and very few of them were "placed" in important academic positions by him. Though he tried desperately in 1846 to convince the Lord Advocate of Scotland that his favourite pupil and nephew, R. D. Thomson, should succeed him, he failed even to pass on his chair to one of his own pupils.[80] Ironically his successor, Thomas Anderson, was a Liebig pupil. Equally significantly both R. D. Thomson and Colquhoun, protégés and relatives of Thomson, eventually failed to find posts in academic chemistry: the former became a medical officer of health in 1856; and in the late 1820s Colquhoun seems to have entered commerce, a traditional occupation in his family.[81] One of his few successes, however, occurred in 1833 when he acted as the well-paid chairman of an advisory committee which recommended to the Senate of Marischal College, Aberdeen, that Clark be appointed professor of chemistry.[82] There would seem little doubt that generally Thomson did not offer to his students the rigorous training and career opportunities that were to be enjoyed under Liebig. Yet ambitious young chemists did at least gain direction and encouragement from him in the early stages of their careers. Graham is a case in point. Having studied under Thomson in 1825–26 Graham published his first three articles in *Annals of Philosophy* a journal over which Thomson still wielded influence.[83] When he moved in 1826 to Edinburgh to further his career Thomson's sealed letters of introduction to Edward Turner (then a

[79] Thomson to Liebig, 18 April 1838, Bayerische Staatsbibliothek, München, Liebigiana Bh.

[80] Thomson's letters of 27 July and 6 August 1846 to Andrew Rutherfurd, the Lord Advocate for Scotland; and Rutherfurd's reply of 3 August 1846 in which he refused to allow Thomson to resign in favour of R. D. Thomson. This correspondence is in the Scottish Record Office.

[81] Colquhoun graduated M.D. 1826, never practised medicine, and seems to have retired from scientific activity in the late 1820s. See W. Innes Addison, *The Matriculation Albums of the University of Glasgow from 1728 to 1958*, Glasgow, 1913, 293.

[82] A. Findlay, *The Teaching of Chemistry in the Universities of Aberdeen*, Aberdeen, 1935, 23–5.

[83] Graham, "On the absorption of gases by liquids", *Annals of Philosophy*, **12**, 69–74, 1826; Graham, "On the heat of friction", *ibid.*, 260–2; Graham, "Alcohol derived from the fermentation of bread", *ibid.*, 369.

private teacher of chemistry and chemical editor of Brewsters' *Edinburgh Journal of Science*) and John Leslie (professor of natural philosophy in the University of Edinburgh) enabled Graham to establish himself more easily and effectively in Edinburgh's scientific life.[84] They also helped him to begin his teaching career when he took over Turner's classes from February to July 1828.[85] Again Crum and Colquhoun first established themselves via the *Annals of Philosophy*; and a few years later Andrews' opening three papers dealt quite explicitly with Thomsonian topics.[86] In general, therefore, Thomson's laboratory was not a finishing school for prospective academic chemists: it was a nursery.

IV

One of the most important elements in the success of a research school could be the availability of simple, quick and reliable experimental techniques which brilliant and average students could apply in a new or growing field of enquiry. There is no doubt that Liebig's apparatus for combustion analysis of organic compounds fulfilled these desiderata though it had to be supplemented by Dumas' method for determining nitrogen. As Hofmann pointed out, this apparatus "is certainly that which has conduced, more than any other of his great discoveries, to facilitate the productive labours of the chemical community, and has been the main source of that marvellous development of chemistry, especially organic, which will be looked back to hereafter as one of the chief glories of our age . . .".[87] It must be stressed that before Liebig perfected his "combustion apparatus" the difficulties facing organic analysts were so formidable that only a few of the best men, such as Gay-Lussac, Thenard, Prout and Berzelius, had overcome them and produced accurate results before 1830. For instance Berzelius determined the carbon in a compound by oxidising it with potassium chlorate to carbon dioxide which he estimated gravimetrically and not volumetrically: he measured the increase in weight of a small bulb containing caustic potash and covered with thin leather, which he introduced into a bell-jar containing the carbon dioxide which he had collected over mercury. This difficult operation required a high degree of experienced manipulative skill. Liebig, however, determined the carbon dioxide by weighing it after he had absorbed it in his well-known five bulbs containing potassium hydroxide solution. These bulbs ensured that the carbon dioxide was totally absorbed;

[84] Graham (73), 15, 29.

[85] *Ibid.*, 31–2.

[86] Crum, "Experiments and observations on indigo", *Annals of Philosophy*, **5**, 81–100, 1823; Andrews, "On the action of a flame urged by the blowpipe on other flames", *Philosophical Magazine*, **6**, 366–7, 1829; Andrews, "On the detection of baryta or strontia when in union with lime", *ibid.*, **7**, 404–6, 1830; Andrews, "Chemical researches on the blood of cholera patients, *ibid.*, **1**, 295–305, 1832; Colquhoun (71).

[87] Hofmann (15), 45.

and the two upper ones acted as safety vessels by preventing any potash solution being lost irrespective of the direction in which gases were being passed into it.[88] This combination of extra-ordinary simplicity and effectiveness characterized many of Liebig's experimental methods or apparatus such as his method of analysing air using an alkaline solution of pyrogallol and "his" condenser. It is not surprising that Liebig was proud of the speed and effectiveness with which about 400 analyses per year were made in his laboratory using his combustion apparatus. Indeed, as he pointed out to Wöhler, his method was not only more reliable than Berzelius' but also twenty times faster: "Er hat 18 Monate mit seinen Analysen der organischen Säuren zugebracht; es sind im ganzen 7, mit den Wiederholungen wollen wir sagen 21. Ich bitte Dich, lieber Freund, in unseren letzten Arbeiten sind im ganzen in drei Monaten 72 Analysen gemacht worden, von denen keine einzige mißlang, daran hätte Berzelius mit seinem alten Apparate fünf Jahre gearbeitet."[89] With practice any determined student could obtain reliable results with Liebig's combustion apparatus. When his students began to apply it and related techniques to the newly emerging field of organic chemistry the result was an explosion of knowledge. By 1846 as many as fifteen students in his laboratory published in just one year no less than thirty-two research papers in Liebig's own *Annalen der Chemie und Pharmacie*.[90] Clearly Liebig's combustion apparatus and its relatives permitted the production of knowledge to take place in a regular routine way; and, it should be stressed, students who were not innately brilliant were enabled by this apparatus to do competent research. The accession of relatively large numbers of students to his laboratory had compelled Liebig to codify and systematize not only the research techniques which he and his students employed but also the preliminary training which he gave to them. By 1837 he had published a guide to organic analysis; and in the following decade, his pupils Will and Fresenius published books on the methods of qualitative and quantitative analysis that were used in the Giessen laboratory.[91]

[88] Partington (17), iv, 234–8; J. L. W. Thudichum, "On the discoveries and philosophy of Liebig: Lecture II", *Journal of the Society of Arts*, **24**, 95–100 (98), 1876.

[89] Liebig to Wöhler, 2 March 1838, in Volhard (7), ii, 225.

[90] Volhard (7), i, 174–5.

[91] Liebig, *Anleitung zur Analyse organischer Körper*, Brunswick, 1837, translated by W. Gregory, *Instructions for the Chemical Analysis of Organic Bodies*, Glasgow, 1839; H. Will, *Anleitung zur qualitativen chemischen Analyse*, Heidelberg, 1846; H. Will, *Outlines of the course of Qualitative Analysis followed in the Giessen Laboratory*, London, 1846; C. R. Fresenius, *Anleitung zur qualitativen chemischen Analyse*, Bonn, 1841, translated by J. L. Bullock, *Elementary Instruction in Qualitative Analysis*, London, 1841; Fresenius, *Anleitung zur quantitativen chemischen Analyse*, Brunswick, 1846, translated by Bullock, *Instruction in Chemical Analysis* (*Quantitative*), London, 1846. It is important to note the rapidity with which these works were translated into English.

In short, Liebig scored a double success: he invented simple, fast and reliable experimental techniques, and these were applied in the emerging field of organic chemistry. Thus his students, both brilliant and mediocre, were enabled to produce reliable chemical knowledge in a systematic way on a large scale. In this sense, the era of Big Science began at Giessen in the early 1840s.

In this particular respect Thomson's work forms a painful contrast. There is no evidence that he devised simple, fast and reliable techniques which a large group of laboratory students applied to a new field. It is true that by 1825 he developed methods of analysing inorganic salts and of determining the specific gravity of gases, but as I have previously stressed the reliability of these methods was severely attacked in public. It may be true, for instance, that Thomson invented the alkalimetrical or centesimal mode of analysis: his method was to determine the reacting quantities of two soluble salts, say solutions of zinc sulphate and barium chloride, by varying the amount of one reactant until the supernatant liquid produced gave no reaction with each reactant.[92] Unfortunately, he ignored the problem of absorption by the precipitate and in some cases wildly misjudged its composition. Again Thomson was quick to see the importance of determining accurately the specific gravity of gases; yet between 1822 and 1826 he put himself into a totally contradictory position on the question of whether the presence of water vapour in hydrogen significantly affected the determinations of its specific gravity to which he had given so much time and effort.[93] Additionally, Thomson attempted to use these unreliable methods in the field of inorganic chemistry in which the fruits were not ready for picking as they were in organic chemistry. Despite his laudable ambitions Thomson never produced a conspicuously successful experimental technique in his research field. This meant that after 1825, when Thomson turned from the analysis of salts and gases to the analysis of minerals, his students lacked a set of routine dependable techniques with which they could occupy and colonise an area of research. From the little we know about what his students worked on in his laboratory one suspects that initially his students worked chiefly on mineral analysis. Though Thomson took odd pupils such as Johnston, who in late 1826 was working on potassium chloroferrocyanide, it seems that between 1825 and 1835 the better students were encouraged to do research in the field of mineralogical analysis; certainly the research work of some thirteen pupils was sufficiently important to be published by Thomson himself.[94] Such students could consult Thomson's manuscript

[92] R. D. Thomson (8), 142–3.

[93] Brock (21), 252.

[94] Graham (73), 27. In Thomson's *Outlines* (24) the mineral analyses done in his laboratory by the following students are cited on the following pages: Birkmire, William: 365; Blythe, (William?): 331, 572; Bruce, (James Hamilton?): 298; Colquhoun, Hugh:

rules of analysis which were available in his laboratory.[95] Indeed by May 1828 Thomson told the publisher Blackwood that he had "made considerable progress in a practical system of chemistry" which he intended as a supplement to the seventh edition of his textbook *A System of Chemistry*.[96] A year later he had dropped the project of writing a separate book on practical chemistry and analysis.[97] It is significant that the nearest he came to producing such a work was the third part of his *Outlines of Mineralogy, Geology and Mineral Analysis* which was added to enable readers to judge the accuracy of the analyses which the first part contained.[98] Thomson also pronounced with characteristic if optimistic élan that it was also a teaching manual for "young British chemists, who were desirous of perfecting themselves in this important branch of practical chemistry".[99] This treatise on analysing minerals shows that Thomson's research students between 1825 and 1835 had nothing like Liebig's combustion analysis method which they could systematically and easily deploy. On the contrary students had to learn a multiplicity of difficult techniques; and only patient, skilfull and pernickety ones were likely to produce reliable results. In any event Thomson's treatise on mineral analysis had been anticipated by H. Rose's *Handbuch* of which an English translation was quickly published in 1831.[100] Perhaps it is significant that the first separately published account of the apparatus and methods used in Thomson's laboratory was given by his nephew and was aimed chiefly at British schools.[101] Compared with works by H. Rose, Will, Fresensius and Liebig himself, this treatise on practical chemistry was elementary in level, less comprehensive in scope, and less systematic in its treatment. The plain fact is that Thomson, whose fluent mastery of systematic and clear writing ensured the unrivalled popularity of his textbook in Britain for about thirty years, was nothing like as successful as a manipulative

---

465; Coverdale, (John?) Dr.: 232, 377; Fairie: 362; Lehunt, Charles: 236, 266, 275, 302, 331, 334, 335, 480; Muir, Thomas: 202, 212, 383, 401, 424, 425, 493; Muir, William: 510; Richardson, Thomas: 140, 244, 262, 309, 354, 365, 410, 477, 487, 506, 614, 615, 678; Short, (John Quircke?): 245; Steel, Andrew: 410; Thomson, R. D.: 244, 339, 379, 436, 473, 573. It is clear that the dominant students in Thomson's second research programme were Richardson, T. Muir, Lehunt and R. D. Thomson.

[95] *Glasgow Evidence*, 203. No copy of these manuscript rules appears to have survived.

[96] Thomson to Blackwood, 29 May 1828, National Library of Scotland, MS 4023, f. 147.

[97] Thomson to Blackwood, 3 December 1829, National Library of Scotland, MS 4026, f. 183.

[98] Thomson (24), i, v.

[99] *Ibid.*, i, v. Thomson, of course, was totally convinced that chemistry had made remarkable progress from about 1780 owing to the improvements made in analytical methods, *ibid.*, ii, 353–4.

[100] H. Rose, *Handbuch der analytischen Chemie*, Berlin, 1829; translated by J. J. Griffin, *A Manual of Analytical Chemistry*, London, 1831.

[101] R. D. Thomson, *School Chemistry*, London, 1848.

chemist. His inability to devise for himself and for his students simple speedy and reliable techniques, first in the field of analysis of salts and gases and then in that of mineral analysis, led to the virtual disintegration of his research school after 1836.

V

The question of publication opportunities is a relatively simple one. During the late 1820s Liebig published his important papers in the *Annales de Chimie et de Physique*, which was conveniently edited by his mentor and friend Gay-Lussac, and in Poggendorf's *Annalen der Physik und Chemie*.[102] In 1832, however, Liebig gained control of totally unimpeded publication by taking over as dominant editor P. L. Geiger's *Magazin für Pharmacie*. Under its new titles *Annalen der Pharmacie* (1832–39) and *Annalen der Chemie und Pharmacie* (1840–73) Liebig published research papers, often concerning organic chemistry, by himself, his pupils and his friends. From his advantageous position as editor, Liebig also surveyed chemistry with an eagle eye and in his editorial criticisms pounced on deviators.[103] In these ways, the *Annalen* rapidly became the journal of the Giessen research school of chemistry. Liebig's students knew this and were encouraged by him to publish under their own names even when he had helped them.[104] He realized acutely that his young students were greatly encouraged by seeing their names in print; and he was sufficiently worldly to realize that a good paper published by one of his students increased his own reputation. For reasons which I have previously discussed the Giessen laboratory produced a large amount of research work which after 1832 appeared predictably in the *Annalen*. It is not surprising that in the 1840s it had outstripped its rivals such as Erdmann's *Journal für praktische Chemie* to become the leading chemical journal of Europe. Liebig's pupils could enjoy therefore a flying start with regard to publication. What better opening to his career could Stenhouse have made than to publish his first five papers in Liebig's *Annalen*?[105]

Thomson's case is paradoxical. Before he assumed in 1817 his post at the University of Glasgow, from 1813 he had edited in London his own *Annals of*

[102] See *Royal Society Catalogue of Scientific Papers*, and Paolini (7).

[103] Partington, (17), iv, 299; and J. P. Phillips, "Liebig and Kolbe, Critical Editors", *Chymia*, **11**, 89–97, 1966.

[104] Good (53), 561.

[105] Stenhouse, "Darstellung und Analyse des Hippursäure-Aethers", *Annalen der Pharmacie*, **31**, 148–51, 1839; Stenhouse, "Ueber eine neue Chlorcyan-Verbindung", *Annalen der Chemie und Pharmacie*, **33**, 92–7, 1840; Stenhouse, "Ueber das sogenannte Künstliche Ameisenöl", *ibid.*, **35**, 301–4, 1840; Stenhouse, "Zusammensetzung des Elemi- und Oli-banumöls", *ibid.*, 304–6; Stenhouse, "Untersuchung des Palmöls und der Cacao-butter", *ibid.*, **36**, 50–9, 1840.

Philosophy, a journal strongly slanted to chemistry. Between 1818 and 1820 inclusive he superintended the journal at a distance and then took it over again.[106] However, with uncharacteristic concern for his own future, he resigned entirely in late 1820 as editor because of his distance from London "which quadrupled, as he said, the labour of the editor, and diminished almost in the same proportion, its successful exertion".[107] Until late 1826 Thomson met no difficulties in placing his papers: between 1821 and 1826 inclusive Thomson published 18 papers exclusively in the *Annals of Philosophy* edited by his friend Richard Phillips who had succeeded him as editor.[108] Unfortunately for Thomson *Annals* ceased publication in 1826. For the next eight years Thomson lacked a regular journal in which he could publish his papers, and indeed had to use journals such as *Philosophical Transactions* and *Transactions of the Royal Society of Edinburgh* whose columns he had conspicuously shunned in previous years. Between 1827 and 1835 his 19 original research papers were published in nine different journals.[109] No wonder then that in 1835 and 1836 he eagerly assisted his nephew R. D. Thomson in editing the *Records of General Science* in which he published exclusively twenty-three papers during those two years in which it was published: he obviously was stimulated by regaining ready and unimpeded access to publication as well as by his desire to keep his nephew well supplied with copy. Unfortunately *Records* ceased publication in late 1836 because the marginal profit it showed was not consonant with the great labour involved in editing it.[110] From then onwards Thomson was again looking for appropriate vehicles for his papers so that fourteen of his papers published between 1837 and 1841 appeared in six different journals.[111] One can understand his enthusiasm for the *Proceedings of the Glasgow Philosophical Society* which were first published in 1841. As the revered President of that Society, Thomson for a third time had ready access to a journal and not unexpectedly most of his last papers were published in its *Proceedings*. Thomson's own career as a publisher of research papers seems therefore to have flourished

[106] Thomson to Dalton, 13 August 1818, in Roscoe and Harden, (21) 171–2.

[107] Crum (8), 253.

[108] See *Royal Society Catalogue of Scientific Papers*.

[109] The nine journals in which he published 19 papers between 1827 and 1835 were the *Edinburgh Journal of Science* (3), *Philosophical Transactions of the Royal Society* (1), *Glasgow Medical Journal* (2), *Philosophical Magazine* (2), *Annals of the Lyceum of New York* (1), *Transactions of the Royal Society of Edinburgh* (7), *American Journal of Science* (1), *History of the Berwickshire Naturalists' Club* (1), and *Annales de Chemie* (1).

[110] R. D. Thomson to Benjamin Silliman, 12 November 1836, Historical Society of Pennsylvania, Gratz Collection, Case 12, Box 13.

[111] These fourteen papers were published in *Reports of the British Association for the Advancement of Science* (8), *Annalen der Pharmacie* (1), *Philosophical Magazine* (2), *American Journal of Science* (1), *Comptes Rendus* (1), and *Bibliothèque Universelle* (1).

when he enjoyed control of a journal or easy access to it. Yet even when he had access to a journal Thomson did not encourage his pupils to publish independently the work they had done in his laboratory. It is significant that the results acquired by his students in each of the two major research programmes he directed were published very largely as two books with Thomson as sole author. He acknowledged the work they did, particularly in analysing minerals, yet attempted to gain credit for himself. Unlike Liebig he regarded the research done by his students in his laboratory under his aegis as his own exclusive intellectual property.[112] Given this sort of possessiveness, which precluded Thomson from suggesting a problem to a student who then gradually made it his own, it is not surprising that Thomson's students lacked the publishing opportunities which Liebig's *Annalen* so generously afforded to his.

VI

The question of power is not one that generally looms largely in analyses of past scientific activity, yet once science began to be institutionalized problems of power and status inevitably arose. In the case of a university teacher who was intent on creating and maintaining a research school, these problems could be pressing. At the least they could deflect him from the running of his school and erode his confidence; at the worst total lack of power could mean that his research programme would remain unimplemented.

In the case of Liebig, some of his problems concerning status and power were quickly solved and the majority solved by the mid 1830s. Initially, of course, during his first and only session as extraordinary professor, Liebig met difficulties.[113] His fellow professors resented the way in which he had been imposed on them by the Grand Duke of Hesse, they suspected his irregular education, and no doubt at the bottom they feared his innovating zeal. W. L. Zimmermann, the ordinary professor of chemistry, regarded him as a petulant upstart and therefore refused to co-operate with him. In addition his vigorous criticisms of the state of chemistry, his proposed remedies, and his hostility to

[112] The exceptions seem to have been his two relatives R. D. Thomson, A. Steel, and Richardson, a close friend of Thomson's son, who all published papers based on research done in Thomson's laboratory. R. D. Thomson, "History and analysis of the Vanadianate of Lead", *Records of General Science*, **1**, 34–5, 1835; R. D. Thomson, "Chemical analysis of Crucilite, *ibid.*, 142–4; R. D. Thomson, "Analysis of Kirwanite, *ibid.*, 219–20; R. D. Thomson, "Examination of Hair Salt, or native sulphate of alumina and iron", *ibid.*, **2**, 55–61, 1835; T. Richardson, "Analysis of Wolfram", *ibid.*, **1**, 449–52, 1835; T. Thomson and A. Steel, "Chemical Analysis of Gadolinite, together with an examination of some salts of Yttria and Cerium", *ibid.*, 403–24.

[113] R. E. Oesper, "Justus von Liebig—Student and Teacher", *Journal of Chemical Education*, **4**, 1461–76 (1466), 1927; E. Berl, "Justus Liebig", *Journal of Chemical Education*, **15**, 553–62 (61), 1938.

the speculative Naturphilosophie of his eminent medical colleague Wilbrand all threatened what they regarded as an unnecessary and disagreeable disturbance of the *status quo*. These early conflicts were unexpectedly resolved when Zimmermann, whose endless chicanery had deeply annoyed Liebig, was accidentally drowned in 1825. As the man who was fortunately on the spot, Liebig was appointed full professor in 1825, a promotion which was welcomed by most of his colleagues who had begun to realize he was an asset to the University and to themselves. From then onwards Liebig's path was less rough, though one of his practises aroused bitter hostility from his colleagues. It seems that the majority of his laboratory students lacked the leaving-certificate based on the classics and awarded by the Gymnasia, which in principle was indispensable for those wanting to attend the University and Liebig's laboratory.[114] Liebig simply ignored what he regarded as restricting bureaucratic pedant y, but most of his colleagues regarded his willingness to admit unqualified students as a pernicious and destructive lowering of standards. Liebig gradually won this particular battle as his laboratory brought increasing fame to the University. In particular Liebig helped to arrest the startling decline in total student numbers which afflicted the University and other small German ones between 1831 and 1836.[115] No doubt Liebig's colleagues realized that traditional admission requirements if imposed would deter some students from attending the University at a time when German universities were in particularly sharp competition with each other for students and for their class fees. However disreputable and even bizarre some of Liebig's attitudes and practises appeared to them, his colleagues were compelled by his successes to acknowledge that warts-and-all he was the university's outstanding feature: they therefore gradually acquiesced in his innovations. Generally there seems little evidence that Liebig's research school was hindered in its style of work and growth by status or power problems with one exception which will be discussed in the penultimate section of this paper: with characteristic aplomb and bravura he exploited to the full what he regarded as his professorial rights. The battles with colleagues in which he engaged did not erode his confidence in his ability to mount a research school or deflect him significantly from his purposes. In some ways, indeed, as a professor of chemistry he was well placed. Ensconsed in the Philosophy faculty of a small university Liebig was not overburdened by

[114] Good (53), 562.

[115] Between 1830 and 1836, the total number of students at Giessen dropped from about 500 to about 300, and the number of medical students from about 90 to about 60. During the same period the number of "registered" students with Liebig rose from about 10 to 20; by 1843 the number had risen to about 65. See Wankmüller (54), 5–6. Between 1830 and 1834 the total number of students at the University of Freiburg dropped from 865 to 434; at Heidelberg it declined from 828 to 518 between 1833 and 1834. See: "List of Universities", *The Quarterly Journal of Education*, **9**, 343–7 (344), 1835.

an excess of low-level teaching. It is true that he taught a variety of lecture courses, such as experimental chemistry, pharmaceutical chemistry to medical students, agricultural chemistry, and stoichiometry all in 1826, and that he taught fairly large numbers of pharmacists at Giessen.[116] Nevertheless these teaching duties did not mulct him of energy and purpose. As Liebig himself confessed, one of Giessen's greatest virtues was that its small university was distinguished by its relative lack of those distractions which tend to be endemic in large universities and towns: "it was as if Providence had led me to the little university. At a larger university or in a larger place my energies would have been divided and dissipated, and it would have been much more difficult, and perhaps impossible, to reach the goal at which I aimed; but at Giessen everything was concentrated in work and in this I took passionate pleasure".[117]

In the case of Thomson his energies were by no means totally devoted to his research school. Though the University of Glasgow in principle attached peculiar importance to chemistry and could boast of a distinguished chemical lineage which began with Cullen and Black, Thomson found himself in a long embittered and unsuccessful dispute about his own status.[118] For Thomson the development of his research school and of his subject became inseparable from the question of his inferior status as a Regius Professor. Compared with the so-called College Professors, the Regius Professors formed a minority group whose privileges and rights were restricted. These Regius Professors were "little better than tolerated aliens" so that the possibilities for abrasive political infighting were enormous.[119] As the most intellectually distinguished of the Regius Professors and probably the fiercest and most experienced polemicist, too, Thomson spent much time and energy in acting as their chief spokesman and activist. Every document and political move concerning their status was engineered by him or was a response to his efforts. He objected with his usual aggressive tenacity to what he regarded as the deliberate degradation by the College Professors of himself and of his subject. It should be noted that the dispute between the Regius and College Professors, which began in earnest in 1807, was not solved until 1858 when the British government at last took action. The incessant intensity of this internecine struggle for power and its eroding effect on Thomson's confidence cannot be overestimated. Quite

[116] H. F. Kilian, *Die Universitaten Deutschlands in medicinisch-naturwissenschaftlicher hinsicht*, Heidelberg and Leipzig, 1828, 288.

[117] Liebig (14), 37.

[118] The Glasgow lineage of Black, Cullen, John Robison, William Irvine, Thomas Charles Hope, Robert Cleghorn and Thomson is described in A. Kent (ed.), *An Eighteenth-century lectureship in Chemistry*, Glasgow, 1950. Morrell (42) gives an account of the question of Thomson's inferior status as a Regius Professor in the University of Glasgow.

[119] The phrase is taken from an official history by J. Coutts, *A History of the University of Glasgow*, Glasgow, 1909, 337.

simply too much of Thomson's energy and time was necessarily spent in university politics and too little on his research school.

In any event as a professor in the medical faculty of Scotland's second largest university, which attracted in the early 1830s about 1,000 students, Thomson was a very busy man.[120] His main teaching duty was lecturing on chemistry one hour a day six days a week for an academic session about half a year long; from 1830 onwards he seems to have taken on a second year class, too.[121] In addition Thomson subjected his keen lecture-class students to an hour's *viva voce* questioning twice a week.[122] Furthermore, at least between 1817 and 1827 and probably beyond that period, Thomson lectured once a week on mineralogy and natural history presumably because he regarded Lockhart Muirhead, the Professor of Natural History, as less than competent.[123] Thomson taught large numbers of students in his first year chemistry class which was obligatory for medical students who intended to graduate. Inevitably therefore for most of these students Thomson's subject was merely one of several pre-clinical ones and subsidiary to their chief aim. On the other hand, owing to the system of Lernfreiheit which then operated in the Scottish universities, any student, matriculated or occasional, could attend Thomson's lecture class if he payed the class fee of £3 3s. 0d. The size of this first-year class during Thomson's vital years at Glasgow is set out below.[124]

1817–8	213	1823–4	122	1829–30	222	1835–6	135
1818–9	190	1824–5	150	1830–1	188	1836–7	138
1819–20	151	1825–6	177	1831–2	175	1837–8	86
1820–1	101	1826–7	175	1832–3	188	1838–9	75
1821–2	153	1827–8	205	1833–4	190	1839–40	50
1822–3	116	1828–9	204	1834–5	156		

No wonder that until 1837 Thomson felt he did more than his fair share of teaching. As an examiner, too, he was so heavily committed that in spring 1826, for instance, he spent about 130 hours orally examining candidates for the M.D.[125] In spite of teaching, tutoring and examining, Thomson managed

[120] In 1830, the University of Glasgow had 20 professors to deal with about 1,000 students in all; at Giessen about 30 professors and 10 Privatdozenten coped with about 500 students in all.

[121] Addison (63) indicates that from 1830 Thomson sometimes ran a second-year class as well as his first-year one; *Glasgow Evidence*, 151.

[122] *Glasgow Evidence*, 203.

[123] *Ibid.*, 152.

[124] The sources for these figures are:
1817 to 1826, *ibid.*, 527; 1826 to 1837, *Report of the Glasgow University Commissioners*, Parliamentary Papers, **29**, (1839), 71; for 1837 and 1838, Thomson to John Lee, 22 December 1838, National Library of Scotland, MS 3442, f. 202; and for 1839–40, Thomson to Rutherford, 12 November 1839, National Library of Scotland, MS 9711, ff. 115–116.

[125] *Glasgow Evidence*, 154.

during his prime to spend during term about five hours a day in the laboratory.[126] It is true that he had a five month summer vacation in which to recuperate travel, research and publish; yet during the university term he was heavily engaged in a multiplicity of tasks which inevitably distracted his attention from his research school far more than was the case with Liebig.

VII

The extraordinary charismatic power which Liebig exerted on his pupils showed in their loyalty to him. Above all their fierce pride in having been a member of his school indicated the preternatural hold he had on them. Examples of this sort of disciple-fetishism abound. Perhaps the most charming and revealing is the tribute paid to Liebig by Hofmann in his famous Faraday lecture (1875) delivered to the Chemical Society of London:

> Like all the great generals of every age, Liebig was the spirit as well as the leader of his battalions; and if he was followed so heartily it was because, much as he was admired, he was loved still more. If I speak somewhat fondly of Liebig, many around me are thinking of him fondly too for we were alike pupils of his. We remember his fascinating control over every faculty, every sentiment that we possessed; and we still, in our manhood now, remember how ready we were, as Liebig's young companions in arms, to make any attack at his bidding, and follow where he led. We felt then, we feel still, and never while we live shall we forget Liebig's marvellous influence over us; and if anything could be more astonishing than the amount of work he did with his own hands it was probably the mountain of chemical toil which he got us to go through. I am sure that he loved us in return. Each word of his carried instruction, every intonation of his voice bespoke regard; his approval was a mark of honour, and of whatever else we might be proud our greatest pride of all was in having him for our master.[127]

This sort of charisma enabled Liebig to exact from his research school a remarkably intense and specialized mode of existence.[128] Indeed those who studied chemistry exclusively formed a distinct clan at the University of Giessen. Liebig's laboratory students lived chemistry all day and every day. By avoiding the traditional student dissipations and amusements, they formed a distinct group detached from the other students. They did not aspire to the liberal humanism enshrined in the University of Berlin (founded 1809) under Wilhelm von Humboldt, a Prussian bureaucrat and classical scholar.[129] Nor were they allowed by Liebig to deviate from the advancement of pure chemical

[126] *Ibid.*, 151.
[127] Hofmann (15), 10.
[128] Oesper (112), 1471–2.
[129] Ashby (1), 25.

knowledge into its impure applications. He offered a broad basic training irrespective of the technical field which any student wanted to enter, and uncompromisingly refused to teach technical chemistry in his laboratory. Yet students were enticed by his vehement assertion that a properly trained chemist would be able to solve technical problems speedily and easily.

Liebig's charisma was apparent in the day to day arrangements which obtained in his laboratory. It was particularly displayed between 1824 and 1835 when Liebig, who lacked a private laboratory, worked in the same room as his students under physical conditions which were far from ideal. During those eleven vital years Liebig's influence on his laboratory students was exerted through close physical and mental contact with them in an informal atmosphere and situation. These were propitious conditions in which his charisma could operate: matters would have been different had Liebig from the start been an encapsulated professor whom his students rarely met or saw. The inadequate laboratory arrangements in those years did not demoralize the laboratory school: on the contrary, inspired by Liebig's example and insistence that talent amounts to will and work they produced among his students a fraternal cohesion.[130] In that sense the unheated balance room, the cramped size of the laboratory, the absence of fume chambers, and the fanned portable coal furnaces were challenges to ingenuity and adaptiveness.[131] So, too, were the pedagogic methods which Liebig employed on his laboratory students throughout his Giessen career. His regime was characterized by its incessantly challenging stimulus and by its promotion of self-reliance and responsibility in the students. As he recalled in his fragmentary autobiography:

> Actual teaching in the laboratory, of which practised assistants took charge, was only for the beginners; the progress of my special students depended on themselves. I gave the task and supervised its execution; as the radii of a circle all have their common centre. There was no actual instruction; I received from each individual every morning a report upon what he had done on the previous day, as well as his views on what he was engaged upon. I approved or made my criticisms. Everyone was obliged to follow his own course. In the association and constant intercourse with each other, and by each participating in the work of all, everyone learned from the others. Twice a week in winter, I gave a sort of review of the most important questions of the day; it was mainly a report on my own and their work combined with the researches of other chemists.[132]

As the charismic centre of the laboratory's activities, Liebig even expected his students to undergo considerable physical pain in the cause of the advancement

[130] Volhard (7), i, 12.
[131] *Ibid.*, i, 62–3.
[132] Liebig (14), 40.

of chemical Wissenschaft. When he first prepared anhydrous formic acid he ordered several students to bare their arms on which he dabbed the corrosive liquid: they complied unflinchingly.[133] Such was the *esprit de corps* he engendered and sustained.

In contrast with Liebig, Thomson can hardly be called a charismatic figure or leader. With the exception of his nephew R. D. Thomson, his laboratory pupils rarely thought of themselves as Thomson disciples. None of his students, therefore, paid to him such a fervent public tribute as Hofmann paid to Liebig though many regarded him with esteem and maybe affection.[134] It is surely significant that between 1857 and 1948 Thomson's career and life aroused no sustained analysis or biography whatsoever: in this respect even his pupils "deserted" him after R. D. Thomson and Crum, his primary obituarists, had paid their respects.[135] His regime, though specialized and devoted to chemistry as an independent science and not a trade, did not promote to a large extent self-reliance in students. Nor did he incessantly provoke them with research challenges. Because he regarded his students to some extent as laboratory assistants doing work for him and not for themselves, he did not try generally to stimulate his students to do independent research as Liebig did. This semi-authoritarian attitude precluded the existence of that informality in which charisma is most effectively exerted. In any case even if he had possessed the desire to encourage his laboratory students to work independently, the means to realize this aim were not perfect: I have already drawn attention to the inadequacies of Thomson's programme, technique and publication opportunities. At bottom, perhaps, Thomson's personality did not allow him to create his own chemical church, though there is no doubt that he successfully communicated the spirit of enquiry to his students and furthered their careers when he could. He was reluctant to pay respect to others, and was proud of his bluntness. His brusqueness, arrogance, ill-temper and jealousy were displayed most conspicuously in the polemical wars he waged.[136] Clearly as a

[133] Good (53), 561–2. Though the story may be apocryphal, it illustrates the contagious and overwhelming effect of Liebig's enthusiasm on his students.

[134] Crum (8), 254.

[135] The revival of interest in Thomson after a lacuna of almost a century was heralded by: H. S. Klickstein, "Thomas Thomson, Pioneer Historian of Chemistry", *Chymia*, **1**, 37–53, 1948; and J. R. Partington, "Thomas Thomson, 1773–1852", *Annals of Science*, **6**, 115–26, 1949.

[136] Both Crum (8), 255, and R. D. Thomson (8), 153, found it necessary to apologize for Thomson's peremptory deportment. His jealousy and ill-temper surprised Constable the publisher: see Constable to John Leslie, 20 February 1822, National Library of Scotland, MS 331, ff. 157–8. In the mid 1830s "as members of the Philosophical Society of Glasgow, Thomson invariably treated Graham with an amount of respect and even deference which that brusque and quick-tempered old philosopher too frequently failed to extend to others": see T. E. Thorpe, *Essays in Historical Chemistry*, 2nd ed., London, 1902, 207.

ublic figure he was neither loved nor admired but respected for his life of stern ectitude, proud independence and unflagging industry. Though his students o doubt regarded him as an enigmatic "card" Thomson's deportment in one rucial respect disturbed strangers and must have hindered the growth of ssential mutual respect between his laboratory students and himself. Sir Robert Christison, who esteemed Thomson highly as a chemist and as a poly- ıath, nevertheless recalled one of Thomson's less attractive features in a way hat explains the limitation of his charisma:

> He was known by his friends to be at bottom a warm-hearted, good-natured man, who did unobtrusively many a kind act. No man could have imagined, to look at him, that the most glaring ingredient in his character, so far as conduct was concerned, was an uncontrollable propensity to sneer—not behind backs, but in presence of his subject. He did so without any appearance of anger, malice, or sense of humour, but rather with a mournful look, as if sorrowing that he should feel called upon to exercise in the particular case his privilege as follower of Thersites. Hence, though his sneers were often bitter, and not infrequently made, his friends, when assailed, only laughed; but strangers were astonished, and if not quick in apprehension, were apt to resent his censorship as insolence.[137]

suspect that even students like Andrews who went to Glasgow specifically to :udy under Thomson were not attracted by his chilling sarcasm.

VIII

The last element in the research school situation is financial support from ı institution. This was, of course, intimately connected with the power, ıarisma, programme and reputation of the director. But I want to discuss in quite arbitrary separation from the other elements I have previously ›nsidered because of its importance in permitting the conversion of a temporary :hool into a permanent institutionalized one. In particular I shall consider ıe three chief aspects of financial support: the director's salary, his laboratory :commodation, and the laboratory expenses granted to him.

In his first year at Giessen, during which his small laboratory in the wing an army barracks was opened, Liebig's salary was 300 florins (£26) and the ıy amount of 100 fl. (£9) was given to him by the University for laboratory :penses.[138] In April 1825 his salary was raised to 500 fl. (£45).[139] After immermann's death in July 1825 and Liebig's promotion, his salary was

[137] Christison (68), i, 366–7. This description refers to 1827 when Christison spent .rt of his honeymoon *chez* Thomson in Glasgow.

[138] Volhard (7), i, 55, 100.

[139] *Ibid.*, i, 101.

increased to 800 fl. (£69) and the laboratory fund to an estimated 400 fl. (£34).[140] For the next ten years until 1835 Liebig's salary and laboratory fund from tl University seem to have been inadequate to meet the steadily increasing co he incurred in running his laboratory. It appears that the annual cost of tl laboratory was met partly by Liebig, who spent 300–400 fl. (£26–34) per yea and by the University.[141] The latter's contribution between 1825 and 183 which from 1828 included the salary of 150 fl. per year paid to the laborator steward, is set out below:[142]

1825	446 fl. (£38)	1829	618 fl. (£53)	1833	619 fl. (£53)
1826	455 fl. (£39)	1830	845 fl. (£73)	1834	594 fl. (£51)
1827	497 fl. (£43)	1831	649 fl. (£56)	1835	774 fl. (£67)
1828	614 fl. (£53)	1832	618 fl. (£53)		

During these ten years the University paid the salary of a laboratory stewar (i.e. Famulus), while Liebig himself paid a laboratory assistant 320 fl. (£28) year.[143] It would appear that in this decade the expenses of the laborator (materials, apparatus and the assistant) were met roughly equally by Liebi and the University, i.e. the government of Hesse Darmstadt. It also seen that the University was not as indifferent to his enterp ise as he suggeste Nor should it be forgotten that Liebig's remuneration was gained from fe paid to him by his students as well as from his salary. Clearly, however, the financial arrangements were unsatisfactory for the energetic, ambitious an anxious Liebig. Not surprisingly in 1829 he unsuccessfully asked the Chancell of Hessen, von Linde, for an increase of salary. By 1833 he was calling for new lecture room, a proper laboratory, and again an increase in salary; additio ally he threatened to resign, and was suffering from nervous exhaustion. Tl Chancellor of the University was reluctant to lose him, promised relief and 1834 raised his salary to 850 fl. (£73).[144]

In 1835, no doubt as a response to the invitation he had received from tl University of Antwerp, his salary was increased to 1250 fl. (£108); and tl University not only continued to pay the laboratory steward but also began pay Ettling, the laboratory assistant, a salary of 300 fl. (£26) which previous Liebig had met from his own pocket.[145] In the same year, at an approxima cost of 5035 fl. (£435) the University converted the old auditorium, partition off a small private laboratory for Liebig, and enlarged the laboratory.[146] Th

[140] *Ibid.*, i, 63, 102.

[141] *Ibid.*, i, 68. Liebig's own view of his situation is set out in his letter of 12 Augu 1833 to von Linde, the Chancellor of the University: see *ibid.*, i, 67–74.

[142] *Ibid.*, i, 64.

[143] *Ibid.*, i, 68.

[144] *Ibid.*, i, 76.

[145] *Ibid.*, i, 80.

[146] *Ibid.*, i, 79.

ɔmbination of better financial arrangements and improved accommodation ı the laboratory permitted Liebig to expand his student numbers at this time: was about 1835, for instance, that the trek of keen young British chemists ɔ the Giessen laboratory began. Fortunately for Liebig his fame was then ıfficient to induce other universities to make attractive offers to him. As a ›yal Hessian, Liebig used these opportunities as levers to prize salary increases om the grudging government. In 1837, for instance, his refusal of an invitaon to go to the University of St. Petersburg enabled him to gain an increase ı salary of 400 fl. to 1650 (£142).[147] It also enabled him in 1839 to have built new larger laboratory to his own design at a cost of 12,000–13,000 fl. (£1,020–120) which was borne by the University. At the same time the laboratory ınd was substantially increased to 1,500 fl. (£130).[148] Liebig's star was then › much in the ascendant that, after he had refused in 1840 an invitation from ıe Austrian government to go to the University of Vienna, his salary was ıised in 1841 to 3,200 fl. (£275) and the laboratory expenses increased in 1843 › 1,900 fl. (£164).[149] It is worth commenting that in the seven years between 333 and 1841 Liebig's salary rose from 800 fl. (£69) to 3,200 fl. (£275) and the boratory expenses paid by the government from about 620 fl. (£53) to 1,500 fl. 130). These dramatic increases resulted from Liebig's fame as a teacher, searcher, editor and writer; from the pressure exerted by the town of Giessen hich gained financially from his presence at the university; and not least om the sharply competitive nature of the European university system which iebig exploited so successfully to his own financial advantage.

There seems little doubt that in 1835 Liebig's university began to take ›me financial responsibility for his research school. By 1839 it had committed self firmly to his enterprise. The implications of this move towards regular stitutional financial support were so important that they were not lost on iebig's contemporaries. For instance, William Gregory, a pioneer British ganic chemist and one of Liebig's first British pupils, saw that the 1839 ıancial arrangements permitted Liebig to run a research school of moderate ze without having himself to meet its cost. Gregory pointed out that when ıe necessarily large expenses of a laboratory were borne by a teacher who ıarged his students a low fee the financial loss he entailed discouraged him om maintaining or enlarging the size of his laboratory class. He also saw ıat, if high and "realistic" fees were charged to cover such expenses, "but few udents study practical chemistry on these terms. In short, the attempt to ırow the burden on the students effectually prevents the formation of an

[147] *Ibid.*, i, 80.
[148] *Ibid.*, i, 81; Gregory (56), 22.
[149] *Ibid.*, i, 80, 84.

efficient school of research".[150] But the government of Hesse-Darmstadt Gregory argued, had broken the impasse by subsidising Liebig's research schoc on a large scale from 1839. In particular, in 1839 Liebig enjoyed a nev enlarged laboratory which could accommodate up to fifty students, an adequat salary of 1,650 fl. (£142), and a government grant for laboratory expenses o 1,500 fl. (£130) which apparently met the cost of having up to fifteen student in the laboratory; and of course from 1835 he had been helped by a salarie laboratory assistant as well as the traditional salaried laboratory steward When Liebig took on more than fifteen laboratory students, he himself had t pay from his salary and fees the increased expenses of a larger laboratory class.[151] The really important point is that from 1839 the Hessian government met th expenses associated with a limited number of laboratory students (fifteen). I this way money was not put directly into Liebig's pocket, yet he could accom modate up to fifteen students in his laboratory without suffering financial loss From the secure financial base established in 1839 and expanded by 184 Liebig was enabled at his discretion to enlarge his research school which wa unprecedented in its size and in its volume of publication. Furthermore thi financial liberality of the Hessian government permitted Liebig from 1839 "t open his laboratory, provided as it is with everything necessary for research, o terms which allow almost every student with ease to avail himself of the oppor tunity".[152] Though his fees were charged at his discretion, it seems that fron 1839 Liebig's laboratory students paid 78 fl. (£6 14s. od.) for a course whicl ran six full days per week for eight to nine months. In short, the financia support for his school which Liebig at last extracted from a reluctant governmen in 1835, 1839 and 1843, permitted him to expand it to an unrivalled degree. Th year 1839 in particular was very significant because in that year the world' outstanding research school in chemistry, and possibly in science as a whole began to be seriously supported financially by its university; and the inadequac of financing a research school solely from a professor's personal initiative an pocket was thereby publicly acknowledged.

Like Liebig Thomson was aggressively persistent in extracting from hi university laboratory accommodation in which students could work. Durin his first session at Glasgow he was irritated by the lack of a laboratory, bu within six months of his appointment the university agreed to furnish the logi class-room as a room for his lecture class and to convert the old chemistr class-room into a laboratory.[153] By autumn 1818 the laboratory, equippe

[150] Gregory (56), 18.

[151] *Ibid.*, 20–2.

[152] *Ibid.*, 20.

[153] Thomson to Napier, 18 March 1818, British Museum, MS 34, 612, f. 176; Records Glasgow College (Faculty Minutes), 26 March 1818.

with good apparatus provided partly by the university and partly by Thomson, was opened to students. It had defects: it was damp and could accommodate only ten students. It should be noted that the British Government, the patron of Thomson's chair, contributed nothing to the cost of this laboratory or to his other departmental expenses of any kind; and between 1818 and 1840 it paid him a salary of only £50 per year. This first laboratory was created by the joint initiative of Thomson and his university, acting without government support. It is clear that in the 1820s the type of his laboratory teaching was such that his annual salary failed to meet his unavoidable laboratory expenses which he alleged constituted a severe drain on his financial resources.[154]

Again like Liebig he pressed hard for better accommodation particularly after 1826. His special lever was the increasing size of his lecture class for which the accommodation was inadequate. By 1827, for instance, his class was so big that extra space for students had to be created in it by partly dismantling some of the improvements made to it the previous year at a cost of £70.[155] In 1828 and 1829 Thomson applied to the university for a new classroom.[156] By the latter year his case was irresistible. In spite of further alterations made by the university to his lecture-room at the beginning of session 1829–30, his class was so big that he was forced to divide it into two groups to which he lectured at a separate hour.

The University, controlled by the College professors, responded to this challenge in an enlightened way.[157] Perhaps they knew that Thomson's refusal to be enticed to the new University of London in 1826 meant that he was determined to stay to develop chemistry at Glasgow, and no doubt they welcomed the increasing number of medical students which he, Hooker and Burns attracted to the university.[158] Perhaps, too, they hoped that their financial munificence in providing a new teaching laboratory as well as a new classroom would embarrass him into rare silence. Whatever their motives, the new building for the chemistry department, erected in Shuttle Street outside the university walls at a cost of about £5,000 was opened to students in 1831. Though Thomson thought that the extra-mural location of his new building was a deliberate attack on his status as a Regius professor, his new teaching and research laboratory was far superior to his previous one: it was not damp and it could accommodate more students. Even the querulous Thomson was

[154] Morrell (42), 254.

[155] Faculty Minutes, 8 June 1826.

[156] Faculty Minutes, 4 January 1828, 15 March 1829.

[157] On the Shuttle Street laboratory, see A. Kent, "The Shuttle Street Laboratories", *Glasgow University Gazette* (1956), number 25.

[158] The growth of the medical school at the University of Glasgow in the 1820s hinged on the work done by Thomson, Hooker, and John Burns (professor of surgery, 1815–50).

satisfied. He had the top three floors of the building for his chemistry department, the ground floor and cellars being rented to tenants and shopkeepers who were occasionally disorderly. With characteristic mercantile acumen the university used part of the Shuttle Street building as a financial investment. Nevertheless it was conspicuously generous to Thomson in providing him in 1831 with new accommodation which cost about three times as much as Liebig's eight years later. It was in this laboratory that Thomson and his school implemented part of his second research programme.

Yet ironically Thomson acquired the Shuttle Street laboratory only when his exhausting career was coming to an end. Apart from the deficiencies of programme, technique, publication, and personality, which I have discussed previously, Thomson was fifty-eight years old in 1831, whereas Liebig was only thirty-six when in 1839 he acquired his new building at Giessen. In any event, between 1835 and 1841 Thomson deliberately threw himself into unsuccessful political agitation for reform of the Scottish universities in general and of the power structure of the University of Glasgow in particular. But after about 1834 several developments over which he had no control reduced the scale of his laboratory school. The sudden death of his wife in late 1834 staggered him.[159] His own pupil Graham at the neighbouring Anderson's University was by this time a powerful and younger rival who attracted students such as Lyon Playfair who apparently never considered enrolling for Thomson's laboratory class.[160] In any event the decline suffered in the late 1830s by the medical school of the university together with Scotland's economic depression from 1837 contributed to the marked reduction of the size of his lecture and laboratory classes. By session 1839–40 he had only fifty in the former and four in the latter. In the late 1830s therefore Thomson's total remuneration from class fees and fixed annual salary of £50 dropped most unpleasantly: in 1833–34 it was £587; six years later it was about £200. Thomson's star was by this time very much descendant: in the very year when the Hessian government gave to Liebig's school favourable financial arrangements, Thomson could not afford a laboratory assistant.[161] No wonder that he demanded from the British government an increase of salary. His persistence was rewarded in 1840 when for the first time in his professorial career his salary was at last raised to £200 per year as a reward for past service. Lacking a retirement pension Thomson held his chair until his death, but from 1841 his protégé R. D. Thomson lectured on organic chemistry and ran the practical class.

It seems that before 1831 Thomson's physical accommodation for his

[159] Crum (8), 254.

[160] T. W. Reid, *Memoirs and Correspondence of Lyon Playfair*, London, 1899, 36.

[161] Morrell (42), 261–2; Thomson to Rutherfurd, 12 November 1839, National Library of Scotland, MS 9711, ff. 115–6.

laboratory students was inadequate: in particular it was so small that he had to turn many prospective students away. After 1831 laboratory accommodation was not a problem, but the joint force of matters previously discussed prevented him from exploiting it to the full as the home of a research school. One other point needs to be stressed. Though the university provided considerable capital outlay in 1818 and in 1831 for Thomson's laboratories, he always met the annual laboratory expenses for materials and assistance and much of the apparatus from his own pocket. For that reason his laboratory class and school necessarily involved him in financial loss.[162] In that sort of situation there was every financial inducement to diminish and not to expand the facilities for practical work. At no stage in his career did Thomson enjoy the services of a laboratory steward and an assistant whose salaries were paid by his institution or by the British government; nor did he ever receive an annual laboratory grant which would have enabled him to take up to a certain number of students without incurring financial loss. The contrast with Liebig is obvious: Thomson's school always cost him money; after 1839 Liebig's, up to a certain size, cost him nothing.

IX

In 1885 Sir William Thomson, professor of natural philosophy in the University of Glasgow (1846–99), asserted that physics laboratories in universities "are now advancing to something of the method and consistent system that Thomas Thomson and Liebig so greatly gave to chemical laboratories".[163] Though he was patently keen to pay tribute to the man whose laboratory he had attended in session 1838–39, Sir William's point was not totally invalid.[164] I have tried to argue that Liebig and Thomson were the first professors of chemistry in their respective university systems who launched research schools during the 1820s and the 1830s. For that reason alone they are worth comparing. Of course Liebig created and developed his school with triumphant success; but Thomson, who was equally thrusting and ambitious, was not by any means totally successful with his school. I have also tried to show that their relative degrees of success can be understood most fully if we take into account the intellectual, technical, institutional, psychological and financial elements in their situations.

The model I have suggested suffers from the limitation that it tends to be an idealizing rationalization of Liebig's success. Inevitably Thomson fares

[162] R. D. Thomson (8), 146.

[163] W. Thomson, "Scientific Laboratories", *Nature*, **31**, 409–13 (411), 1885.

[164] S. P. Thompson, *The Life of William Thomson, Baron Kelvin of Largs*, London, 1910, i, 174.

badly in the comparison, even though these two pioneers of the 1820s shared some aims. Yet the model does emphasize and reveal why and how Thomson innovated: the features of his research school are thereby more sharply delineated. For this reason the model may illuminate the careers of other nineteenth-century chemists and groups. For instance I would agree that the Society of Arcueil may be regarded as a private embryonic research school whose programme was to solve problems concerning capillarity, light, heat and chemical affinity in a framework of short range attractive and repulsive forces.[165] It may also help us to understand the larger problem of the detailed way in which in the 1830s leadership in chemistry began to pass from France to the German states and their universities. It may illuminate the failure of French chemists such as Gay-Lussac, Dumas, Chevreul, and that ill-fated pair Laurent and Gerhardt, to establish institutionalized research schools. It emphasizes the decisive contribution to the professionalization of chemistry made in Germany by Liebig, Wöhler, Bunsen, and later by Hofmann and Kolbe. It gives point to the well-known individualism of British scientists as displayed by Davy, Dalton, Faraday and Graham, none of whom founded research schools.[166] It draws attention to the important pioneering British research schools run by Thomson, Hofmann, and H. E. Roscoe. In short it may help to throw light on one of the most important and difficult problems posed by nineteenth-century science, i.e. the comparative history of its professionalization.

Acknowledgements

For valuable help and criticism I am indebted to Drs. W. H. Brock, W. V. Farrar, and Arnold W. Thackray. For permission to refer to manuscripts and to quote from them I am grateful to: The Trustees of the British Museum; the Historical Society of Pennsylvania, Philadelphia; the Trustees of the National Library of Scotland; the Royal Society of Edinburgh; the Scottish Record Office; the Clerk of Senate and the Reference Librarian of the University of Glasgow; Mrs. Seton Dickson, Symington, Ayrshire, the owner of the Pollok-Morris manuscripts; and the Bayerische Staatsbibliothek, München.

[165] Crosland (15), 297–308; O. Hannaway's review of Crosland, *Isis*, **60**, 578–81, 1969 and R. Fox, "The Laplacian Programme for Physics", *Boletin de la Academie Nacional de Ciencias de la Republica Argentina*, **48**, 429–37, 1970.

[166] J. B. Morrell, "Individualism and the Structure of British Science in 1830", *Historical Studies in the Physical Sciences*, **3**, 183–204, 1971.

Addenda

p.6, line 17: *insert* of *after* teaching.

p.19, column 1, line 23: *insert* James Finlay Weir Johnston.

IX

PRACTICAL CHEMISTRY IN THE UNIVERSITY OF EDINBURGH, 1799–1843

"THE showman in the other corner"—such was the pejorative description given by John Leslie, Professor of Natural Philosophy in the University of Edinburgh, of his colleague Thomas Charles Hope (1766–1844), Professor of Chemistry and Medicine from 1799 to 1843.[1] Yet the career of this flamboyantly popular teacher has received curiously little attention. For instance recent articles on Hope are heavily dependent on the basic biography compiled 120 years ago by his colleague T. S. Traill.[2] Hope, a protégé of Joseph Black,[3] occupied an important chair of European reputation in the metropolitan University of Scotland when chemistry was changing rapidly and British science was undergoing incipient professionalization. Many aspects of his work would repay close study: one could adduce his rapid espousal of Lavoisier's ideas and his sustained interest in the chemical facets of the Huttonian–Wernerian dispute. This paper is however deliberately limited to a study of one feature of Hope's career, i.e. the teaching of practical chemistry in the University of Edinburgh during his incumbency. Such a subject is not merely parochial. In 1799 when Hope fully assumed the responsibilities of the Edinburgh chair its standing and perhaps potentialities were second to none in Europe. When he died in 1844, however, Liebig, Wöhler and Bunsen at the Universities of Giessen, Göttingen and Marburg had established their hegemony with regard to teaching methods and the development of research schools of chemistry. This change of leadership was associated not only with German initiatives stimulated by Liebig's pioneering work at Giessen from the mid-1820s, but also with the difficulties experienced at Edinburgh in developing the teaching of practical chemistry. Accordingly my aim in this paper is to give an account of these difficulties which culminated in abortive

[1] R. A. Smith, *The Life and Works of Thomas Graham*, Glasgow, 1884, 9.

[2] J. Kendall, "Thomas Charles Hope, M.D.", in A. Kent (ed.), *An Eighteenth Century Lectureship in Chemistry*, Glasgow, 1950, 157–63; R. H. Cragg, "Thomas Charles Hope (1766–1844)", *Medical History*, **xi**, 186–9, 1967; T. S. Traill, "Memoir of Dr. Thomas Charles Hope, late Professor of Chemistry in the University of Edinburgh", *Transactions of the Royal Society of Edinburgh*, **xvi**, 419–34, 1849.

[3] In addition to Traill, *op. cit.* (2), see Hope's letter of 18 October, 1793, to Joseph Black (Black Correspondence, iii, 277–8, University of Edinburgh Library) in which he asked his former professor to examine his famous paper on strontia before reading it to the Royal Society of Edinburgh.

efforts made in 1833 and 1834 to establish an independent chair and lecture-ship in practical chemistry; and to explore the implications of these events together with their aftermath.

I

There is no doubt that Hope was one of the most popular and successful chemistry lecturers of his time, a feat which exacted tribute from his contemporaries. The young and highly critical Charles Darwin excluded Hope from his strictures on the dullness of the lectures he heard at Edinburgh between 1825 and 1827.[4] Some years earlier Marcet had pointed the contrast between Hope and Leslie: "Hope enseigne bien, mais n'a point de génie; et Leslie a du génie, mais il enseigne mal".[5] The self-same Leslie decried the decline of his own class numbers: "the taste of hard study being evidently on the decline—the glare of chemistry obscures everything else."[6] Hope certainly held the limelight and delighted big audiences. His spectacular and punctiliously organized lecture demonstrations, using large apparatus specially designed for the purpose,[7] ensured that he exploited the popularity of chemistry in Edinburgh to such an extent that on eight occasions more than 500 enrolled for his course.[8] As a demonstrator in the lecture-room Hope in his prime was allegedly unsurpassed in Europe except by Thenard in Paris.[9] He sustained a testing programme: over a period of six months for five days a week, each lecture was illustrated to the full by experiments. Hope simplified and popularized chemistry without vulgarizing it.[10] He himself insisted that

[4] C. Darwin, "Autobiography" in F. Darwin (ed.), *The Life and Letters of Charles Darwin*, London, 1887, 36.

[5] Marcet's letter of 15 January, 1822, to Berzelius, H. G. Söderbaum (ed.), *Berzelius Bref*, Stockholm and Uppsala, 1914, i (Part 3), 227.

[6] Leslie's letter of 25 December, 1813 to James Brown (Leslie Correspondence and Papers, University of Edinburgh Library). I am indebted to Dr. A. C. Chitnis of the University of Stirling for this reference.

[7] *The Life of William Allen with Selections from his Correspondence*, London, 1846, i, 355. In a note dated 11 May, 1818, Allen recorded *inter alia* that the bulbs of Hope's differential thermometers were almost two inches in diameter and that his receiver for oxygen had a capacity of ten to twelve gallons.

[8] Evidence, Oral and Documentary, taken before the Commissioners for visiting the Universities of Scotland with Appendix and Index. The University of Edinburgh. *Parliamentary Papers*, **xxxv** (1837), Appendix 130. Hope's biggest class numbered 55[illegible] in 1823–4. In subsequent references this volume will be called *Edinburgh Evidence*.

[9] L. Playfair, *A Century of Chemistry in the University of Edinburgh*, Edinburgh, 1858, 23.

[10] G. Wilson and A. Giekie, *Memoir of Edward Forbes*, Edinburgh and London, 1861, 99.

he spent several hours a day in superintending the preparations for the lecture next day, a claim which examination of his lecture notes substantiates.[11]

Several characteristics of the Scottish Universities in general and of the University of Edinburgh in particular encouraged, even if they did not necessitate, the style of work adopted by Hope. The lack of entrance examinations for students, in accord with the Scottish tradition of democratic intellect, together with their youth, provided opportunities for professors to be elementary, spectacular and popular in their teaching. Hope's audience varied exceptionally in age and composition: it included medical students for whom his lectures were compulsory and many of the Edinburgh public who attended out of general curiosity.[12] Furthermore, like some of his medical colleagues at Edinburgh, Hope received neither salary nor capital and running expenses which he therefore met himself.[13] Clearly he was heavily reliant on the fees paid by the members of his class. An unsalaried professor like Hope depended on the financial rewards of gaining popularity with a large number of students. As Brewster vehemently asserted, such a professor "is forced to become a commercial speculator, and under the dead weight of its degrading influence, his original researches are either neglected or abandoned".[14] For many years Hope's emoluments were the highest received by a professor in a Scottish University, his remuneration from class fees hovering around £2,000 a year. Given this sort of financial independence it is not surprising that professors tended to be monopolistic, jealously guarding their disciplines against both internal and external competition.[15] Hope was no exception in this regard: he allowed his tutorial assistant to use his apparatus for explanation but not for demonstration;[16] and he regarded the proposal made by the Scottish Universities Commission (1826), that medical students could attend private teachers for an imperative second course of chemistry, as a condemnation of his efficiency as well as an attack on his professorial rights.[17]

[11] Edinburgh Evidence, *op. cit.* (8), 267; Packets 116 and 117 in Hope Papers, Gen. 270–1, University of Edinburgh Library.

[12] Edinburgh Evidence, *op. cit.* (8), 266 and Appendix, 130; A. Bower, *The Edinburgh Student's Guide: or an account of the classes of the University, arranged under the four Faculties; with a detail of what is taught in each*, Edinburgh, 1822, 42–5 (42). After about 1815 it is clear that Hope attracted about a hundred students in excess of the number who attended the other basic medical classes. For details see footnote 54.

[13] Edinburgh Evidence, *op. cit.* (8), 279 and Appendix, 169.

[14] D. Brewster, "Decline of Science in England", *The Quarterly Review*, **xliii**, 305–42 (326), 1830.

[15] L. J. Saunders, *Scottish Democracy 1815–1840. The Social and Intellectual Background*, Edinburgh and London, 1950, 331.

[16] Edinburgh Evidence, *op. cit.* (8), 267.

[17] *Ibid.*, Appendix, 230.

Until 1823 the teaching of chemistry at the University of Edinburgh was conducted exclusively by lecturing, a deficiency which was exploited by the private teachers in the city. As early as 1800 Thomas Thomson and John Thomson were successfully lecturing on chemistry in Edinburgh.[18] At least from 1807 until 1811 Thomas Thomson had capitalized on the weakness in Hope's teaching by mounting practical classes, an omission further emphasized in 1818 when Thomson, by that time Professor of Chemistry at the University of Glasgow, opened a laboratory for teaching and research.[19] Two years later Andrew Fyfe, later Professor of Chemistry at King's College, Aberdeen, opened a private laboratory for teaching the basic skills of practical chemistry and pharmacy. Though initially discouraged by the small size of his classes, Fyfe persisted so that in the summer of 1822 he ran five separate practical courses all of which were well attended.[20] In that year there were at least three extra-mural lecturers to rival Hope: Andrew Fyfe, John Deuchar and John Murray the younger, of whom the first two ran practical classes which offered opportunities unavailable in the University.[21]

Hope's reluctance to develop the practical teaching of his subject is hardly puzzling. The extent of his pharmaceutical and clinical work[22] shows that in his opinion chemistry was ancillary to medicine whose dominance would inevitably have been partially undermined by the growth of expensive and time-consuming practical chemistry. Perhaps, too, Hope was secretly embarrassed by his failure between 1805 and 1835 to publish any papers on the little research he was then doing. In addition his expository gifts were

[18] See the *D.N.B.* articles on Thomas and John Thomson; and W. Hanna, *Memoirs of the Life and Writings of Thomas Chalmers*, Edinburgh, 1850, i, 473. Both Thomsons became professors, John holding in turn the chairs of Military Surgery and General Pathology in the University of Edinburgh. The extramural field was a forcing-ground for promising young scientists. Thomas Thomson, John Thomson, Andrew Fyfe, William Gregory, Edward Turner and George Wilson all became professors and began their teaching careers during Hope's incumbency as extramural teachers of chemistry in Edinburgh. Some of the private teachers of chemistry in Edinburgh were associated with the extra-mural medical lecturers. The whole question of extramural teaching of natural philosophy and medicine in early nineteenth century Scotland requires detailed investigation.

[19] For an assessment of Hope's great rival in Scotland see J. B. Morrell, "Thomas Thomson: Professor of Chemistry and University Reformer", *The British Journal for the History of Science*, June, 1969.

[20] A. Fyfe, *To the Right Honourable The Lord Provost, the Magistrates, and other members of the Town Council of Edinburgh, Patrons of the University*, Edinburgh, 1833, 2.

[21] Bower, *op. cit.* (12), 143–4.

[22] Hope wrote the chemical part of the *Edinburgh Pharmacopoeia* (10th edn., Edinburgh, 1817) as he confessed in his "Remarks on Mr. Phillip's Analysis of the Pharmacopoeia Collegii Regii Medicorum Edinburgensis", *Annals of Philosophy*, **i**, 187–94, 1821. For several years he lectured on clinical medicine, as Traill stressed: Traill, *op. cit.* (2), 426.

tarnished by a cold, pompous and affected manner.[23] Whatever his motives were he definitely did not encourage promising young chemists: as an example his practical room was open to none but his assistant.[24] One obvious result of this exclusive policy was that, as Robert Christison pointed out, "Dr. Hope, with all his ability as a teacher, made very few chemists, because he never encouraged practical study".[25] Some students tried to meet this deficiency by forming their own societies for performing experiments, the best known being that organized in 1815 by Christison himself and James Syme.[26] Some of Hope's best students, like Christison, Edward Turner and later William Gregory, left Edinburgh for Paris to study analytical organic and pharmaceutical chemistry under Robiquet, some years before the trek of British students to the German Universities began.[27]

II

In 1823, however, the teaching of practical chemistry and pharmacy was started in the new Adam-Playfair building by Dr. John Wilson Anderson, an Edinburgh manufacturing chemist, who as Hope's assistant was sanctioned by his professor to give what were in effect private classes within the University. It seems that Hope tolerated but hardly encouraged this class in spite of his assertions to the contrary before the University Senate.[28] Between 1823 and 1828 Anderson and Longstaff, who in turn were Hope's part-time

[23] Smith, *op. cit.* (1), 14 and 35; Wilson and Giekie, *op. cit.* (10), 99; and Chalmers' account of the way in which in 1801 Hope tried to squash his enthusiasm for natural philosophy in Hanna, *op. cit.* (18), 470.

[24] R. Christison, *The Life of Sir Robert Christison, Bart., ed. by his sons*, Edinburgh and London, 1885, i, 58.

[25] *Ibid.*, 62. Wilson and Giekie, *op. cit.* (10), 101, were quite open in explaining Hope's indifference to practical chemistry: "Dr. Hope gave little or no encouragement to the new movement, which ran counter to his personal tastes, and did not promise to serve his pecuniary interests".

[26] A. Grant, *The Story of the University of Edinburgh during its first three hundred years*, London, 1884, ii, 398. Christison served the University of Edinburgh for fifty-five and a half years first in the chair of Medical Jurisprudence and then in that of Materia Medica. James Syme became a distinguished occupant of the chair of Clinical Surgery in the University of Edinburgh.

[27] Christison and Turner studied in 1820–1 under Robiquet whose methods, etc., are described by Christison, *op. cit.* (24), i, 267–70. Gregory migrated to Paris in 1827–8: see W. Gregory, *Testimonials in favour of William Gregory as a candidate for the vacant chair of chemistry in the University of Edinburgh*, Edinburgh, 1843, 4.

[28] College Minutes, 1 May, 1823, University of Edinburgh Library; but see Christison, *op. cit.* (24), i, 343, and J. W. Anderson, *Letter to the . . . Town Council of Edinburgh . . . in reference to the contemplated establishment of a Lectureship of Practical Chemistry*, Edinburgh, 1834, 23.

assistants, taught the practical class at their own responsibility and risk, being excluded from using the meagre University materials and apparatus.[29] As attendance at this class was not compulsory for the University medical students, it was poorly attended and therefore barely lucrative to its directors[30] who no doubt felt the additional competition of the private practical classes organized between 1824 and 1828 by Edward Turner.[31] Hope seems to have regarded the practical class as an optional extra which bore no necessary relation to his lecture course, a view directly opposed to the steadily spreading attitude in Edinburgh which saw that practical chemistry was essential as well as advantageous.[32] Certainly he did not conceive it as a source of promising young chemists who would work in a research school under his aegis.[33] It is not surprising that, when the Scottish Universities Commission began in 1826 to collect evidence in Edinburgh, the state of the practical class was attacked by Brewster and Christison. The former confessed that the low standard of mineralogical analysis in Scotland had obliged him from 1816 to send minerals abroad to be analysed.[34] Christison, too, was embarrassed by the situation. Aware that Edinburgh chemistry was inferior to that in Paris where opportunities for practical chemistry were greater and at £4 per month for a full course considerably cheaper, Christison made in 1826 the lethal point that "There is a great deal of general chemical knowledge in Scotland, but there are very few chemists".[35] Positively, however, he proposed that the laboratories for training and research run by Robiquet in Paris and Thomson in Glasgow had shown the way forward.[36]

[29] D. B. Reid, *Remarks on Dr. Hope's "Summary", Presented to the Patrons of the University*, Edinburgh, 1833, 9.

[30] "Veritas" in *The Scotsman*, 12 June, 1833, asserted that between 1823 and 1828 the average attendance at the practical class lay between twelve and twenty.

[31] R. Christison, *Biographical Sketch of the late Edward Turner*, 2nd ed., Edinburgh and London, 1837, 19. Turner left Edinburgh to become the first professor of chemistry at University College, London.

[32] See Edinburgh Evidence, *op. cit.* (8), 284, 285, 341, 448, 508, 569 for the views about the place of practical chemistry held by Hope, James Russell, William Wood, George Bell, J. H. Davidson and Daniel Ellis respectively. Russell, Bell, Davidson and Ellis urged that practical chemistry should be imperative for University medical students.

[33] *Ibid.*, 284 and Hope's peroration to his lectures (Packet 113 in Hope Papers, Gen. 270, University of Edinburgh Library).

[34] *Ibid.*, 557.

[35] *Ibid.*, 291–2.

[36] Thomson in his "History and Present State of Chemical Science", *The Edinburgh Review*, **1**, 256–76 (276), 1829, explained the decrease in the number of active British chemists after 1800 and the increase in the number of their French and German equivalents in terms of the inadequate method of mere lecturing often employed in Britain.

III

In 1828 the teaching of practical chemistry under Hope's nominal supervision moved into a new phase with the appointment as Hope's assistant of David Boswell Reid, a former pupil of Hope and Anderson.[37] Reid who had taught privately from 1826 was thoroughly convinced that practical chemistry was of paramount importance. In spite of Hope's discouragement he brought such energy to the running of the practical class that in 1828–9 about 120 students attended it. This class was directed by Reid in a room which he rented from the University; its expenses, too, were met by Reid whose status was clearly that of a permitted independent teacher.[38] In early 1829, however, his status became ambivalent when the Royal College of Surgeons of Edinburgh decreed that potential candidates for its licentiate would henceforth be required to attend a suitable course of practical chemistry lasting three months. As Reid was not at this time an M.D., a University Professor, or a member of the Edinburgh College of Surgeons, his class could not be recognized by the Surgeons even though it was conducted with his professor's permission within the University walls. This dilemma was solved by a second arrangement which Hope and Reid made in 1829 to qualify Reid's winter course of that year. The ticket for the practical class was issued as a joint one carrying the names of both Hope and Reid. The former agreed to give an introductory lecture to the practical class which was conducted in Hope's preparation room specially converted by him; he spent £153 on new fixed apparatus which remained his property. In return for qualifying Reid's class and merely giving an introductory lecture, Hope exacted one-third of the profits drawn from the class. Between 1829 and 1832 he took £420 from the practical class, though it was totally conducted by Reid who met at least two-thirds of the expenses and provided portable apparatus at a cost of £300. Reid's weak bargaining power is apparent in these arrangements associated with the joint practical course, which the Surgeons initially refused to recognize

[37] H. Reid, *Memoir of the late David Boswell Reid*, Edinburgh, 1863. Reid's work and career deserve detailed study. His use of cheap small-scale apparatus in his practical classes from the early 1830s allowed him to develop practical chemistry in the popular education movement of this time. See D. B. Reid, "Education—Study of Chemistry", *Chambers Edinburgh Journal*, **v**, 138–9, 158, 1836.

[38] The account of the Reid–Hope arrangements has been chiefly inferred from: D. B. Reid, *A Memorial to the Patrons of the University on the Present State of Practical Chemistry*, Edinburgh, 1833; and T. C. Hope, *Summary of a Memorial to be presented to the Right Honourable The Lord Provost, Magistrates, and Council, respecting the Institution of a Professorship of Practical Chemistry in the University of Edinburgh*, Edinburgh, 1833. There is no reference in the Town Council Minutes to this Memorial by Hope.

on the grounds that Hope's involvement in it was palpably scanty. Nevertheless they were so generally impressed by Reid's work that as a temporary dispensation they agreed to recognize his class until he should become officially qualified. In 1830 Reid gained his M.D. and membership of the College of Surgeons, yet the arrangement he had made in 1829 with Hope persisted until 1832 when Reid resigned. Clearly Reid was prepared to pay a heavy price for his continuing association with the University and its large body of medical students. Perhaps he felt that the Report of the Scottish Universities Commission (October, 1831), if implemented, would permanently secure the position of practical chemistry in the University.[39] In any event his class was popular: on average about 200 students per year attended it. Meanwhile Hope had further compromised himself by proclaiming to his students and to the Scottish Universities Commission that he was determined to give status to practical chemistry, without even bothering to attend the class except in 1829.[40]

IV

Perhaps for these reasons and Hope's reluctance to change his assistant, Reid was able to obtain better terms in yet a third arrangement with Hope which took effect from 1 November, 1832, for the winter session.[41] From the aggregate fees £270 for Reid and all current expenses were deducted, the remainder being equally divided between Reid and Hope who each received £81. As before Reid conducted the class after Hope had given his solitary introductory lecture. Realizing that his practical class with 201 students was as popular as before and that he had just squeezed better terms from Hope, Reid acted decisively in January, 1833, when he addressed a memorial to the Town Council of Edinburgh, then the patrons of the university responsible for its general supervision including matters of curriculum. He proposed that the time was ripe for the Town Council to create a new, independent, and permanent chair of practical chemistry in the University.[42]

Reid forcibly argued that practical chemistry was essential vocationally,

[39] Scottish Universities Commission: the Report relative to the University of Edinburgh, *Parliamentary Papers*, **xii** (1831), 106 recommended: "The Chemical Class is admirably taught; but it would be desirable that the Medical Students should be brought more acquainted with Practical Chemistry, and that a thorough acquaintance with it should be held essential for obtaining a Medical Degree. This, however, would be best derived from private teachers . . .". For a variety of reasons the Report was not implemented.

[40] D. B. Reid, *A Letter to the Honourable The Burgh Commissioners, on the Evidence of Dr. Christison*, Edinburgh, 1835, 8.

[41] Hope, *op, cit.* (38), 15.

[42] Reid, *op. cit.* (38).

it functioned as a branch of liberal education by developing mental and physical skills, the Army and Navy Medical Boards now insisted that potential candidates for their diplomas attended a practical chemistry course, and that in the past the provision in the University for teaching practical chemistry had been precariously irregular. To him there was only one answer: that he should be the first occupant of the chair whose foundation he proposed. The subsequent negotiations, disputes, memorials and counter-memorials involving Hope, Reid, Fyfe, the University Senate and the Town Council are tortuously complex.[43] By 5 June, 1833, however, the matter appeared to be settled. The College Committee of the Town Council by the casting vote of its chairman had recommended that Reid's proposal be rejected; and the Town Council in turn, by the casting vote of the Lord Provost, also decided that the creation of a chair of practical chemistry was inexpedient.[44] Hope, it seemed, had preserved his monopoly at the cost of publicly displayed ill-feeling between his assistant Reid and himself. Such intra-mural hostility and malignance was hardly conducive to the future development of practical chemistry within the University, nor was it likely to encourage the growth of a research school.

One crisis associated with practical chemistry was more than enough; but in November, 1833, a second furore erupted again inspired by Reid who had reverted to private teaching.[45] The situation in the University was that Anderson had returned as Hope's assistant and director of the practical class. Fees were as usual: £4 7s. od. for Hope's lectures; £3 3s. od. for Anderson's class. In the extramural field the announced fee for a combined theoretical and practical course was £6 6s. od., in strict accord with precedent. Reid, however, stole a march on his competitors by offering a practical course for £3 3s. od., and a long theoretical course at only £1 1s. od. instead of the standard £3 3s. od. to those who attended his practical class. Even though the Royal College of Surgeons, previously generous to Reid, disapproved of his action he remained intransigent. In response to Reid's aggression the extramural

[43] The probable order of publication of memorials was as follows: (*a*) Reid, *op. cit.* (38); (*b*) Fyfe, *op. cit.* (20); (*c*) Appendix to Reid, *op. cit.* (38); (*d*) Hope, *op. cit.* (38); (*e*) D. B. Reid, *A Reply to the Report of the Senatus Academicus of the University of Edinburgh, upon Dr. Reid's Memorial to the Honourable the Patrons of the University*, Edinburgh, 1833; (*f*) Reid, *op. cit.* (29). The course of events can be followed from the above, Edinburgh newspapers such as *The Scotsman* and *The Edinburgh Evening Courant*, the College Minutes, and the Town Council Minutes. The critical use of this wide range of independent sources permits one to distinguish between fact and polemic.

[44] Town Council Minutes, 5 June, 1833.

[45] By late 1833 Reid had erected rooms for teaching a new integrally related theoretical—practical course on ground behind the Surgeons' Hall. See: C. H. Creswell, *The Royal College of Surgeons of Edinburgh, Historical Notes from 1505 to 1905*, Edinburgh, 1926, 95–6; H. Reid, *op. cit.* (37), 11.

teachers in self-defence reluctantly undercut him by dropping the total cost of their courses from £6 6s. od. to £3 3s. od. Hope refused to compromise the respectability of the University and himself by reducing his fees. Inevitably Hope's lecture-class suffered some diminution, but the winter practical class was decimated to 8 compared with 111 the previous session! By April, 1834, it had become slowly apparent that, owing to the persistently low fees charged by the extramural teachers, the University practical class would probably not run in the summer session. Accordingly the Town Council, seizing on the possibility of practical chemistry being untaught, decided without consulting the unco-operative Hope to establish a separate and independent lectureship in practical chemistry in the University.[46] As in the previous year the University Senate supported Hope's opposition to the Town Council's scheme admist yet another flurry of accusing pamphlets;[47] but in addition the affluent Hope was so thoroughly determined to prevent interference with his professorial monopoly that he reserved the privilege of taking steps against the bankrupt Town Council to maintain his legal rights.[48] The patrons were impressed. On 5 August, 1834 they resolved by 19 votes to 10 that the lecturer in practical chemistry should hold his appointment from Hope whose professorial privileges would not be infringed.[49] Sensing victory Hope then stone-walled by not making an appointment so that in late August the Town Council decided to advertise the post.[50] The result was quite unambiguous: not one application for the post of lecturer in practical chemistry in the University of Edinburgh was received.[51] Even though chemistry was a popular subject and there was no shortage of competent private teachers in Edinburgh, no chemist was willing to be subject to obvious insecurity or to

[46] Town Council Minutes, 22 April, 1834.

[47] The account of the price-cutting war is based on the following which are listed in probable order of publication: (*a*) Anderson, *op. cit.* (28); (*b*) D. B. Reid, *A letter to the Lord Provost . . . on the present state of practical chemistry*, Edinburgh, 1834; (*c*) J. W. Anderson, *Postscript containing Remarks on a Pamphlet by Dr. Reid*, Edinburgh, 1834; (*d*) W. Gregory, *Observations on the Proposed Appointment of a Teacher of Practical Chemistry in the University; with Remarks on some passages in Dr. Reid's letter to the Council on the subject*, Edinburgh, 1834; (*e*) J. W. Anderson, *Additional observations on the proposed appointment of a teacher of practical chemistry in the University*, Edinburgh, 1834; (*f*) D. B. Reid, *A Letter to the Right Hon. the Lord Provost Magistrates, and Council of Edinburgh, in reply to Observations by Dr. Gregory*, Glasgow?, 1834; (*g*) Evidence of Robert Christison printed in the General Report of the Commissioners appointed to inquire into the State of Municipal Corporations in Scotland, *Parliamentary Papers*, **xxix** (1835), 364–71; (*h*) Reid, *op. cit.* (40).

[48] Report of Town Council meeting of 29 July, 1834, in *The Scotsman*, 30 July, 1834.

[49] Town Council Minutes, 5 August, 1834.

[50] *Ibid.*, 26 August, 1834.

[51] *Ibid.*, 23 September, 1834.

offer himself as a football to be kicked by the contending University and Town Council.

V

The two disputes of 1833 and 1834 not only discredited the University's course of practical chemistry, but they also affected the reputation of the systematic chair. Eminent chemists such as Professors Christison, Edward Turner, and Thomas Thomson all agreed in their evidence to the Municipal Corporations Commission (1835) that the position of the Edinburgh chair of chemistry had become unenviable: its future was uncertain in view of changes which the Town Council could make at its discretion. Both Turner and Thomson laid most blame on the Town Council for unwisely interfering in academic matters; the chemistry chair, formerly regarded as the most important one in the University, would no longer be the object of ambition for the best chemists.[52] These mournful predictions were not incompatible with the subsequent history of practical chemistry in the University. Until Lyon Playfair acceded to the chair in 1858 no significant improvements in practical chemistry took place.[53] The reasons for this stagnation seem clear. Lacking a retirement pension, Hope who was 68 years old in 1834 continued to occupy the chair for nine years and could scarcely be expected at that age to rival younger competitors in Scotland. At a time when the number of students studying medicine and chemistry in the Scottish Universities was declining,[54] Thomas Graham at Anderson's University, Glasgow, and to a less extent

[52] *Op. cit.* (47g), 365, 403, 405, 407. It is significant that Christison and Thomson, both of whom realized the deficiency in Hope's mode of teaching, nevertheless condemned the Town Council's attempt to create a separate chair of practical chemistry. Their criticism was based to a considerable extent on the view that the Town Council had unjustifiably tried to erode the rights and privileges attached to Hope's chair.

[53] L. Playfair, *op. cit.* (9), 29–30; T. W. Reid, *Memoirs and Correspondence of Lyon Playfair*, London, 1899, 179–80; A. Logan Turner, *History of The University of Edinburgh 1883–1933*, Edinburgh and London, 1933, 267.

[54] The size of Hope's class during his incumbency is set out below:

1799, 293;	1808, 382;	1817, 493;	1826, 479;	1835, 211;
1800, 337;	1809, 412;	1818, 475;	1827, 453;	1836, 182;
1801, 345;	1810, 422;	1819, 502;	1828, 493;	1837, 163;
1802, 335;	1811, 473;	1820, 479;	1829, 432;	1838, 165;
1803, 270;	1812, 441;	1821, 497;	1830, 430;	1839, 113;
1804, 329;	1813, 515;	1822, 554;	1831, 395;	1840, 138;
1805, 342;	1814, 477;	1823, 559;	1832, 366;	1841, 129;
1806, 317;	1815, 508;	1824, 519;	1833, 234;	1842, 118;
1807, 386;	1816, 522;	1825, 505;	1834, 215;	

The figures for years 1799 to 1829 inclusive are taken from Edinburgh Evidence, *op. cit.* (8), Appendix, 130; those for the remaining years have been kindly given to me by Mr. C. P. Finlayson, Keeper of Manuscripts, University of Edinburgh Library.

Thomson at the University of Glasgow attracted young chemists; and the challenge offered by the Edinburgh extramural teachers was considerable.[55] Within the University changes were made only with difficulty: from at least 1824 until 1858 when the Universities (Scotland) Act was passed, the University Senate and the Town Council were generally at war. The former asserted its academic freedom; the latter autocratically exerted when possible its legally sanctioned rights of patronage and supervision.[56] Both sides were prepared in extreme cases to pursue expensive litigation in order to break dead-lock. The prevalence of such bitter suspicion and dissension limited the possibilities of academic reform.

VI

In retrospect it is clear that the debates and decisions of 1833 and 1834 reveal a delicately complex situation in which neither Hope nor Reid was totally to blame. On Reid's side it is apparent that he rapidly increased the popularity of the University practical class by offering an intensive course concerned mainly with basic skills of manipulation such as filtration and analysis with the blow-pipe. Even his opponents such as Anderson and William Gregory acknowledged his qualities.[57] Unlike Hope he encouraged his students to ask questions, an attitude which compensated his drill-sergeant method of teaching.[58] From his point of view he was doing the work while Hope scooped in the profits like a tax-collector, particularly from 1831 when Hope tried to gain credit from his class. To Reid, Hope was a lazy, rich reactionary not interested in practical chemistry which he neither supported nor directed.[59] Explicitly linking his efforts to the age of reform in which entrenched privileges and exclusive institutions were scrutinized, Reid argued that he merely wanted Hope to be replaced by the Town Council as the patron of the new chair: the future of practical chemistry was too important to be merely left to the personal whims of the professor. The force of Reid's position is shown for instance by the Whig support he received

[55] Graham's students at Anderson's included Stenhouse, Playfair, Gilbert, the Griffins and Crum (Smith, *op. cit.* (1), 66). At Edinburgh in 1835 at least four classes of practical chemistry were conducted by William Gregory (who had pioneered a separate lecture course on organic chemistry from 1831), Kenneth Kemp, Andrew Fyfe, and the irrepressible David Boswell Reid.

[56] A. Grant, *op. cit.* (26), ii, 14–83.

[57] Anderson, *op. cit.* (47c), 8; Gregory, *op. cit.* (47d), 8.

[58] Christison, *op. cit.* (24), i, 344.

[59] Traill, *op. cit.* (2), 427, admitted: "Dr. Hope had always endeavoured to impress his pupils with the importance of Practical Chemistry, and introduced it into the University classes for the cultivation of that branch of study; but, from increasing years, and *love of ease*, this department he soon almost wholly abandoned to his assistants" (my italics).

from *The Scotsman.*[60] In contrast Hope was unimpressed by Reid's reforming zeal: the professor saw his assistant as a brash upstart who suffered from inflated delusions of grandeur.[61] After only four full years as director of the University practical class Reid's unconcealed self-interest had led him to propose the establishment of an independent chair. Hence Hope chiefly relied on arguments such as the infringement of his legal professorial monopoly, the inevitable reduction of his income owing to competition from the proposed chair, and the likely decrease in status of his chair in the future. Furthermore in the 1830s Hope and the Senate continued to see chemistry as an ancillary subject. Various versions of Hope's introductory lecture to the practical class show that he conceived practical chemistry as a technically useful tool in a wide range of activities from pharmacy to surveying.[62] The subsidiary place of chemistry to medicine was also stressed by the Senate in its Report of 30 April, 1833, to the Town Council.[63] The University pointed out that the only practical chemistry course of use in a medical school was one in which students merely repeated the experiments used as illustrations in the lectures given by the professor of chemistry and medicine. For the Senate chemistry was only one of many subjects in a crowded medical curriculum and the time already spent on it was quite sufficient. Consequently the Senate unanimously agreed that it would be absurd to increase the time devoted to the subordinate subject of chemistry in any form. There is no doubt that the medical ambience of chemistry restricted its development as an autonomous subject.

This theme was developed in a little-known, but significant, pamphlet[64] published in 1842 by William Gregory, then Professor of Medicine and Chemistry at King's College, Aberdeen, who in 1844 succeeded Hope in the

[60] "Proposed Chair of Practical Chemistry", *The Scotsman*, 4 May, 1833. This editorial brushed Hope's interests to one side: "Must all improvements be proscribed, for the sake of preserving the professor's emoluments! And must the mode of teaching remain at the point where it stood thirty years ago, when Dr. Hope got his chair, until he die or resign!" It must be said that Hope's indifference to practical chemistry allowed Reid's supporters to argue on the basis of Hope's behaviour that theoretical and practical chemistry could validly be separated.

[61] Anderson, *op. cit.* (47c), 12.

[62] One of Hope's introductions to the practical class (Packet 118 in the Hope Papers, Gen. 271, University of Edinburgh Library) which must date from 1829 asserts that practical chemistry is useful in the following: chemical research, physiology, pathology, pharmacy, toxicology, civil and military engineering, industrial chemistry, mineralogy, valuation of land; and it provides indoor "rational amusement" for country gentlemen in wet weather.

[63] Senate Minutes, 30 April, 1833.

[64] W. Gregory, *Letter to the Right Honourable George Earl of Aberdeen on the state of the schools of chemistry in the United Kingdom*, London, 1842.

Edinburgh chair. In an appeal addressed to the Earl of Aberdeen, at that time Foreign Secretary and Chancellor of King's College, Gregory contrasted the lack of cheap opportunities for laboratory training and research in Britain with those readily available under Liebig at the University of Giessen where he had studied. The relevance of Gregory's pamphlet to this paper is that Gregory showed *inter alia* how different financial arrangements could encourage or inhibit the growth of schools of research organized to produce professional chemists. Gregory stressed that the Scottish Universities paid the capital outlay for a laboratory, while the professors met their annual expenses for materials, apparatus and assistance from their own pockets. The expenses being high, low fees were likely to reduce the professor's income, high ones to prohibit attendance by all except rich students. In this situation there was no inducement to the professor to expand the facilities for practical work. At Giessen, however, Liebig had been enabled by the liberality of the Duke of Hesse-Darmstadt "to open his laboratory, provided as it is with everything necessary for research, on terms which allow almost every student *with ease* to avail himself of the opportunity".[65] In detail it seems that the state provided Liebig with a free house, a large salary, expensive laboratory equipment, annual running expenses of £130 per year, a salaried assistant and a salaried laboratory steward. Consequently the Giessen course of pure practical chemistry, which ran for six full days per week for eight to nine months, cost only £6 14s. 0d.[66] In contrast, for a course of practical chemistry orientated towards pharmacy Edinburgh students paid £3 3s. 0d. for tuition one hour a day for five days per week for three months. No wonder Giessen attracted British students. Edinburgh, of course, possessed no equivalent to the generosity displayed in Hesse-Darmstadt. All the Scottish Universities were poor, but the biggest one, Edinburgh, with its large and costly medical school, was a special case. Its recent historian stresses that "the financial situation deteriorated markedly in the years after 1831. In 1835 a memorial from the Senatus begging for government help was brusquely rejected by the Lords of the Treasury. By this time the bankruptcy of the town council had been publicly acknowledged. . .".[67] Quite apart therefore from the personal quirks

[65] *Ibid.*, 20 (my italics). Note that Gregory was describing the post–1835 situation at Giessen.

[66] *Ibid.*, 22. Gregory had previously pointed out that for a full-time course of practical chemistry the usual fee in Paris for a course of eight months was £60 and in London for one of six months it was about £50 (*ibid.*, 18). Even if Gregory had cited the highest Paris and London fees, it remains obvious that Liebig's course was the best buy financially and in other ways.

[67] D. B. Horn, *A Short History of the University of Edinburgh* 1556–1889, Edinburgh, 1967, 168.

of Hope and Reid and other matters previously discussed, there were formidable financial obstacles to the development at Edinburgh of a research school on Giessen lines. At least on this issue the British policy of self-help was manifestly inadequate.[68]

ACKNOWLEDGEMENTS

I am indebted to the following for their valuable help: the Librarian and the Keeper of Manuscripts of the University of Edinburgh; and the Archivist of Edinburgh Corporation. This article was read to the Society for the Study of Alchemy and Early Chemistry 22 March, 1969.

[68] The conditions in which Thomas Thomson and Liebig ran their practical classes were strikingly different. Thomson's laudable enterprise, in mounting a practical class for a small group of full-time students at the relatively cheap rate of £1 per month, brought him little profit: the fees he took barely covered his expenses. In any event, as at Edinburgh his subject was constrained by its medical context. He bore the heavy burden of giving frequent lectures to medical students; but Liebig, ensconced in the Philosophy faculty at Giessen, taught informally mainly in his laboratory. Again Thomson could offer no qualification to his successful laboratory students, whereas Liebig's could quickly gain the coveted Ph.D. (I am indebted to Dr. W. V. Farrar for stressing this last point.)

The Patronage of Mid-Victorian Science in the University of Edinburgh*

During the nineteenth century the intellectual activity known as science was transformed into a profession. Though national and indeed local differences were apparent, this process seems to have been associated with several characteristic features. Firstly, specialization grew rapidly. Secondly, those who pursued positive knowledge and understanding of nature became self-conscious about the aims and the characteristics of their work. One obvious indication of this self-awareness was that in 1834 William Whewell coined the term 'scientist' to designate collectively those who studied nature; from that time scientists slowly began to displace natural philosophers, cultivators of science, and men of science.[1] Thirdly, the related search for public recognition of scientists and of their work became intensified. This quest for social justification and legitimation showed itself most obviously in the formation of societies and pressure groups of which the best known in this country was the British Association for the Advancement of Science which was founded in 1831. The aims of this Association were quite clearly defined from the start:

> To give a stronger impulse and a more systematic direction to scientific enquiry,—to promote the intercourse of those who cultivate Science in different parts of the British Empire, with one another and with foreign philosophers,—to obtain a more general attention to the objects of Science, and a removal of any disadvantages of a public kind which impede its progress.[2]

* For much valuable criticism I am indebted to Dr R. M. MacLeod, the referees and my colleague, Dr D. Fraser. A first draft of this paper was written for a conference on 'The Patronage of Science in the Nineteenth Century', organized by the Past and Present Society and by the British Society for the History of Science, held on 14 April 1972 at the Royal Society of London. For permission to use and quote from material under his care I am grateful to Mr C. P. Finlayson, Keeper of Manuscripts, University of Edinburgh Library.

[1] S. Ross, 'Scientist: the Story of a Word', *Annals of Science,* **18** (1962), 65–85 (71–2).

[2] The objects and rules of the British Association were always printed immediately after the list of contents in any *Report of the British Association for the Advancement of Science.*

Fourthly, as the century passed more full-time jobs in scientific work became available. Lastly, by the mid-century experimental science had secured itself as an intellectually legitimate activity in some European universities: the teaching of practical science in laboratories had been successfully launched and research schools based on laboratories had emerged.[3]

If we confine ourselves to Britain, the astonishing growth of specialization in science, of self-consciousness shown by scientists, and of public recognition of both science and scientists, is graphically illustrated by the increase in the number of societies devoted to advancing and diffusing science. In 1760, England, Wales, Scotland and Ireland mustered just a dozen formal groups which concerned themselves either centrally or marginally with science. By 1870, the number had increased from twelve to about 125, of which fifty-nine were restricted to particular sciences.[4] In particular cities as for example Edinburgh, such a dramatic increase in the number of societies also took place: in 1780 there was only one formally constituted scientific society; ninety years later, at least eight societies were active. These included the Royal Society of Edinburgh (chartered 1783) which was the most prestigious, the Geological Society of Edinburgh (founded 1834), the Botanical Society of Edinburgh (founded 1836), the Royal Scottish Society of Arts (founded 1821), the Scottish Meteorological Society (founded 1856) as well as fringe groups such as the Medico-Chirurgical Society (founded 1821), the Scottish Society of Antiquaries (chartered 1783), the Highland and Agricultural Society (founded 1784), and the Royal Medical Society (founded 1737, chartered 1778) which was run by and for students.

I

For much of the nineteenth century, the virtues of individualism, libertarianism, voluntarism and, above all, self-help were lauded in Britain from Adam Smith in 1776 to John Stuart Mill and Samuel Smiles in 1859. It was widely accepted as a principle or as an aspiration that government should depart from the ideal state of *laissez-faire* only in those hopefully exceptional circumstances in which individual action was unable to satisfy an overwhelming need. Indeed, the social philosophy of early and mid-Victorianism

[3] J. B. Morrell, 'The Chemist Breeders: the Research Schools of Liebig and Thomas Thomson', *Ambix*, **19** (1972), 1–46.

[4] A. Thackray, 'Reflections on the Decline of Science in America and on Some of its Causes', *Science*, **173** (1971), 27–31 (29).

saw the persistent apotheosis of the Smilesian virtues of work, thrift, duty, respectability and self-help. Yet by 1870 intervention by the central government, in order to establish the conditions necessary for civilized social life, was firmly established. The age in which unfettered individualism flourished as a social philosophy paradoxically witnessed a long series of reforms on which, by about 1870, the foundations of a centralized social-service state had been laid.

This apparent contradiction has generated a variety of explanations and the debate still continues.[5] If, however, we are concerned to understand why the British government by 1870 was still unwilling to disturb the individualism which was prevalent in the organization of British science, we must apprehend all the possible circumstances which were likely to provoke collective action by the state. Generally it seems that state intervention took place when at least one of four conditions was fulfilled: first, when the existence of an intolerable situation, such as children working in mines, deeply stirred humanitarian consciences; second, when apposite opportunities arose for the deployment of Benthamite utilitarianism, which could subsume both collectivism and individualism in different proportions depending on the context of its application; third, when opportunities or needs existed which could be exploited in the interests of desirable social control, of which an obvious example was public education conceived as an insurance against unrest or discontent in the future; fourth, when certain aspects of life were deemed a threat to national security and supremacy. These four situations were, of course, not totally separable and could fuse into each other. In addition it must be stressed that when any one or all four of these situations occurred, the response of the state was generally practical, unplanned and basically *ad hoc*. Whether the means adopted were ideologically acceptable or dubious, the mid-Victorian administrative state had to solve pressing and disagreeable problems by devising appropriate administrative expedients. The patent deficiencies of an urbanizing and industrializing society provoked a series of piecemeal responses by the state,

[5] A. V. Dicey, *Lectures on the Relation between Law and Public Opinion in England during the Nineteenth Century*, 2nd edn. (London, 1914); J. B. Brebner, 'Laissez-faire and State Intervention in Nineteenth-century Britain', *Journal of Economic History*, Supplement to **8** (1948, 59–73; O. O. G. M. MacDonagh, 'The Nineteenth-Century Revolution in Government: A Reappraisal', *The Historical Journal*, **1** (1958), 52–67; H. Parris, 'The Nineteenth-Century Revolution in Government: A Reappraisal Reappraised', *The Historical Journal*, **3** (1960), 17–37; J. Hart, 'Nineteenth-Century Social Reform: A Tory Interpretation of History', *Past and Present*, **31** (1965), 39–61; R. M. MacLeod, *Treasury Control and Social Administration* (London, 1968); D. Fraser, *The Evolution of the British Welfare State* (London, 1973).

whether these were unwelcome or unexpected. As a result of these measures various groups in society became protected from the extreme pressures of a competitive capitalist society: for instance, paupers, women workers, and lunatics were the direct beneficiaries of state action.

If we look at British science *circa* 1870, its condition did not provide three of the four circumstances under which state intervention was likely to occur. Compared with, say, problems of public health or even overhauling of the judiciary, the financial problems faced by some British scientists seemed trivial, peripheral, and therefore dispensable. Nor is it clear that British science in 1870 provided signally favourable opportunities or abuses out of which widespread and vigorous concern could be rapidly generated by Benthamite utilitarians. Again it is not clear that many aspects of science, with the exception of scientific-cum-technical instruction for the working class, could be exploited in the interests of desirable social control. With respect to British science *circa* 1870 there is therefore little doubt that three pre-requisites for state intervention did not occur. Yet, the fourth condition for state action, that of a perceived threat to national security or supremacy, could be made relevant to the condition of British research and teaching in science in the mid-Victorian period. Indeed the connection between the state of British science and the possible erosion of British technical supremacy had been tenuously established paradoxically at the time of the Great Exhibition of 1851.

Though that Exhibition celebrated the zenith of Victorian technical achievement, some warning voices were raised.[6] Prince Albert and Lyon Playfair in particular urged that Britain would retain her economic supremacy only if she gave much more attention to technical training and to the scientific basis of technical innovation and advance. Albert's peroration to his presidential address delivered in 1859 to the British Association for the Advancement of Science summarized his attitude:

> We may be justified in hoping, however, that by the gradual diffusion of Science, and its increasing recognition as a principal part of our national education, the public in general, no less than the Legislature and the State, will more and more recognize the claims of Science to their attention; so that it may no longer require the begging-box, but speak to the State, like a favoured child to its parent, sure of his parental solicitude for its welfare; that the State will recognize in Science one of its elements of strength and prosperity, to foster which the clearest dictates of self-interest demand.[7]

[6] D. S. L. Cardwell, *The Organisation of Science in England* (London, 1957), 58–62.

[7] The Prince Consort, 'Presidential Address', *Report of the British Association for the Advancement of Science: 1859* (London, 1860), lix–lxix (lxviii).

Albert indeed put one point quite clearly: that British science had to elevate its relation with government from being a beggar to being a favoured child. But of course the onus for making a compelling case for extensive state patronage of science did not lie with government, as Albert hinted, but with the scientists themselves. Invariably the mid-Victorian Parliament did not move until a compelling case had been irrefutably substantiated by some private or official body: the norm was self-help; any proposed deviation from that norm had to be buttressed with irresistible evidence and argument.

Fortunately for scientists and propagandists such as Playfair, the bogey of possible loss of British technical supremacy could be, and was, invoked during the 1860s.[8] In particular, the poor performance of some British manufacturers at the Great International Exhibition held in Paris in 1867 produced such alarm that the movement for more and better technical instruction was vigorously launched by early 1868. Simultaneously, Colonel Alexander Strange opened a campaign for more state support of research in physical sciences appropriately before the British Association in 1868. As a result of the initiative of Strange and of the support given to his programme by the small yet influential group of London scientists known as the 'X-Club', the British Association approached the Government in late 1869 for a formal enquiry concerning the national provision made for scientific instruction and the advancement of science. In February 1870 Gladstone agreed to appoint the famous Devonshire Commission to root out the facts of the matter. The Playfair-school and its brethren, though divided on the question of salaries from government to scientific researchers, had successfully used two main levers to prise from a reluctant government the typical Victorian device of a Royal Commission: they had wounded national pride by drawing attention to the possible loss of British technical and economic dominance, and by making invidious and embarrassing comparisons between the patronage of research in Britain and Germany. The Devonshire Commission sat for six years and did a very thorough job. It recommended *inter alia* that State laboratories and increased research grants for private individuals be provided, and urged the establishment of a Ministry of Science and Education with a Council of Science to assist it. The Government ignored most of the costly recommendations made by the Devonshire Commission so that the voluntarist tradition of the organization of British science continued.

[8] *Op. cit.* note 6, 84–98; R. M. MacLeod, 'The Support of Victorian Science: The Endowment of Research Movement in Great Britain, 1868–1900', *Minerva*, **9** (1971), 197–230 (200–6); *idem*, 'The X Club: A Social Network of Science in late-Victorian England', *Notes and Records of the Royal Society of London*, **24** (1969), 305–22.

Yet during the 1860s and early 1870s the state was by no means inactive in patronizing, both formally and tacitly, some forms of scientific activity. If we confine ourselves to the less obscure government institutions, it is clear that from the 1850s in particular considerable expenditure had been consciously devoted to science. Characteristically much of this spending by government was justified in terms of commercial, military, or national benefit. As this patronage was administered by a variety of government departments, there was of course no pervading system by which government expenditure on scientific institutions was regulated. The parliamentary estimates for 1874–5, listed in Table 1, bring out clearly the extent and purpose of regular expenditure by the state on its chief scientific institutions.[9]

In addition to this regular expenditure on institutions, considerable sums

TABLE 1

Department	*Organization*	*Estimate (£s)*
Treasury (Office of Works)	Topographical Survey	132,000
Admiralty	Hydrographical Survey	121,055
Privy Council	Geological Survey	22,920
Admiralty	Astronomy: Greenwich Observatory	5,642
Admiralty	Astronomy: Cape of Good Hope Observatory	3,371
Treasury (Office of Works)	Astronomy: Edinburgh Observatory	690
Meteorological Committee, Admiralty, Treasury	Meterology	12,082
Treasury (Office of Works)	Botanical Gardens: Kew, Edinburgh, Dublin	21,470
Board of Trade	Standards Department	2,063
Total		321,293

Source: Eighth Report of the Royal Commission on Scientific Instruction and the Advancement of Science [*c.* 1298], Parlimentary Papers, xxviii (1875), 49–50.

[9] *Eighth Report of the Royal Commission on Scientific Instruction and the Advancement of Science* [*c.* 1298], Parliamentary Papers, xxviii (1875), 49–50. Furthermore, State intervention via legislation and the accompanying growth of a centralized administration created posts for scientists. See the list of departments and commissions existing in 1854 in: D. Roberts, *Victorian Origins of the British Welfare State* (Hamden, Conn., 1969), 93–5; R. M. MacLeod, 'The Alkali Acts Administration, 1863–1884: The Emergence of the Civil Scientist', *Victorian Studies*, **11** (1965), 86–112.

of money had also been spent from time to time, especially by the Admiralty and the War Department, on a variety of enterprises from the *Challenger* voyage (1872–6), the transit of Venus expedition (1874), to the experiments on armour-plate and explosives done for the army and navy. Perhaps, therefore, with pardonable exaggeration, an editorial in *Nature* concluded that 'the fact of an expenditure, reaching probably about half a million, annually, without any pretence of a system to regulate it, is one in itself deserving very serious consideration'.[10] Though this expenditure seemed unco-ordinated, the rationale behind it was clear: that is, in pursuit of prospective commercial, military and national benefits, various government departments had set up, on an *ad hoc* basis, permanent or temporary institutions to do scientific work for those departments. Indeed, throughout the nineteenth century successive governments and the Treasury regarded the Geological Survey as being a merely temporary public service which should cease to exist once all the United Kingdom had been geologically mapped.[11]

The salient features of the support for scientific work given by mid-Victorian governments become even more comprehensible if we keep in mind the characteristics of the government's wider responsibilities in the general field of social policy. The basis of a centralized bureaucratic social-service state had been laid by 1870 not as the result of implementing enlightened ideals but, on the contrary, by a series of unplanned, *ad hoc*, piecemeal responses by the state to urgent social problems. If the response to the pressing problems of public health was *ad hoc*, then the response to the less pressing problem of state patronage of science was likely to be even more so. In any event, the case of some relatively well-heeled scientists begging money from the state was different in kind from the deprivation suffered by drunkards, prostitutes, exploited children, lunatics, and genuine paupers. Until scientists could mount an overwhelming case for extended and regular state patronage of science, the appropriate department of government was unlikely to open its coffers except when it occasionally indulged in some piecemeal response to a particular request or situation. Given the general circumstances which provoked collective action by the various mid-Victorian British governments, it would be unhistorical to berate them for their alleged parsimony and occasional haphazard benevolence towards pure science. The burden of justification lay not with the state but with those scientists who urged the case of more state patronage.

10 *Nature*, **12** (1875), 305.
11 A. Geikie, *A Long Life's Work: An Autobiography* (London, 1924), 304.

II

I want now to turn to the University of Edinburgh during the 1860s and early 1870s in order to see how one very important institution exemplifies the themes which I have already enunciated. My reasons for choosing this particular institution are quite simple. From the 1720s onwards it had deliberately cultivated medicine and science as its chief magnets to students. By the early 1770s it had become for science perhaps the pre-eminent university in the English speaking world as a result of a deliberate policy of recruiting professors who were both competent scholars and proved teachers.[12] From the 1820s onwards the University had faced severe problems of two different kinds: new and refurbished institutions, both at home and abroad, energetically challenged its scientific reputation and competed for students; and within Edinburgh a thirty years' war was fought between the Senate and Town Council, the latter being responsible for the supervision and maintenance of the University including appointments to most chairs.[13] That strife for sovereignty ended only in 1858 when the Universities (Scotland) Act was passed by Parliament.

In 1860 the University began to recover its reputation. Other British universities housed some science professors who were distinguished in both research and teaching, such as William Thomson, professor of natural philosophy at the University of Glasgow. At Edinburgh during the 1860s and early 1870s all its science professors were active in research and many were formidable teachers. It may have been true, as Edward Frankland suggested to the Devonshire Commission, that the slow progress of original research in England was chiefly the result of 'the entire non-recognition of original research by any of our Universities'.[14] The situation at Edinburgh was, however, somewhat different: the scientific professors were paid primarily to teach; though the research ethos was nothing like as intense and as compelling as in German universities, without exception these professors used their chairs to do research. During these years, the medical school of the University acquired again its high reputation and became the

[12] J. B. Morrell, 'The University of Edinburgh in the late Eighteenth Century: its Scientific Eminence and Academic Structure', *Isis*, **62** (1971), 158–71.

[13] J. B. Morrell, 'Individualism and the Structure of British Science in 1830', *Historical Studies in the Physical Sciences*, **3** (1971), 183–204; *idem*, 'Science and Scottish University Reform: Edinburgh in 1826', *British Journal for the History of Science*, **6** (1972), 39–56.

[14] *Third Report of the Royal Commission on Scientific Instruction and the Advancement of Science* [*c*. 868], Parliamentary Papers, xxviii (1873), 58.

largest in Britain in terms of student numbers. By 1874–5 the number of medical students had almost reached nine hundred, of whom 333 were born in England, twenty-one in Ireland, fifty-seven in India, ninety-seven in the colonies, eighteen in foreign countries, and only 369 in Scotland.[15] Though the medical school was the chief attraction of the University to students, the University's decline from international importance is shown by the low proportion (2%) of foreigners in the medical student body. The medical school was imperial but not international in character. Yet Edinburgh, the third largest British university, was like most of the other three Scottish universities in being financially impoverished, particularly relative to the aggregate wealth of the colleges of Oxford and Cambridge. Again in contrast with the old English universities, medical and physical sciences at Edinburgh had been central to the life and attractions of the University for decades. In no other British university at the time was there such a contrast between ambition and capacity with respect to research and teaching in science; and the problems concerned with the expansion of university scientific research and teaching were more sharply felt there than elsewhere in Britain. To facilitate discussion, information about the Edinburgh professoriate in science and medicine between 1860 and about 1875 is arranged by faculty and given in Table 2.[16]

By the early 1870s the University housed thirty-six professors under the principalship of Sir Alexander Grant (1868–84), who had succeeded Sir David Brewster (1859–68), the first physicist to be appointed head of any British university. Four of these chairs belonged to the Faculty of Theology, six to Law, twelve to Medicine, and fourteen to Arts. No separate Faculty of Science existed until 1893, matters concerning science being the province of a Committee of the Faculty of Arts.

In order to understand the organization of scientific teaching and research in the mid-Victorian University of Edinburgh, we must first analyse its peculiarly Scottish internal structure as it related to science. An Edinburgh professor was nominated to his chair either by the Crown or by the seven Curators of Patronage, of whom three were elected by the University Court and four by Edinburgh Town Council. Once he was ensconced in his chair he enjoyed, at least intra-murally, the legal monopoly of his subject. As intra-mural competition within a field was not permitted,

[15] *Report of the Royal Commissioners appointed to enquire into the Universities of Scotland: Returns and Documents* [*c.* 1935–III], Parliamentary Papers, xxxv (1878), 523.

[16] Table 2 is based on: A. Grant, *The Story of the University of Edinburgh* (London, 1884); A. Logan Turner, *History of the University of Edinburgh, 1883–1933* (Edinburgh and London, 1933); *Edinburgh University Calendar: 1871–1872* (Edinburgh, 1872).

TABLE 2

Chair	*Faculty*	*Founded*	*Patron*	*Incumbent(s) 1860–75*
Botany	Medicine	1676	Curators	John Hutton Balfour 1845–79
Institutes of Medicine	Medicine	1685	Curators	John Hughes Bennett 1848–74
Practice of Medicine	Medicine	1685	Curators	Thomas Laycock 1855–76
Anatomy	Medicine	1705	Curators	John Goodsir 1846–67 William Turner 1867–1903
Chemistry	Medicine	1713	Curators	Lyon Playfair 1858–69 Alexander Crum Brown 1869–1908
Midwifery	Medicine	1726	Curators	Sir James Young Simpson 1840–70 Alexander Russell Simpson 1870–1905
Natural History	Medicine	1767	Crown	George James Allmann 1855–70 Charles Wyville Thomson 1870–82
Materia Medica	Medicine	1768	Curators	Sir Robert Christison 1832–77
Clinical Surgery	Medicine	1803	Crown	James Syme 1833–69 Joseph Lister 1869–77
Medical Jurisprudence	Medicine	1807	Crown	Thomas Stewart Traill 1832–62 Andrew Douglas MacLagan 1862–97
Surgery	Medicine	1831	Curators	James Miller 1842–64 James Spence 1864–82
Pathology	Medicine	1831	Curators	William Henderson 1842–69 William Rutherford Sanders 1869–81
Natural Philosophy	Arts	1708	Curators	Peter Guthrie Tait 1860–1901
Practical Astronomy	Arts	1786	Crown	Charles Piazzi Smyth 1846–89
Agriculture	Arts	1790	Lords of Session, Curators, & University Court	John Wilson 1854–88
Engineering	Arts	1868	Crown	Henry Charles Fleeming Jenkin 1868–85
Geology	Arts	1871	Crown	Archibald Geikie 1871–82

Source: A. Grant, *The Story of the University of Edinburgh* (London, 1884); A. Logan Turner, *History of the University of Edinburgh, 1883–1933* (Edinburgh and London, 1933); and *Edinburgh University Calendar: 1871–1872* (Edinburgh, 1872).

Edinburgh professors were protected from the bracing rivalry which the *privatdozents* so conspicuously provided in the German universities. There was no question of having several teachers lecturing concurrently on sub-divisions of a subject, a practice by that time well established in the larger German universities such as Berlin: each professor enjoyed exclusive possession of his subject and carried the appropriate burdens. From the 1850s, however, some professors had been helped in their teaching by assistants appointed by the University as distinct from the traditional personal assistants to particular professors. By the mid-1870s about forty-five assistants were employed in the University, two-thirds of them being attached to scientific or medical chairs.[17] Of this group of thirty, only one was paid by the government, and then at a salary of only £100 per year. Six enjoyed constant salaries totalling £550 per year from the University Fund. The others were paid fluctuating salaries either from the University Fund by an annual allocation by Senate of from their professor's own pocket. Irrespective of the sources of his salary, each assistant was totally subject to his professor's control, whether as deputy-lecturer, tutor, examiner, laboratory assistant, or research assistant.

This system of professorial monopoly was closely related to the system of remuneration which was adopted until 1893 in the Scottish universities generally, and in a more extreme form at Edinburgh. An Edinburgh science professor derived his emolument, out of which he frequently met some of the expenses of his class, mainly from the class-fee which each of his students paid directly to him. His basic salary was usually low: indeed until 1858, five medical professors received no salary whatsoever; after 1858, as a result of the Universities (Scotland) Act, only the professor of anatomy remained without salary. The class-fee system encouraged professors to be student-orientated and to keep themselves in business as teachers. Not surprisingly, many professors, like many of the public, saw teaching as their primary function, and any moves which might have reduced the number of students were strenuously resisted. The class-fee system stimulated ambitious professors to acquire and maintain large classes, and of course it discouraged sinecuring. In sharp contrast to the German universities, it was associated with the absence of admission requirements for most of the classes which allowed many professors to recruit classes sufficiently big to ensure adequate remuneration. It also harmonized with the privilege of *lernfreiheit*: provided his pocket and his professor allowed him, any person of any age and training could attend any of the classes in whatever number

[17] *Op. cit.* note 15, 347–55.

and order best suited him. Though graduation in medicine had become the norm during the 1870s, only one in five or six students graduated in arts. Hence the nature of his subject affected each professor profoundly. If he taught a subject which was compulsory for graduation as well as being fashionable, he possessed a guaranteed audience whose size he could hopefully increase from year to year. If, however, his subject was not compulsory for graduation he was thrown into the academic market-place to search for students. No wonder that some classes were far more remunerative than others. Table 3 shows that in the mid-Victorian period the University professors succeeded in their search for students, particularly medical ones.[18] Table 4 provides information about the greatly varying sizes of the science classes during the early 1870s.[19] Table 5 demonstrates with striking clarity

TABLE 3

Year	*Arts Students*	*Divinity Students*	*Law Students*	*Medical Students*	*Total Number of Students*
1861–2	623	94	202	543	1,462
1862–3	613	76	272	549	1,510
1863–4	616	77	278	509	1,480
1864–5	637	74	254	475	1,440
1865–6	660	67	292	458	1,477
1866–7	708	64	296	457	1,525
1867–8	665	65	338	445	1,513
1868–9	661	75	311	517	1,564
1869–70	702	67	343	586	1,698
1870–1	687	68	335	678	1,768
1871–2	729	57	343	725	1,854
1872–3	737	58	329	782	1,906
1873–4	711	59	321	839	1,930
1874–5	793	66	318	899	2,076
1875–6	774	58	337	896	2,065
1876–7	894	70	317	1070	2,351

Source: Report of the Royal Commissioners appointed to enquire into the Universities of Scotland: Returns and Documents [*c.* 1935–III], Parliamentary Papers, xxxv (1878), 335.

18 *Ibid.*, 335.
19 *Ibid.*, 336–40.

TABLE 4

Year	Natural Philosophy Lecture	Natural Philosophy Advanced	Natural Philosophy Laboratory		Agriculture Lecture	Geology Lecture	Engineering Lecture	Engineering Mechanical Drawing	Engineering Surveying	Materia Medica Lecture
1871–2	180	4	9		21	41	20	16	9	132
1872–3	183	9	13		26	18	29	14	9	143
1873–4	198	9	19		19	22	21	20	9	150
			W	S						
1874–5	213	11	10		30	32	33	11	16	165
1875–6	229	7	12	14	32	26	35	15	9	170
1876–7	219	7	14	10	34	25	32	9	13	167

TABLE 4 (*contd.*)

Year	*Chemistry Lecture*	*Chemistry Advanced*	*Chemistry Demonstration in a Laboratory*		*Chemistry Laboratory*		*Physiology Lecture*	*Physiology Laboratory*		*Practical Astronomy Lecture*	*Anatomy Lecture*	*Anatomy Practical W*
			W	S	W	S		W	S			
1871–2	195	6	14	107	4	5	147	26	103	0	305	334
1872–3	203	7	9	118	12	9	161	21	105	0	311	357
1873–4	222	6	7	124	10	12	151	23	108	0	280	351
1874–5	216	9	22	143	9	16	161	18	107	0	313	383
1875–6	243	9	34	169	16	23	187	38	120	0	336	392
1876–7	264	9	35	172	15	21	242	52	133	0	324	435

TABLE 4 (*contd.*)

Year	*Anatomy Demonstrations*	*Anatomy Practical and Demonstrations*	*Pathology Lecture*	*Pathology Laboratory*		*Natural History Lecture*		*Natural History Laboratory*	*Botany Lecture*	*Botany Laboratory*
	W	S		*W*	S	W	S	S		
1871–2	149	106	128	—	22	31	219	21	283	38
1872–3	133	137	140	—	17	—	246	39	307	36
1873–4	99	123	146	—	—		266	17	354	43
1874–5	109	135	151	—	—	—	350	20	343	65
1875–6	145	126	157	7	58	—	317	12	343	66
1876–7	121	172	167	63	95	54	411	33	389	57

Key: W means Winter Session (November–April); S means Summer Session (May–July).

Source: Report of the Royal Commissioners appointed to enquire into the Universities of Scotland: Returns and Documents [*c.* 1935–III], Parliamentary Papers xxxv (1878), 336–40.

TABLE 5

Chair	Salary (nearest £)	Government Contribution to Salary by Parliamentary Grant (£)	CLASS FEES (£) 1871–2	1872–3	1873–4	1874–5	1875–6
Natural Philosophy	202 *from 1874* *268*	180	570	603	664	671	745
Agriculture	350 *from 1873* *370*	150	88	109	79	126	134
Geology	400	200	150	67	105	122	75
Engineering	400	200	155	193	190	190	236
Materia Medica	100	100	530	509	612	673	667
Chemistry	200	200	1,225	1,329	1,429	1,578	1,879
Physiology	150	150	—	no data	—	1,047	1,235
Practical Astronomy	300	300	0	0	0	0	0
Anatomy	0	0	2,277	2,409	2,323	2,510	2,645
Pathology	100	100	680	703	715	748	774
Natural History	196	160	750	756	798	1,162	957
Botany	200	160	1,020	1,097	1,276	1,256	1,320
		£1,900					

Source: Reports of the Royal Commissioners appointed to enquire into the Universities of Scotland: Returns and Documents [*c.* 1935–III], Parliamentary Papers, xxxv (1878), 360–7; *Devonshire Evidence* II, Appendix 5, 10–11.

the wide disparities in professorial emoluments and identifies the more remunerative chairs for the same period.[20]

One comment on Table 4 and three comments on Table 5 are perhaps necessary. Firstly, formal advanced classes, which might have prepared students for research, were given in only chemistry and natural philosophy. These advanced classes attracted a small proportion of those who had attended the main lecture class. In most subjects, a prospective research student jumped the big gap between the main lecture course and laboratory research; in these, therefore, there was no gradual transition from learning the elements of a subject to researching in it. In medical subjects, a research qualification was available; in non-medical sciences, however, the D.Sc. became available only in 1895 and the Ph.D., on the European and American model, only as late as 1919. Secondly, by the mid-1870s only six of the twelve scientific chairs in the University were worth £1,000 per year, a sum which Gladstone as Chancellor of the Exchequer had stated in 1865 should be the minimum emolument of every chair.[21] Thirdly, the professor of practical astronomy, Charles Piazzi Smyth, did not teach a class because very few students ever applied to take his course, and because he was additionally Astronomer Royal for Scotland, whose duties were incessantly demanding both by day and by night. Though Smyth cultivated paradox to the highest degree and enjoyed the rare double distinction of F.R.S. elected (1857), F.R.S. resigned (1874), his position was intolerable. Not unexpectedly, Smyth, who lacked a teaching assistant, had chosen the advancement of science and not its diffusion: indeed his commission of 1846 as Regius Professor of Astronomy and as Astronomer Royal for Scotland exacted from him onerous and important duties in his second capacity while it imposed no specific duties on him as professor; additionally it gave him a salary of £300 per year without indicating how much each of

[20] *Ibid.*, 360–7; *Royal Commission on Scientific Instruction and the Advancement of Science. Minutes of Evidence, Appendices, and Analyses of Evidence*, II [*c.* 958], Parliamentary Papers, xxii (1874), Appendix V, 10–11. In future references this work will be called *Devonshire Evidence*, II. In the *Seventh Report of the Royal Commission on Scientific Instruction and the Advancement of Science* [*c.* 1297], Parliamentary Papers, xxviii (1875), Appendix III, 54–8, slightly different figures for the class fees for session 1874–5 are given from those quoted in Table 5. The former figures were supplied by Principal Grant in summer 1875; the latter by him in session 1876–7. The reasons for these discrepancies, which do not change the hierarchy of reward from students, are administrative incompetence by the professors who supplied the figures and the confusion shown by some of them in failing to distinguish consistently between gross and nett class-fees.

[21] Reported in *Minutes of the Senate of the University of Edinburgh*, 22 December 1866.

his two posts was worth.[22] Given that ambivalent situation, Smyth had become full-time Astronomer Royal and from the 1860s had wisely

> limited himself to receiving (on the day announced in the University Calendar for opening the course) all matriculated applicants for Practical Astronomy, ascertaining their calibre and objects, and then advising or assisting such young men afterwards in their studies at various periods throughout the session, according to circumstances, and gratuitously.[23]

Lastly, from 1861, as a result of the Universities (Scotland) Act, the state had become the chief source from which Scottish professors' salaries were paid.[24] This situation arose partly because the Senate had accepted the supremacy of the University Court, founded by the same Act, as a condition of securing more financial support from the government. Indeed that Act allocated £10,000 by parliamentary grant for the improvement of the Scottish universities, a total of £3,345 being allotted to Edinburgh. Three years later the Edinburgh University Property Act (1861) completed the transfer of the University from the Edinburgh Town Council by stripping the former of nearly all its old endowments. By 1871 the state contributed £1,900 to the salaries received by eleven Edinburgh science professors, yet, with the exception of natural philosophy for which £100 was allowed, no grants for their departmental expenses were made from state funds.

In this respect the state had made a move towards supporting science in the University: in the mid-Victorian period it gave £2,000 per year chiefly as professorial salaries and slightly as departmental expenses. This may be contrasted with the grants made by government to other scientific institutions in Edinburgh.[25] Not unexpectedly the Museum of Science and Art was treated best: the estimates for 1873–4 revealed a total allocation of £9,230, of which £4,380 was spent on salaries and wages, £750 per year being the Director's salary. The same estimates revealed that £1,750 went to the Botanical Garden and £805 to the Royal Observatory. At the bottom of the list, the Royal Society of Edinburgh from 1836 received an annual government grant of £300 to pay the rent of its rooms, while the Scottish Meteorological Society was allowed the use of two small rooms in the attic of the Edinburgh General Post Office. For these the latter paid £30 per

22 Grant, *Story of the University of Edinburgh*, I, 341–4.

23 *Devonshire Evidence*, II, Appendix 5, 9.

24 *Op. cit.* note 22, II, 133; D. B. Horn, *A Short History of the University of Edinburgh, 1556–1889* (Edinburgh, 1967), 169–73.

25 *Fourth Report of the Royal Commission on Scientific Instruction and the Advancement of Science* [*c*. 884], Parliamentary Papers, xxii (1874), Appendix I, 25–6; *Devonshire Evidence*, II, Appendix 14, 67–9; *op. cit.* note 9.

year and gave the government such meteorological information as the Scottish Registrar General required.

III

The general financial caution shown by the government towards the University of Edinburgh meant that self-help had still to be its main source of money. Accordingly the University's income was derived from many sources: interest on capital funds; annual payments from slowly increasing parliamentary grants, and the Leith Dock dues; matriculation and graduation fees; and endowments by public and private bodies. In 1869–70, for example, the University's total income was £19,916, of which £12,541, including the government contribution of slightly over £6,000, was already ear-marked by deed, statute, or ordinance.[26] The disposable income of the University Fund was therefore only £7,375. About half of this (£3,664) was derived from graduation and matriculation fees (£1,642 matriculation fees; £1,694 medical graduation fees; and £328 from other graduation fees). These fees constituted a variable and precarious source of almost half the University's disposable income. Table 6 shows that they were indeed the chief source of the gradual increase in the University's disposable income, a fact fully appreciated at the time by the professoriate which was attracting more students to the University and consolidating the value of the medical degrees.[27]

The chief items of expenditure from the University Fund may be gauged from the breakdown for 1869–70 which in its proportions is representative of the 1860s and 1870s. The chief beneficiaries from the available total of £7,375 were as follows: buildings, £1,827; library, £1,584; administration, £981; assistance for classes, decreed by ordinance of the Commission which implemented the 1858 Act, £735; service, £595; assistance for classes, allocated by Senate, £568; printing, £366; and prizes, £207. Given this wide range of demands, the Senate was compelled to be cautious and practise financial economy. As many unavoidable charges had to be met from the University Fund, the amount available for science teaching, either as salaries of assistants or as departmental expenses, was necessarily

[26] *Edinburgh University Calendar: 1871–1872*, 292–7, gives details of income and expenditure for 1869–70.
[27] *Op. cit.* note 15, 407.

TABLE 6

Income (£)	1866–7	1867–8	1868–9	1869–70	1870–1
Matriculation fees	1,496	1,491	1,525	1,642	1,719
Medical graduation fees	1,539	1,372	1,521	1,694	2,078
Total disposable income	7,298	7,973	8,025	7,375	7,851

	1871–2	1872–3	1873–4	1874–5	1875–6
Matriculation fees	1,801	1,841	1,858	1,992	1,994
Medical graduation fees	2,098	2,267	2,412	2,375	2,629
Total disposable income	8,218	8,470	8,600	8,811	9,366

Source: Report of the Royal Commissioners appointed to enquire into the Universities of Scotland: Reports and Documents [c. 1935–III], Parliamentary Papers xxxv (1878), 407.

limited. Sir Alexander Grant put the matter clearly to the Devonshire Commission: 'The funds at the disposal of the University are altogether insufficient . . . in many cases to obtain the necessary materials, and to give an adequate remuneration to the Class Assistants.'[28]

The University was also unable to employ as many assistants as its professors would have liked. In the case of those popular subjects in which practical laboratory training was available, additional assistants paid by the professor himself were often appointed to cope with the large numbers of students. In the case of anatomy, by 1872 Turner himself paid three assistants; and that part of the class expenses met by himself totalled about £350. Similarly in chemistry Crum Brown paid about £400 per year from his own pocket mainly for assistants' salaries.[29] Nor, of course, was the University Fund sufficiently large to pay the expenses necessarily involved in mounting lecture courses, never mind laboratory classes. In the case of physiology, as early as 1848 Bennett had opened a University physiology laboratory in which practical histology using the microscope, experimental physiology using modern physical instruments, and chemical physiology were rapidly made available.[30] Between 1848 and 1868 Bennett

28 *Devonshire Evidence*, II, Appendix 5, 13–14.

29 *Ibid.*, 2, 6 and 9.

30 Reported in *Senate Minutes*, 21 December 1867 and 30 January 1869. See also J. G. McKendrick, 'John Hughes Bennett', *Edinburgh Medical Journal*, **21** (1875–6), 466–74.

had spent about £950 from his own pocket on histological specimens, optical apparatus, and teaching diagrams.

During the 1860s, Senate was as incapable as the Town Council had been previously of meeting the expenses incurred by a British pioneer in the laboratory teaching of practical physiology. Furthermore, the creation of new chairs of engineering and of geology, though desirable *per se*, put additional demands upon the already stretched University Fund. This was not proportionately increased by the number of students attending the new classes because each student contributed to that Fund a matriculation fee of £1 per year, irrespective of the number of classes he attended. Given this situation, in which teaching expenses could not be met from the University Fund, it was inevitable in what was primarily a teaching University that no special financial provision was made for research done by either professors or assistants. Quite simply the cost of materials, apparatus, and instruments had to be borne by the individuals concerned. In an expensive subject like chemistry the cost of materials, rather than the difficulty or type of the problem, had already and often restricted the choice of research investigation to be undertaken by advanced students or assistants.[31] As far as professors were concerned, the matter had been raised in 1866 by Bennett who wanted the University to pay for a combustion chamber he intended to install in the laboratory for his own research purposes. In reply, Senate decided that as a matter of financial expediency appliances for 'private investigation, or for special individual purposes, not required by the class' were not chargeable to the University Fund.[32]

The inability of the University to meet the costs of research was felt particularly acutely by those who had high ambitions for it. Brewster, who had been a prime mover in the founding of the British Association, was one of these. In his second address as Principal, he strongly supported the proposition that research was essential to any university: 'A University which teaches only what has been known, and from which no new light passes into the mind of the student, and irradiates the intellectual world, is unworthy of the name.'[33] Edinburgh, of course, was worthy in that respect: all its science professors prosecuted research. As a result the financial inadequacy of the University and the insufficiency of professorial reward were highlighted.

No wonder then that in 1864, when Brewster thundered once more

[31] *Op. cit.* note 28, 10.

[32] *Senate Minutes*, 27 January 1866.

[33] D. Brewster, *Introductory Address on the Opening of Session 1860–1861* (Edinburgh, 1860), 9.

against the obstinate parsimony of the government apropos the Scottish universities, the Association for the Better Endowment of the University of Edinburgh was founded as a local pressure group.[34] The general platform of the Association was that the revenues of the university were scanty and inadequate for the proper encouragement of learning and research in the Scottish metropolis. It aimed therefore to found research fellowships, to increase the endowment of existing chairs, and to found new ones. The professoriate was, of course, especially sympathetic to the second of these aims. By May 1865 the Endowments Committee of Senate, in urging Gladstone to increase the endowments of Edinburgh chairs, failed to disturb his publicly expressed suspicion 'that endowment gravitates towards torpor as its natural consummation . . .'.[35] On the accession in June 1866 of Lord Derby's third administration, private lobbying was resumed and in May 1867 a deputation led by the Earl of Dalhousie argued the case for better endowments with the Prime Minister.[36] Derby's response was chilling: he suggested that the government grant begun in 1858 was too recent in origin to be added to, asserted that the University was overstocked with professors, and urged that local efforts be made. The deputation was probably right in concluding from Lord Derby's negative and ignorant refusal that he had neither read the relevant documents nor enquired into the case of the University. The sustained pressure brought during the 1860s by the University for more financial support from successive governments did, however, bear some fruit in 1869 when a parliamentary grant of £500 per year for the maintenance and repair of the University buildings was established.[37]

Though endowments of chairs remained generally unchanged between 1860 and 1875, the teaching staff was increased, new chairs being exclusively created by private benefactions from alumni, well-wishers and Scottish patriots. In 280 years down to 1862 only two chairs had been established at Edinburgh by private benefaction, but in the next ten years in a laudable display of self-help four chairs were founded from private sources: Sanskrit

[34] D. Brewster, *Introductory Address at the Opening of Session 1864–1865* (Edinburgh, 1864), 3, 4, 6 and 19.

[35] The meeting with Gladstone was recorded in Senate Minutes, 22 December 1866; his view on endowments is in: *Inaugural Address as Rector of the University of Edinburgh* (Edinburgh, 1860), 20.

[36] The rebuff from Lord Derby is reported in *Senate Minutes*, 28 June 1867.

[37] Horn, *Short History of the University of Edinburgh*, 174. In January 1867, for instance, the Treasury had rejected the proposal made by a deputation from the University that the expense of maintaining and repairing the buildings should be transferred to the Board of Works (*Senate Minutes*, 24 November 1866 and 29 January 1867).

(1862), Engineering (1868), Geology (1871), and Political Economy (1871).[38] The first of these set the general pattern of private endowment supplemented by help from the Treasury. Appropriately, Dr John Muir, a Sanskrit scholar who had retired from the Indian Civil Service, endowed the Sanskrit chair with 40,000 rupees. This yielded £200 per year interest, to which the 1858 University Commissioners added an annual parliamentary grant of £200. Six years later, Sir David Baxter, the Dundee linen manufacturer who had made a fortune from his introduction in 1836 of power-loom weaving, endowed a chair in engineering to which Fleeming Jenkin was elected.

Though the foundation of this chair may be seen as part of the same movement, launched by industrialists and engineers, which had also endowed a chair in engineering for Osborne Reynolds at Owens College, Manchester, in 1868, it was not the first effort of its kind made at the University of Edinburgh. From 1855 until his death in 1859, George Wilson held the joint office of Regius Professor of Technology and Director of the Museum of Science and Art in Edinburgh (founded 1854).[39] On Wilson's death, the government immediately suppressed the Chair of Technology in the University, and appointed as Director of the Museum Thomas Archer who was responsible to the Department of Science and Art at South Kensington. Though Wilson had attracted no less than eighty-five students by November 1859, the government was clearly keen to gain total control of the Museum once its viability had been established by Wilson. In this move the government was indeed aided by Senate which put to the government the view that instead of having a replacement for the chair it would be better to allow the professors of chemistry, botany, and natural history to lecture in the Museum. By autumn, 1860, Brewster implicitly condemned this short-sightedness of the Senate when he averred in public that the University ought to teach Technology and Civil Engineering.[40]

In late 1867, Baxter proposed to the Senate the foundation of a chair of engineering which he would endow with £5,000.[41] In welcoming this benevolence, Senate recommended that the annual interest on £4,000 be allocated to the chair, and that £1,000 be spent on the expenses of the class in order to avoid pillaging the University Fund. Senate also asked the Treasury to add £200 per year to the chair so that the University would be able at last to mount adequate technical instruction spanning engineering,

[38] *Op. cit.* note 22, II, 134, 148–50 and 154.
[39] *Ibid.*, 354–61. [40] *Op. cit.* note 33, 17–29.
[41] The account of the founding of the chair of engineering draws on *Senate Minutes*, 21 December 1867, 20 and 25 January 1868, 8 February 1868, and 29 February 1868.

agriculture, chemistry, physics, and mathematics. At the same time Brewster drew the attention of the Treasury to the benevolence of the Highland and Agricultural Society of Scotland, which had offered to add £150 per year to the chair of agriculture of which the annual salary then was only £50. Impressed by this flurry of self-help, the government rapidly added its own contributions of £200 per year to the engineering chair and £150 per year to that of agriculture; it also accepted Brewster's proposal that the first nomination be Baxter's, subject to the approval of the Crown, but held that subsequent nominations were to be exclusively the Crown's.

The chair attracted two outstanding applicants: Jenkin, professor of engineering at University College, London (1865–8), and an expert on submarine telegraph cables; and William John MacQuorn Rankine, professor of civil engineering and mechanics at the University of Glasgow (1855–72). Doubtless Jenkin was elected because Baxter and Senate thought him more likely and able to fulfil Baxter's *desiderata*: the linen manufacturer

> hoped it would be made obligatory on the new Professor to teach as part of the course the application of Engineering to manufacturing industry. It would also be pleasing to him if the Professor would make practical excursions, with his students, taking them into the field to teach them surveying and going with them to large workshops and manufactories for the purpose of bringing them into direct contact with industrial operations.[42]

It is clear that the founding of this chair was an important part of the movement for technical education which erupted in late 1867.

In March 1871 the chair of geology was established through the initiative of Sir Roderick Impey Murchison, Director General of the Geological Survey (1855–71), who succeeded in placing in it his protégé, Archibald Geikie, Director of the Geological Survey of Scotland (1867–81).[43] As with the chair of engineering, that of geology had been discussed for some years before it was established. From the mid-1850s it had been widely realized that the chair of natural history could usefully become one of zoology provided geology and mineralogy could be separated from it. During the 1860s, Murchison himself had unsuccessfully lobbied the government about

[42] *Senate Minutes,* 29 February 1868.

[43] The account of the founding of the chair of geology draws on: A. Geikie, *Life of Sir Roderick I. Murchison*, II (London, 1875), 340–1; *op. cit.* note 11, 142–5; D. Milne Home, 'Opening Address, Session 1870–71', *Proceedings of the Royal Society of Edinburgh*, **7** (1869–72), 232–307 (236–238); *Senate Minutes,* 23 December 1865, 25 October 1870, 28 January 1871, 11 February 1871 and 25 March 1871.

the desirability of a separate chair of geology. Others were also active: in 1865 and 1866 both the Royal Society of Edinburgh and the Senate unsuccessfully petitioned government on the same issue. In August 1870, however, Allman resigned the chair of natural history. Murchison saw this as an opportunity of carrying out in his lifetime a proposal which he had already provided for in his will. As a patriotic Scot and as an admirer of Geikie, who at that time was reviving the Scottish tradition of studying igneous rocks, Murchison suggested in October 1870 to Principal Grant that the natural history chair be split into those of biology and of geology. He offered £6,000 as the endowment of the latter chair and hoped the government would add to it. Murchison also stressed to Grant that 'the nomination of the first person to occupy that chair is to be *made by myself*. That is the only condition!'[44]

Strongly supported by Edinburgh's leading scientific societies, the University applied to the Treasury, urging the division of the natural history chair, of which the Crown was patron, and asking for half the total endowment of the proposed chair to be provided by the government. The Treasury, however, was not as compliant as in 1868. This time it objected to the private donor of a large part of the endowment having the nomination of the first professor: it argued that it could not 'permit an appointment supported in part by public money to be vested in any person [i.e. Murchison] acting under no recognized and defined responsibility to the Public . . .';[45] it stressed that the precedents of Muir and Baxter, having the patronage of the first incumbents of the chairs they had endowed, were wrong in principle; and the Home Office supported the Treasury's view that the prerogative of the Crown ought not to be infringed. Moreover, the Department of Science and Art raised the question of whether Geikie ought to retain his post as Director of the Scottish Geological Survey should he be elected to the proposed geology chair.

Though Murchison had been struck down by paralysis in November 1870, his views were ably supported by Lyon Playfair who at that time was newly elected MP for the Universities of Edinburgh and St Andrews. By February 1871, under pressure the government had capitulated on these issues. On 10 March 1871, the Royal warrant, founding the geology chair and appointing Geikie to it, was issued. Not surprisingly the financial arrangements were the same as those associated with the engineering chair

[44] Murchison to Grant, 7 October 1870, reported in *Senate Minutes*, 25 October 1870. The italics were Murchison's.

[45] Treasury to Senate, 5 January 1871, reported in *Senate Minutes*, 28 January 1871.

of 1868: £200 p.a. from private benefaction, £200 p.a. from government and, though the Crown was patron of the chair, £40 p.a. for class expense was provided from Murchison's endowment.

IV

While deeply involved in the negotiations associated with the geolog chair, Principal Grant delivered, on 16 January 1871, at the Royal Societ of Edinburgh an address on the educational system of Prussia.[46] In hi opinion the problem facing British higher education was how to tap th state's resources without becoming a victim of centralizing bureaucracy Nevertheless he clearly stated his view that Prussian higher education was s advanced largely because the state was heavily involved in its maintenance He ruefully compared the University of Berlin with that of Edinburgh i order to show how comparatively small was the proportion of financia support given by the state to his own university. This lack of state suppor had indeed become particularly apparent during the 1860s when labora tories, sometimes involving considerable capital outlay, had been introduce into the University: in addition to the established laboratories in anatomy chemistry, physiology and botany, the period saw the creation of new one in natural philosophy (1868), pathology (1870), zoology (1872), geolog (1876) and materia medica (1877). Laboratories at that time were, of course becoming *de rigeur* not only for the practical teaching of students but als as the location of research schools. In the more alert German universities, th capital and running expenses of laboratory teaching were paid by the state

At Edinburgh, however, the difficulties attending the creation an expansion of laboratories were exacerbated by a shortage of money and o space which were endemic in the University as a whole: the Universit Fund was decidedly inadequate to the claims for capital and runnin expenses made upon it; and the University had only one already crowde building in which new classes and laboratories had to be accommodated

[46] A. Grant, 'On the Educational System of Prussia', *Proceedings of the Royal Societ of Edinburgh*, **7** (1869–72), 309–35 (327–8, 335). Grant stated that for the University o Berlin in 1864–5, its total income was about £30,000 of which £28,842 was a gran from the government; at Edinburgh in 1870–1, the total income was £20,351 of whic £6,329 came from parliamentary grants. From *Devonshire Evidence*, II, Appendix 17 72 it is clear that in 1869 the total income of the ten Prussian universities (Berlin Breslau, Bonn, Halle, Königsberg, Griefswalde, Münster, Göttingen, Marburg, Kiel) wa 1,225,481 Th. (*c.* £163,000) of which 859,661 (*c.* £115,000) came from governmen grants.

Indeed, William Turner, in his evidence to the Devonshire Commission, made a simple point which is often forgotten, namely, that teaching laboratories 'take up a large comparative amount of space, because you cannot pack the students as you do in a lecture room; they must have space to move about in'.[47] The sizes of the laboratory classes have already been given in Table 4, from which it is clear that only in anatomy and physiology did a majority of students regularly take the laboratory as well as the lecture class. This situation merely reflected the sizes of the laboratories in different subjects. In all cases severe problems tested professorial patience and resource to the full. In anatomy, for instance, the presence of some two hundred students at a time in the imperfectly ventilated and crowded dissecting rooms produced discomfort and anxiety.[48] In chemistry the accommodation for practical work was so inadequate that Crum Brown had suggested that a temporary shed in the quadrangle be erected. Moreover, as he sadly confessed to the Devonshire Commission, 'we have but one room in which to carry on analyses, the preparation of specimens, and furnace operations, three departments of work which ought certainly to be accommodated in different rooms'.[49] Nevertheless, Crum Brown had been compelled to dissuade students from attending the practical class because the laboratory could accommodate only twelve people at a time.

In the case of the natural philosophy laboratory, formerly the pathology classroom, the accommodation was probably worst of all: when Tait took more than ten practical students in it, the extra ones worked among Tait's own collection of apparatus in the lecture-room. Tait himself was so short of space that his instruments were 'in two or three places piled in strata about the room . . .'.[50] The general congestion was so great that it prohibited

47 *Devonshire Evidence*, II, 4.

48 *Ibid.*, 5. Laboratory work in anatomy is described by A. Logan Turner, *Sir William Turner: A Chapter in Medical History* (Edinburgh and London, 1919), 65–6, and 121–31.

49 *Ibid.*, 108, and also 7–11.

50 *Ibid.*, 13, and also 12–16. R. Sviedrys, 'The Rise of Physical Science at Victorian Cambridge', *Historical Studies in the Physical Sciences*, **2** (1970), 127–51 (138) has rightly stressed that during the years 1866 to 1873 a flush of at least eight physics laboratories appeared in British universities or university-level institutions. Tait's laboratory, for which he had been pressing from at least 1865, was established in 1868 as a result of a large, incidental and quite exceptional surplus of £569 for session 1865–6 in the University General Fund. This unexpected surplus was largely spent on fitting up Tait's laboratory (£150) and on buying for the University the late Professor Goodsir's own collection of anatomical specimens and apparatus (£340). See *Senate Minutes* for 28 July 1865, 30 March 1867, 6 April 1867 and 21 December 1867. From the start Tait publicly asserted that the funds for his laboratory were inadequate and that the prospects were not encouraging: see P. G. Tait, 'Establishment of a Physical Laboratory', *The Scotsman*, 3 November 1868.

several kinds of work being done simultaneously. For instance, when one powerful electromagnet was used the galvanometers throughout Tait's accommodation were disturbed. No wonder that Tait stressed to the Devonshire Commission that lack of space was basically a question of lack of money. Like Crum Brown he had to turn prospective practical students away. In the cases of the recently instituted chairs of engineering and geology, no laboratories were provided. Quite characteristically, the government contributed only to the salaries attached to these two chairs and not to departmental expenses of any kind. On the other hand Senate tended to spend money from the inadequate University Fund on laboratories in well-established and well-attended subjects. Jenkin and Geikie to some extent solved this problem by initiating practical work which could be done either without a laboratory or in a class-room temporarily converted to a laboratory. In engineering, Jenkin rapidly made available mechanical drawing and practical surveying. In geology Geikie initially lacked a laboratory as well as a separate class-room and even specimens, which he himself had to collect or buy. However, he immediately began practical work in the field by exploiting Edinburgh's exceptional advantages for instruction of this type. Five years later he opened his practical class in blow-pipe analysis; and in 1877 he established the first British university class in practical petrography in which thin slices of igneous rocks were studied with microscopes.[51]

One solution to the pressing problems of accommodation was to acquire money for new buildings. The buildings in use in the 1860s were those devised in the late eighteenth century when the University housed about a thousand students and twenty-one professors. By the early 1870s almost two thousand students were taught by thirty-six professors and forty-five assistants. Indeed forty distinct courses of instruction were given in only eighteen class-rooms. Clearly the development of practical work in laboratories required new buildings.[52] Accordingly between 1874 and 1883, £130,000 was raised by private subscription and £80,000 contributed by the government to build a new medical school near the newly-built Royal

[51] *Op. cit.* note 11, 152–3; *Edinburgh University Calendar: 1876–1877* (Edinburgh, 1877); and *Edinburgh University Calendar: 1877–1878* (Edinburgh, 1878).

[52] This was the chief basis of the plea made to the Devonshire commission on 12 May 1874 by a Deputation from a Committee of the general public appointed to promote the extension and improvement of the buildings of the University of Edinburgh. See *Royal Commission on Scientific Instruction and the Advancement of Science: Minutes of Evidence, Appendices, Analyses and General Index to Evidence* [*c.* 1363], Parliamentary Papers xxviii (1875), 60–3.

Infirmary.[53] Self-help was far more in evidence in meeting the cost of these new buildings than it had been decades before when the Adam-Playfair building was erected between 1789 and 1827. This had cost £161,000, towards which the government had contributed a total of £131,000; this was composed of £5,000 granted in 1801 by royal warrant, £120,000 in annual parliamentary grants between 1815 and 1826, and £6,000 as a supplementary grant made in 1831.

There is no doubt that, by the 1870s, shortage of money, space, and equipment did little to reduce the gap between ambition and capacity as far as teaching was concerned. In the case of research, the situation was equally pressing. Generally, European governments made no direct provision to their universities exclusively for research, and in this respect Edinburgh was normal in that the British government did not support research there. But particularly in German universities the facilities for teaching paid for by the state were used by enterprising professors for research. At Edinburgh, however, the state's grant of £100 to the natural philosophy class was its sole contribution to the University's departmental expenses. Crucially, Edinburgh lacked state subsidies given for teaching which could be used for research. Furthermore, teaching expenses could not be met from the University Fund; and the University, always alive to the necessity of attracting students, devoted its very limited funds to items used in teaching. The cost of research in the form of materials, apparatus and instruments had therefore to be borne by individual professors. Each professor who was active in research had, of course, a means of supporting himself financially from his teaching. At Edinburgh, however, each science professor usually lectured one hour each day of the week for at least half the year, and spent much extra time in preparing his lecture-demonstration experiments and in supervising practical work. In the case of Tait, for instance, it is clear that, owing to shortage of assistance, he spent about nine months of each year on teaching, leaving only three months for research and a holiday. No wonder that in 1872 Tait argued that the Scottish

[53] *Op. cit.* note 22, II, 208–15. In the 1870s private subscriptions were primarily responsible for new buildings of the University of Glasgow and of Owens College, Manchester. At Glasgow £174,000 was subscribed by private philanthropists, and £120,000 granted by government: J. D. Mackie, *The University of Glasgow 1451–1951* (Glasgow, 1954), 286. In Manchester private subscription to the Extension Fund of Owens College totalled £211,000; the government provided nothing. See J. Thompson, *The Owens College: Its Foundation and Growth* (Manchester, 1886), 338, 339, 491 and 644. Though Edinburgh apparently fares badly in the comparison with Glasgow and Manchester, it must be remembered that by 1870 £75,000 had been publicly subscribed for the new buildings of the Royal Infirmary: see A. L. Turner, *Story of a Great Hospital: The Royal Infirmary of Edinburgh, 1729–1929* (Edinburgh, 1937), 254.

universities needed more chairs per subject, and that the salaries of professors should be more than half their total emolument.[54] Indeed as long as the class-fee remained the primary source of the emolument of professors, keeping themselves in business as teachers inevitably consumed much professorial effort and time. Research was therefore usually squeezed into the intervals between teaching.[55]

For financial support, each professor had to acquire a patron, earn extra money, or dip into his own pocket. At Edinburgh, various solutions to this problem were advanced. Four professors enjoyed a possible advantage over their colleagues in that they held double offices: the Professor of Botany was also Regius Keeper of the Royal Botanic Gardens, Edinburgh; the Professor of Natural History was Regius Keeper of the Natural History section of the Edinburgh Museum of Science and Art; the Professor of Practical Astronomy was Astronomer Royal for Scotland; and the Professor of Geology was Director of the Scottish Geological Survey. Three of these four professors used or tried to exploit their second post for research. Geikie was perhaps the most conveniently situated: the job of mapping the geology of Scotland, at the state's expense and at a salary of at least £400 per year, provided data and problems central to his main research interest in ancient British volcanoes and in the stratigraphy of the old red sandstone. Though a very conscientious teacher, Geikie regarded the Scottish Geological Survey as his most important charge.[56]

The Professor of Practical Astronomy, as has already been explained, went further than Geikie and made his second office his exclusive concern.[57] Whereas Geikie seems to have been content with the Survey and its staff of thirteen, Smyth was extremely unhappy about the indifference shown by the government to the Royal Observatory at Edinburgh. An expert in

54 *Devonshire Evidence*, II, 14; *The Life and Scientific Work of Peter Guthrie Tait*, C. G. Knott (ed.) (Cambridge, 1911), 77 and 248. From 1868, Tait gave over a hundred different lectures a year (five per week) to the junior class of natural philosophy, more than sixty a year (three per week) to the advanced class, and supervised the laboratory for about 25 hours a week.

55 I am indebted to Professor N. Campbell of the University of Edinburgh for stressing that the Edinburgh conviction of 'teach first, research second' persisted well into this century. He has drawn my attention to Sir James Walker (professor of chemistry 1908–28), a distinguished researcher in his prime, who surprisingly deviated from this conviction in 1920 when he allowed an assistant to have Wednesday afternoons free from teaching in order to do research.

56 *Op. cit.* note 11, 167.

57 This summary of Smyth's troubles draws on: A. S. Herschel, 'Some Notes on the late Professor Piazzi Smyth's Work in Spectroscopy', *Nature*, **62** (1900), 161–5; *Report of The Commissioners appointed in 1876 to inquire into the state of the Royal Observatory at Edinburgh*, Parliamentary Papers xxxiii (1877); and *Devonshire Evidence*, II, Appendix 5, 14–16.

spectroscopic astronomy, he campaigned so incessantly that in 1876 a government commission was appointed to inquire into the state of the Royal Observatory at Edinburgh. It recommended a substantial increase to every item of the government grant to the Observatory. Nothing was done, however, so that the Observatory's pauperism and inefficiency remained. With just two assistants to help him, Smyth envied the relative affluence and large staff of seventeen assistants enjoyed by the Greenwich Observatory. Indeed, much of the research done by Smyth as Astronomer Royal for Scotland was subsidized from his own pocket.

In the case of Balfour, professor of botany, the government was far more co-operative.[58] In the early 1850s the Commissioners of Woods and Forests had supported his pleas for a proper laboratory and a museum of economic botany, the nucleus of which had been given by Balfour himself and by his gardener James McNab. In 1855 these same Commissioners secured £6,000 from the government for the erection of a new Palm House. Though he was paid only £120 per year as Regius Keeper of the Botanical Garden, the materials and some equipment for his own research were available there. With characteristic self-help, he added to the former through his field excursions, during which specimens suitable for cultivation were collected by his students and himself.[59]

Wyville Thomson was less fortunate in his capacity as Regius Keeper of the Natural History section of the Edinburgh Museum of Science and Art. As a result of a demarcation dispute with the Museum's Director, Thomson enjoyed neither control of materials there nor access to them.[60] In any event, the Museum's resources were marginal to his research interest in the distribution of species and physical conditions in the depths of oceans. Fortunately for Thomson, by mounting the famous *Challenger* expedition (1872–6) the government, through the Admiralty, extensively patronized his research.[61] The chief purposes of this famous expedition were to sound and dredge in the three great ocean basins, to collect all possible flora and fauna at all depths, and to study rarely-visited oceanic islands. After the successful laying of the Atlantic cable in 1866, oceanic telegraphy had

58 Balfour's campaigns, which were strongly supported by Sir William Gibson Craig, MP for Edinburgh, are described in H. R. Fletcher and W. H. Brown, *The Royal Botanic Garden Edinburgh 1670–1970* (Edinburgh, 1970), 141–3.

59 *Ibid.*, 130–3.

60 *Devonshire Evidence*, II, 66–74.

61 C. Wyville Thomson, *The Voyage of the 'Challenger'. The Atlantic* (London, 1877), I, 1–92. The book was published by the authority of the Admiralty and for good measure it was dedicated to G. J. Goschen, First Lord of the Admiralty 1871–4. The Challenger expedition is well covered in M. Deacon, *Scientists and the Sea 1650–1900: A Study of Marine Science* (London, 1971), 333–65.

developed rapidly. Hence, research into the physical and biological conditions in the depths of the ocean could be justified on utilitarian grounds. Not surprisingly the *Challenger* was given a naval surveying staff to which was added a civilian scientific staff of six headed by Thomson as Director at a salary of £1,000 per year. After spending only two years in his Edinburgh chair, he enjoyed the next four on the *Challenger* which was splendidly equipped with laboratories and apparatus. For good measure, his substitutes, T. H. Huxley and Professor Carus of Leipzig, increased the popularity of the natural history class during his absence. Clearly the *Challenger* expedition was a conspicuous example of the way in which research could be supported by the state as part of a larger and traditional concern with naval and colonial dominion. It was also an example of the way in which such an arch opponent of endowment as Robert Lowe, Chancellor of the Exchequer from 1868–73, was prepared to support an important research project if it was of a kind quite beyond the reach of private enterprise.

Most professors, of course, neither experienced the government patronage which Wyville Thomson enjoyed, nor occupied a second post which they could exploit for their own research. Inevitably these men paid the cost of research from their own emolument, or they cast about for additional sources of income. For an Edinburgh professor, one obvious and traditional source came from writing textbooks and popular works.[62] As Sir William Thomson sadly noted, this practice could be 'likened to an army in which the general is employed in teaching the goose step to recruits.'[63] A second extra source of income was consultancy or professional practice, which was of course traditional for the medical professors. For instance, Fleeming Jenkin was a professional engineer who between 1858 and 1873 specialized in the development of electric cables for marine telegraphy, partly in conjunction with Sir William Thomson.[64] This income enabled him to pursue his research in his own house in lieu of a laboratory provided by the University.[65]

62 Some of these were much more than routine compilations as Tait's works of the 1860s show: W. Thomson and P. G. Tait, *A Treatise on Natural Philosophy*, I (Oxford, 1867); P. G. Tait, *An Elementary Treatise on Quaternions* (Oxford, 1867); *idem, Sketch of Thermodynamics* (Edinburgh, 1868).

63 *Devonshire Evidence*, II, 111.

64 From S. P. Thompson, *The Life of William Thomson, Baron Kelvin of Largs*, I (London, 1910), 552–3, it is clear that from the mid-1860s Thomson and Jenkin were closely associated and well rewarded as co-owners of patents and as partners as consulting engineers.

65 T. J. N. Hilken, *Engineering at Cambridge University 1783–1965* (Cambridge, 1967), 108–9; R. L. Stevenson, *Memoir of Fleeming Jenkin* (London, 1924), 67.

In the case of natural philosophy, whose utilitarian appeal was not so apparent, little consultancy work was available for Tait or even desired by him. He knew, too, that private benefactors of the University usually endowed a chair for the purpose of advancing instruction, and that they rarely thought of making a contribution to the cost of research. No doubt he regretted the inability of the Royal Society of Edinburgh, of which he was a key member, to assist any research other than by publishing it. Like some of his colleagues, however, he was supported by the British Association, which during the late 1860s and early 1870s divided about £1,000 p.a. between selected individuals for specific pieces of research: between 1868, when he first acquired a laboratory, and 1876, Tait received no less than £345 from the British Association for research on the conductivity of metallic bars and on thermo-electric phenomena.[66] Less happily, in 1866 and 1867 Tait had applied for financial support from the annual government grant of £1,000 which a committee of the Royal Society of London allocated.[67] Though the grant was established in 1850 to meet the expense of apparatus and materials incurred by British individuals in their research, the awards usually went to Fellows who lived in or near London. Tait was not an FRS and lived in Edinburgh: not surprisingly he joined Henry Enfield Roscoe, professor of chemistry at Owens College, Manchester, as the second distinguished provincial whose application was refused during the mid-1860s. With the exception of the research supported by the British Association, Tait therefore confined his attention to those research problems which he could finance from his own pocket; and he ran his laboratory from the same source. Good work was done in it not only by Tait but also by Sir William Thomson and Jenkin, who used it for their experiments concerned with testing and laying telegraphic cables to the West Indies and Brazil.[68] No wonder that in 1876 Tait mournfully referred to the value of the work done in his laboratory, even with the excessively imperfect means at his disposal.

[66] *Report of the British Association for the Advancement of Science*: 1868 (London, 1869), 1, £30; *ibid.*, 1869, lxxx, £20; *ibid.*, 1870, lxiv, £20; *ibid.*, 1871, lxxiv, £25; *ibid.*, 1872, lix, £50; *ibid.*, 1873, lx, £50; *ibid.*, 1874, lvi, £50; *ibid.*, 1875, lviii, £50; *ibid.*, 1876, lvii, £50.

[67] R. M. MacLeod, 'The Royal Society and the Government Grant: Notes on the Administration of Scientific Research, 1849–1914', *The Historical Journal*, **14** (1971), 323–58 (334–5).

[68] From 1870 Tait began to publish accounts of research done by named pupils under his supervision in his laboratory: P. G. Tait, 'Notes from the Physical Laboratory of the University', *Proceedings of the Royal Society of Edinburgh*, **7** (1869–72), 206–8. See also *Report of the Royal Commissioners appointed to inquire into the Universities of Scotland* [c. 1935–I], Parliamentary Papers xxxiii (1878), 150.

Perhaps the most telling feature of research in science done at the University of Edinburgh in the mid-Victorian period was the absence of those institutionally supported research schools which had evolved in the leading German universities. Chemistry provides an apposite and ironic example of the University's incapacity to meet the German challenge. In 1858 Lyon Playfair, apostle of the inosculation of science and the arts, pioneer propagandist for technical education, and from 1855 Secretary to the Department of Science and Art at a salary of £1,000 per year with annual expenses of £350, was appointed to the chemistry chair.[69] He took the only chair he regarded as worth having in order to devote himself more exclusively to science. As he judged the chair to be the chief ambition of scientific chemists in Britain, he succeeded in establishing a teaching laboratory in the inadequate accommodation the University could give him. Presumably Playfair had in his mind the creation of a research school of the sort first established by Liebig under whom he had taken his doctorate. Yet, like his successor Crum Brown, who had studied under Bunsen at the University of Heidelberg and under Kolbe at the University of Marburg, Playfair founded no research school, though he himself fitted his research between teaching and onerous work for the government on various commissions.[70] Playfair was financially independent as a result of a wise second marriage; unlike many of his colleagues he could afford to subsidize his laboratory to the extent of spending the whole of his professorial income on it during his first year. Even so the laboratory was too small; no doubt Playfair looked enviously at the new chemistry laboratory for 132 students which was opened at the University of Leipzig for Kolbe in 1868. It is significant that in 1869 he resigned his chair not because of age or ill-health but because he had decided it was more worth-while to cultivate a political career.

V

During the mid-Victorian period critics of British universities frequently looked to the German universities for inspiration and for models. It was

69 The account of Playfair is based on: T. W. Reid, *Memoirs and Correspondence of Lyon Playfair* (London, 1899), 142, 164, 177–81, 429; L. Playfair, *A Century of Chemistry in the University of Edinburgh* (Edinburgh, 1858), 29–30.

70 During the 1860s Playfair's work as a commissioner embraced such varied problems as the health of towns, herring fishery, cattle plague, endowed schools, and Thirlmere water. In this respect he continued his work as a scientific civil servant during his incumbency of the Edinburgh chair.

clear to them that one reason for the rise of science in those universities was that they were supported, though not controlled, by the appropriate states. Indeed, German universities were generally state-supported institutions from their foundation. During the eighteenth century they existed chiefly to produce trained specialists in law, in medicine, and in theology. In the following century these universities, usually from their philosophy faculties, began to produce additionally another group of trained specialists: the scientists. During the nineteenth century the chief purpose of eighteenth-century German universities was simply enlarged and not basically changed. Given the long tradition of involvement by German states in the production of trained experts, it is not surprising that by the 1870s these states were patronizing the teaching of science in their universities. In particular many universities enjoyed a plurality of professors per scientific subject: they also received from the state capital expenses for laboratories, and running expenses for laboratory teaching.

In the case of Edinburgh, however, there was no sustained tradition of state patronage of the University. This relative lack of state support underlay the persistent and frustrating disparity between ambition and capacity in both teaching and research in science in the mid-Victorian University of Edinburgh. There was generally little reluctance on the part of the Senate or the professors to innovate. Their chief difficulty lay in implementing their aims and ideals: for that reason I have drawn attention to the restraints which hampered these eager science professors in their two chief roles as teachers and researchers. Many of these restraints were ultimately reducible to the extreme poverty of the University. In particular, improved or new laboratories, both adequately equipped and sufficiently big, were desperately expensive and beyond the University's resources. Hence the laboratories were usually too small and run on a financial shoe-string. Though the Devonshire Commission and others had urged that far greater financial aid from the government be provided for better salaries, more assistance, and proper laboratories, such help was not forthcoming. Successive mid-Victorian governments clearly expected that the stimulus of private competition and the liberality of private patronage should be utterly exhausted before state subsidies should be given to the University. Thus the government from 1858 merely provided low salaries for the professors, and from 1869 part of the expense of maintaining the buildings. Quite characteristically, the government made a contribution of no more than half the total cost of new chairs and of new buildings, and that only when substantial private efforts had already been made. In some vital spheres of social life, such as public health, government interference proliferated in the years allegedly characterized by decentralization and localism.[71] In the case of the University of Edinburgh, which failed to make a compelling case to the government for state subsidies of a kind given by German and American states, self-help and localism were therefore by no means fading or irrelevant aspirations. They were generally the staple of its expansion in student numbers, in modes of teaching, in research, in the limited improvement and establishment of laboratories, and ultimately in buildings. Indeed, Gladstone in an address as Rector, bluntly epitomized the course of the mid-Victorian University of Edinburgh by drawing attention to its mode of survival: 'In the history of the University of Edinburgh, we may clearly trace the national character of Scotland—we find there all that hardy energy, that gift of extracting much from little, and husbanding every available provision—of supplying the defects of external appliances and means from within by the augmented effort and courage of man'.[72]

[71] R. Lambert, *Sir John Simon 1816–1904 and English Social Administration* (London, 1963), 607.

[72] W. Gladstone, *Inaugural Address as Rector of the University of Edinburgh*, 20–1.

XI

Individualism and the Structure of British Science in 1830

Over half a century ago the polymathic J. T. Merz produced his monumental classic on the intellectual history of nineteenth-century Europe. One of its most welcome features remains his account of the different ways in which science had been institutionalized in France, Germany, and England.[1] Merz saw, inter alia, that science is not merely positive knowledge which has been rigorously acquired and then patiently accumulated in textbooks and journals, but also that it is a socially organized intellectual activity. Accordingly he concerned himself with scientific institutions as well as scientific ideas. Particularly since 1960 this aspect of Merz's approach has enjoyed a belated revival. In their different ways, Cannon's exploration of the intellectual network centred on the University of Cambridge during the 1830's, Mendelsohn's survey of the professionalization of science in Europe, Ben-David's insistence on the competitive nature of the German university system, Crosland's examination of Napoleonic patronage of science, and Ackernecht's appraisal of the Paris clinical school have all drawn attention to and illuminated key aspects of

I am grateful to the University of Pennsylvania for the tenure of a visiting professorship in spring 1970 when this paper was written. For help and encouragement I am indebted to the faculty and students of its Department of History and Philosophy of Science, particularly to Dr. R. McCormmach and Dr. A. W. Thackray, to Professor H. Guerlac, Dr. W. H. Brock, Dr. W. F. Cannon, Dr. D. Fraser, and to the members of seminars held at Johns Hopkins University on 6 March 1970 and the University of North Carolina on 13 March 1970 to whom preliminary versions of this paper were read.

1. J. T. Merz, *A History of European Thought in the Nineteenth Century* (London, 1904; reprint, New York, 1965), *1*, 89-301.

the changing social structure of nineteenth-century science.[2] In the previous decade, too, Cardwell had usefully scrutinized the organization of science in England in a pioneering and indispensable book published (one notes) in a series dedicated to sociology.[3]

It appears that much recent social history of nineteenth-century science has been focused on the European continent, if one excludes quite arbitrarily the genre of heroic biography.[4] Perhaps, therefore, it would be advantageous to turn to nineteenth-century British science, and to survey its organization not over the whole century but in and around a particular year. I have chosen 1830 because crucial changes in both British science and British society took place then or thereabout. In that climacteric year Charles Babbage vehemently denounced the Royal Society of London, which was suffering traumatic internal dissent apropos its future development and the related question of the election of its next president. In the following year the British Association for the Advancement of Science, the first national pressure group for professionalizing science, was established at York. Shortly afterward the Reverend William Whewell obligingly coined the term "scientist" to acknowledge those changing or novel characteristics and aims which were inadequately conveyed by the term "cultivator of science." The year also saw the accession of William IV to the British throne and the first gleams of the Age of Reform. My aim in this paper is therefore to analyze the leitmotiv and the related institutional structure of British science, not merely English science, in 1830 and immediately afterward. To clarify the discussion, my paper is divided into four related sections. First I draw attention to the prevalence of individualism as a social and political ideology in Britain around 1830. Second I argue that the conditions under which the British govern-

2. W. F. Cannon, "History in Depth: The Early Victorian Period," *History of Science, 3* (1964), 20-38; *idem,* "Scientists and Broad Churchmen: An Early Victorian Intellectual Network," *Journal of British Studies, 4* (1964), 65-88; E. Mendelsohn, "The Emergence of Science as a Profession in Nineteenth-Century Europe" in K. Hill, ed., *The Management of Scientists* (Boston, 1964), 3-48; M. Crosland, *The Society of Arcueil, A View of French Science at the Time of Napoleon I* (London, 1967); J. Ben-David, "Scientific Productivity and Academic Organization," *American Sociological Review, 25* (1960), 328-343; E. H. Ackernecht, *Medicine at the Paris Hospital, 1794-1848* (Baltimore, 1967).

3. D. S. L. Cardwell, *The Organization of Science in England* (London, 1957).

4. The outstanding example from the last decade is L. P. Williams, *Michael Faraday* (London, 1965).

ment was likely to disturb the dominant individualism by state intervention were palpably not fulfilled with regard to the alleged decline of British science. Third I describe the institutional structure of British science, which reflected the individualism prevalent if not pervasive in 1830. In this third section I try to give a synoptic anatomical view, illustrated with apposite but not exhaustive detail; and I take the liberty of stressing those provincial and Scottish institutions and influences whose importance seems to me to be frequently underestimated. Lastly, as a coda, I emphasize the provincial origins of the British Association for the Advancement of Science; and I analyze the apparent paradox that the Association generally shunned the question of state support for science.

I

Writers from Babbage onward, including the redoubtable Merz, seem dazzled by the successful efforts made by the French governments between 1794 and 1808 to create de novo and sometimes to refurbish an impressive set of scientific institutions of which the Ecole Polytechnique was the enviable pinnacle.[5] Certainly the professionalization of French science was achieved through centralized bureaucratic innovation and revival which was organized and supported by the state, a tradition previously characteristic of enlightened despotism. In contrast with French science, that of Germany became professionalized chiefly through the decentralized University system operated by the various states in a spirit of cultural competition. It was after all in the small provincial University of Giessen in Hesse-Darmstadt that the messianic Justus von Liebig started and developed those two basic aspects of professionalized science, laboratory teaching and the research school. Though the German universities were largely autonomous intellectually, they were administratively state institutions of which the capital and running expenses were borne by the appropriate government. We must realize that in both France and the German states the professionalization of science occurred mainly in organizations which were both sponsored and managed by the state: patronage by the relevant

5. C. Babbage, *Reflections on the Decline of Science in England* (London, 1830), passim; Merz, *op. cit.*, pp. 243 and 245.

government maintained both the Ecole Polytechnique and the University of Giessen. Clearly if one measures British science against this criterion culled from the French and German modes of practice, the results will be hopelessly inappropriate.

Again, from Babbage onward one senses that the diversity of the organization of British science and the motive behind it have been persistently underestimated.[6] Babbage himself gave scant attention to University College London, the mechanics' institutes, popular scientific education, and the provincial scientific societies. For polemical reasons he simplified the structure of British science and exaggerated some of its alleged defects. Yet his dissatisfaction with the intellectual and ethical standards adopted by the Royal Society of London and his protest about lack of public recognition for science both show the self-awareness that was increasingly displayed by British scientists from about 1830. It must not be forgotten that the growth of self-consciousness—the realization of collective identity—is probably the most important element in the professionalization of an activity.[7] At the personal level, Babbage's specialism was higher mathematics and its applications, a field which featured prominently in his book. As his difficulties with the Treasury in connection with his calculating machine were increasing in 1830, his plea for munificent state patronage of higher mathematics was scarcely concealed self-interest. Furthermore his envy of Edward Sabine, named in 1828 as one of the Admiralty's three advisers along with Thomas Young and Michael Faraday, was shown in his attacks on Sabine's competence and character. It is clear that Babbage's book confirms the old adage that personal testimony is not necessarily reliable evidence. One of the most serious defects of his book was his exclusion of the Scottish universities, among which Edinburgh and Glasgow were distinguished in scientific research and teaching, embarrassingly so to Babbage. Perhaps he had a valid excuse: until about 1850 obtuse writers used "England" to include "Scotland," and "English" to subsume "Scottish," heinous practices which linguistic Scottish nationalism eradicated in mid-century. For polemical and personal

6. Merz appreciated individualism in the English character, but failed to see the rich variety of institutions it produced: Merz, *op. cit.*, pp. 264-275 and 279.

7. G. Millerson, *The Qualifying Associations: A Study in Professionalization* (London, 1964), pp. 10-12.

reasons Babbage revealed a limited awareness of the sheer variety of ways in which science was organized in England, not to mention those frequently ignored Celtic fringes called Scotland and Ireland.[8]

A necessary antidote to the narrow perspective dispensed by Babbage et alii is the recognition that basic traits in British society in 1830 were self-help, voluntarism, individualism, and libertarianism. All these characteristics implied the tenet and belief that individuals should initiate and support their own activities at the grass-roots level by exercising their own powers of will, choice, and action, as opposed to looking to state intervention or control. The persistence of this voluntarist tradition is shown by the wide span of time through which it was enunciated and elaborated. From Adam Smith in 1776 to John Stuart Mill and Samuel Smiles in 1859, libertarianism was noisily lauded, and the domestic function of government was generally seen as negative restriction and not positive action. Indeed, the opening pages of Smiles's famous homily *Self-Help* unambiguously identified the chief source of British power:

> "Heaven helps those who help themselves" is a well-tried maxim, embodying in a small compass the results of vast human experience. The spirit of self-help is the root of all genuine growth in the individual; and, exhibited in the lives of many, it constitutes the true source of national vigor and strength. Help from without is often enfeebling in its effects, but help from within invariably invigorates. Whatever is done *for* man or classes, to a certain extent takes away the stimulus and necessity of doing for themselves; and where men are subjected to over-guidance and over-government, the inevitable tendency is to render them comparatively helpless. . . . The solid foundations of liberty must rest upon individual character; which is also the only sure guarantee for social security and national progress. John Stuart Mill truly observes that "even despotism does not produce its worst effects so long as individuality exists under it; and whatever crushes individuality *is* despotism, by whatever name it be called."[9]

8. As early as the 1830's Whewell's wholesale disregard of Scottish achievements in science was angrily corrected by David Brewster, "Whewell's History of the Inductive Sciences," *The Edinburgh Review, 66* (1837), 110-151 (147-149). It would be invidious to mention recent writers who, failing to distinguish between Scotland and England, have blithely described Brewster as English.

9. See particularly A. Smith, *The Nature and Causes of the Wealth of Nations* in *The Works of Adam Smith* (London, 1811), *4*, 41-43; J. S. Mill, *On Liberty* (London, 1859), pp. 21-22; and S. Smiles, *Self-Help* (London, 1859), pp. 1-3.

II

Adoration of British liberty had been markedly strengthened by the fervid reaction against the excesses committed by the Jacobins during the Terror.[10] It shone in contrast with the intolerance and despotism which allegedly were bringing ruin upon France, so that the deep-seated British suspicion of the arbitrary prerogative of the state was conspicuously reinforced. By 1830, at the dawn of the Age of Reform, it was generally if not totally accepted that the state would be imprudent or iniquitous to undertake actions and duties which were already adequately performed by individuals free from state control. When Lord Melbourne, who was twice British prime minister during the 1830's, put the question "Why can't you let it alone?" he was not for once exposing his incontrovertible indolence but expressing trust in individualism. This emphasis on personal responsibility was clearly not the sole property of one political group such as the Whigs or Benthamites; and it was consolidated by the corresponding and widespread appeal to personal religion made by the thriving Evangelical movement.

Yet owing to the rapid pace of social change, state intervention and collectivism had begun inevitably to gather force in the mid-1820's and within ten years were well launched. It seems that the British government disturbed the prevalent spirit of individualism when at least one of two not totally separable conditions was fulfilled: first, when intolerably cruel or unsafe situations outraged humanitarian consciences; second, when apposite opportunities arose for the deployment of Benthamite ideology, which was deeply motivated by the desire of its middle-class adherents to gain power. In opposing deliberate and wanton cruelty, Benthamite utilitarians, Whig philanthropists, Tory humanitarians, and bristling Evangelicals willingly joined forces during the 1820's when inter alia the

10. The parts of this section which deal with the general conditions for state intervention have been synthesized from such standard sources as: P. A. Brown, *The French Revolution in English History* (London, 1918); L. Woodward, *The Age of Reform 1815-1870* (Oxford, 1964); A. Briggs, *The Age of Improvement 1783-1867* (London, 1959); E. Halévy, *The Growth of Philosophic Radicalism* (London, 1949); *idem, The Triumph of Reform 1830-1841* (London, 1961); A. V. Dicey, *Lectures on the Relation between Law and Public Opinion in England during the Nineteenth Century*, 2nd ed. (London, 1914); J. B. Brebner, "Laissez Faire and State Intervention in Nineteenth-Century Britain," *Journal of Economic History,* Supplement to *8* (1948), 59-73.

public whipping of women was abolished and measures for the protection of children were introduced. It was, of course, a basic element in the Benthamite creed that pain should be minimized and if possible eliminated. The success enjoyed by various juntos in initiating the Age of Reform, aided by the persistently enunciated doctrines associated with utilitarianism, shows that pressure-groups used state intervention for their own not disreputable ends. In short, state action in Britain around 1830 was likely to occur only when intolerable conditions or opportunities for Benthamite legislation could be exploited by powerful and united pressure-groups.

If we consider British science at this time, it hardly provided examples of outrageous circumstances likely to arouse shame, wrath, and action from conscience-stricken humanitarians. Compared with large imminent issues such as slavery, working conditions in factories, the deficiencies of the Poor Law, the inadequacy of municipal administration, sanitary conditions in towns, and other problems concerning the patent misery and discontent of the working classes, the allegations made by Babbage about the decline of science in England were insultingly trivial and eminently dispensable. Nor did the organization of British science provide signally favorable opportunities which benevolent Benthamite legislators could appropriate and use for political ends. Their chosen targets were usually obvious abuses out of which widespread and energetic concern could be generated. In any event, except when humanitarian questions arose, the utilitarians generally tried by legislation to extend and not to curtail individual liberty and rights. Furthermore, that minority among scientists which urged either occasional or persistent state intervention in British scientific activity did not form a pressure group sufficiently well represented or active in government to achieve it.[11] In any event it is doubtful whether the condition of scientific instruction and institutions was at this time a party question. With respect to science there is no doubt that the two prerequisites for state intervention rarely occurred. It should be remembered, too, that such an important national matter as the education of English children was organized exclusively on the voluntarist system until 1833. Even a reforming Lord Chancellor,

11. Among politicians important in 1830 only Sir Robert Peel, Henry Brougham, and maybe Lord Althorp were strongly interested in science.

Henry Brougham, argued strongly in that year that "The efforts of the people are still wanting for the purpose of promoting Education; and Parliament will render no substantial assistance, until the people themselves take the matter in hand with energy and spirit, and the determination to do something."[12] Indeed when in 1833 the government granted £20,000 to two religious groups—the National Society and the British and Foreign School Society—for the building of new schools, the grant was available only if voluntary contributions met half their cost. If the state was slow and cautious in entering the field of national education, it is no wonder then that the state generally left British science to run itself in a voluntarist way.

The British government did, however, support scientific activity of various kinds when national security, internal need, and intermittently, sheer prestige were felt to be either directly or obliquely at stake. For decades the government's concern with navigation and cartography had led it to patronize observational astronomy and voyages of discovery. Quite traditionally, therefore, a number of the Admiralty's enterprises abroad, such as giving a five-year honorary research fellowship to Charles Darwin in 1831, occasionally patronized scientists at a time when the British were seeking to extend their naval and colonial dominion.[13] Less directly the state patronized science abroad through the East India Company, whose president had been a member of the British cabinet from 1812. For instance, the Company not only maintained observatories at Madras, Bombay, and St. Helena, but also supported the Calcutta Botanical Gardens of which the botanist Nathaniel Wallich was the superintendent. On the domestic front security and need jointly motivated the government's continuing creation of Regius chairs of medicine at the Universities of Edinburgh and Glasgow during the opening decades of the nineteenth century. It wanted trained and competent medical manpower. Yet quite characteristically these Regius professors received a low salary or none at all from the Crown, which relied on the ability of the professors and their universities to meet

12. Cited by G. Combe, *Lectures on Popular Education* (Edinburgh, 1833), p. 1.
13. Cannon, "Scientists and Broad Churchmen," pp. 82-83.

the heavy expenses associated with their activities.[14] Sometimes government departments, such as the Boards of Excise and Ordnance, turned to chemists for data which would serve as the basis of legislation or employed them for reasons of safety. The military schools, too, employed scientists: we find that in 1830 James Inman was resident professor of mathematics at the Royal Naval College, Portsmouth, and Michael Faraday was a visiting lecturer at the Royal Military Academy, Woolwich. Finally, less irregular patronage was dispensed to major national institutions for reasons associated with prestige and sometimes utility. Establishments such as the Royal Observatory, the British Museum, the Mint, the Botanic Gardens at Kew, Edinburgh and Dublin, the Natural History Museums at Edinburgh and Dublin, and the Royal Dublin Society were partly or totally financed by the government.[15] Yet this state patronage only nibbled incidentally and innocuously at the total body of scientific activity in Britain. Compared with the amounts which the governments of France and the German states were willing to spend on scientists and scientific institutions, the British government's contribution in 1830 was characteristically erratic and possibly niggardly: with few exceptions it expected people and organizations to look after themselves, as its recent closing of the Board of Longitude in 1828 had conspicuously shown.

The result of putting what may be called Smilesian virtues to work has been readily appreciated by general historians of Britain during the first industrial revolution. For example, Pollard and recently Musson and Robinson have forcibly argued that the

14. A. Duncan, *Memorials of the Faculty of Physicians and Surgeons of Glasgow, 1599-1850* (Glasgow, 1896), pp. 162-186; J. Coutts, *A History of the University of Glasgow* (Glasgow, 1909), pp. 512-569; A. Grant, *The Story of the University of Edinburgh during Its First Three Hundred Years* (London, 1884), *1*, 321-328.

15. The financing of science by the British government remains to be investigated, though H. F. Berry, *History of the Royal Dublin Society* (Dublin, 1915) contains useful information on Ireland. The variability of government patronage may be judged from the annual grants given in 1830 to the Botanic Gardens in Edinburgh and the Natural History Museum, both of which were associated with the University of Edinburgh: the former received £819; the latter received £100. In both cases Professors Graham and Jameson met the annual deficits as best they could. See: *Report of the Royal Commission of Inquiry into the State of the Universities of Scotland, Parliamentary Papers, 12* (1831), 151 and 177.

entrepreneurs of the industrial revolution, while not enjoying state sponsored and formalized technical training, frequently availed themselves of local opportunities which were usually sufficient for their immediate purposes.[16] If this sort of thesis is extended to the organization of science in Britain in 1830, then the effects derived from voluntarism and individualism were understandably great variety and apparent confusion. This diversity frequently emanated from local initiative which was exercised in response to local conditions and pressures. Such bewildering disorder should not be regarded as a regrettable deviation from the French and German patterns of professionalization. On the contrary it represented a distinctly national style of science of which individualism was the chief leitmotiv. Nor was the disorder really haphazard and bewildering. If differences of function, location, and social class are made, the variegated structure of institutionalized British science at the accession of William IV seems almost tailor-made to satisfy the needs and aims of professionals, devotees, and amateurs alike. Correspondingly the commitment to science shown by institutions and the degree of professionalization of the sciences cultivated in them varied widely, being frequently dependent on the extent to which private initiative could create or exploit local opportunities, traditions, and contingencies. What then was this structure and how did it reflect the dominant individualism?

III

First, at the national level, each of the three metropolitan societies—the Royal Society of London, the Royal Society of Edinburgh (f. 1783), and the Royal Irish Academy (f. 1786)—possessed its own characteristic membership, degree of professionalization, and favored fields of interest.[17] For example, the Edinburgh Society gained intellectually and socially from the contribution and expertise

16. S. Pollard, *The Genesis of Modern Management: A Study of the Industrial Revolution in Great Britain* (London, 1965); A. E. Musson and E. Robinson, *Science and Technology in the Industrial Revolution* (Toronto, 1969).

17. The Royal Society of London has been served by C. R. Weld, *A History of the Royal Society* (London, 1848) and H. Lyons, *The Royal Society 1660-1940* (Cambridge, 1944). Serious studies devoted to the remaining metropolitan societies are still required.

readily given by the city's leading cultural and professional groups, the University professoriate, the lawyers, and the medicals. It contrasted sharply with the Royal Society of London where the gentry, clergy, and military officers were trying to ensure that the dominant ethos remained dilettante and amateur: a greater proportion of its members published, and the cohesion provided by the unique combination of its three leading groups seems to have prevented the sort of internal dissension which so troubled its London counterpart in 1830. Second, as a result of group initiative a galaxy of specialized societies flourished chiefly in two of the three metropolitan centers. One can instance the following London societies: the Medical (f. 1773), Linnean (f. 1788), Mineralogical (f. 1799), Medical and Chirurgical (f. 1805), Geological (f. 1807), Astronomical (f. 1820), Zoological (f. 1826) and Geographical (f. 1830), not forgetting the Society of Arts (f. 1754) and the Institute of Civil Engineers (f. 1818).[18] At their best the style of work and composition of membership of these specialized societies subversively threatened the hegemony relished by the Royal Society of London, whose acute premonition had led it to try to suppress the embryonic Geological and Astronomical Societies in 1807 and 1820 respectively.[19] Elsewhere in England the dominance of natural history and allied fields, which every man could cultivate, is seen in the Geological Society of Cornwall (f. 1814) and the Natural Historical Society of Manchester (f. 1821). In Scotland, however, more emphasis was placed on medicine and related subjects, many of the societies being predictably associated with universities often in the form of student societies whose activities were nurtured by the professoriate. At Edinburgh alone one can point to the Royal Medical Society (f. 1734), the Harveian Society (f. 1752), the Royal Physical Society (f. 1771), the Wernerian Natural History Society (f. 1808), the Scottish Society of Arts (f. 1821), the Plinian Society (f. 1823), and the Hunterian

don, 1907); J. L. E. Dreyer and H. H. Turner, *History of the Royal Astronomical Society 1820-1920* (London, 1923); D. Hudson and K. Luckhurst, *The Royal Society of Arts, 1754-1954* (London, 1954).

19. See, e.g., M. J. S. Rudwick, "The Foundation of the Geological Society of London: Its Scheme for Co-operative Research and Its Struggle for Independence," *The British Journal for the History of Science, 1* (1963), 326-355.

18. Though indispensable, histories of these societies are usually narrow and hagiographical: A. T. Gage, *History of the Linnean Society of London* (London, 1938); H. B. Woodward, *The History of the Geological Society of London* (Lon-

Medical Society (f. 1824).[20] By contrast, for reasons which remain obscure, specialist societies in Ireland were rare.

Third, again as the result of group initiative, a multitude of provincial general scientific societies, often carrying the ennobling title "Literary and Philosophical Society," had burgeoned in the English manufacturing towns and also in traditional regional centers. It is probable that Charles Lyell did not exaggerate when he asserted that compared with the specialist London societies the provincial ones constituted "a still more novel and characteristic feature of the times."[21] A sample list culled from the North of England is impressive even allowing for qualitative differences: Manchester (f. 1781), Liverpool (f. 1812), Newcastle (f. 1813), Leeds (f. 1818), Yorkshire, Sheffield, Hull, Whitby (all f. 1822), and Scarborough (f. 1830). Scotland and Ireland could each boast at least a pair: Perth (1784) and Glasgow (1802), Cork (f. 1819) and Belfast (f. 1821).[22] Naturally these societies varied widely in membership and technical competence: for instance, in 1830 the Philosophical Society of Glasgow was still dominated in its membership by intellectually isolated craftsmen and manufacturers who generally neither attended meetings nor offered papers. Indeed the Society slid from crisis to crisis until in 1834 its renovation began with the election to membership and immediate office of distinguished professors from the University of Glasgow and Anderson's University who had previously ignored it.[23] Yet the provincial societies provided a local focus of activity where meetings, lectures, a library, sometimes apparatus, an opportunity for publication, social legitimation, and the satisfactions of power, vanity, and emulation were all to be savored.

20. C. P. Finlayson, "Records of Scientific and Medical Societies preserved in the University Library, Edinburgh," *The Bibliotheck: A Journal of Bibliographical Notes and Queries Mainly of Scottish Interest, 1* (1958), 14-19.

21. C. Lyell, "Scientific Institutions," *The Quarterly Review, 34* (1826), 153-179 (163).

22. The list is taken from A. Hume and A. I. Evans, *The Learned Societies and Printing Clubs of the United Kingdom* (London, 1853). It would appear that the call issued by Schofield for more social history of nineteenth-century British science, based on these societies, has remained largely unheeded: R. E. Schofield, "Histories of Scientific Societies: Needs and Opportunities for Research," *History of Science, 2* (1963), 70-83. But see two studies of ephemeral societies: W. H. Brock, "The London Chemical Society 1824," *Ambix, 14* (1967), 133-139; and N. G. Coley, "The Animal Chemistry Club," *Notes and Records of the Royal Society, 22* (1967), 173-185.

23. A. Kent, "The Royal Philosophical Society of Glasgow," *The Philosophical Journal, 4* (1967), 43-50.

A fourth category was constituted by those institutions, devoted equally to teaching and research, which were created and maintained by individual initiative or jeu d'esprit. Founded as a philanthropic establishment for artisans by Count Rumford in 1799, the Royal Institution in 1830 combined popular teaching and specialized research. Under Sir Humphry Davy and then Michael Faraday it had capitalized on fashionable London's interest in physical and chemical science; in its laboratory brilliant individual work flourished, but Faraday led no research school.[24] Its frequently ignored Irish equivalent, the Royal Dublin Society (f. 1731), was furnished with a devoted staff, led by Charles Giesecke, which specialized in natural history. Its English imitators and descendants, such as the London, Surrey, Liverpool, and Birmingham Institutions, served a mainly middle-class audience with the lectures and libraries which were such characteristic features of an age of self-improvement.

When one turns to organizations which were avowedly concerned with teaching, those that taught some science are best understood in terms of the class needs they fulfilled, as Cardwell has clearly demonstrated with respect to England alone.[25] Though a variety of establishments diffused science, it should be noted as an indicator of the degree of professionalization of British science in 1830 that not one of them gave a qualification solely in science. Nor was the context of science teaching uniform: some subjects such as natural philosophy appeared in the arts curriculum, some like botany in the medical program, and flexible ones like chemistry in both. Again in some institutions a scientific subject could be irrelevant to the process by which a degree was acquired: the geology class at the University of Cambridge was run by Sedgwick as a nongraduating one. In other establishments such as the Scottish universities the students enjoyed the privilege of *Lernfreiheit* and attended classes in science, whether graduating or nongraduating ones, according to their intellectual preferences and pockets.

Within these diverse patterns, the constituent colleges of Oxford and Cambridge Universities, Trinity College Dublin, and King's College London provided some education in science largely for those

24. T. Martin, *The Royal Institution* (London, 1961).
25. Cardwell, *Organization of Science in England*, pp. 28-29.

aspiring to the status of the cultivated English gentleman.[26] There were, however, sharp differences between these four institutions. By 1830 an increasingly powerful group of research-oriented teachers at Cambridge had not only modernized the mathematics tripos, then the dominant degree, but were also rejuvenating natural historical fields. In the former activity George Biddell Airy (Plumian professor of mathematics and natural philosophy) and Babbage (sinecurist Lucas professor of mathematics) were prominently supported by William Hopkins, a private tutor, and George Peacock and the Reverend James Challis, both of whom were Fellows of Trinity College Cambridge. In the latter activity those two key patrons of Darwin, the Reverend Adam Sedgwick (professor of geology) and the Reverend John Stevens Henslow (professor of botany), scorned their sinecures by developing field methods of instruction. The link between the mathematicians and the natural historians was provided by the voraciously versatile Whewell, then professor of mineralogy. With the exception of the Observatory no great institutional demands for accommodation or apparatus were found to be necessary. At Oxford, which was oriented toward classics and about to be racked by tractarianism, only two men, the Reverend William Buckland (professor of mineralogy and geology) and Charles Daubeny (professor of chemistry), ranked equally with the Cambridge group. Both the charismatic Buckland in field and cave and Daubeny in his laboratory at Magdalen College worked hard and to little long-term effect in a deteriorating situation. In the Emerald Isle the solitary William Rowan Hamilton (professor of astronomy) saved Trinity College Dublin from total scientific obscurity. Lastly, King's College London, founded in 1828 by Anglican and Tory groups as an immaculate rival to University College London, functioned mainly

26. This paragraph is based on relevant works previously cited and others such as: C. E. Mallet, *A History of the University of Oxford* (Oxford, 1924-1927), *3;* D. A. Winstanley, *Unreformed Cambridge* (Cambridge, 1935); C. Maxwell, *A History of Trinity College, Dublin* (Dublin, 1946); J. F. C. Hearnshaw, *The Centenary History of King's College, London, 1828-1928* (London, 1929); N. Barlow, ed., *The Autobiography of Charles Darwin* (London, 1958); N. Barlow, ed., *Darwin and Henslow* (London, 1967); J. W. Clark and T. M. Hughes, eds., *The Life and Letters of the Reverend Adam Sedgwick* (Cambridge, 1890); E. O. Gordon, *Life and Correspondence of William Buckland* (New York, 1894); R. T. Gunther, *A History of the Daubeny Laboratory Magdalen College Oxford* (London, 1904); F. S. Taylor, "The Teaching of Science at Oxford in the Nineteenth Century," *Annals of Science, 8* (1952), 82-112; and the indispensable portraits provided by the *Dictionary of National Biography.*

as a theological and classical preparatory department for the Universities of Oxford and Cambridge. Accordingly it placed less emphasis on science than its London competitor, though in 1830 the recruitment of Charles Lyell and John Frederic Daniell to the chairs of geology and chemistry was imminent.

Science for the middle classes and above was more widely available at the six Scottish universities, at University College London, and tenuously at their Ulster offspring, the Belfast Academical Institution's collegiate department.[27] Great qualitative differences existed among the three pre-Reformation universities of Glasgow, St. Andrews, and King's College Aberdeen, the late sixteenth-century pair of Edinburgh and Marischal College Aberdeen, and that late eighteenth-century monument to private enterprise, Anderson's University in Glasgow. Of these, Edinburgh and Glasgow were pre-eminent in offering inexpensive and secular studies which spanned liberal, useful, and vocational fields. Though in 1830 the University of Edinburgh was losing its reputation as the outstanding English-speaking University in the world of science, its medical school remained internationally important. Of its scientific professoriate, John Leslie (natural philosophy), Thomas Charles Hope (medicine and chemistry), Robert Jameson (natural history), and Robert Graham (medicine and botany) were outstanding professors who had initiated or expanded effective use of lecture demonstrations or of field work in spite of financial and other constraints.[28] Laboratory

27. Histories of these universities vary widely in quality. For the eight institutions in question, H. H. Bellot, *University College, London 1826-1926* (London, 1929) is exemplary. Also useful are: D. B. Horn, *A Short History of the University of Edinburgh 1556-1889* (Edinburgh, 1967); Grant, *op. cit.;* J. D. Mackie, *The University of Glasgow 1451-1951* (Glasgow, 1954); Coutts, *op. cit.;* T. W. Moody and J. C. Becket, *Queen's, Belfast 1845-1949: The History of a University* (London, 1959). R. G. Cant, *The University of St. Andrews, A Short History* (Edinburgh, 1946) contains little about science. R. S. Rait, *The Universities of Aberdeen: A History* (Aberdeen, 1895); J. Muir, *John Anderson, Pioneer of Technical Education and the College He Founded* (Glasgow, 1950); and A. H. Sexton, *The First Technical College: A Sketch of the History of "The Andersonian"* (Glasgow, 1894) are now dated.

28. See: *Evidence, Oral and Documentary, Taken and Received by the Commissioners for Visiting the Universities of Scotland: The University of Edinburgh, Parliamentary Papers, 35* (1837), passim; M. Napier, *Biographical Notice of Sir John Leslie* (Edinburgh, 1836); J. B. Morrell, "Practical Chemistry in the University of Edinburgh, 1799-1843," *Ambix, 16* (1969), 66-80; L. Jameson, "Biographical Memoir of the late Professor Jameson," *The Edinburgh New Philosophical Journal, 57* (1854), 1-49; and C. Ransford, *Biographical Sketch of the Late Robert Graham* (Edinburgh, 1846).

work was available only in chemistry, but Hope led no research team. However, the much maligned Robert Jameson was remarkably successful in producing a notable group of students, probably as a combined result of his rigorous training in the field and of his seminars held in the Natural History Museum of which he was Keeper. Westward at Glasgow, the scientific reputation of the medical school had risen dramatically through the ambitious efforts of Thomas Thomson (professor of chemistry) and William Jackson Hooker (professor of botany).[29] The former's valiant attempt to establish a research school had foundered on political rocks and on his inability to devise basic techniques which his students could systematically apply to a new field; but the practical training in chemical analysis which he had given for twelve years to his laboratory class was unique in a British university. At Anderson's University, founded in 1796 by John Anderson to remedy the defects of the University of Glasgow and to extend the availability of useful knowledge, the outrageously spectacular Andrew Ure (professor of chemistry and natural philosophy) was about to be replaced by the broodingly introspective Thomas Graham, whose new laboratory was soon to be a mecca for keen young Northern chemists.[30]

South of the border in 1826 the ideological drive and political agility of dissenters, chiefly Whig alumni of the University of Edinburgh, had disturbed Oxbridge's dominance by their private enterprise in founding University College London as a joint-stock company which offered an attractive rate of interest.[31] Its organizational characteristics and intellectual emphases showed its Scottish and particularly Edinburgh origin: a wide range of modern subjects, liberal and professional, was taught in a secular context by lectures to nonresidential students who had free access to single courses; and professors were remunerated by small salaries plus student fees. The debt to Edinburgh was particularly strong in the professoriate,

29. J. B. Morrell, "Thomas Thomson: Professor of Chemistry and University Reformer," *The British Journal for the History of Science, 4* (1969), 245-265.

30. R. A. Smith, *The Life and Works of Thomas Graham* (Glasgow, 1884) is disappointing on Graham's Glasgow period; but W. S. C. Copeman, "Andrew Ure," *Proceedings of the Royal Society of Medicine, 44* (1951), 655-662, is enticing.

31. This paragraph is largely based on: Bellot, *op. cit.;* and C. W. New, *The Life of Lord Brougham to 1830* (Oxford, 1961).

in the stress placed on medicine and science, and not least in the internecine quarrels which disturbed its opening years. Indeed in 1830 University College London was only four years from building, on the Edinburgh model, the first hospital attached to an English university to be used for clinical teaching of medical students. Just four years after its foundation, though smarting from the autocratic wardenship of the Whig geologist Leonard Horner, the first scientist to head a British university, it was furnished with seven professors of science. The spectrum was wide: it ranged from their doyen Charles Bell (physiology) through the painstaking Edward Turner (chemistry) and John Lindley (botany) to the intellectually stagnant Robert Edmond Grant (comparative anatomy and zoology), the flamboyantly fashionable Dionysius Lardner (natural philosophy), and the execrably incompetent Granville Sharp Pattison (morbid anatomy). None of these led a research school, but it was symptomatic that, for example, Turner, a master of exact analysis, had just opened a practical laboratory class.[32]

The artisan classes were also catered for by 1830.[33] Inspired by the success of George Birkbeck's popular lectures to working men at Anderson's University between 1800 and 1804 and by the enterprise of Leonard Horner in founding the Edinburgh School of Arts in 1821, the London Mechanics' Institute had been created largely by Birkbeck himself, Thomas Hodgskin, and Lord Henry Brougham in 1823. Supported by dissenters and radicals, and supervised by Whigs who feared the rebellious propensities of the uneducated urban masses, the mechanics' institute movement had reached its peak in 1830 shortly before it was appropriated by the bourgeoisie. Aided by the popular education groups, such as Brougham's Society for the Diffusion of Useful Knowledge, and by encyclopedias ranging from the *Britannica* to the *Metropolitan*, the movement constituted a remarkable national attempt on a self-help basis to educate the populace at a time when the state was manifestly indifferent.

32. H. Terrey, "Edward Turner, M.D., F.R.S. (1798-1837)," *Annals of Science, 2* (1937), 137-152.

33. My interpretation is indebted to: New, *op. cit.;* T. Kelly, *George Birkbeck: Pioneer of Adult Education* (Liverpool, 1957); M. Tylecote, *The Mechanics' Institutes of Lancashire and Yorkshire before 1851* (Manchester, 1957); and J. N. Hays, "Science and Brougham's Society," *Annals of Science, 20* (1964), 227-241.

Finally two types of teaching institution, the national medical colleges and the private tutor, complete the broad picture. Wide differences of social class and professional aims existed among the six metropolitan Colleges of Physicians and of Surgeons which flourished in London, Edinburgh, and Dublin.[34] Yet their concern with teaching preclinical medical subjects and the continuing importance in science of the medical profession of which they were the pinnacles are frequently ignored. For example, the first Edinburgh medical institution to make a laboratory course of practical chemistry compulsory for its students—in 1829—was significantly the Edinburgh College of Surgeons and not the prestigious University with its distinguished chemical lineage.[35] Again, in 1830 the Hunterian Museum of the Royal College of Surgeons in London employed and gave facilities to William Clift and the young Richard Owen who acted as its chief and assistant curators. Of the increasing body of private teachers of science performing in 1830, only that arch entrepreneur John Dalton was a nationally known figure.[36] Generally second-order men prospered in metropolitan or regional centers where a fashionable or interested audience could be attracted, and they flourished as private pre-clinical medical teachers.

IV

The tradition of self-help did not die immediately after 1830, but on the contrary persisted with characteristic vigor. It is true that the 1830's witnessed an acceleration in the status and recognition afforded to science, a movement in which the British Association for the Advancement of Science (f. 1831) was conspicuously active.

34. Competent accounts are given by: G. N. Clark, *A History of the Royal College of Physicians of London* (London, 1964-1966), *2;* J. D. H. Widdess, *A History of the Royal College of Physicians of Ireland 1654-1963* (Edinburgh and London, 1963); *idem, The Royal College of Surgeons in Ireland and its Medical School 1784-1966* (Edinburgh and London, 1967). Z. Cope, *The Royal College of Surgeons of England: A History* (London, 1959) is less satisfactory. C. H. Creswell, *The Royal College of Surgeons of Edinburgh: Historical Notes from 1505-1905* (Edinburgh, 1926) is fragmentary. Both Edinburgh Colleges would repay detailed study.

35. J. B. Morrell, "Practical Chemistry," p. 72.

36. A. W. Thackray, "Fragmentary Remains of John Dalton, Part I: Letters," *Annals of Science, 22* (1966), 145-174.

Yet the British Association itself, in spite of being a body devoted inter alia to the professionalization of science, strikingly shows the continuing vitality of local private enterprise in its origins and crucially successful first meeting. Its foundation primarily reflected provincial Northern initiative and not the struggle for power which split the Royal Society of London during 1830.[37]

Several elements in its creation and early history may be easily distinguished. First, up to and including 1830 but especially from 1827, such diverse figures as John Playfair, John Frederick William Herschel, Davy, David Brewster, Babbage, and Daubeny had expressed concern about the status of scientists and the concomitant public support of some kinds of science. Brewster in particular repeatedly pressed hard for increased recognition for scientists and science through the columns of his periodical, the *Edinburgh Journal of Science*.[38] The deaths of William Hyde Wollaston, Thomas Young, and Davy within the space of six months between December 1828 and May 1829 not only staggered him but confirmed his view that an era in British science had ended.[39]

Second, in his famous critique of Babbage's book Brewster proposed in October 1830 that an "association of our nobility, clergy, gentry and philosophers" should be formed to remedy the depressed state of science.[40] Third, by spring 1831 Brewster, who at that time

37. My interpretation is merely an extension of W. F. Cannon, "History in Depth," pp. 24-25. It is implicit in O. J. R. Howarth, *The British Association for the Advancement of Science: A Retrospect 1831-1931,* 2nd ed. (London, 1931), and the early *Reports of the British Association for the Advancement of Science.* Cf. L. P. Williams, "The Royal Society and the Founding of the British Association for the Advancement of Science," *Notes and Records of the Royal Society, 16* (1961), 221-233. The foundation of the British Association in 1831 was paralleled by the establishment by Charles Hastings in 1832 of the Provincial Medical and Surgical Association which was later renamed the British Medical Association. Both these groups aimed to improve professional status, and both were founded in the provinces by the exertions of alumni of the University of Edinburgh.

38. See: Brewster, "Memoir of the Life of M. Le Chevalier Fraunhofer," *Edinburgh Journal of Science, 7* (1827), 1-11; Brewster, "Exhibition of the National Industry of France," *ibid., 8* (1828), 344-346; Brewster, "Mr. Dalton's System of Chemical Philosophy," *ibid., 8* (1828), 346-355; G. Harvey, "On the Science of Ship-building," *ibid., 9* (1828), 298-300; Babbage, "Great Congress of Philosophers at Berlin," *ibid., 10* (1829), 225-234.

39. Brewster to Ørsted, 24 June 1829, M. C. Harding, ed., *Correspondance de H. C. Ørsted avec divers savants* (Copenhagen, 1920), *2,* 282.

40. In his "Decline of Science in England," *The Quarterly Review, 43* (1830), 305-342 (341), Brewster reached a large Anglican and Tory audience.

lacked means, prospects, and a permanent post commensurate with his achievements, had gained for his project the support of John Phillips, Secretary to the Yorkshire Philosophical Society, and of Roderick Murchison, the Scottish President of the Geological Society of London. Largely through the efforts made by Phillips and his colleague, the Reverend William Vernon Harcourt, Vice-President of the Yorkshire Philosophical Society and conveniently a son of the then Archbishop of York, ably supported by three Scots, John Robison (jnr.), James Finlay Weir Johnston, and James David Forbes, the first meeting at York was arranged and social ostracization avoided.[41] Not unexpectedly that first meeting was strongly Northern and Scottish in its inspiration, composition, and initiative: Harcourt, "the soul of our meeting" as Brewster called him, laid down the objects and rules of the association whose title he invented.[42] As Murchison recalled: "It was then and there resolved that we were ever to be *Provincials*. Old Dalton insisted on this —saying that we should lose all the object of diffusing knowledge if we ever met in the Metropolis."[43] Indeed, London scientists with the exception of the geologists were absent; the University of Oxford was represented by the solitary Daubeny; and the Universities of Cambridge, Edinburgh, Glasgow, and London held themselves totally aloof. Clearly many of the savants associated with the old and new British universities, keen to maintain their aristocracy, were doing more than weighing the upstart provincial association; they were also holding back through resentment of embarrassing allegations about the decline of British science and the accompanying call for

41. Brewster, "Great Scientific Meeting to be Held in York," *Edinburgh Journal of Science, 4* (April 1831), 374; Brewster, "Observations on the Decline of Science in England," *ibid., 5* (July 1831), 1-16; Brewster, "Proposed Scientific Meeting at York," *ibid., 5* (July 1831), 180-182; Brewster, "Decline of Science in England," *ibid., 5* (October 1831), 334-358; J. W. F. Johnston, "Scientific Meeting at York," *ibid., 6* (January 1832), 1-33; A. Giekie, *Life of Sir Roderick I. Murchison* (London, 1875), *1,* 184-189; J. C. Shairp, P. G. Tait, and A. Adams Reilly, *Life and Letters of James David Forbes* (London, 1873), pp. 75-79; M. M. Gordon, *The Home Life of Sir David Brewster* (Edinburgh, 1869), pp. 141-149; I. Todhunter, *William Whewell, D.D.: An Account of His Writings with Selections from His Literary and Scientific Correspondence* (London, 1876), *2,* 126-132, and 237-238.

42. Gordon, *Brewster,* p. 144.

43. Giekie, *op. cit. 1,* 187-188. The italics are Murchison's.

state attention to be given to science, which to them constituted explicit criticism of what they regarded as their own adequacy and success. It must be stressed that the London institutions and the University of Cambridge (including Babbage) supported the British Association from 1832 only after it had become apparent that the fledgling group was sufficiently important to be invaded and remodeled on less contentious lines.[44] Accordingly direct national encouragement of science, one of the Association's original aims, was quietly and quickly dropped in spite of Brewster's public opposition.[45] During the 1830's, therefore, the Association rarely approached the government, the chief exception being the successful recommendation it made in 1838 to Lord Melbourne's administration that an Antarctic expedition be mounted. Not surprisingly the first British national pressure-group for science and scientists relied extensively on voluntary support and individual zeal; and its membership embraced savants and sciolists alike. Quite simply the very diverse local and personal interests in the Association wanted to preserve opportunities in which their own initiative could be exercised; any profound surrender of autonomy was fundamentally anathema to their own concerns, however badly coordinated at a national level their activities might have been.

Self-help as a motive inherent in the organization of British science persisted well into the Age of Reform, its inability to cope with the problems of scale and expense of professionalized science becoming slowly visible. Yet it had hardly sunk into its geriatric phase in 1851 when the Great Exhibition dazzlingly confirmed the superiority of British manufacturing enterprise. In that same year the senior British scientific civil servant, the Astronomer Royal, was

44. Giekie, *ibid.*, p. 188. Buckland, President of the British Association's Oxford meeting in 1832, ensured that its social tone was effortlessly superior: see, e.g., E. C. Curwen, *The Journal of Gideon Mantell, Surgeon and Geologist* (Oxford, 1940), pp. 102-104. It is apparent from Clark and Hughes, *op. cit., 1,* 390 and 407, that Sedgwick reluctantly attended the 1832 meeting because of the pressure put on him by his Oxford equivalent, Buckland, and by Murchison. The next year as president of the Association, which met at Cambridge, he was its animating spirit.

45. Brewster, "The British Scientific Association," *Edinburgh Review, 60* (1835), 363-394; *idem,* "British Association for the Advancement of Science," *North British Review, 14* (1850), 235-287; *idem,* "Presidential Address," *Report of the British Association for the Advancement of Science, 19* (1850), xxxi-xliv.

far from singing the requiem of the libertarian tradition in his presidential address to the British Association. On the contrary Airy's words epitomized a feeling almost as prevalent then as in 1830: "this absence of Government-Science harmonizes well with the peculiarities of our social institutions. In Science, as well as in almost everything else, our national genius inclines us to prefer voluntary associations of private persons to organizations of any kind dependent on the State."[46]

Addenda

pp. 196, 199: the dismissals of Trinity College, Dublin, and of Robert Edmond Grant, should not be taken seriously.

46. Airy, "Presidential Address," *Report of the B.A.A.S., 20* (1851), xxxix-liii (li).

XII

LONDON INSTITUTIONS AND LYELL'S CAREER: 1820–41

In offering a contribution to a session concerned with 'the background to Lyell's work', I want to begin by launching a caveat against the notion of 'background'. If, in the case of Lyell, 'background' features remained in obscurity then they can be dismissed; if, however, 'background' features were important then they become foreground. This point is not merely linguistic pedantry, because if we look at the scientific institutions of London in the period 1820–41, it is too easy to assume, with naïve optimism, that if they existed they must have been functionally effective for scientists. This was not necessarily so. We have to discover, as a matter of contingent reality, the ways in which particular institutions actually affected the careers of individual scientists. In this paper, therefore, I shall offer some general observations on London scientific institutions; and then I shall analyse Lyell's varying allegiances to them in terms of his ambitions concerning the shape and direction of his career.

During Lyell's lifetime, science in Western Europe was at once developing its cognitive structure and establishing an equally important social structure: considered as a socially organized intellectual enterprise, it was slowly transformed from an occasional avocation of a few individuals into a regular vocational pursuit. This process assumed different forms in France, the German states, and Britain, the three leading scientific countries at that time. In France the typical scientific career became that of teacher, examiner, or consultant in a state-supported and state-controlled bureaucracy which was centralized in Paris: French *savants* were often state functionaries. In the German states, however, the dominant scientific career became that of a professor in a university, which was invariably state-supported but rarely state-controlled. Whereas the French scientific mecca was inevitably Paris, the German equivalent could be a small provincial town such as Giessen. Compared with France and Germany, Britain offered in Lyell's lifetime a more fluid situation: formal state support for scientists and their organizations grew relatively more slowly; a plurality of scientific institutions flourished mainly on a voluntary basis; and no typical career structure can easily be discerned. It was still possible in Britain for the enthusiastic devotee who lacked formal scientific training to make a great contribution to science, as the case of Murchison reminds us. At the age of 31 and a bored retired army officer

For valuable help and criticism I am indebted to John Christie, Jonathan Hodge, Roy Porter, and Martin Rudwick. For permission to cite manuscripts, I am grateful to the Devon Record Office, the Geological Society of London, the Royal Society of London, Trinity College, Cambridge, the Trustees of the British Museum, and the University Library, Cambridge.

of independent means, Murchison perceived, with the help of Sir Humphry Davy, 'that a man might pursue philosophy without abandoning field sports'; fifteen years later, in 1838, his great tome on the Silurian system justly crowned him King of Siluria.[1] Murchison's is by no means the only example in the early nineteenth century of a gentleman achieving as a devotee the highest intellectual standards in science without being dependent on it for a living. Indeed during the most creative part of Lyell's career, namely c. 1825 to c. 1841, the relative absence of formal career structures allowed individuals to indulge in bizarre eccentricity. Perhaps the best example of unpredictable erratic behaviour was the way in which Sir James South extinguished his astronomical research, and lost £8,000, by smashing to pieces the mounting, made by Troughton, of his famous telescope. For good measure, in 1836, he printed a scurrilous poster in which those fragments were offered for sale by auction.[2] Such unLyellian behaviour showed that South was more concerned with emotional release than with the maintenance of his scientific career.

It was indeed the lack of formal state support and the absence of regular career structures which *inter alia* aroused the ire of the declinists who in the early 1830s lamented the condition of British science. Though the grumbletonians such as Babbage and Brewster frequently founded their case on their own jealousies and frustrations, there was genuine disagreement among working scientists about the sort of encouragement government should give to scientific research.[3] Generally Babbage's opponents argued that the state should patronize research, especially of a useful kind, only where private exertion was demonstrably inadequate; but where individuals were exerting themselves, government support would be useless and hurtful. Babbage's critics could point to the fashionability and wide diffusion of a taste for science, and to the existence of private wealth sufficient to sustain that taste: in Basil Hall's view, science in France would die without government support, whereas in England such state support 'would be like dashing with the oar to accelerate the cataract'.[4]

Too much attention has been given, in my opinion, to the rather intractable problem of whether Babbage was right or wrong in his strictures on the state of English science. Equally important was the deep concern indisputably felt about the present state and future prospects of English science, a feeling shown more in private correspondence than in public stance. For instance, Whewell refused to rally publicly under Dr Brewster's banners; and though keen to reform the Old Lady, the Royal Society of London, by supporting Herschel for the presidency in 1830, he is not usually seen as a member of the Babbage-Brewster axis.[5] Yet privately he confessed to Murchison in 1831 that there was indeed 'a dearth of great men, and laborious experimenters' and he therefore persistently recommended as a palliative his notion that the Royal Society ought to produce annual reports on the progress of different sciences.[6] One suspects that Whewell was not alone in being publicly an anti-declinist but privately a jeremiah. Such self-awareness on the part of the cultivators of science, such questioning, almost pathological preoccupation with the condition of science, especially characteristic of the late 1820s and the 1830s, showed itself historiographically, institutionally, and linguistically. Historiographically, that period witnessed the consolidation of the view that between c. 1795 and 1830 British geology became a science. In 1831 Sedgwick, as President of the Geological Society, canonized William Smith as the Father of English Geology; eight years later Whewell in the same capacity enunciated the triple division of Descriptive Geology into the Fabulous, Heroic, and Historical periods; and, of course, one reason for the establishment of the *Proceedings of the Geological Society* in 1826 was to 'furnish a connected history of the Society'.[7] Institutionally, the most conspicuous example of self-awareness was the founding, in 1831, of the British Association for the Advancement of Science. This first national pressure-group tried to promote science intellectually by coordinating and directing research via its system of reports and peripatetic meetings; while socially it gave research grants to selected workers and occasionally lobbied public bodies for patronage.[8] Linguistically, Whewell came to the aid of British science in 1834 when he deplored the division of the soil of science into small allotments. In reviewing Mrs Somerville's *Connexion of the physical sciences*, Whewell pointed out that one curious result of insulated specialization in science

> may be observed in the want of any name by which we can designate the students of the knowledge of the material world collectively. We are informed that this difficulty was felt very oppressively by the members of the British Association for the Advancement of Science, at their meetings at York, Oxford, and Cambridge, in the last three summers. There was no general term by which these gentlemen could describe themselves with reference to their pursuits. *Philosophers* was felt to be too wide and too lofty a term, and was very properly forbidden them by Mr. Coleridge, both in his capacity of philologer and metaphysician; *savans* was rather assuming, besides being French instead of English; some ingenious gentleman proposed that, by analogy with *artist*, they might form *scientist* . . . but this was not generally palatable; others attempted to translate the term by which the members of similar associations in Germany have described themselves, but it was not found easy to discover an English equivalent for natur-forscher. The process of examination which it implies might suggest such undignified compounds as *nature-poker*, or *nature peeper*, for these *naturae curiosi*; but these were indignantly rejected.[9]

The ingenious gentleman was, of course, Whewell himself. His neologism 'scientist' epitomizes that self-consciousness which was pervasive in the 1830s.

In 1830 Granville published an anonymous critique of the Royal

Society entitled *Science without a head.*[10] Yet, if we look at the explosion of new scientific institutions between 1819 and 1841 in London alone, science appeared not headless but a hydra. That institutional expansion, mainly voluntarily supported and specialist-orientated, shows the extent to which science gained public recognition during two central decades of the Age of Reform. Consider the situation in London in 1819. The main institutions ostensibly devoted to scientific research and/or publication were seven in number: Royal Society (f. 1660), Royal Observatory (f. 1675), Royal Society of Arts (f. 1752), British Museum (f. 1753), Linnean Society (f. 1788), Royal Institution (f. 1799), and the Geological Society (f. 1807). Regular institutionalized teaching of science in the metropolis was largely restricted to the Royal Institution and its local imitators. By 1841, however, that situation had been transformed. The successful establishment of the Astronomical Society in 1820 at once confirmed that the Royal Society was powerless to halt the erosion of its hegemony and inaugurated a rash of fifteen specialist societies: witness the Asiatic (f. 1823), the Phrenological (f. 1823), the Zoological (f. 1826), the Geographical (f. 1830), the Entomological (f. 1833), the Statistical (f. 1834), the London Clay Club (f. 1836 and the precursor of the Palaeontographical), the Meteorological (f. 1836), the Aborigines Protection (f. 1837), the Ornithological (f. 1837), the Agricultural (f. 1838), the London Electrical (f. 1838), the Botanical of London (f. 1838), the Microscopical (f. 1839), and the Chemical (f. 1841). Such a list is not exhaustive and it arbitrarily omits medical and technical organizations. Moreover, though the annual meetings of the British Association for the Advancement of Science were peripatetic, its Council met in London, usually at the Geological Society, and to that extent it was based in London. Even the government had shown enterprise by providing the Museum of Economic Geology (established 1837) and the Mining Record Office (f. 1839) as a local habitation for the Geological Survey (f. 1835). Though in 1841 government dismantled the Kew Observatory, there was compensation that very year when Kew Gardens were put on a new footing under the elder Hooker as director. This extraordinary expansion of new societies or institutions, ostensibly devoted to the advancement of science, was not paralleled by the establishment of their equivalents devoted to the teaching of science. Nevertheless, the London Mechanics' Institute (f. 1823), University College London (f. 1826), King's College London (f. 1828), and a host of Literary and Scientific Institutions, of which the Eastern Atheneum at Stepney was the most curious, supplemented the teaching given by private lecturers; and, though actual teaching did not begin until 1851 at the Museum of Economic Geology, in 1839 the Treasury had sanctioned that innovation.

The burgeoning of London's scientific societies, paralleled in the provinces by the growth of literary and philosophical societies, even in such unlikely places as Barnsley and Bradford, was not to everyone's taste. No less a figure than John Herschel refused to join the first meeting of the British Association on the grounds that already too much of his time and effort had been dissipated and exhausted as an official in existing scientific societies.[11] And William Vernon Harcourt, sensing the fullness of the scientific arena, was always keen to declare that 'The Association contemplates no interference with the ground occupied by other Institutions'.[12] This proliferation of societies indicates that shifts in the cultural uses of science were taking place, which in the particular case of London remain unexplored in detail. Nevertheless, this institutional expansion in London was probably based on the ways in which patrons of science perceived it as being natural truth, polite knowledge, technical agent, theological edification, social anodyne, and cultural affirmation.[13] For performers who published scientific papers, those institutions also offered libraries, specimens, sometimes apparatus, relatively informed audiences, critical evaluation, peer group encouragement, and the possibility of creating intellectual disciples. At the same time, through this organizational pluralism, more people could hope to gain intellectual reward or at least to participate in organized culture; and in those societies dominated by wealthy clubability, social advancement was not a pipe-dream. Most importantly, however, many of the societies were publishing societies in which the expense of printing papers was met not by the contributor but by the societies from their subscriptions. Between 1820 and 1840 in London the range of publication opportunities in the journals of scientific societies was enlarged at no cost to the contributors themselves, who were in addition protected from the financial risk inherent in commercial publication.

It is indeed publication which shows more clearly than anything else that between 1820 and 1841 the new and old specialist societies in London usurped much of the ground previously held by the Royal Society. At a time when the Royal Society was in any event enduring internal difficulties and vacillations concerning its functions and Fellowship, its *Philosophical transactions* had become, by the 1830s, chiefly devoted to experimental philosophy for which no specialist society existed.[14] The basic allegiance of leading geologists was palpably shown by the publication pattern of men such as Buckland, Sedgwick, Murchison, and Lyell. Having given the Bakerian Lecture at the Royal Society, Lyell was no doubt obliged to publish it as his only contribution to the *Philosophical transactions*; otherwise he reserved his papers primarily for the *Proceedings* or the *Transactions* of the Geological Society and, secondarily, for British Association meetings.[15] Indeed, the intense allegiance felt by many of the leading Fellows of the Geological Society to its two journals received presidential expression. In 1831 Sedgwick stressed that the *Transactions* represented the Society 'in the great republic of science; and without them, beyond our own immediate circle, we possess neither voice nor animation'.[16] Eleven years later Murchison felt sufficiently sure of his ground to rebuke Mantell for depriving the Geological Society by publishing in the *Philosophical transactions*.[17] Private opinions were more forthright. While refereeing a paper submitted to the *Philosophical transactions* Murchison asked Buckland: 'Why do such bunglers go to the R.S.? because they cannot cram their stuff down our throats at the Geo.'.[18] Such comments were representative of the confidence felt by the hammermen about their Society and its journals: that security contrasted sharply with the situation in 1809, when control of publication was one of the chief issues dividing the suspicious Royal Society and the young Geological Society, which was committed to independence of action and the division of scientific labour.[19]

In the short compass of this paper it is impossible to give a blow-by-blow account of the origins, the aims, the financing, and the facilities of that plethora of new and existing scientific institutions which graced the metropolis between 1820 and 1841. In any case, as I have already stressed, we need to discover which institutions were deemed desirable, neutral, or hostile by particular scientists.[20] Different men, of course, nursed different ambitions and expectations: when faced with the same institutional structure, they therefore responded to it differently. It is for this basic reason that the technique of prosopography, or collective biography, has recently been used in the study of scientific institutions in the hope of making valid generalizations about them and their members.[21] Some of the benefits of such an approach become apparent, I think, even if we look at the intersection of institutional features and just one individual career. In Lyell's London there was an abundance of institutions to choose from. What, then, were Lyell's choices?

If we turn first to voluntary societies devoted primarily to scientific research and publication, we find that Lyell was a Fellow of the Geological, Royal, Linnean, Zoological, and Geographical Societies, and a member of the British Association, to all six of which he had compounded for life membership by 1832 at the considerable cost of almost £200. Additionally he was, like Murchison, a founder member of the Atheneum Club, welcoming the services of its library, and savouring its then unique combination of intellectual respectability, social exclusiveness, and a 'genteel elegantly served dinner for 2.6^{d} with all the newspapers'.[22] He also supported warmly the soirées held by Babbage and by Murchison because they helped to give to science its due importance in London's polite society.[23] But, of course, it was the Geological Society which received his prime allegiance. Though office holding in the Geological Society was thought by Babbage to be more burdensome than elsewhere, Lyell accepted heavy administrative duties, being a Secretary (1823–5), Foreign Secretary (1829–35), and President (1835–7). Lyell clearly saw office holding as necessary for the good of the Society but as a sacrifice of his research: he successfully resisted the temptation of being President in 1833–5 but then reluctantly succumbed the next biennium.[24] In advising Darwin, Lyell revealed his own motives and attitudes with brutal frankness:

> Don't accept any official scientific place, if you can avoid it, and tell no one that I gave you this advice, as they would all cry out against me as the preacher of anti-patriotic principles. I fought against the calamity of being President as long as I could . . . my question is, whether the time annihilated by learned bodies ('par les affaires administratives') is balanced by any good they do . . . At least, work as I did, exclusively for yourself and for science for many years, and do not prematurely incur the honour or penalty of official dignities. There are people who may be profitably employed in such duties, because they would not work if not so engaged.[25]

Nevertheless, Lyell did incur the penalty of office holding at the Geological Society not only because it was the relevant specialist society for him but also because he subscribed to its features and ethos. Indeed, even such a fierce critic of London institutions as William Swainson exempted the Geological Society from his general stricture that the republic of science had degenerated into an aristocracy of wealth: for him, the laws and management of the Geological Society constituted an admirable model for all other societies.[26] Babbage, too, praised the Geological Society for lively discussions at its meetings.[27] These geological conversations, which had no equivalent in any other London scientific society, were proverbial and contrasted sharply with the irresistible monotony of the meetings of the Royal Society. At their best, they attracted a remarkable galaxy of talent, as when in 1840 at one meeting Buckland, Murchison, Agassiz, Lyell, Greenough, John Edward Gray, and Whewell all held forth on the glacial hypothesis until 11.45 p.m.[28] Such urbane geological warfare, in which scientific and personal victory could be achieved, was not merely instructive and entertaining: as Murchison pointed out, 'The ordeal, therefore, our writings have to pass through in the animating discussions . . . within these walls, may be considered the true safeguard of our scientific reputation'.[29] Moreover, the discussions were usually characterized by manly vigour, tempered always by good manners.[30] Other features of the Society were no doubt amenable to Lyell, such as its published financial accounts, its biennial presidency, and its *Proceedings* containing the presidential addresses in which progress was summarized and desiderata suggested. Of all the London specialist scientific societies during the 1830s, it was the most adaptable: its leaders encouraged and consolidated the early British Association rather than jealously holding aloof from the upstart provincial fledgling.[31] Nor should we forget that in 1830 six of its Presidents, Fitton, Sedgwick, Murchison, Greenough, Lyell, and Whewell, worked diligently on behalf of Herschel in the contested election for the Presidency of the Royal Society.[32] The peppery Paddy Fitton even went to the extreme of publishing anonymously a pamphlet deploring court intrigue in that election, and of criticizing Murchison for 'ratting' when Murchison agreed to serve on the Council of the Royal Society in late 1831.[33]

If all these features show that the Geological Society was an enterprising liberal learned society, it was at the same time a gentleman's geological club dominated by a coterie. Though this oligarchy was based on merit and not rank, gentlemen of secure income, such as Lyell, Murchison, Broderip, Fitton, Greenough, and Darwin, aided by academics such as Sedgwick, Buckland, and Whewell, dominated the meetings of the Society, dictated its social tone, and engineered key appointments such as the Presidency.[34] Few mining engineers and surveyors were either key members of the Society or close associates of Lyell, excepting John Taylor the Treasurer. This select nature of the Geological Society during the 1830s was emphasized by the Society's refusing to permit publication by independent reporters of their celebrated discussions; even the reports for the *Literary gazette* and *The Atheneum* were apparently supplied by the Secretaries who carefully avoided all allusion to the discussions.[35] I suspect that the combination of genteel Fellowship and intellectual meritocray of the Geological Society was especially attractive to Lyell: not surprisingly, he was a founder member of the élite Geological Society Club, yet he approved of the meritocratic attitude of the Society in conferring its Presidency on working geologists and not on social rank.[36]

Lyell's involvement in the British Association was an example of how he acted on the advice given to Darwin: until 1838 he managed to avoid responsibility as either a Councillor or as a President of the Geological Section. Indeed, before the 1838 meeting at Newcastle Lyell had attended only one meeting of the British Association, at Edinburgh in 1834.[37] There is no doubt that he approved its sectional proceedings, and the way it publicized and popularized science; yet he always felt that these benefits were obtained at the considerable cost of the time and energy of 'the real good and true workers in science'.[38] Compared with many fellow geologists such as Phillips, Sedgwick, Murchison, Buckland, Taylor, Edward Turner, Fitton, Greenough, Yates, and Lonsdale, Lyell made a minimal contribution to the running of the British Association in its early crucial years. In a similar way, though he attended the meetings of the Royal, the Zoological, the Linnean, and the Geographical Societies, his administrative work for those societies was negligible: Lyell was really justifying himself when he asserted paradoxically that Herschel's failure to be elected President of the Royal Society was a boon for British science because it left Herschel free to pursue his research in South Africa.[39]

The 1830s saw a most important development in the patronage by government of geological research and publication with the establishment of the Geological Survey and the Museum of Economic Geology, followed by the Mining Record Office and eventually, in 1851, the School of Mines and Science applied to the Arts.[40] It was, of course, entirely characteristic that the state's patronage of geological research was usually not ostensible but incidental, occasional, and indirect. One can instance Darwin's post as naturalist to the *Beagle*, Sedgwick's prebendal stall at Norwich, Buckland's canonry at Christ Church, Oxford, and Jameson's Regius chair at Edinburgh University. When the government did patronize scientific research directly and ostensibly, a powerful case, usually involving considerations of utility, had usually been made by groups or individuals who often had shown that the research in question was viable. The Geological Survey and its Museum illustrate that general point. Pre-Survey maps by geologists such as William Smith, Greenough, and Griffith, had shown both the strengths and the limits of voluntary individual effort. The Geological Survey was the government's response to the work already done by De La Beche and to his careful lobbying in which he stressed the utility and cheapness of his schemes. In realizing his vision of a British School of Mines, De La Beche wisely worked by establishing its components one by one. Having lost an independent income of £3,000 per year by about 1832, he had economic incentive to earn his livelihood with his geological skills. Between 1832 and 1835 he established temporary links with the Ordnance Survey by colouring eight sheets for £300 as expenses; in spring 1835, supported by the Ordnance Board and by Spring-Rice, Chancellor of the Exchequer, De La Beche was appointed Director of the Geological Survey with a salary of £500 per annum and estimated expenses of £1,000 a year. Having at last acquired a permanent appointment, De La Beche immediately and successfully lobbied Spring-Rice for a Museum of Economic Geology which was established in 1837 in Craig's Court. Two years later, as a result of pressure exerted by Sopwith and the British Association, De La Beche was put in charge of the adjacent Mining Record Office which opened in 1840. Until 1839 De La Beche had worked on the Survey virtually single handed, but by 1841 he had gained several assistants including W. T. Aveline, A. C. Ramsay, and John Phillips. Within only six years of the founding of the Survey, De La Beche was well on the way to implementing his plan of a government supported museum which would be a centre for geological teaching and research. His success marked the second stage in the development of continued patronage of science by the government, the first being the Royal Observatory which was likewise founded for practical reasons.

Lyell's attitude to the Geological Survey was at best lukewarm. Whereas Buckland enthusiastically supported plans for a Museum of Economic Geology, a Mining Record Office, and eventually a School of Mines, and whereas Murchison in 1841 was responsible for Ramsay's appointment to the Survey, Lyell, in contrast, took little interest in applied geology. Consequently he neither guided promising young bachelors into the Survey nor helped it voluntarily himself. Indeed, in his second presidential address to the Geological Society in 1837, Lyell virtually ignored the Survey except to affirm that he did not distrust De La Beche's skill or experience in geological surveying; simultaneously he eulogized the developing work of Murchison and Sedgwick on Devonian geology.[41] Such allegiance was quite harmonious with Lyell's insistence on the crucial importance of organic remains which in De La Beche's opinion had been overestimated to the detriment of mineral composition of strata and their actual superposition as directly observed.[42] This was merely one example of the sustained intellectual differences between the two men, epitomized by Lyell's commitment to 'uniformitarianism' which De La Beche ridiculed as premature system-building.[43] These divergent theoretical commitments were, moreover, reinforced by contrasts of career and institutional affiliation. From 1831 Lyell seemed to fear De La Beche as a potential plagiarist and as a formidable literary competitor.[44] Certainly after 1835 De La Beche spent much of his time in South-West England making a full-time living as a surveyor, while Lyell remained a London-based gentleman-geologist primarily interested in geological dynamics. One suspects that Lyell feared that a permanent state-supported Geological Survey under the undoubtedly ambitious De La Beche would not only erode the dominance exerted by the élite of the voluntary Geological Society but also might exclusively annex certain key areas such as Devon. As early as 1835 Colby had assured Murchison that the Survey would not trespass on Murchison's 'district' for at least four years.[45] Two years later Sedgwick, a true Yorkshireman, always forthright but never mean, put the question bluntly by asking if all his research had to stop

> because an *official* person has had the misfortune to publish a bad map? . . . De La Beche complains that Murchison does not wish to cooperate with the Trigonometrical Survey. How is it possible to cooperate? In our opinion Devonshire is radically wrong, as it is now published. Are we to shut our mouths and let the error continue to be propagated?[46]

Lyell's support of these sentiments was shown in February 1837, when he disregarded Greenough's plea that in his forthcoming presidential address he (Lyell) should ignore the Devonian work done by Murchison and Sedgwick. De La Beche, however, clearly felt that the Survey was being attacked behind his back, without the possibility of rapid reply, by envious men such as Murchison and Lyell who he thought were intent on removing him from his job as director. Indeed, the souring of personal relations associated with the Devonian question reached its apogee in 1837 when Murchison told Sedgwick: 'De La B is a dirty dog, there is plain English & there is no mincing the matter. I knew him to be a thorough jobber & a great intriguer & *we* have proved him to be thoroughly incompetent to carry on the survey'.[47] Such antipathies rumbled on into the 1840s, and were only to be expected simply because the creation of the Geological Survey disturbed the dominance previously exerted by the clerisy within the Geological Society. The establishment of the Survey was therefore during the late 1830s the occasion of bringing into sharp focus questions relating to geological motives, conduct, property, and careers, as well as those concerning the relations between state-supported and voluntarily supported geology.[48]

Lyell's shrewd perception of the shape and direction of his career was also shown by the nature of his attachment to the three teaching institutions with which he was potentially or actually associated, namely the Royal Institution, University College London, and King's College London. At the Royal Institution, where he lectured in spring 1833 to a mixed audience, Lyell supplemented the fashionable physics of Faraday; but, as he wished to concentrate and not dissipate his efforts, he never repeated his successful performance there.[49] With respect to University College London, Lyell saw, as early as 1828, that the College did not offer sufficient basic salary to tempt men of the calibre of Hooker and Babbage to teach financially unprofitable classes.[50] A year later, in scotching a rumour that he was a candidate for the geology chair, Lyell told Horner firmly that 'every lecturer who has not a good class rather does harm to the Institution and one cannot expect it in geology yet'.[51] Given these strong views, it is not surprising that Lyell's initial enthusiasm for his chair at King's College began to wane well before he began to teach in spring 1832. In April 1831 Lyell had anticipated that, as a professor, his situation would be agreeable, influential, and respectable; but by the end of that year he concluded that the most effective influence was to be exerted not from his chair but through independent research and publication.[52] Though Lyell no doubt approved the gentlemanly tone of King's, he was nevertheless planning to resign even before he began to teach. Besides having Phillips in mind to succeed him, he saw clearly that a Lyellian school of geology at King's was not a viable proposition. As he told Murchison: 'I had at first some little regret at relinquishing the notion of being a sort of founder of a school which shd follow up the "modern cause" system yet I am sure that in the present state of science in England there is not a sufficient field open to satisfy the reasonable ambition of any gentleman who shd undertake such a task in London'.[53] The sporadic nature of the geology teaching at King's College and University College during the 1830s shows how acute Lyell's premonition was. In any event, the College was almost bankrupt and kept in existence only by the success of the school: the painfully frequent resignations and even simple disappearance of professors, and the discontinuing in 1834 of the chair of natural history and zoology held by James Rennie, were the more public symptoms of the College's struggles with adversity during its opening years.[54]

In this paper I have argued that Lyell's varying attachment to institutions can be understood in terms of his perceptions about their utility for him. Compared with other British geologists of his generation, Lyell, like Murchison, was more conscious of the shape and direction of his career. Whereas others like Sedgwick dissipated their energies, Lyell concentrated on his science and his career, suffering neither interference nor distraction.[55] Granted he had advantages: wealth which allowed him to travel widely in a way impossible for a poor provincial like John Phillips; good social position; a tamed wife; no distracting children; few family neuroses; and good health, except for his weak eyes. But he capitalized on these by putting aside all temptations which interfered with his work: his successful avoidance of premature office-holding showed a laudable concern for not having a working day cut to shreds by meetings.[56] Though interested in politics, Lyell was not a party man, partly because as a young man he saw in the case of Cuvier the dangers of mixing science with administration, with place-hunting, and with 'the dirty pool of politics'.[57] He consistently tried to avoid the disabling annoyance of politics and invitations, both of which were inimical to steady work.[58] Even at the height of his success as both a writer and a teacher, he detached himself from King's College and the Royal Institution, cutting the cockneys in order to address his prime audience of geological peers with publications.[59] With singular steadiness of purpose he pursued his aims of gaining geological knowledge, income, respect, fame, and command of society.[60] In 1830 Babbage had lamented that in England science was not a profession, but in 1832 Lyell was determined 'to make science a profession'.[61] That determination provided a protective mechanism for Lyell, an ambitious expatriate Scot who felt that he rarely met congenial souls even among geologists.[62] More positively, it not only enabled him to produce 'the big book' in his early thirties, but also to make a crucial contribution to the evolving consciousness of English science and scientists.

REFERENCES

1 Archibald Geikie, *Life of Sir Roderick I. Murchison* (2 vols., London, 1875), i. 94: Horace B. Woodward, *The history of the Geological Society of London* (London, 1908), pp. 168–9. The literal enthronement took place in 1849.

2 J. L. E. Dreyer and H. H. Turner (eds.), *History of the Royal Astronomical Society 1820–1920* (London, 1923), pp. 52–5. Sir James South's poster of 1836 is in the Royal Society of London (MM.10.7).

3 'On the alleged decline of science', *The Caledonian mercury*, 15 September 1831, pinioned Babbage, Brewster, and South for being either unpardonably ignorant or culpably disingenuous; and stressed that Babbage had received from government £6,000 for his machine, South a knighthood, and Brewster a pension of £100 per year.

4 [Basil Hall], 'Beechey's voyage to the Pacific and Beering's Straits', *Quarterly review*, xlv (1831), 57–97 (57–9).

5 I. Todhunter, *William Whewell. An account of his writings with selections from his literary and scientific correspondence* (2 vols., London, 1876), i. 41; ii. 121–2.

6 Whewell to Murchison, 16 November 1831, Geological Society of London, Murchison Papers.

[7] Adam Sedgwick's speech, 18 February 1831, announcing the first award of the Wollaston Prize to Smith, *Proceedings of the Geological Society of London*, i (1834), 270–9 (279); Whewell, Anniversary Address, 15 February 1839, *Proceedings of the Geological Society of London*, iii (1842), pp. 61–98 (96); and Council announcement, 9 April 1827, *Proceedings of Geological Society of London*, i (1834), 1. For the historiography of geology established by Fitton, Conybeare, and Lyell, see Rachel Bush, 'The development of geological mapping in Britain from 1795 to 1825' (London University Ph.D. thesis, 1974), and Roy Porter, 'The making of the science of geology in Britain, 1660–1815' (Cambridge University Ph.D. thesis, 1974).

[8] O. J. R. Howarth, *The British Association for the Advancement of Science. A retrospect 1831–1931* (London, 1931).

[9] [Whewell], 'Mrs. Somerville on the connexion of the sciences', *Quarterly Review*, li (1834), pp. 54–68 (59–60).

[10] [A. B. Granville], *Science without a head; or, the Royal Society dissected* (London, 1830).

[11] Herschel to William Vernon Harcourt, 5 September 1831, in E. W. Harcourt (ed.), *The Harcourt papers* (14 vols., Oxford, 1880–1905), xiii. 244–8 (247–8). Herschel's point was based primarily on his experience as Foreign Secretary of the Astronomical Society (1820–7), Secretary of the Royal Society (1824–7), and President of the Astronomical Society (1827–9).

[12] This assertion always introduced the explicit statement of the objects of the British Association printed in its annual *Reports*.

[13] This classification of the cultural uses of science is derived from Arnold W. Thackray, 'Natural knowledge in cultural context: the Manchester model', *The American historical review*, lxxix (1974), 672–709.

[14] A. B. Granville, *The Royal Society in the XIXth. century* (London, 1836), tables facing pp. 59 and 138.

[15] [Mrs] K. M. Lyell (ed.), *Life, letters and journals of Sir Charles Lyell, Bart.* (2 vols., London, 1881), ii. 479–82.

[16] Sedgwick, Anniversary Address, 19 February 1830, *Proceedings of the Geological Society of London*, i (1834), 187–212 (189).

[17] Murchison, Anniversary Address, 18 February 1842, *Proceedings of the Geological Society of London*, iii (1842), 637–87 (653).

[18] Murchison to Buckland, 23 January 1832, Royal Society of London, MS. 251, no. 44.

[19] M. J. S. Rudwick, 'The foundation of the Geological Society of London: its scheme for co-operative research and its struggle for independence', *The British journal for the history of science*, i (1962-3), 326–55.

[20] Roger Hahn, 'Scientific careers in eighteenth-century France', in M. P. Crosland (ed.), *The emergence of science in Western Europe* (London, 1975), pp. 127–38.

[21] Steven Shapin and Arnold Thackray, 'Prosopography as a research tool in the history of science: the British scientific community, 1700–1900', *History of science*, xii (1974), 1–28.

[22] Lyell, op. cit. (15), i. 322; Leonard G. Wilson, *Charles Lyell. The years to 1841: the revolution in geology* (New Haven and London, 1972), pp. 135–6, 318. The establishment, in 1824, of the Atheneum for literary men was yet another indication of London's cultural expansion in the 1820s; see Humphry Ward, *History of the Atheneum 1824–1925* (London, 1926). The fact that Lyell compounded for life membership of six scientific institutions presumably indicates his long-term commitment to science by the early 1830s.

[23] Lyell, op. cit. (15), i. 371, 375, 377, 383, 466; ii. 13; B. W. Richardson, *Thomas Sopwith, with excerpts from his diary of fifty seven years* (London, 1891), pp. 170–1.

[24] Buckland to Murchison, 12 November 1832, Devon County Record Office, D.138 M/F 239; Lyell, op. cit. (15), i. 235, 251, 384–5. Though Lyell was not enamoured of Greenough as a geologist, he nevertheless looked to Greenough's nomination as President 'as *a fixed thing*' probably to avoid the office himself: Murchison to Greenough, 17 November 1832, Cambridge University Library, Greenough Papers, Add. 7918.

[25] Lyell to Darwin, 26 December 1836, in Lyell, op. cit. (15), i. 474–5.

[26] William Swainson, *A preliminary discourse on the study of natural history* (London, 1834), pp. 299, 313, 314, 429.

[27] Charles Babbage, *Reflections on the decline of science in England, and on some of its causes* (London, 1830), pp. 45–6.

[28] Woodward, op. cit. (1), pp. 138–42.

[29] Murchison, Anniversary Address, 15 February 1833, *Proceedings of the Geological Society of London*, i (1834), 438–64 (464).

[30] Whewell, Anniversary Address, 16 February 1838, *Proceedings of the Geological Society of London*, ii (1838), 624–49 (648–9).

[31] Of senior London scientists, only Murchison, Greenough, and Yates attended the first meeting of the British Association. The Presidents of the second and third meetings were geologists, namely, Buckland and Sedgwick.

[32] Wilson, op. cit. (22), p. 304; Geikie, op. cit. (1), i. 197–9; John Willis Clark and Thomas

McKenny Hughes, *The life and letters of the Reverend Adam Sedgwick* (2 vols., Cambridge, 1890), i. 365–6; Todhunter, op. cit. (5), i. 41.

33 [W. H. Fitton], *A statement of circumstances connected with the late election for the Presidency of the Royal Society* (London, 1831); Fitton to Babbage, 19 November 1831, British Library Add. MS. 37186, ff. 152–3.

34 From Clark and Hughes, op. cit. (32), i. 333–4, 463; Buckland to Murchison, 12 November 1832, Devon County Record Office, D. 138M/F 239; and Lyell to Whewell, 25 January 1837, Trinity College, Cambridge, Whewell Papers, a. 208[126], it is clear that the outgoing President could effectively appoint his successor: 1828, Fitton fixed on Sedgwick; 1832, Murchison on Greenough; 1836, Lyell on Whewell.

35 Woodward, op. cit. (1), pp. 145–6; Abraham Booth, *The stranger's intellectual guide to London, for 1839–40* (London, 1839), pp. 77–8. In contrast, the discussions held at the geological section of the British Association were reported via officials of the section. This difference between the Geological Society and the geological section of the Association shows that in the former there was more to the restriction than a wish to retain the informal vitality of unreported discussion. Irrespective of the internal reasons for the non-reporting of the discussions held at the Geological Society, an impression of exclusiveness was given to outsiders.

36 Woodward, op. cit. (1), p. 65; Lyell, op. cit. (15), i. 472–3.

37 Lyell attended the meetings of 1834, 1838, 1839, 1840; sat on Council 1838–40; and acted as President of the geological section in 1838 and 1840. Murchison's difficulty in inducing Lyell to act as President of the geological section of the British Association in 1838 is clearly shown in Murchison to Babbage, 5 August 1838, British Library Add. MSS. 37190, ff. 511–12: 'In regard to Lyell I can only say, that when Horner was last in this house 6 weeks ago I distinctly said "we must place Lyell in a high station" on which H. said "if you do rely on it, he will run away &c.—as he particularly wishes to be free" . . . If, however, Lyell should have no objection to hold office, there is no man on earth who I would rather see leading the Geologists, and that is the place he would have occupied, had he been at the two last meetings of the British Association'.

38 Lyell, op. cit. (15), i. 350, 442, 445, 457 (quoted); ii. 42–6.

39 Ibid., i. 465, 475; Lyell to Babbage, 25 May 1832, British Library Add. MSS. 37186, f. 428.

40 My account is synthesized from John Smith Flett, *The first hundred years of the Geological Survey of Great Britain* (London, 1937), pp. 11–56; Edward Bailey, *Geological Survey of Great Britain* (London, 1952), pp. 17–51; Archibald Geikie, *Memoir of Sir A. C. Ramsay* (London, 1895), pp. 34–64.

41 Lyell, Anniversary Address, 17 February 1837, *Proceedings of the Geological Society of London*, ii (1838), 479–523 (491–6). Having been consulted by the Ordnance Board, in June 1835, Buckland, Sedgwick, and Lyell, as President of the Geological Society, had recommended that De La Beche's geological mapping be extended. This recommendation, which was at least condoned by Lyell, is not incompatible with my intepretation of Lyell's hostility to De La Beche. In June 1835 Buckland, as always, strongly supported De La Beche. Sedgwick *at that time* was not convinced that De La Beche was wrong on the Devonian question. Only in September 1835, having seen Murchison's recent sections of Pembrokeshire, did Sedgwick begin to think that Murchison might be right on the Devonian question; and in any event he saw the correction of De La Beche and Williams as entirely a matter for Murchison and not for himself; see Murchison to Buckland, 11 September 1835, Geological Society of London, Murchison Collection; and Sedgwick to Lyell, 20 September 1835, in Clark and Hughes, op. cit. (32), i. 446–8. Close attention to chronology reveals, therefore, that in June 1835 Sedgwick had no evidence for suspecting De La Beche's competence. Lyell, who at that time opposed De La Beche's interpretation of the Devonian culm-measures, would have been in a minority in questioning De La Beche's competence. In any case, as the elected President of the Geological Society, he was hardly in a position to doubt De La Beche's capabilities.

42 H. T. De La Beche, *How to observe. Geology* (London, 1836), pp. 220, 238.

43 Wilson, op. cit. (22), p. 456; H. T. De La Beche, *Researches in theoretical geology* (London, 1834), pp. 359–61; De La Beche, *A geological manual* (London, 1831), pp. 97, 129; M. J. S. Rudwick, *The meaning of fossils* (New York and London, 1972), pp. 194–6; idem., 'The Devonian System 1834–1840. A study in 'scientific controversy', *Actes du XIIme Congrès International d'Histoire des Sciences; Paris, 1968* (Paris, 1971), vii. 39–43.

44 Wilson, op. cit (22), p. 343. Certainly by late 1834 these fears had been transformed into personal dislike which Lyell did not bother to conceal; see De La Beche to Sedgwick, 11 December 1834, Cambridge University Library, Sedgwick Papers, Add. 7652, I.A. 125, written shortly after Murchison and especially Lyell had attacked his paper on Bideford anthracite read to the Geological Society on 3 December 1834.

45 Buckland to Murchison, 12 June 1835, Devon Record Office, D.138 M/F 221.

46 Clark and Hughes, op. cit. (32), i. 478–9; my italics.

47 De La Beche to Greenough, 20 November 1836, 8 and 16 April 1837; Colby to De La Beche, 3 April 1837; all in Cambridge University Library, Add.MS.7918. The attitudes of

Murchison and Lyell are set out in Murchison to Sedgwick (transcript), 2 February 1837, Cambridge University Library, Sedgwick Papers, Add.7652, III.D.13. See also Geikie, op. cit. (1), i. 249–50.

[48] For the notion of a gentleman's clerisy I am indebted to Roy Porter, 'The industrial revolution and the rise of the science of geology', in M. Teich and R. M. Young (eds.), *Changing perspectives in the history of science* (London, 1973), pp. 320–43. The threat to that clerisy from the Geological Survey was clear to Murchison: 'It was always to be feared that the employment of public means and authorities would swamp our Society and individual efforts and here we have a crushing proof of it'. See Murchison to Sedgwick (transcript), 7 February 1839, Cambridge University Library, Sedgwick Papers, Add.7652, III.D.21.

[49] Lyell, op. cit. (15), i. 397–8.

[50] Ibid., i. 178; H. H. Bellot, *University College, London 1826–1926* (London, 1929), p. 38.

[51] Lyell, op. cit. (15), i. 257–8.

[52] Ibid., i. 318, 357, 359; Wilson, op. cit. (22), p. 340. See especially Martin J. S. Rudwick, 'Charles Lyell, F.R.S. (1797–1875) and his London lectures on geology, 1832–33', *Notes and records of the Royal Society of London*, xxix (1975), 231–63. Rudwick's interpretation of Lyell as a non-venal careerist, to which I am indebted, is entirely compatible with my paper.

[53] Lyell to Murchison, 22 December 1831, Geological Society of London, Murchison Papers.

[54] J. F. C. Hearnshaw, *The centenary history of King's College, London, 1828–1928* (London, 1929), pp. 72–3, 89–90, 96–125. It was ironic that in 1831 Rennie had published declinist views in denouncing the parrot-learning of mathematics in British universities and in deploring the extinction of philosophical zoology by Linnean shackles; see George Montagu, *Ornithological dictionary of British birds with a plan of study, and many new articles and original observations by James Rennie* (2nd edn., London, 1831), pp. ix, xxv, xxx.

[55] In 1832 Lyell delivered a lethal estimate of Sedgwick: 'He has not the application necessary to make his splendid talents tell in a work. Besides every one leads him astray'; see Lyell, op. cit. (15), i. 375.

[56] T. G. Bonney, *Charles Lyell and modern geology* (London, 1895), p. 121.

[57] Lyell, op. cit. (15), i. 137, 143, 146, 249.

[58] Ibid., i. 352, 355, 367, 375–6.

[59] Ibid., ii. 465.

[60] Ibid., i. 326, 360, 373. Lyell's sensitivity about his being in total control of his career was shown in 1831 when he denied strongly that Murchison had converted him to geology from law and that Murchison had helped him financially; Murchison to Lyell, no date [1831], Green Folder, Geological Society of London, Murchison Papers.

[61] Ibid., i. 376; Babbage, op. cit. (27), pp. 10–11.

[62] Lyell to Sedgwick, 21 April 1837, in Clark and Hughes, op. cit. (32), i. 484.

XIII

Brewster and the early British Association for the Advancement of Science

A bi-centennial celebration can fill one with gloom, especially if one is recruited to dilate upon a savant who is, historically speaking, rather tedious and unproblematic. In the case of Sir D.B., as his friends called him, we have a welcome exception and indeed a glorious opportunity: Brewster was never dull; and this Symposium has revealed that his extraordinary career poses many interesting historical problems. Perhaps one aspect of his work has not been sufficiently stressed today, namely, that at his best Brewster is one of the great writers of English prose, particularly in that characteristically Victorian genre, the long essay review. In his zealous and obsessed moods, when his pen could hardly keep pace with his mind, or with grammar, his writing was fiery and persuasive. Here is one of my favourite gobbets from Brewster, his denunciation in 1830 of the iniquities of the patent law:

> a system of vicious and fraudulent legislation, which . . . places the most exalted officers of the state in the position of a legalized banditi, who stab the inventor through the folds of an act of parliament, and rifle him in the presence of the Lord Chief Justice of England.[1]

For the historian such splendid prose is a pleasure to read but it presents problems of handling. With respect to the British Association the problem is acute because by 1851 Brewster had put into print three retrospective accounts of its origins and early history; the first in the *Edinburgh Review* in 1835, the second in the *North British Review* in 1850, and the third in his Presidential address to the Association also in 1850.[2] At the factual level, these accounts can be misleading, sometimes seriously so. For instance, in the 1850 article Brewster made much of the views on the decline of science allegedly proclaimed by William Vernon Harcourt in his inaugural speech to the Association in September 1831. This 1850 account of Harcourt's speech was followed by Mrs. Gordon in her biography of Brewster.[3] More recently Derek Orange rightly characterised Brewster's 1850 version as odd.[4] This oddity is explained if we turn to contemporary newspaper accounts of Harcourt's speech and contemporary correspondence, from which it is clear that Brewster's memory deceived him. Nineteen years after the event, Brewster cited a *letter* Harcourt wrote in late November 1831 to Lord Milton, a copy of which Harcourt sent to Brewster, as being what Harcourt *said* in his speech of September 1831. In our book on the early Association, to which this paper is deeply indebted for empirical material and interpretative framework, Arnold Thackray and I were particularly careful when exploiting Brewster's retrospective public accounts: we found them very stimulating for his polemical perceptions and acute insights, but whenever possible they were checked against published and unpublished contemporary documents.[5]

One of Brewster's most imaginative and successful experiments was to instigate the British Association for the Advancement of Science. In this paper I want to look at the changing relations of Brewster to the Association, beginning with his proposing the formation of an association of nobility, clergy, gentry, and philosophers to remedy the depressed state of British science. He led the northern lights at the inaugural York meeting of the Association in 1831, and by the second meeting at Oxford in June 1832 he was as enchanted as ever with it: he had successfully drawn attention to the importance of establishing a Council, his report on optics confirmed his high intellectual position in the Association, he was one of two Vice-presidents at the 1832 meeting, and along with three other religious dissenters he had received during the meeting the rare accolade of an honorary doctoral degree from the University of Oxford. Then, I shall argue, the Association for which Brewster had campaigned so energetically began to be used against him. In early 1833 his protégé, James David Forbes, drew considerably on his own Association contacts to defeat Brewster in a contest for the chair of natural philosophy at the University of Edinburgh. At the Cambridge meeting in 1833 the advocates of Fresnel's wave theory of light, mainly drawn from Trinity College, Cambridge, and Trinity College, Dublin, began to promulgate that theory in Section A of the Association, thus challenging Brewster's previous dominance there. By 1834 it was patently clear to Brewster, a Vice-president that year, that the Cambridge invasion of the Association meant that it would not be the reforming body he envisaged. In 1835 he vented his spleen in the *Edinburgh Review*, an act of apparent disloyalty which provoked Thomas Romney Robinson to refer publicly at the 1835 meeting to Brewster as one who wielded 'the concealed dagger of a lurking assassin'.[6] There was indeed rich irony in Brewster's relation to the early Association: though at its centre until 1832, he had been edged to its periphery only two years later.

I

By the late 1820s, when he was almost 50 years old Brewster; had earned a living for thirty years as an editor, author, encyclopaedist, inventor, and consultant. Though he acquired in 1829 a government pension of £100 per year, Brewster felt he lacked regular recognition commensurate with his talents. From the early 1820s he had been irritably dissatisfied with the treatment of scientific men by government; and in the late 1820s he took every opportunity, *via* his periodical, the *Edinburgh Journal of Science*, to press for increased state patronage of science and scientific men. If such concerns were generalisations from his own case, the deaths of William Hyde Wollaston, Thomas Young, and Humphry Davy, in just six months between December 1828 and May 1829, staggered him; they also confirmed his view that an era in British science had ended and that the time was ripe for the scientific millennium to be at last ushered in.

With respect to organised science in the Scottish metropolis, Brewster was irritated in the late 1820s with the Royal Society of Edinburgh of which he was Secretary for six years. He thought its elections were mismanaged. He deplored the refusal of the Society to elect as a Fellow his young protégé, James David Forbes; he resented the difficulties concerning the election of another protégé, the chemist James Finlay Weir Johnston. He was outraged by the reluctance of the Society to pay the legal costs generated by his attempts as Secretary to extract the Society's property from the University museum where Robert Jameson zealously guarded his geological booty. And Brewster reprobated the annual rent of £260 for its apartments which the Society paid to government.[7]

By 1829, then, Brewster's restlessness made him receptive to Charles Babbage's article about the 1828 Berlin meeting of the Gesellschaft Deutscher Naturforscher und Ärzte which from 1822 had met annually in a different German city.[8] Like Babbage, he was inspired by the German congress of savants and brooded on the idea of a European scientific academy. Again like Babbage he was obsessed with the question of the decline of science, for him a heart-breaking subject. It was not surprising that in early 1830 when Babbage had begun writing his book, *Reflections on the Decline of Science in England*, he turned to Brewster for ammunition. In reply Brewster tried without success to interest Babbage in organising 'an association for the purpose of protecting and promoting the *secular* interests of science'.[9] When Babbage's book was published in late spring 1830, Brewster returned in private to the notion that an association should be set up to revive science and to act as a pressure group on government. Publicly he reviewed Babbage's book in the October 1830 issue of the *Quarterly Review*: in a long article on the general decline of science, he proposed that an association of nobility, clergy, gentry and philosophers should be formed to remedy the depressed state of science. Brewster remained convinced that ultimately government alone was capable of patronising science properly, so that for him his proposed association was a necessary preliminary vehicle which would arouse government to its responsibilities. Brewster's *Quarterly Review* article also carried some cavalier remarks about English universities and roused the wrath of both William Whewell and George Biddell Airy. By late 1830 Brewster's zealous excitability had earned for him the hostility of the two leading Cambridge mathematical physicists.[10]

Early in 1831 Brewster received for his journal an article from Johnston about the 1830 Hamburgh meeting of the German naturalists. This account confirmed Brewster's opinion that it was desirable to have an equivalent British institution.[11] On 21 February 1831 he wrote to Babbage, specifying York and July/August as the time and place of the first meeting; and with crass naivety he suggested for President, John Herschel, who had just been defeated by the Duke of Sussex in a contested election for the Presidency of the Royal Society of London. Two days later he optimistically informed John Phillips, secretary of the Yorkshire Philosophical Society, that arrangements for the meeting to be held at York were 'in progress'.[12] Brewster's views about the date, the size, the finances, and the aims of the Association, were not to be implemented. But through these two letters of February 1831 he tolled the bell that called together two groups which were to be of central importance at the first meeting; the Edinburgh savants (himself, Forbes, Johnston, John Robison and Sir Thomas Makdougall Brisbane); and the Castor and Pollux of York science (Harcourt and John Phillips).

Proposing is one thing, disposing another. From February 1831 until late September 1831 when the Association met in York, Brewster maintained his roles as propagandist and projector but declined that of organiser. Encouraged by the enthusiastic response from York, in April 1831 Brewster gave notice of the meeting in his own journal, making it public that in his view the Association was to be modelled on the German gathering, was to meet in July at York, and that Robison (the Secretary of the Royal Society of Edinburgh) was to be interim secretary. Having passed the difficult organising of a novel event to Robison, Brewster become so absorbed with his spectroscopic researches that, as Robison complained, he became a member of an anti-corresponding society. In July 1831 Brewster emerged by publishing in his journal his draft plan of nine regulations for the constitution of the proposed body, borrowing heavily from the German model. With characteristic unpredictability, he called publicly on Robison, Johnston, and especially the Yorkshire Philosophical Society to be prepared in September with a code of laws. Agitation of this kind ensured that the proposed meeting was seen by Brewster's opponents as heavily identified with him. That was the chief reason why the constellation of savants from Trinity College, Cambridge, did not attend the York meeting: to them, going to York was equivalent to rallying round Brewster's standards, that is, subscribing to his views on the decline of science. In fact, from early July 1831 the lead in organising the meeting and framing its constitution was taken not by Brewster but by Harcourt, a masterly politician who could be all things to all men without seeming disingenuous: a man capable of seeming a declinist to Brewster yet able to win Whewell to the cause of the Association. At the York assembly Harcourt's dominance was such that even Brewster acknowledged there and then that Harcourt had been the soul of the meeting. As Harcourt himself was to encapsulate the matter in 1853, it was Brewster who proposed that a craft be built for the united crew of British science, but it was Harcourt who manned the ship, constructed her charts, and piloted the vessel.[13]

At the 1831 meeting one of Harcourt's master strokes was to name Brewster and Whewell as Vice presidents for the 1832 meeting at Oxford. Between these two meetings, Brewster both promoted and embarrassed the fledgling Association. He recruited a few Scottish members, though nothing like as many as Forbes who induced forty men to join. In April 1832 Brewster told Harcourt that the Association ought to be governed by a permanent Council, modelled on the French Institute, through which of course he hoped to lobby for his pet scheme of a state-supported physical laboratory, to be established especially for him.[14] Brewster also realised the advantages of having a small decision-making body to act between meetings. The Association, characterised by Brewster as Frankenstein's monster, needed a flywheel. This notion was highly agreeable to those from Cambridge, Oxford and London who wished to increase their control of the *parvenu* Association. At the 1832 meeting, constitutional revision was therefore smoothly and quietly accomplished when the Council was established to run the Association 51 weeks of the year. Ironically, the Council which Brewster proposed was one means by which the Cambridge/London/Oxford axis, conspicuously absent in 1831, took over the Association from 1832.

Brewster also caused Harcourt some embarrassment in late 1831 and early 1832. Though Harcourt *privately* maintained that British science was stagnating and *privately* favoured direct state patronage of individuals, *publicly* he adopted a position which put him in neither the declinist nor the anti-declinist camp. In Harcourt's view the issue of state patronage was prospectively divisive. That is why he tried to mute Johnston's account of the York meeting published in Brewster's *Edinburgh Journal of Science* in January 1832. Brewster thought Johnston had written in a good spirit, but Harcourt disagreed. He had just managed to recruit Whewell to the Association and he felt there was a real danger that Johnston would alienate the Cantabs who were so essential to Harcourt's plans, for instance, as reporters on the state of science. Johnston refused to be muzzled by Harcourt:

he referred pointedly to jealousy of the Association by leading savants; and he argued that the Association should try to arrest the decline of science in Britain. Moreover Johnston accused Lord Milton, the Association's first President, of being out of touch with general opinion when in his speech at York the nobleman had reprobated the *direct* encouragement of science by government.[15]

Despite Brewster's continued obsession with the debate on the decline of science, and his support for Johnston's views, he was a central figure at the 1832 meeting at Oxford. He produced his report on optics, and along with three other religious dissenters (Robert Brown, Michael Faraday and John Dalton) he received an honorary Doctor of Civil Law degree from the University of Oxford.[16] This was a highly political act, just after the third Reform Bill had become law: it allowed the University to make a timely answer to accusations of bigotry and reaction, though at the cost of seeming to make a move which might lead to the abolition of religious tests at Oxford. The Association boasted about its absence of religious barriers, and thus presented a model of benign toleration to Oxford, the renowned citadel of the established church. No doubt Brewster was delighted with his Oxford degree as a personal accolade, just as he welcomed it as another victory for dissent, for whiggery, and for reform.

II

As a loyal Whig Brewster was knighted in late 1831, an honour which did little to improve his finances. Lacking private means and a regular profession, in spring and summer 1832 he turned to his patron Lord Brougham for either a better pension or an English church living. In Brewster's view the latter would permit scientific research better than writing or inventing. After negotiations involving the Archbishops of York and Canterbury, the astronomer John Brinkley (then Bishop of Cloyne) and Harcourt, Brewster finally rejected this particular way out of his financial difficulties.[17]

In late 1832 the chair of natural philosophy at the University of Edinburgh became vacant through the death of Sir John Leslie. Though he had been a stern critic of Scottish universities, Brewster became a candidate because he was desperate for a job. To his astonishment Brewster discovered that his own candidature was opposed by James David Forbes, a well-off son of the late Sir William Forbes, the leading Edinburgh banker. Forbes was an ambitious and ingratiating man, much younger than Brewster, greatly his inferior in scientific reputation and of course heavily indebted to Brewster, his chief Scottish scientific patron. Nothing daunted, Forbes launched his canvas with the Town Council of Edinburgh, the electors to the chair. He desperately needed evidence *via* testimonials that he was a national figure. It was here that Forbes exploited his contacts in the Association and the work he had done for it, such as his 1832 report on meteorology. Testimonials from Harcourt and Whewell, for instance, were in the Forbes's hands before Brewster had even applied to them.

By the end of 1832 Forbes had printed 59 testimonials to himself. No fewer than 14 of these referred glowingly to his work for the Association. From York, Harcourt stressed that Forbes was a valued friend, while Phillips went so far as to speak fulsomely on behalf of the Association about Forbes. Phillips subsequently regretted this rash assertion: fearful of conflict between Brewster, the Scottish instigator of the Association, and Forbes, its chief Scottish activist, he privately hoped Brewster would be appointed because that would be less dangerous to the Association's peace. For his part, in response to Brewster's plea, Harcourt stressed to the Lord Provost of Edinburgh that at the 1831 meeting Brewster had displayed considerable power as a public speaker, the Forbes' camp having rumoured that Brewster was incapable of lecturing because of nervousness. Having given a testimonial to Forbes, Harcourt was clearly trying to disable Forbes' use of the Association as an electioneering resource. Harcourt's action was subsequently followed by Phillips, Johnston and Robison, each of whom testified publicly to Brewster's prowess in *extempore* exposition. But the damage had been done. Partly through his Association contacts Forbes amassed about seventy testimonials. Another candidate, Thomas Galloway, too busy teaching at Sandhurst to attend the meetings of the Association, produced only eleven, mainly from Scottish professors, none of whom was active in the Association.[18]

In the event, the Town Council elected Forbes to the chair primarily because of personal contacts between its members and the Forbes' banking house and because the Tory Town Council supported the Tory Forbes against the Whig Brewster. Yet the Town Council's wishes were legitimated by the testimonials of English philosophers, especially Cambridge and Oxford academics who were impressed by Forbes' work for the Association. For Brewster there was bitter irony in the way in which Forbes had accomplished what Brewster called 'the most scandalous job that the history of science records'.[19] After all Forbes had exploited the Association of which Brewster, first his mentor and then his opponent, was the principal instigator.

As if this were not enough, by summer 1833 at the Cambridge meeting of the Association, Brewster found himself involved in a fierce battle about Fresnel's wave theory of light. The location of the controversy was Section A, devoted to mathematical and physical sciences, a section which occupied the commanding pinnacle of the Association's hierarchy of sciences. For the Cambridge faction and its Dublin allies, the wave theory exemplified the new mathematical physics. These Cambridge and Dublin mathematical physicists sought to promote the wave theory and they found in Section A a leading instrument for propagating their views. On the other hand, Brewster, the instigator of the Association who resented the Cambridge invasion of it, found Section A an equally natural vehicle for objecting both to a new style of enquiry which threatened his position and to what he regarded as the unwarranted dogmatism of Fresnel's Cambridge supporters. At the 1832 meeting in his report on optics Brewster expressed his doubts about the wave theory. He acknowledged its power and beauty, but felt it could not cope with absorption spectra. His own recent work on nitrogen dioxide, which had almost blinded him, showed that its absorption spectrum contained more than a thousand *specific* dark lines. For Brewster, a wave theory implied the physical existence of an ether to carry the waves. He could not conceive how an ether, modified by the particles of nitrogen dioxide which contained it, could *selectively* absorb over a thousand *specific* waves of light, while transmitting the rest.

Between the 1832 and 1833 meetings the supporters of the wave theory moved into the attack, through the work of William Rowan Hamilton and Humphrey Lloyd in Dublin, of Airy in Cambridge, and of Baden Powell in Oxford. When the Association met at Cambridge in 1833, the Cambridge/Dublin coterie seized its opportunity. In his address as local secretary, Whewell stressed that the wave theory, with its correlating and predictive powers, belonged on the same level as Newton's law of gravity. Though Whewell did not mention Brewster by name, he did acknowledge that the wave theory could not begin to explain absorption spectra. A few days later, Section A brought together most of the leading protagonists: Hamilton, Lloyd, John Herschel and Airy on the one hand, *versus* Brewster, Richard Potter and John Barton on the other. In a telling discussion of absorption spectra, Herschel argued that ether particles *could* be connected with the molecules of substances to form complex vibrating systems which would resonate only to particular wavelengths. This analogy with sound, which Herschel illustrated experimentally on the spot, forced Brewster to acknowledge the problems of the emission theory of light and to admit that the facts of absorption were not incompatible with the wave theory. Very craftily Whewell and his allies commissioned a report by Lloyd on physical optics for the 1834 meeting. I suspect that Lloyd's report was deliberately intended to replace Brewster's own 1832 report on optics and it ensured that from 1834 the wave theory became the new orthodoxy of Section A. To call for and obtain a second report on a topic by a different author, within just two years of the first report, was unique in the early annals of the Association; and it doubtless added insult to the injury inflicted on Brewster.

These polemics in Section A, and their successors, showed that at the extremes contrary career investments were at stake, Brewster's in experimental optics and Whewell's in mathematical physics. Each party was strong where the other was weak: Brewster was no expert in analytical mathematical methods; Whewell had little talent for sustained delicate experimentation. Brewster resented the polemical, arrogant and partisan idea that the undulatory theory was on a par with Newton's theory of gravitation; and he deplored the rashness with which Whewell asserted the physical existence of an ether, which for Brewster was both unobservable and unimaginable. Thus the optical disputes in Section A revealed animosities of methodology, of person, of career, and of style.[20]

By 1834 it had become clear to Brewster that the Association, his own brain-child, was relatively indifferent to the question of direct national provision for men of science. He was disappointed that it had neglected or renounced key issues such as government research posts, scientific Members of Parliament, pensions for scientists, honours for scientists, never mind reform of the patent laws. This emasculation of his original aims he ascribed mainly to the Cambridge invasion of the Association, an explanation which Arnold Thackray and I think is essentially correct but incomplete.

Let Brewster himself have the last words about the early British Association. At the 1842 meeting he declared publicly and ominously that learned societies, meaning the Royal Society of London and the Association, were subject to 'the incubus of the undulatory theory'.[21] He thus revived the metaphor he had used in his 1835 *Edinburgh Review* article to denigrate the Cambridge coterie. In that article he had complained that there was 'an incubus pressing on the vitals of the Association with its livid weight . . . a congestion somewhere near its heart, impeding its respiration, and disturbing its most vital functions. Is it political, ecclesiastical, or personal, or is it all of them combined?'.[22] Brewster's use of the same metaphor, that of the incubus, to describe both the Cambridge faction and the undulatory theory shows how deeply he felt that he had become the odd man out, and had lost intellectual and organisational control of the Association he had so enthusiastically initiated.

Notes and References

For permission to cite from manuscripts in their care I am grateful to the Trustees of the British Library, the British Association for the Advancement of Science, and the Library of University College, London .

1. [David Brewster], 'Decline of Science in England', *Quarterly Review* 43 (1830), 333.
2. 'The British Scientific Association', *Edinburgh Review* 60 (1835), 363–393; 'British Association for the Advancement of Science', *North British Review* 14 (1850), 235–287; 'Presidential Address', *Report of the British Association for the Advancement of Science . . . 1850* (London, 1851), xxxi–xliv.
3. M. M. Gordon, *The Home Life of Sir David Brewster* (2nd edition, Edinburgh, 1870), 147–48.

4. A. D. Orange, 'The Origins of the British Association for the Advancement of Science', *British Journal for the History of Science* 6 (1972), 152–176, on 173.
5. J. Morrell and A. Thackray, *Gentlemen of Science: Early Years of the British Association for the Advancement of Science* (Oxford, 1981), 142 for details of Brewster's inadvertence.
6. Robinson, speech at the Dublin meeting, 15 August 1835, *Athenaeum* 8 (1835), 642.
7. Morrell and Thackray, *op. cit.* (5), 43–44.
8. C. Babbage, 'Great Congress of Philosophers at Berlin', *Edinburgh Journal of Science* 10 (1829), 225–234.
9. C. Babbage, *Reflections on the Decline of Science in England, and on some of its causes* (London, 1830); Brewster to Babbage, 24 February 1830, British Library, Add. Ms. 37185, f 72.
10. Brewster, *op. cit.* (1), 341; Morrell and Thackray, *op. cit.* (5), 51–52.
11. Johnston, 'Account of the Meeting of Naturalists at Hamburgh', *Edinburgh Journal of Science* 4 (1831) 189–244.
12. Brewster to Babbage, 21 February 1831, British Library, Add. Ms 37185, ff 481–482; Brewster to Phillips, 23 February 1831, Foundation volume, British Association archives, Bodleian Library, Oxford.
13. Morrell and Thackray, *op. cit.* (5) 58–94, give full details of the respective roles assumed by Brewster and Harcourt before and at the 1831 meeting.
14. On the creation of the Council, see Morrell and Thackray, *op. cit.* (5), 298–302.
15. Johnston, 'Account of the Scientific meeting at York', *Edinburgh Journal of Science* 6 (1832), 1–32; Morrell and Thackray, *op. cit.* (5) 143–144.
16. David Brewster, 'Report on the Recent Progress of Optics', *Report of the British Association for the Advancement of Science . . . 1832* (London, 1833), 308–322; Morrell and Thackray, *op. cit.* (5), 232, 390–391.
17. Gordon, *op. cit* (3), 157; Brewster to Babbage, 26 March, 8 April 1832, British Library, Add. Ms 37186, ff 297–298, 321–323; Brewster to Brougham, 9 May, 28 May, 30 August 1832, Brougham Papers, 15728, 26616, 15730, The Library, University College, London.
18. *Testimonials in favour of David Brewster as a candidate for the chair of natural philosophy in the University of Edinburgh* (Edinburgh, 1832); *Testimonials in favour of Thomas Galloway . . .* (Edinburgh, 1832); *Testimonials in favour of James D. Forbes . . .* (Edinburgh, 1832); Morrell and Thackray, *op. cit.* (5), 431–3. I am preparing a detailed study of this fascinating election.
19. Brewster to Babbage, 3 February 1833, British Library, Add. Ms 37187, ff408–411.
20. For the disputes on the wave theory see: G. N. Cantor, 'The Reception of the Wave Theory of Light in Britain: a Case Study Illustrating the Role of Methodology in Scientific Debate', *Historical Studies in the Physical Sciences* 6 (1975), 109–132; T. L. Hankins, *Sir William Rowan Hamilton* (Baltimore and London, 1980), 88–95, 129–171; Morrell and Thackray, *op. cit.* (5), 466–472.
21. *Literary Gazette* (1842), 534.
22. [David Brewster], 'The British Scientific Association', *Edinburgh Review* 60 (1835), 392.

XIV

Economic and ornamental geology: the Geological and Polytechnic Society of the West Riding of Yorkshire, 1837–53

Recent work on institutionalized provincial science during the first English industrial revolution has suggested that, even in industrial areas, science was pursued and patronized more as polite learning and as a mode of cultural affirmation than as a direct agent of technical and economic change.[1] It has been likewise argued that during this period British mining contributed little to the creation of the science of geology and that geology aided mining even less.[2] In this essay I consider the extent to which such findings are illuminated by the early history of the Geological and Polytechnic Society of the West Riding of Yorkshire which was founded in 1837 by local coal-mine and iron-furnace owners and managers. At the same time I hope to add a few nuances to the detailed account in Davis's standard history of the Society by drawing on unpublished sources which were not available to him.[3]

I

Critics who scourged the state of English science in the early 1830s often singled out geology as the happy exception. Likewise the Geological Society of London (f. 1807) was depicted as a model scientific society for others in the metropolis to emulate. There is no doubt that compared with other disciplines geology was then extremely buoyant; and that the Geological Society tried to act as a metropolitan leader in English geology through its *Proceedings*, its *Transactions* and the famous discussions at its meetings. At the same time it was a gentleman's geological club dominated by a meritocratic oligarchy based on scholarship and not on rank. Gentlemen of secure and in some cases fabulous income, such as Lyell, Murchison, Fitton, Darwin and Greenough, aided by Oxbridge clerical academics such as Sedgwick, Buckland and Whewell, dominated the Society: they led the manly discussions, dictated the social ethos, and shared the administrative spoils. With the obvious exception of John Taylor, the doyen of Cornish mining who was Treasurer from 1823 to 1843, surveyors, engineers, and mine owners were not key Fellows. Given the occupational composition of the Geological Society's oligarchy, its romantic wanderlust, its love of elevated and elevating scenery, it is not surprising that this metropolitan coterie generally neglected coal formations and mining areas.[4] In the 1830s the Geological Society of London nurtured the work on the Cambrian, Silurian and Devonian systems done by Sedgwick and Murchison, and on tertiary formations by Lyell and Fitton, without encouraging comparable work on either mining areas or the carboniferous coal measures.

Yorkshire geology had not been ignored by the metropolitan and Oxbridge geologists. In the early 1820s Buckland, Professor of geology at Oxford, had made Kirkdale cave and others famous for the fossil teeth and bones they contained. His sensational discoveries were, however, quite different from the sustained research programme pursued by Sedgwick, the Yorkshire-born Professor of geology at Cambridge. Sedgwick had worked on Yorkshire geology, but as a means and not an end. His study of Yorkshire magnesian limestone had attempted to establish its relation to what were subsequently called the Permian marls; and his research on the carboniferous Pennine chain of hills was undertaken not on its own account but primarily to illuminate the stratigraphical and dynamical geology of the Cumbrian mountains.[5]

This emphasis on polite Yorkshire geology was not confined to the Geological Society coterie. In the 1820s the Yorkshire Philosophical Society (f. 1822) had devoted itself to the geology of Yorkshire and the antiquities of York by collecting pertinent materials in its Museum at York. Taking advantage of both local opportunity and pride, the self-conscious provinciality of the Yorkshire Philosophical Society achieved rapid success: having appointed John Phillips as the Keeper of its Museum in 1826, his classic work of 1829 on the geology of the Yorkshire coast was both an advertisement for the Museum and its first fruit.[6] Though Phillips's career prospered nationally in the 1830s, York remained his base and Yorkshire his research area. He did publish on the lower coal measures, but the chief thrust of his work was the structure of the carboniferous limestone in the north west of the county.[7] It is significant that in 1837 he surveyed the Ingleton area of Yorkshire for coal as a commission and not on his own initiative; while surveying he was more interested in the Bowland anticlines than in locating coal.[8] Thus the two leading publishers on Yorkshire geology focused on the coast and the north-west dales and not on the coal-field.[9]

The non-mining geology pursued by Phillips and by the Yorkshire Philosophical Society was of course quite appropriate to an ancient cathedral city and county centre before the intrusion of Hudson's railways. Yet the philosophical societies of the major West Yorkshire manufacturing towns, all situated on the coal measures, followed this pattern of polite ornamental non-industrial geology. Of the active members of the Leeds Philosophical and Literary Society (f. 1818) only E. S. George had cultivated the geology of the local coal-field: when the Leeds Society launched its solitary volume of *Transactions* in 1837 the only paper on that subject was a posthumous one by George.[10] Yet it did show a brief spasm of interest in local coal geology in late 1837 just when the Geological and Polytechnic Society of the West Riding of Yorkshire was being formed. On 8 December 1837 J. G. Marshall capitalized on eight lectures on geology then being delivered in Leeds by James Finlay Weir Johnston, Reader in chemistry and mineralogy at the University of Durham, by establishing a geological group to cover Leeds geology and especially the coal-mining area of Middleton in south Leeds. After a brief flurry of activity and co-operation with T. W. Embleton, the Manager of the Middleton collieries, this Leeds geological group was defunct by 1839; and Marshall had already begun to study the metamorphic rocks of the Lake District where he had a large country house.[11] In Sheffield a similar lack of interest in coal-field geology was apparent. From its inception in 1822 to 1837, the Sheffield Literary and Philosophical Society mustered only Charles Morton, an engineer and colliery manager, with any sustained research interest in coal geology and mining technics.[12] By the late 1830s both the Sheffield and Leeds Societies were encouraging belles-lettres: local practical men were especially reluctant to give research level papers on local manufacturing and its technical problems, though without doubt they participated in the scientific enterprise as patrons, audience, and diffusers.[13] Wakefield was the most important town nearest to the centre of the worked coal-field, but there the question was the desperate one of survival: established in 1826 as a polite debating circle, the Wakefield Lit. and Phil. evaporated in 1838. Out of over 100 papers delivered to it, only three dealt with coal geology and mining problems.[14] At Bradford no regular scientific society existed until

1839 when William Sharp, senior surgeon at the Infirmary, established the first Bradford Philosophical Society.[15] It is therefore indisputable that before 1837 the chief West Yorkshire Lit. and Phils. in manufacturing towns actually on the county's large coal-field gave scant institutional encouragement to research and publication concerning its geology. This patent indifference to geological knowledge concerning Yorkshire's most important mineral resource was paralleled in the specialist geological societies founded in the 1830s in the Irish and Scottish capitals (Dublin 1831; Edinburgh 1834) which were devoted primarily to polite geology. The former was founded and run chiefly by Dublin academics who were not indifferent to Ireland's possible economic development but were mainly interested in the geological structure of their country. Likewise, the Edinburgh Society, composed of businessmen, existed 'to dignify and adorn their hours of recreation by scientific pursuits'; accordingly it gave negligible attention to the geology of the adjacent Lothian coal-field.[16]

There were, however, by 1837 two provincial specialist scientific societies, the Royal Geological Society of Cornwall (f. 1814) and the Natural History Society of Northumberland, Durham, and Newcastle upon Tyne (f. 1829), which placed their main emphasis on local geology with special reference to local mining. The former published a mixture of pure geology, mineral analyses, mining technology and statistics in its *Transactions*; and brought together local gentry and mine owners to an extent unknown in the Yorkshire literary and philosophical societies. Much of its success was due to men such as John Henry Vivian, a cultivated gentleman and mining entrepreneur who was familiar with the great continental mining academies. Even with this propitious social composition, however, the Cornwall Society had not fulfilled its own stated aims of completing a geological map of the county, of establishing a mining records office, and of setting up a mining school. Retrospectively the Cornish Society seems to have been as well placed as any local geological society could have been to promote effective co-operation between geologists, mine owners, and mine managers, and to encourage the study of local geology with particular reference to mining problems. Its failure to meet its chief desiderata shows that during the 1820s and 1830s such a programme faced colossal difficulties.[17]

The Natural History Society of Northumberland nurtured similar ambitions. Indeed, it was founded in 1829 as a splinter group from the Newcastle Literary and Philosophical Society to give greater attention to the geology of the North-Eastern Coal-field, then the most productive in Britain. This Society's commitment to coal-field geology was shown particularly in its proposed map of the whole of Northumberland, Durham, and Cumberland, which was to be on such a scale that 'the out-crop of each principal bed of coal, sandstone, or limestone, shall be minutely laid down, together with the range and direction of the principal dykes and veins which intersect them, and this to be accompanied with various sections through the strata to the greatest depth ascertained by the several mines now in course of working'.[18] The chief protagonist of this ambitious programme was John Buddle, the mining engineer who had earned the sobriquet 'King of the coal trade' for his practice of dividing coal workings into panels and especially for his system of compound ventilation.[19] Buddle was worried that in different parts of the North-Eastern Coal-field, the same coal seams were called different names, so he pushed hard not only for a map showing dykes but also for sections showing the direction, bendings, and "throws" of these dykes. Buddle also was the prime mover of a scheme for making the Society's Museum a depot for the records of former workings of exhausted or relinquished collieries as a guide to posterity by which expense and accidents might be avoided.[20] Even though these two schemes were powerfully advocated by Buddle, neither was implemented in the 1830s by the Natural History Society of Northumberland. Sensing failure in Newcastle, Buddle turned to the British Association for the Advancement of Science when it visited Newcastle in 1838; having revealed his own map and sections of the Newcastle coal-field, he joined Thomas Sopwith in successfully urging the British government via the Association to establish the Mining Records Office which opened in London in 1840. As with the Cornwall Geological Society, the Newcastle one had a propitious social composition which embraced mining men led by Buddle, clerics such as William Turner, the aristocrat W. C. Trevelyan, the independent gentleman Selby, the land surveyor Hewitson, the lawyer Adamson, the insurance agent William Hutton, the medical bureaucrat Winch, and the provision merchant Alder.[21] Nevertheless most local mine owners and managers did not share Buddle's enthusiasm for making public the geological details of the Newcastle coal-field; hence the failure in the 1830s of the Newcastle Society, like that of the Cornwall one, to produce a local geological map and to establish a local mining records office.

Yet Buddle himself had shown that it was possible though difficult for one man to combine fruitfully economic geology and mining technics, while earning the plaudits of the metropolitan geological coterie: at the Newcastle meeting of the British Association for the Advancement of Science in 1838, he became one of the few mining men to hold a vice presidency in the geological section.

II

The programme and indeed title of what became the Geological and Polytechnic Society of the West Riding of Yorkshire were not easily defined. The Society was formed on 1 December 1837 with the naive Baconian inductivist aim of collecting, recording, and comparing geological and mechanical information pertinent to the Yorkshire coal measures and coal trade. Its geological model was the Natural History Society of Northumberland; its mechanical one was the Royal Polytechnic Society of Cornwall (f. 1833) which with the varied inducements of very low membership fee (5s.), of prizes, and of exhibitions, devoted itself to encouraging Cornish arts and industry, especially mining and pilchard fishing.[22] In order to give body to its general aims, the Yorkshire Society turned for advice to two leading Northern savants, John Phillips and James F. W. Johnston. The presence of Phillips at the Society's second meeting on 14 December 1837, and Johnston's absence from it, ensured that in the circular of 16 December accompanying the rules of the Society its title was 'The Geological Society of the West Riding of Yorkshire'; there was also more than a hint that Phillips was to be the great Baconian interpreter who would "methodize" the geological data to be accumulated by the Society. Johnston, however, gave different private advice: though himself interested in Yorkshire coal-field geology, he shrewdly sensed that given the intellectual resources of the Society the polytechnic programme might be less quickly exhausted than the geological one. He therefore recommended that the Society should devote itself to the practical working and economy of coal-mines, their products, and ancillary industries, as well as to the exclusively geological programme advocated by Phillips. Faced with these two different agenda, the Society stuck to its original aims: by spring 1838 the prospectus of the retitled 'Geological and Polytechnic Society of the West Riding of Yorkshire' made clear that the Society intended to cover more than specialist geology without embracing general science. Fortunately the pressure of Phillips's lecturing engagements prevented an embarrassing conflict with Johnston, who in a lecture in June 1838 set out the ideology of the Society with the entire concurrence and positive assistance of its leading members.[23]

The most striking feature of Johnston's lecture was its studied avoidance of polite gentlemanly geology: the very title which permitted him to embrace the triptych of geology, polytechnics, and philanthropy, was witness to his sustained directly utilitarian thrust. For the known part of the coal-field Johnston set out a very ambitious programme modelled on Buddle's work in the north east: the identity of Yorkshire coal seams, their disturbances, dislocations, and "heaves", plus the relations between the Yorkshire and Lancashire coal-fields, all to be recorded in maps and sections. For the unknown part of the coal-field, Johnston urged borings east of the known coal-field 'at the expense of a common fund' to discover seams at greater depths than hitherto worked. Given his own preoccupations, Johnston called for the compilation of statistics of coal-mining and for systematic chemical study of coal. Of course, he advocated a Museum not just for the preservation of fossils, but more as a repository for mining records past and present. In buttressing his desiderata with the example of Buddle, Johnston was clearly trying to conjure up a Yorkshire imitator from the assembled mining interest.

In expounding the polytechnic part of the Society's programme, Johnston pointed to the ventilation and draining of mines as key areas, and especially to the development of anemometers and the improvement of the Davy safety-lamp. He also advocated the related study of possible improvements in iron manufacture, starting with the geology of ironstone beds and continuing with the question of the hot blast which he strongly supported. Of course, Johnston again invoked Buddle, this time as a model mining engineer; but, rather surprisingly, he recommended as a model of experimental technical research and publication on the properties of iron, the work on the strength of materials for steam boilers done by Alexander Dallas Bache under the auspices of the Franklin Institute in Philadelphia. In contrast with the geological and polytechnic components of the Society's programme, the philanthropic one received scant attention from Johnston who recommended a paternalism designed to solve mine owners' problems with their labour forces, such as luddism and insubordination, allied to collecting local economic and medical statistics. His models here were John Taylor's views on the management of miners and the inquiries encouraged by the Statistical Society of London (f. 1834). The overall nature of this programme was clearly a far cry from the gentlemanly geology of Somerset House.[24] This difference was explicitly adumbrated by Thomas Wilson who told Lord Morpeth that the object of the YGS was 'not so much to cultivate *theoretical* geology, as to investigate thoroughly the mineral seams, both of coal and ironstone, that cover so large a portion of this Riding, with reference to their *economic* value'.[25] The programme of the YGS also implied that it did not intend to compete with the general scientific societies in the area.

The Society's most successful effort to implement its ambitious aims was its published *Proceedings*. Here the YGS scored a coup. Clearly it could not rival the Geological Society of London which published both *Transactions* and *Proceedings*; but it did surpass the West Yorkshire Lit. and Phils. who either published memoirs sparsely or not at all. Its *Proceedings* appeared regularly from late 1839, showing a commitment to the advancement of science which the local general scientific societies could not equal. From its inception to 1843, the Society managed to mount its statutory four meetings per year, before declining to three a year in 1844, and to two a year in 1847. The papers published or delivered between 1838 and 1843 represent therefore the high point of the Society's activity. To what extent, however, did they implement the Society's programme?

Of the seventy-three contributions made in six years, a third was devoted to mining technics, including ventilation, safety-lamps, wire ropes, boilers of steam engines, and mining waste, the leading contributors being mainly West Yorkshire coal-mine or iron-furnace owners and managers, with the clear exception of Sopwith, the Newcastle land and mining surveyor, who recommended his pet subjects of isometrical projection and models of mining districts. The second most popular category was the geology of the West Yorkshire coal-field to which twenty-two papers were devoted, the main contributors again being mine and furnace men who clearly took seriously Johnston's desiderata for the known part of the coal-field. Problems of iron manufacture, mainly dealing with the relative merits of iron produced by the hot and cold air blast furnaces, attracted eight papers almost entirely given by local iron-masters. Agriculture, especially in its putative connections with geology, was energetically promoted by Thorp. In general, about two-thirds of all papers dealt with the geology of the coal-field and the technics of the coal industry. Yet already polite geology had made a small appearance: J. T. Clay had been quick to apply Agassiz's glaciation theory, promulgated at the Glasgow meeting of the British Association in 1840, to the questions of Yorkshire erratic boulders and "drift" gravel; and Sopwith expounded the glacial theory warmly. Even so, this intrusion of polite geology, inspired by Agassiz, hardly disturbed the dominance of coal-field papers, especially as general science other than geology and chemistry was totally unrepresented.[26]

In two other respects, however, the Society was less successful in achieving its manifest purposes during its opening six years. Though guided by Phillips and especially by Greenough, and having good local exemplars at Leeds and Newcastle to copy, the Museum of the Society, which cut across the local museums, did not prosper as much as its leaders wished. Earl Fitzwilliam, the President, had launched the Museum with a generous donation of money and specimens; but by 1841 Embleton, the Honorary Curator, in deploring the lack of donors of specimens, set out a list of desiderata to be fulfilled. To implement these aims, Martin Simpson, an expert on Yorkshire coast fossils, was appointed Curator at £50 per annum from summer 1842 to summer 1843 when the Society decided to put its Museum (cases of specimens in temporary accommodation in Wakefield) into the care of a West Yorkshire Lit. and Phil. because it could not afford a salaried Curator. By summer 1844 the YGS Museum had effectively been combined with that at Leeds. While many Lit. and Phils. existed primarily to support their museums and not to publish papers, the reverse was the case with the YGS.[27]

The second instance of incomplete success concerned the collaborative research by members of the Society, in co-operation with the Manchester Geological Society (f. 1838), on a section across the Pennine chain which would show the mutual relations of the Yorkshire and Lancashire coal-fields.[28] Greenough, an old-style mapper, then completing yet another geological map of England and Wales, supported the project warmly, urged exclusive concentration on the coal-field part of Yorkshire, and recommended a common vertical but not horizontal scale for the section.[29] After considerable discussion involving chiefly Morton, Embleton, Hartop and Thorp, by summer 1841 the line and scales of the section were decided with the revised aim of procuring that section most illustrative of the Yorkshire coal-field rather than that permitting the best comparison between the two coal-fields. The section across the Yorkshire coal-field was almost complete by late 1843, being apparently available for reference but not published.[30] As had happened at Newcastle with Buddle, it was left to an interested individual, Thorp, to publish *c.* 1847 a series of sections of the Yorkshire coal-field in connection with a projected work on it. The Society thus did not entirely succeed in producing a map and sections of the coal-field; and, concomitantly, it did not establish a depository of mining records.[31]

III

Even so, it is clear that between 1838 and 1843 the YGS, of which ordinary membership was restricted to West Riding residents, avoided the precariousness which afflicted much of the Lit. and Phil. movement from about 1840. This was chiefly due to a core-group of members: Thomas Wilson, the Secretary and Treasurer until 1842, who administrated the Society with high-minded zeal and relentless efficiency; and a small group of performers, that is men who gave papers at the quarterly meetings and promoted the Society's collaborative research. By late 1843 the Society nominally totalled 299 members, yet a quintet of performers (Thorp, Hartop, Embleton, Morton, Briggs) conducted by Wilson, constituted the small band largely responsible for the Society's fortunes.[32] Their most signal characteristic was their involvement in the Yorkshire coal and iron trade, chiefly the former, as mine owners or managers mainly in the Wakefield–Barnsley area; the Reverend Thorp, it should be noted, being a partner in a colliery as well as vicar of Womersley. Wilson, Briggs, Morton and probably Embleton, were mainstays of the West Yorkshire Coal Owners Association. Indeed, it was at a meeting of this Association at Wakefield on 1 December 1837 that the YGS was established. Unfortunately very little is known about the Association which was apparently devoted to problems of negotiating with colliers and to the maintenance of coal prices, at a time when the Yorkshire coal trade was exposed to great competition. Though its title proclaimed inclusiveness, only about one fifth of all Yorkshire coal owners were members of it.[33] There is unfortunately no evidence that the Association *per se* tried to map the county's coal measures, to establish a depot for local mining records, or to promote investigations into technical mining problems such as ventilation. Politically it was dominated by ardent free-traders and Liberals who, as defenders of commercial and civil liberty, vehemently opposed the state interference and espionage endorsed in the Mines Act of 1842.[34]

The YGS, as an offshoot of a trade association, was initially controlled by coal and iron men; not by a mixture of academics, independent gentlemen, medics, clerics, lawyers and merchants, as in other geological and scientific societies. Some of them had indeed a strong economic motive. In the 1830s Wilson, who had previously worked shallow seams at Silkstone, staked his capital in trying to find coal north-eastwards at Darton at greater depths than then usually contemplated; this risky venture depended on assumptions he made about the identity and direction of certain coal seams. Unfortunately his Kexborough pit, near Darton, failed disastrously because the shaft was sunk just where a "throw" occurred, leaving him no alternative but to withdraw from mining and from the secretaryship of the YGS in 1842.[35] His close friends Briggs and Morton were, however, successful in sinking pits eastwards. In 1836 Briggs sank the first ever successful pit through the magnesian limestone to the coal underneath at Newton near Castleford. From 1841 in partnership with Morton he successfully worked the Whitwood collieries near Normanton, which were deeper than his Flockton pits and adjacent to the new Sheffield–Leeds railway. Embleton, too, was obsessed with the question of identity of coal seams not least because the near exhausted seams of the Middleton colliery near Leeds, which he managed from 1830, prevented him from competing with the more successful Barnsley pits.[36] There is, then, enough evidence to suggest that the majority of these mine owners and managers, at least half of whom were working deeper mines than average, hoped that, if a comprehensive summary in some form of the relations of the various seams could be compiled from previously scattered local information, then the sinking of new deeper shafts would be less hazardous financially. No doubt the bigger capitalists among them hoped to acquire knowledge of the deeper seams which only they had the financial capacity to exploit. No doubt, too, the financial stringency, falling prices, unemployment, and labour troubles which erupted in 1837 combined to strengthen their awareness of the financial risks they faced.[37]

Given this vital economic motive, it is not surprising that most of the mining core-group enjoyed few contacts with organized polite science in either the metropolis or in the provinces. None was FRS,

FGS, or connected with the Yorkshire Philosophical Society. With the single exception of Morton who worked conspicuously in the Sheffield Literary and Philosophical Society from 1833 to 1838, they were not active in their local Lit. and Phil. From 1839 the YGS was dependent on these local scientific societies because it used their premises as it moved from town to town for its meetings; yet Wilson believed that most provincial scientific societies were 'powerless to advance the bounds of science, or even to communicate what is already known . . .'.[38] With the solitary exception of Hartop, none was known before 1837 by his publications or by appearances at public gatherings of scientists such as the meetings of the British Association. Hartop had given papers to the Association on the geology of the Don valley which resulted in an unimplemented resolution about the desirability of sections and plans of the South-West Yorkshire coal-field.[39] Their relative isolation before 1837 was not, however, the result of educational inferiority. After all, Wilson and Thorp were Cambridge graduates, while Morton and perhaps Embleton had spent a year at Edinburgh University, the others being probably autodidactic and trained by apprenticeship. In short, they formed a distinct and coherent group because of their occupational interest in mining geology and its associated technical problems such as ventilation and ropes.

In the opening phase of 1837–43, the managers of the YGS contrived to induce local West Yorkshire residents to be the Society's performers. This was largely due to the incessant zeal shown by Wilson in soliciting papers. In May 1841, for instance, the prospects for the June Leeds meeting looked gloomy: 'I have written to ask Mr. Teale, who cannot help; Mr. West, who does not answer; Mr. Holt, who says he has not data. . . . Could Mr. Chantrell be spurred up; Mr. Thorp says flatly he has not time . . . . Our brethren at Manchester are I think ahead of us now, they seem to have no difficulty in getting papers.'[40] With the exception of the core-group, mine and furnace managers and engineers certainly did not stampede to offer papers. Rather they had to be cajoled by Wilson who publicly regretted that most members, feeling that only a long and elaborate paper was appropriate for a learned society, were deterred from making brief factual communications.[41]

At the same time the YGS leaders were concerned to create, establish, and if possible expand the local audience for its performers. This was a considerable problem because the membership was scattered over the West Riding and subscriptions were difficult to collect. Furthermore, while lecture courses were by then the staple diet of Lit. and Phils. the YGS disdained this stratagem.[42] It tried, however, to increase its membership of non-performers by offering a low subscription rate of half a guinea, and from 1839 by holding its meetings in turn in all the major towns of the Riding. Given the long-standing interest shown by the gentry in science if it was orientated towards agriculture, it was inevitable that the YGS should try from 1840 to attract the landed interest by cultivating agricultural geology and agricultural chemistry, and by running joint meetings with the Yorkshire Agricultural Society (f. 1837). Wilson himself had grave doubts about the utility of geology in reference to agriculture, yet in 1841 he even contemplated a merger with the Yorkshire Agricultural Society because the popularity of agriculture would ensure a supply of funds sufficient to implement the YGS's aims and to procure paid research staff.[43] A further device Wilson wished to employ was to induce non-local geological stars to attend meetings, or even to perform. He kept looking to Phillips as a visitor from York who would bolster both attendance and meetings. Embleton, however, viewed the idea of importing star performers as ultimately debilitating. As he told Wilson, 'Prof Phillips' absence [from the Leeds meeting of December 1839] will be the means of lessening the attendance at the evening meeting, but I think we ought always to depend upon papers from the members instead of relying upon the assistance of "Professors of Geology".'[44] In the opening six years, Embleton's view prevailed: Johnston, the expositor of the Society's aims, and Sopwith, a mining engineer, were the solitary imported star performers, both from Newcastle; while metropolitan and Oxbridge lions, such as Sedgwick, Buckland and Greenough, accepted invitations to "roar" merely as discussants at meetings, of which the annual ones were arranged to fall near the times of meeting of the British Association in order to capture its stars. Wilson caught such geological giants chiefly through his friend Sopwith and the President Earl Fitzwilliam whose scientific tastes, menagerie, pits, furnaces, and lavish hospitality made his house at Wentworth near Rotherham a favourite port-of-call for passing geologists. Indeed, the YGS did not scruple to put the date of its autumn 1840 meeting into Sedgwick's hands in order to ensure his presence.[45]

For advice on its Museum the YGS turned outside the Riding to Phillips and to Greenough; and for guidance on its proposed section of the Yorkshire coal-field primarily to Greenough and secondarily to Sopwith. Clearly the YGS felt the necessity of taking outside advice only from selected individuals who had a particularly appropriate experience, such as Greenough's in mapping, Sopwith's in section work, and Phillips's in curatorship, which could further the Society's aim of cultivating not theoretical but economic geology. With respect to institutions as well as individuals outside the Riding, the YGS cultivated sturdy northern self-help as much as possible. It collaborated with the Manchester Geological Society on the projected Pennine section work; and perforce it occasionally joined forces with the Yorkshire Agricultural Society with which none the less it refused to be amalgamated. While it never contemplated imitating the Geological Society of London, with which its contacts were negligible, it did support the British Association with whose geological and statistical sections it shared some common aims.

IV

The second phase of the Society's history covered the years 1844–6 inclusive, when only three out of the statutory four meetings per year were held. This lapse was caused partly by two changes of Secretary: in 1842 Clay replaced Wilson, but owing to family bereavement and growing business responsibilities he resigned in 1844. Morton and William West were apparently approached to succeed Clay but both refused. Thorp came to the rescue, being assisted from 1845 by Henry Denny, Curator of the Museum of the Leeds Phil. and Lit. and Lecturer in botany in the Leeds school of medicine.[46] In any event, these three years witnessed distinct changes in the areas covered by papers and in the identity of performers, as well as a decline in productivity from about twelve to nine papers a year.

The most obvious shift was the growth of general science and of general geology, with the associated decline of mining technics, of coal-field geology, and of iron manufacture. Indeed, a third of the papers was devoted to general science, presumably to avoid lacunae caused by the relative dearth of papers on mining geology and technics. By far the leading general contributor was William Scoresby, the vicar of Bradford from 1839 to 1847, who could always be relied upon for interesting experimental demonstrations concerning magnetism and indeed for extemporaneous communications. He was supported by William Sykes Ward, John

Deakin Heaton, and William West, three Leeds men who were all key members of the Leeds Philosophical and Literary Society. Through Scoresby and the Leeds trio, polite general science, which was an anathema to the early managers, became the leading area covered. Mining technics, especially ventilation, were represented on a smaller scale, the leading performers of the previous phase remaining silent. There was a similar decline in Yorkshire coal-field geology, Embleton, Morton and Briggs offering no papers but contributing to discussion. Only one third of the papers dealt with mining geology and technics, the two chief areas purportedly cultivated by the Society; and only Thorp of the first core-group continued to perform regularly. Hartop, Embleton, Morton and Briggs, who gave twenty-three papers in the opening six years, produced only two contributions in the subsequent three years. While the coal men were becoming inactive, Yorkshire non-coal geology and general geology were promoted by two imports, Phillips and Edward Charlesworth, who were successive curators of the York Museum. Clearly in this second phase, the coal and iron men who had previously run the Society had lost intellectual steam or enthusiasm, or developed new interests and careers. As the Society imported few star performers from outside the Riding – York excepted – inevitably it had to transform itself partly into a peripatetic Lit. and Phil. offering an eclectic menu of polite general science and ornamental geology as well as mining geology and technics. Hence it depended increasingly on such local performers in the Yorkshire Lit. and Phil. and Mechanics' Institute networks as Scoresby, Phillips, West and Ward, none of which was occupationally involved in the coal trade.[47]

The third phase of the Society's fortunes covered 1847–53 when no more than two meetings per year were staged. Indeed, by 1854 it became almost defunct.[48] This was partly due to the migration in 1848 of Thorp, the Secretary and Treasurer, from Womersley near Pontefract to the vicarage of Misson in North Nottinghamshire, where he was inconveniently distant from the Society's area of operation. Once again there was a distinct shift in the areas covered by papers and in the identity of performers, as well as a further decline in productivity to about six papers per year. The most striking feature was the almost total disappearance of coal-field geology, the previous stalwarts being entirely inactive. Yorkshire non-coal geology and general geology flourished, being dominated by the wealthy Sheffield devotee Henry Clifton Sorby who favoured the Society with important pioneering papers on petrology.[49] Mining technics were, however, the most popular field, ventilation being the key problem covered: Thorp, the former doyen of coal-field geology, gave more attention in these years to mining technics. A much increased interest in applied science was largely due to Ward, who also revived interest in iron manufacturing. General science lost its previous dominance, becoming the exclusive domain of Leeds savants. What happened *vis à vis* performers was that Scoresby and Phillips, having left Yorkshire, were not available; only Thorp of the original core mine-owning group survived actively into the third phase. Not surprisingly the Society became even more dependent on Leeds men such as Ward, West, Denny and Thomas John Pearsall, and on such Sheffield savants as Sorby and James Haywood.[50] With the exception of Pearsall, all these men were active as performers and as administrators in their two respective Lit. and Phils. There was indeed some overlap of papers; but the YGS was saved from being a mere extension of the Leeds and Sheffield Societies because unlike them it published *Proceedings* and gladly offered an outlet for papers on applied science. None of this third core-group, with the exception of Thorp, was engaged in the coal trade. The utter collapse of the coal-field research programme was confirmed by the total absence of any paper on this topic between 1850 and 1853 inclusive; and it is significant that the polytechnic programme was maintained not only through the steady support of mining men such as Thorp and Benjamin Biram, but also through that given by non-mining savants such as Ward and West.[51] In short, of Johnston's three chief desiderata adumbrated on behalf of the Society, the polytechnic programme was partly implemented, though not with exclusive regard to the coal and iron trades; after a vigorous start, the coal-field geology programme entirely collapsed; while the philanthropic one was never even launched properly. At the same time, as the mining interest withdrew from giving papers to the Society, it became more and more dependent on local savants in the two major West Yorkshire towns. By June 1854 even Thorp thought the Society should wind up because of few contributors, slack members, poor attendance, and debt through having to pay rent to the Leeds Phil. and Lit. as well as a salary to Denny as Assistant Secretary. Shortly afterwards his resignation as Secretary and replacement by Ward signalled the extinction of the mining interest in running the Society.

V

For all of the Society's more active performers, the *Proceedings* was their sole or chief publishing outlet for their papers on geology, at a time when the Leeds Phil. and Lit. published no papers and the Sheffield one offered abstracts of papers only from 1850. This was, one suspects, a strong inducement to savants in those two towns, such as Ward, West and Sorby, to support the YGS as well as their local scientific society. Yet the demise of the mining geology programme after such a vigorous start calls for explanation. There was, of course, the sheer difficulty of the geological problems involved, basically due to the bending of the coal seams, their varying thickness, and the faults which dislocate them, to which attention was often drawn. On such an important matter as the geology of the Don valley the Society produced no consensus. There was also the vexing problem of inducing mine owners in general to proffer detailed local information. The Society's frequent calls for mining facts were widely ignored, partly because of the pervasive belief in the coal trade that secrecy served competitive capitalism best: Wilson regarded the proposed government mining inspectorate as a system of espionage; and probably many local mine owners regarded the Society's call for the production of accurate and detailed local maps, plans, sections, models and records, as another form of espionage. For these men in particular, economic entrepreneurship was incompatible with Baconian co-operative inductivism. In any event, many mines possessed no written records of important features such as the amount and direction of the throw of a fault; and when sections existed, they were sometimes merely general.[52] Though many mine owners did join the Society, their membership was mainly passive and nominal: only a small proportion of the mining membership was prepared to divulge and able to discuss local geological information. The active core of mining men who were performers was unable to renew itself by recruiting converts from the coal trade, and was consequently small. Why did these men, initially prolific, fail to sustain their programme?

It seems that for men of merely local knowledge the pursuit of local geology, like extractive mining, was subject to the law of diminishing returns; practical men such as Embleton, Briggs and Hartop apparently had geological knowledge of only a particular part of the coal-field, leaving only Thorp and probably Morton who possessed more than such local information. Hence most of the active mining men simply ran out of data when they had described their own immediate locality. Perhaps the vehicle of a voluntary learned society was inappropriate for a programme which was concerned with ambitious industrial research and development: certainly some of the active mining coterie diverted their attention to other fields, Briggs developing an interest in agriculture and Morton a career as a mines inspector; Embleton, who moved into mining consultancy, probably became disenchanted with the Society and its Museum; and in 1844 Hartop left Sheffield and the baffling study of the river Don's geology to manage the Bowling iron works at Bradford. One also surmises that Wilson's spectacular financial failure as a mine owner did not convince the practical men who had warned him against disaster that it was in their interest to join his Society. On the other hand, Briggs's pioneering ventures in deeper mining were economically successful without apparently drawing on the geological work done by the YGS. For all these reasons the Society could not sustain a programme devoted to creating a body of geological knowledge applicable to coal-mining, though its polytechnic work revealed the greater feasibility of applying scientific procedures to the engineering problems of the industry.[53] In sum, this most explicity utilitarian and economically motivated Society, active in an industrial and mining area, succumbed considerably as a *pis aller* to the lure of science as ornamental learning.

Table 4 *Topics and number of papers presented to the YGS, 1838–53*

Topics	*1838–43*		*1844–6*		*1847–53*	
	no. of papers	*papers /yr*	*papers*	*papers /yr*	*papers*	*papers /yr*
West Yorkshire coal geology	22	3.7	4	1.3	1	0.1
West Yorkshire non-coal geology	4	0.7	1	0.3	6	0.9
General geology	2	0.3	4	1.3	3	0.4
Mining technics	24	4.0	5	1.7	10	1.4
Iron manufacture	8	1.3	0	0.0	3	0.4
General technics	0	0.0	1	0.3	8	1.1
Coal chemistry	2	0.3	1	0.3	1	0.1
Non-coal chemistry	1	0.2	0	0.0	2	0.3
Agriculture	6	1.0	2	0.7	4	0.6
Philanthropy, statistics and public health	1	0.2	1	0.3	2	0.3
General science	0	0.0	8	2.7	4	0.6
Architecture	3	0.5	1	0.3	0	0.0
Totals	73	12.2	28	9.3	44	6.3

Table 5 *Topics and authors of papers presented to the YGS, 1838–53*

Topics	*1838–43* *Author (no. of papers)*	*1844–6* *Author (no. of papers)*	*1847–53* *Author (no. of papers)*
West Yorkshire coal geology	Thorp (10) Embleton (4) Morton (3) Hartop (2) Briggs (1) Simpson (1) Teale (1)	Thorp (2) Hartop (1) Denny (1)	Denny (1)
West Yorkshire non-coal geology	Clay (2) Alexander (1) Lee (1)	Phillips (1)	Sorby (3) Denny (1) Thorp (1) T. West (1)
General geology	Sopwith (1) Mackintosh (1)	Binney (1) Charlesworth (1) Phillips (1) Solly (1)	Sorby (3)

Table 5 – *continued*

Topics	*1838–43* *Author (no. of papers)*	*1844–6* *Author (no. of papers)*	*1847–53* *Author (no. of papers)*
Mining technics	Hartop (4) Morton (3) Biram (2) Briggs (2) Embleton (2) Fourness (2) Sopwith (2) Fletcher (1) Hanson (1) Holt (1) Holmes (1) Lucas (1) Roberts (1) Ward (1)	Barker (1) Biram (1) Fourness (1) Ward (1) West (1)	Thorp (3) Nasymth (2) Biram (1) Bodington (1) Ramsden (1) Ward (1) West (1)
Iron Manufacture	Hartop (2) Todd (2) Graham (1) Leah (1) Scoresby (1) Solly (1)	————	Ward (2) Solly (1)
General technics	————	Roberts (1)	Ward (4) Broadrick (1) Dalton (1) Dresser (1) Pearsall (1)
Coal chemistry	West (2)	Lucas (1)	W. L. Simpson (1)
Non-coal Chemistry	West (1)	————	Haywood (1) West (1)
Agriculture	Thorp (5) Hamerton (1)	Briggs (1) Haywood (1)	Briggs (1) Haywood (1) Thorp (1) Wilkinson (1)
Philanthropy	Nowell (1)	Thorp (1)	Alexander (1) Haywood (1)
General science	————	Scoresby (5) Heaton (1) Ward (1) West (1)	Ward (2) Heaton (1) Pearsall (1)
Architecture	Wallen (3)	Wallen (1)	————

Acknowledgements

For valuable help and criticism I am indebted to Stella Butler, Ian Inkster, John Pickstone, Roy Porter, and to the members of seminars at the Universities of Leeds, Oxford, Pennsylvania, and Johns Hopkins, to whom a preliminary version was given. For permission to cite unpublished sources, I am grateful to the Council of the Yorkshire Geological Society (archives, minute books), the University Library Cambridge (Greenough papers), Leeds Public Libraries Archives (Wilson papers), the Yorkshire Philosophical Society (Council minutes), and the Leeds Philosophical and Literary Society (minute book of transactions).

Notes and references

(Details of individuals are given only for those not recorded in *DNB*, *DAB*, or *DSB*.)

1 A. W. Thackray, 'Natural knowledge in cultural context: the Manchester model', *American Historical Review*, 1974, **79**, 672–709; S. Shapin, 'The Pottery Philosophical Society, 1819–1835: an examination of the cultural uses of provincial science', *Science Studies*, 1972, **2**, 311–36.

2 R. S. Porter, 'The industrial revolution and the rise of the science of geology', in M. Teich and R. M. Young (eds.), *Changing Perspectives in the History of Science*, London, 1973, pp. 320–43.

3 J. W. Davis, *History of the Yorkshire Geological and Polytechnic Society, 1837–1887. With Biographical Notices of Some of its Members*, Halifax, 1889 (henceforth *Davis*). Yorkshire was then divided into three parts called Ridings.

4 J. B. Morrell, 'London institutions and Lyell's career: 1820–41', *British Journal for History of Science*, 1976, **9**, 132–46; R. Burt, *John Taylor: Mining Entrepreneur and Engineer 1779–1863*, Buxton, 1977; R. S. Porter, 'Gentlemen and geology: the emergence of a scientific career, 1660–1920', *The Historical Journal*, 1978, **21**, 809–36.

5 W. Buckland, *Reliquiae Diluvianae*, London, 1823, pp. 1–51; J. W. Clark and T. M. Hughes, *The Life and Letters of the Reverend Adam Sedgwick*, Cambridge, 1890, **i**, pp. 294–7, 531, and **ii**, p. 503; T. Sheppard, *Bibliography of Yorkshire Geology*, London, Hull and York, 1915, which is *Proceedings of the Yorkshire Geological Society*, 1915, **18** (henceforth *PYGS*).

6 A. D. Orange, *Philosophers and Provincials: The Yorkshire Philo-*

sophical Society from 1822 to 1844, York, 1973; J. Phillips, *Illustrations of the Geology of Yorkshire*: part 1, *The Yorkshire Coast*, York, 1829.

7 cf. Phillips 'On the lower or ganister coal series of Yorkshire', *Philosophical Magazine*, 1832, **1**, 349–53; and *Illustrations of the Geology of Yorkshire*: part 2, *The Mountain Limestone District*, London, 1836.

8 J. Phillips, *A Report on the Probability of the Occurrence of Coal and Other Minerals in the Vicinity of Lancaster. Addressed to the Lancaster Mining Company*, Lancaster, 1837.

9 H. C. Versey, 'History of Yorkshire geology', *PYGS*, 1973–6, **40**, 335–52 (338).

10 E. S. George, 'On the Yorkshire coal-field', *Transactions of the Leeds Philosophical and Literary Society*, 1837, **1**, 135–91; published annual *Reports of the Council of the Leeds Philosophical and Literary Society*, Leeds, 1820–38. On Edward Sanderson George (1801–30), Leeds chemical manufacturer, see E. K. Clark, *The history of . . . the Leeds Philosophical and Literary Society*, Leeds, 1924, pp. 12–13, 29, 42, 146.

11 General minute book of transactions of the Leeds Philosophical and Literary Society, 1821–41 (entry for 8 December 1837); *Eighteenth Report of Council of Leeds PLS*, Leeds, 1838, pp. 8–10; *Nineteenth Report of Council of Leeds PLS*, Leeds, 1839, p. 11; *Twentieth Report of Council of Leeds PLS*, Leeds, 1840, p. 6; *Davis*, pp. 180–2; W. G. Rimmer, *Marshalls of Leeds, Flax-Spinners 1788–1886*, Cambridge, 1960, pp. 182, 221–2; *The Athenaeum*, 1839, p. 646. James Garth Marshall (1802–73); Thomas William Embleton (1809–93), mine manager, obituary in *PYGS*, 1892–4, **12**, 335–9.

12 Published *Annual Reports of the Sheffield Literary and Philosophical Society*, Sheffield, 1824–38; published *Annual Reports of the Sheffield Mechanics' Institute*, Sheffield, 1833–7. On Morton (1811–82), see *Davis*, pp. 61–3; J. Goodchild, 'The first mines inspector in Yorkshire. Part I', *South Yorkshire Journal of Economics and Social History*, 1971, part 3, 15–17.

13 *Seventeenth Report of the Sheffield LPS*, Sheffield, 1840, p. 4; I. Inkster, 'The development of a scientific community in Sheffield, 1790–1850: a network of people and interests', *Transactions of the Hunter Archaeological Society*, 1973, **10**, 99–131.

14 Programmes for 1826–36 held in Wakefield City Archives; *West Riding Herald*, 13 January 1837 and 28 April 1837.

15 J. James, *The History of Bradford and Its Parish*, London and

Bradford, 1866, pp. 245–8; W. Scruton, *Pen and Pencil Pictures of Old Bradford*, Bradford, 1889, pp. 90–3.

16 G. L. Davies, 'The Geological Society of Dublin and the Royal Geological Society of Ireland 1831–1890', *Hermathena*, 1965, no. c, 66–76; 'Memoir of the Society', *Transactions of the Edinburgh Geological Society*, 1870, **1**, 1–6 (1).

17 R. S. Porter, *The Making of Geology: Earth Science in Britain, 1660–1815*, Cambridge, 1977, pp. 134–5. John Henry Vivian (1785–1855) was head of Vivians, the copper smelters.

18 T. R. Goddard, *History of the Natural History Society of Northumberland, Durham and Newcastle upon Tyne 1829–1929*, Newcastle, 1929, p. 39.

19 See the copious evidence of Buddle printed in *Report from the Select Committee on Accidents in Mines*, Parliamentary Papers, 1835, **5**, 1–373 (131–88, 215–23).

20 J. Buddle, 'Synopsis of the several seams of coal in the Newcastle district', *Transactions of the Natural History Society of Northumberland, Durham and Newcastle upon Tyne*, 1831, **1**, 215–24; *idem*, 'Reference to the sections of the strata of the Newcastle coal field', ibid., 225–40; *idem*, 'Suggestions for making the Natural History Society a place of deposit for the mining records of the district', paper read at a meeting of the Natural History Society of Northumberland, Durham, and Newcastle upon Tyne, 23 December 1834, and printed in their *Transactions*, Newcastle, 1838.

21 Buddle, 'Observations on the Newcastle coal-field', *Report of the Eighth Meeting of the British Association for the Advancement of Science*, London, 1839, pp. 74–6; ibid., p. xxiii; *Report of the Ninth Meeting of the British Association for the Advancement of Science*, London, 1840, p. 174.

22 *Second Annual Report of the Cornwall Polytechnic Society*, Falmouth, 1834, pp. 9–13; G. W. Roderick and M. D. Stephens, *Science and Technical Education in Nineteenth-Century England*, Newton Abbot, 1972, pp. 119–33; *Davis*, pp. 2–4.

23 *Davis*, pp. 3–14; Wilson to Phillips, 9 December 1837; Wilson to Johnston, 22 January 1838; Wilson to Phillips, 10 February 1838; Wilson to Johnston, 5 March 1838, in Wilson Papers, DB 178/23.

24 J. F. W. Johnston, *The Economy of a Coal-Field: An Exposition of the Objects of the Geological and Polytechnic Society of the West Riding of Yorkshire, and of the best means of attaining them*, Durham, 1838. For Bache's work see B. Sinclair, *Philadelphia's*

Philosopher Mechanics: A History of the Franklin Institute 1824–1865, Baltimore, 1974.

25 10 July 1839, Wilson papers, DB 178/23, italics in original. Thomas Wilson (1800–76), *Davis*, pp. 49–52.

26 Tables 4 and 5, pp. 249 and 250. Clay, 'Observations on the occurence of boulders of granite, and other crystalline rocks, in the valley of the Calder, near Halifax', *PYGS*, 1839–42, **1**, 201–6 (read June 1841), and 'Observations on the Yorkshire drift and gravel', ibid., 338–51 (read December 1841); Sopwith, 'On the evidence of the former existence of glaciers in Great Britain', ibid., 419–42 (read March 1842). Joseph Travis Clay (1805–92) was a Quaker who founded the worsted coat trade in Brighouse.

27 *Davis*, pp. 150–67; J. E. Hemingway, 'Martin Simpson, geologist and curator', in H. B. Browne, *Chapters of Whitby History 1823–1946*, Hull and London, 1946, pp. 93–105.

28 For the early Manchester Society see R. H. Kargon, *Science in Victorian Manchester: Enterprise and Expertise*, Baltimore, 1977, pp. 24–7, 30–4.

29 Wilson to Greenough, 26 October 1839, Greenough Papers, Add 7918(8); Greenough to Wilson, 4 November 1839, Wilson papers, DB 178/27.

30 *Davis*, pp. 89–118. On Henry Hartop (1786–1865), furnace manager, see G. Mee, *Aristocratic enterprise: The Fitzwilliam Industrial Undertakings 1795–1857*, Glasgow, 1975, pp. 45–63; Reverend William Thorp (1804–60), *Davis*, pp. 213–15, 382–6.

31 YGS Council minutes, 18 December 1839. Thorp's map survives in Wakefield City Archives.

32 Henry Briggs (1797–1868) for details of whom I am indebted to an unpublished typescript by Mr J. Goodchild, Curator of Wakefield City Archives; *Davis*, pp. 60–1.

33 Evidence of Wilson in *Children's Employment Commission: Appendix to First Report of Commissioners. Mines. Part I.* Parliamentary Papers, 1842, **16**, 205.

34 Wilson to Committee of Yorkshire coal owners, 7 February 1842, Wilson Papers, DB 178/22; circular of Wilson to coal owners of the West Riding of Yorkshire, 26 May 1842, Wilson Papers, DB 178/27; *Report of the Committee Appointed at a Meeting of the Yorkshire Coal-Owners. . .on 21 May 1841, to Take into Consideration the Commission of Enquiry into the Employment of Children and Young Persons in Mines and Manufactories. . .*, Barnsley, June 1841, Wilson Papers, DB 178/27.

35 Account of Wilson in unpublished volume 2 of J. Wilkinson, 'Worthies, families and charities of Barnsley and the district', London, n.d., in Wakefield City Archives.
36 W. G. Rimmer, 'Middleton colliery, near Leeds, 1770–1830', *Yorkshire Bulletin of Economic and Social Research*, 1955, **7**, 41–58.
37 A. D. Gayer, W. W. Rostow and A. J. Schwartz, *The Growth and Fluctuation of the British Economy 1790–1850*, Oxford, 1953, **i**, 242–76.
38 Wilson to secretaries of Yorkshire Philosophical Society, 9 February 1842, Wilson papers DB 178/23, reproduced in YPS Council minutes, 14 February 1842.
39 *1833 Report of the British Association*, xxxiv, 478; *Proceedings of the Fifth Meeting of the British Association for the Advancement of Science, held in Dublin*, Dublin, 1835, 107.
40 *Davis*, pp. 172–3. Thomas Pridgin Teale (1800–67), Leeds surgeon, *Davis*, pp. 54–8; William West (1792–1851), Leeds chemical consultant, *Davis*, pp. 238–40; Henry Holt (1812–69), Wakefield mining engineer and surveyor, *Davis*, pp. 52–3; Robert Dennis Chantrell (1793–1872), Leeds architect.
41 *PYGS*, 1839–42, **1**, 37.
42 Wilson to Murray, 5 October 1838, Wilson Papers, DB 178/23.
43 Wilson to Fitzwilliam, 31 December 1840; Wilson to Johnston, 3 January 1841; Wilson to Fitzwilliam, 21 January 1841, all in Wilson Papers, DB 178/22; Wilson to Fitzwilliam, 9 May 1841, Wilson Papers, DB 178/28.
44 YGS Council minutes, 1 November 1839; Embleton to Wilson, 13 November 1839, YGS Archives.
45 *PYGS*, 1839–42, **1**, 79–81, 338; ibid., 1842–8, **2**, 41; *Davis*, pp. 81, 115, 171–3, 226; YGS Council minutes, 8 August 1838, 8 February 1839.
46 YGS Council minutes, 28 May 1844.
47 Tables 4 and 5, pp. 249 and 250. William Sykes Ward (1813–85), Leeds lawyer and inventor, *Davis*, pp. 241–2; John Deakin Heaton (1817–80), Leeds physician, T. W. Reid, *A Memoir of John Deakin Heaton*, London, 1883; Edward Charlesworth (1813–93); T. Stamp and C. Stamp, *William Scoresby: Arctic Scientist*, Whitby, 1976.
48 *Davis*, pp. 259–60; Thorp to Wilson, 19 June 1854, Wilson Papers, DB 178/30.
49 Tables 4 and 5, pp. 249 and 250. N. Higham, *A Very Scientific Gentleman: The Major Achievements of Henry Clifton Sorby*, Oxford, 1963; for example, Sorby, 'On the microscopical structure of

the calcareous grit of the Yorkshire coast', *PYGS*, 1849–59, **iii**, 197–206 (read June 1851).

50 Thomas John Pearsall (1805–83) was then a Leeds consulting chemist and lecturer for the Yorkshire Union of Mechanics' Institutes; James Haywood (d. 1854), was a Sheffield consulting chemist and lecturer.

51 Benjamin Biram (1804–57), coal viewer, who like Hartop worked for Earl Fitzwilliam: Mee, *Aristocratic Enterprize*; A. K. Clayton, 'The Elsecar Collieries under Joshua and Benjamin Biram', unpublished typescript, 1964, Sheffield Public Library.

52 A. H. Green, 'On the coal measures of the neighbourhood of Rotherham', *PYGS*, 1859–68, 4, 685–98 (686–7). cf. Green *et al.*, *Memoirs of the Geological Survey. England and Wales. The Geology of the Yorkshire Coalfield*, London, 1878, pp. 4–7.

53 cf. P. Mathias, 'Who unbound Prometheus? Science and technical change, 1600–1800', in Mathias (ed.), *Science and Society, 1600–1900*, Cambridge, 1973, pp. 54–80; *idem*, 'Science and technology during the industrial revolution: some general problems', *Proceedings of the sixth International Economic History Congress*, Copenhagen, 1978, pp. 104–9.

XV

Wissenschaft in Worstedopolis: Public Science in Bradford, 1800–1850

I TAKE as my text today an epistle of John—John Phillips writing from Birmingham in 1839: 'in quieter towns like . . . York . . . peace, good order, [and] leisure favour the expansion of a philosophical spirit'.[1]

Some of you no doubt think that it is pointless to study science in places which have not been associated with eminent savants and their discoveries. Others may regard provincial science as a hyperborean cave from which the talented were fortunately released by a beckoning metropolis. Prima facie the case of science in Bradford in the nineteenth century seems to support this first view capitally: science as a cultural formation was so fragile that there appears little to study. For the historian of Whiggish persuasion there seems no paean to sing, only a threnody. The contrast with Manchester is simply dismal. If Manchester was Lancashire's shock city of the industrial revolution, it was also a city of science; whereas Bradford was Yorkshire's shock city but not apparently a scientific town. Though it nurtured distinguished Georgian virtuosi such as Abraham Sharp and Richard Richardson, in the nineteenth century it lacked renowned heroes equivalent to the Daltons, Joules and Roscoes, who remain secure in the scientific pantheon. Institutionally it lagged behind: the first Bradford Philosophical Society to last more than four years was launched in 1864, when the Manchester Lit and Phil was approaching its centenary. The Bradford Technical College, opened in 1882, came a generation after Owens College, *the* prototype British provincial science-based university.[2] Bradford's record in producing scientific journals was

This is an unrevised version of the Presidential Address delivered at a meeting of the Society, on the theme of 'Science, technical change and work', in Manchester on 12 May 1984.

Acknowledgements: For valuable comments and criticism I am indebted to James Donnelly, Ian Inkster, Tony Jowitt, and Roy Porter. For permission to cite or refer to manuscripts, I am grateful to the curator of Geological Collections, University Museum, Oxford (Phillips papers), York Minster Library, the British Library, Bradford Public Library, and the Keeper of Manuscripts, Cambridge University Library (Greenough papers). Like everyone else who works on Bradford's history I have benefitted from the exemplary services provided by the staffs of the local studies and archives departments of the City of Bradford Public Library. The research on which this paper is based has been facilitated by a grant from the Royal Society of London to whom I am grateful.

[1] Phillips to Ann Phillips, 11 August 1839, Phillips papers, reproduced in J. B. Morrell and A. W. Thackray (eds), *Gentlemen of Science: early correspondence of the British Association for the Advancement of Science*, London, 1984, p. 322.

[2] An excellent account is given by J. F. Donnelly, 'The development of technical education in Bradford, 1825–1900', unpublished MEd thesis, University of Leeds, 1982, of which pp. 17–44 deal with scientific activity and education in Bradford before 1867.

miserable: none of its philosophical societies ever published separate memoirs or proceedings; and the town's first enduring journal came as late as 1884 when the Society of Dyers and Colourists was formed.[3] For a general science journal one waits until this century (1904) when the *Bradford Scientific Journal* was launched by the Bradford Scientific Association.[4] Even writers sympathetic to the West Riding of Yorkshire have either found little to say about Bradford science or deprecated the town's philistinism. In his important study of Yorkshire's contribution to science, Sheppard noted rightly that the spirit of Yorkshire science had moved around the county, but it never alighted on Bradford.[5] In recent years, Musson and Robinson have examined scientific aspiration as well as achievement; but they offered only one reference, and a passing one at that, to Bradford.[6] Two of the best local Victorian historians lamented the town's lack of encouragement to intellectuals. John James noted sadly that by 1840 science and literature still did not walk hand in hand with the genius of trade;[7] while in 1889 William Scruton stressed that the obsessive pursuit of commercial prosperity and material success had relegated science and philosophy to a subordinate position, even though the town was vastly wealthy and densely populated.[8] The popular object of worship in Bradford was not Minerva but what Ruskin in a speech at Bradford called 'the great Goddess of "getting on"'.[9] T. S. Eliot in *The Waste Land* merely reinforced a dominant image when describing a carbuncular young man as

> 'One of the low on whom assurance sits
> As a silk hat on a Bradford millionaire.'

And, of course, from the 1820s immigration and emigration helped to make the town into a settlement of strangers. Certainly there has been for decades a march of mind from the city. One remembers Fred Delius, Rothenstein, Sir Edward Appleton, J.B. Priestley, John Braine, Barbara Castle, Alan Bullock, Vic Feather, and that doyen of emigrants, my distinguished predecessor as President, Robert Fox. But some of us have steadfastly stayed where we were born, following the admirable example of

[3] F. M. Rowe and E. Clayton (eds), *The Jubilee issue of the Journal of the Society of Dyers and Colourists: 1884–1934*, Bradford, 1934.

[4] The Bradford Scientific Association, like the Bradford Natural History Society, was founded in 1875. It specialised at the research level in geology, leaving field biology to the Naturalists.

[5] T. Sheppard, *Yorkshire's contribution to science, with a bibliography of natural history publications*, London, 1916, p. 8.

[6] A. E. Musson and E. Robinson, *Science and technology in the industrial revolution*, Manchester, 1969, p. 181.

[7] J. James, *The history and topography of Bradford, (in the county of York,) with topographical notices of its parish*, London and Bradford, 1841, p. 19. This was not just routine rhetoric: pp. vii, ix, revealed that he could not publish by subscription because of the poor local response and that his research had not been greatly assisted by Bradfordians.

[8] W. Scruton, *Pen and pencil pictures of old Bradford*, Bradford, 1889, pp. 107–8.

[9] J. Ruskin, *The crown of wild olive*, London, 1906, p. 97, from his lecture 'Traffic' delivered in Bradford, 21 April 1864 (first published 1866).

the Bronte sisters, including the forgotten fourth sister, Doreen, alias Mavis, alias Dawn, alias Tracey, alias Julie, Bradford's answer to Mary Somerville.[10] All this seems to indicate that Bradford offers little scope for a Kargon-like study stressing enterprise and expertise or a Thackray-like analysis of cultural geography.[11] This conclusion will be welcome to those who think provincialism is a regrettable state of mind, but unacceptable to those who see provincialism as instructing us to recognise the complexities which the yearning for metropolitanism obscures.[12]

The historian of local urban science will gain much from Lord Briggs' classic study of Victorian cities. He stressed that industrialisation did not standardise towns but differentiated them. He demonstrated the importance of separate provincial cultures until the 1890s. He saw that lit and phils represented what *he* called 'the local cultural élite', a phrase subsequently bandied about by others. He has some splendid pages on Bradford, buried in a chapter on the civic pride of Leeds.[13] This is, of course, a historical solecism because when writing to Leodensians Victorians always addressed their letters 'Leeds, near Bradford'. In the last twenty years the value of local studies has become apparent through works which have managed to avoid the Scylla of antiquarianism and the Charybdis of boosterism because they have been informed by an awareness of national features and of historiographical issues. One of the most fruitful areas has been local administration, important in this country because much national legislation was implemented locally. In any case local bodies themselves had or could acquire considerable powers. That was why G.M. Young could assert that the change from early to late Victorian England was symbolized by the contrast between Manchester, home of free trade, and Birmingham with its civic gospel.[14] Matters such as incorporation of boroughs, sanitary reform, factory act agitation, chartism, elementary education, and the new poor law took different forms in different places: locality determined whether paupers lived in palaces or hovels.[15] Even more strikingly, some historians have mounted general theses of national scope on the basis of mainly local evidence. The most important contribution of the last twenty-five years to our understanding of class was made in 1963 by E.P. Thompson. This book was written in Yorkshire and coloured by sources from the West Riding of Yorkshire.[16] In any event, two years ago my predecessor discoursed eloquently on science,

[10] It is inexplicable that E. C. Patterson, *Mary Somerville and the cultivation of science 1815–1840*, The Hague, 1983, fails to mention Doreen Bronte.

[11] R. H. Kargon, *Science in Victorian Manchester. Enterprise and expertise*, Baltimore, 1977; A. W. Thackray, 'Natural knowledge in cultural context: the Manchester model', *American historical review*, 1974, **79,** 672–709.

[12] R. Hoggart, *Speaking to each other. Volume 1. About society*, London, 1970, p. 74.

[13] A. Briggs, *Victorian cities*, Harmondsworth, 1968, pp. 43, 47, 140–163.

[14] G. M. Young, *Victorian England: portrait of an age*, Oxford, 1953, p. 124.

[15] D. Fraser (ed), *The new poor law in the nineteenth century*, London, 1976; A. Digby, *Pauper palaces*, London, 1978.

[16] E. P. Thompson, *The making of the English working class*, Harmondsworth, 1968, p. 14–15.

industry, and the social order in Mulhouse, concluding inter alia that history from the periphery is necessary to demolish shibboleths.[17] I intend to follow his approach by discussing some telling episodes in the annals of public science in Bradford, of Wissenschaft in Worstedopolis. At the same time I shall try not to ignore today's theme of science, technical change and work, though I do reserve for myself the Presidential prerogative of relative independence.

During the first half of the nineteenth century Bradford became one of the major towns of Victorian England on the basis of the mechanisation of the worsted textile industry and its concentration there. In 1801 it was a small place with a population of c13,000; by 1851 its population had topped the 100,000 mark, making it the seventh largest English town outside London, with an astounding population growth rate of more than 50% per decade from 1811.[18] After 1851 population growth was less rapid. Not surprisingly the decades from 1820 to 1850 were ones of turmoil. In 1825 the textile industry was in a state of transition: spinning was fully mechanised but combing and weaving hardly at all. Fearful of mechanisation, the combers and weavers launched the great strike of 1825 which ensured that class antagonism henceforth never abated until the 1850s.[19] It was this class antagonism which fuelled riots against the Poor Law in 1837, fed Owenite socialism which flourished from 1837 to about 1842, encouraged the Chartist disturbances of 1839 and 1848, prompted the plug riots of 1842, and most obviously made Bradford one of the leading centres for the factory reform movement. It was after all in Bradford that in 1830 Richard Oastler was awakened to the enormity of white slavery.[20] The mechanisation of weaving by 1850 and the slump which began in 1837 produced simultaneous structural and cyclical unemployment, which together ensured that industrialisation and its effects on different classes remained dominant issues in the town throughout the 1840s.

Socially Bradford was bottom-heavy. It was a raw and rough place. Its middle class was overwhelmingly commercial and manufacturing, but small in comparison to the vast lower-middle class and working class around it. Bradford was a town of migrants. In 1851 51% of the population had been born outside it, a far higher proportion than elsewhere in Yorkshire; of the population aged over 20, 70% had been born elsewhere. Roughly 10% of the population came from Ireland desperate for unskilled

[17] R. Fox, 'Science, industry, and the social order in Mulhouse, 1798–1871', *British Journal for the history of science*, 1984, **17,** 127–68.

[18] The population figures were: 16,000 in 1811; 26,000 in 1821; 44,000 in 1831; 67,000 in 1841; 104,000 in 1851. See *Census of Great Britain, 1851. Population tables. I. Numbers of the inhabitants, in the years 1801, 1811, 1821, 1831, 1841, and 1851*, Parliamentary Papers, 1853, **85,** cxxvi–cxxvii.

[19] For general material on Bradford there are two excellent recent books: D. G. Wright and J. A. Jowitt (eds), *Victorian Bradford: essays in honour of Jack Reynolds*, Bradford, 1982; J. Reynolds, *The great paternalist: Titus Salt and the growth of nineteenth-century Bradford*, Hounslow, 1983. D. G. Wright, 'Politics and opinion in nineteenth-century Bradford 1832–1880', unpublished PhD thesis, University of Leeds, 1966, is also very valuable.

[20] C. Driver, *Tory radical: the life of Richard Oastler*, New York, 1946, pp. 36–70.

work, giving Bradford the largest Irish population in Yorkshire and the 'Orange' disturbance of 1844.[21] It was a parvenu place full of strangers who lived in a settlement rather than a community, so that persons of taste found it difficult to become known to each other.[22] The machinery of social intercourse and the means of improving the small and beleagured middle classes were not prominent.[23] Moreover, as Bradford was little more than an overblown village in 1800, it had a thin eighteenth-century heritage on which the burgeoning nineteenth-century industrial town could draw.[24]

Ecclesiastically and politically Bradford was a cock-pit of conflict, especially in the 1830s and 1840s. Renowned nationally as a citadel of dissent, in 1851 Bradford had the third highest proportion of nonconformists in urban England.[25] Most of these were evangelical nonconformists, the Congregationalists, Baptists, and Methodists, with the rational dissenters, Quakers and Unitarians, in a minority. Chapel-church strife reached its peak in the early 1840s with the seven-years long church-rate controversy won by the dissenters, many of whom politically were Liberals. In the 1840s the Liberals were in the ascendant in the town: they nourished *The Bradford Observer*, Bradford's first enduring newspaper, founded in 1834 as its analogue to Baines' *Leeds Mercury;* and after a long struggle against the Conservatives in the 1840s, they achieved the incorporation of Bradford in 1847 and municipal hegemony. In this decade several issues such as public health provided occasions for *local* party political battles between the Liberal incorporators and their Conservative opponents.[26] The flavour of the deep hostility between Conservative and Liberal was exquisitely revealed in 1834 when Richard Oastler launched a diatribe against the Liberal millocracy which founded *The Bradford Observer*. Its flavour may be judged from its title, *A letter to those sleek, pious, holy, devout dissenters, Messrs. Get-all, Keep-all, Grasp-all, Scrape-all, Whip-all, Gull-all, Cheat-all, Cant-all, Work-all, Sneak-all, Lie-well, Swear-well, Scratchem, etc, the shareholders in the 'Bradford Observer'* . . .

Physically and socially the town was offensive. It lay in a basin, a geographical fact which was associated with appalling housing, bad sanitation, air pollution, low life expectancy, and high infant mortality. In the 1840s these things were noted by a variety of observers, from public officials such as Chadwick and James Smith to private individuals such as

21 A. Elliott, 'Social structure in the mid-nineteenth century' in Wright and Jowitt, *Victorian Bradford*, pp. 101–113.

22 *Bradford observer*, editorial, 4 August 1859; *The Bradfordian*, editorial, 1860, **1**, 30.

23 Behrens, J. (ed), *Sir Jacob Behrens 1806–1889*, London, n.d., p. 38; *The Bradford Review*, editorial, 22 December 1864.

24 I owe this important point to Tony Jowitt. In 1838 Behrens thought Bradford, with a population of about 60,000 was still an overgrown village: Behrens, *Behrens*, p. 38.

25 J. A. Jowitt, 'The pattern of religion in Victorian Bradford' in Wright and Jowitt, *Victorian Bradford*, pp. 37–61.

26 W. Cudworth, *Historial notes on the Bradford Corporation*, Bradford, 1881; A. Elliott, 'The establishment of municipal government in Bradford 1837–1857', unpublished PhD thesis, University of Bradford, 1976; G. B. Hurst, *Closed chapters*, Manchester, 1942, pp. 4–5. 18.

Engels and Weerth. Their general verdict was that Bradford was a 'most filthy town'.[27] Here are the impressions of a German immigrant, Georg Weerth, in the 1840s:

> 'Every other factory town in England is a paradise in comparison to this hole. In Manchester the air lies like lead upon you; in Birmingham it is just as if you were sitting with your nose in a stove pipe; in Leeds you have to cough, because of the dust and the stink, as if you had swallowed a pound of Cayenne pepper at one go; but you can still put up with all that. In Bradford, however, you think you have been lodged . . . with the Devil incarnate . . . If anyone wants to feel how a poor sinner is . . . tormented in Purgatory, let him travel to Bradford.'[28]

Morally, too, the town's promiscuity and drunkenness were notorious. The ratio of brothels to all places of worship was about 1·4 to 1.[29] Drunken fighting was endemic and was the speciality of the Irish: whereas Yorkshiremen sensibly laid still and grunted when knocked down, the belligerent Hibernians, full of war and whisky, jumped up again and felled their antagonists.[30] The deterioration of the town was so alarming that in 1849 Titus Salt, then Mayor, launched an enquiry into the best means of improving its moral, social and religious condition. The report of 1850 drew attention to the infidelity rampant in the lower orders, but reserved its heaviest fire for the beershops and brothels, with their vicious and enervating pleasures; and it proposed measures (some implemented) for raising the town's moral and intellectual character which it saw (like beershops and brothels) as being intimately connected. Salt's own reaction was instructive. In 1851, having decided that the town's problems were intractable, he began building his own industrial township of Saltaire, on the salubrious banks of the river Aire, away from Bradford's various pollutions.[31]

In the turbulent, divided, and violent town there was no shortage of pressure groups especially after the 1820s devoted to alleviating or removing intolerable social evils. Besides the obvious example of factory reform agitation, there was in the town a strong temperance movement. Indeed, in February 1830 Henry Forbes, a worsted merchant of Scottish provenance, established in Bradford the first English temperance society. It inspired neighbouring Leeds to follow suit, and (for a time) Anglicans and dissenters, Liberals and Conservatives worked in harmony in it. In 1837 the Bradford Temperance Society was the first in England to build a

[27] *Second report of the Commissioners for inquiring into the state of large towns and populous districts. Appendix. Part II*, Parliamentary Papers, 1845, **18,** 315.

[28] Quoted in J. Reynolds, *Saltaire: an introduction to the village of Sir Titus Salt*, Bradford, 1976, p. 8.

[29] I. and P. Kuczynski (eds), *A young revolutionary in nineteenth-century England: selected writings of Georg Weerth*, Berlin, 1971, p. 187. Georg Weerth (1822–56).

[30] G. Firth, *Poverty and progress: social conditions in early and mid nineteenth century Bradford*, Bradford, 1979, p. 6.

[31] For Salt's report, see *Bradford observer*, 7 March 1850; on Saltaire, Reynolds, *Titus Salt*, especially pp. 88–147 for penetrating analysis of the period 1834–1850, which he designates as years of crisis. Titus Salt (1803–76), *DNB*.

permanent temperance hall. Like the anti-slavery movement on which it was modelled, the temperance movement was devoted to moral and religious issues, though in a textile town like Bradford it also promised the secular advantages of security of property, a more disciplined work force, and an expanded home market in worsted goods (not alcohol!).[32]

Evangelical fervour against intolerable evils was one thing; the creation of groups devoted to intellectual ends, such as science, another. With the exception of its private Subscription Library (founded 1774), its Choral Society (founded 1823), and its second Mechanics' Institute (founded 1832) cultural formations were difficult to establish and to maintain. The history of organised science in Bradford until the mid 1860s is mainly one of struggling ephemerality. The first lit and phil lasted from 1808 to 1810, the second lasted only a few months in late 1822, and the third four years from 1839 to 1843. Bradford did not contribute to the county-wide boom of the lit-and-phil movement in the 1820s; and its enduring mechanics' institute came as late as 1832.[33] Compared with Sheffield and Liverpool it spawned relatively few scientific groups.[34] Compared with Mulhouse, on which my predecessor dilated so eloquently, it had no equivalent to the Société Industrielle (founded in 1826) until the Society of Dyers and Colourists was established partly on the Mulhouse model in 1884. Science as a cultural mode was not dominant as it apparently was in Manchester: the Bradford 'team' of performers in a county peripatetic organisation such as the Yorkshire Geological Society (founded 1837) was small compared with the Leeds and Sheffield contingents, membership of the British Association for the Advancement of Science was low, and that philosophical carnival waited until 1873 before visiting the town. Even that visit by the touring scientific lions did little to disturb the town's apparent apathy in all scientific and literary matters.[35] Privately Bradfordians were not conspicuous as patrons of scientific books about Yorkshire: in 1836 John Phillips' classic study of the limestone part of the county attracted only five subscribers from Bradford.[36] Even by 1860, as a local cultural pundit put it, science and literature were still 'the

[32] For the Bradford temperance movement see: B. Harrison, *Drink and the Victorians*, London, 1971, pp. 95–97, 104–5, 191; *Second annual report of the Bradford Temperance Society. Presented June 29, 1832*, Bradford, 1832, pp. 9–13; *Proceedings at the opening of the Bradford Temperance Hall on . . . 27th and 28th February, and 1st and 2nd March 1838*, Bradford, 1838. Henry Forbes (1794–1870).

[33] The dates of foundation of the principal Yorkshire lit and phils were: Leeds, 1818; York, Sheffield, Hull, and Whitby, 1822; Scarborough, 1827. H. Dirks, *Popular education: a series of papers on the nature, objects, and advantages of mechanics' institutions*, Manchester, 1841, p.3, stressed that 1823–24 was the boom session, with large towns vieing with each other.

[34] On Sheffield and Derby and much else see I. Inkster, 'Studies in the social history of science in England during the industrial revolution', unpublished PhD thesis, University of Sheffield, 1977.

[35] *Bradford observer*, editorial, 2 May 1874. Contrast the National Association for the Promotion of Social Science which held its third annual meeting in Bradford in 1859, and the British Association which held its 43rd annual meeting in the town in 1873.

[36] J. Phillips, *Illustrations of the geology of Yorkshire. Part II. The mountain limestone district*, London, 1836, pp. v–vii. The Bradford subscribers were John Armistead, John Wilmer Field, Samuel Hailstone, Henry Leah and John Hustler.

drudges of social necessities': the town had no philosophical society, no antiquarian or historical society, no literary society, no public museum, and no free library.[37] Another commentator, the weaver poet Ben Preston, attributed what he called the 'mental degradation' of the town to the long hours spent in the mills: Bradford was full of perpetual workers, both masters and hands, who exemplified the motto chosen by the Corporation, 'Labor omnia vincit'.[38] Clearly the scientific enterprise at the savant level was fragile in the period of Bradford's rise to international economic importance; though as Dame Mabel Tylecote stressed years ago the 1832 Mechanics' Institute was remarkably resilient.[39] Why was this? To answer this question let us now turn to what is very much work in progress on public science in Bradford.

The first Bradford Literary and Philosophical Society, which lasted from 1808 to 1810, was explicitly industrial in its aims. It was in intention devoted not only to science but mainly to the improvement of mechanical arts and manufactures. Not surprisingly it was dominated by men with industrial interests, especially those from the Low Moor and Bierley Iron Works both of which flourished during the Napoleonic period through manufacturing armaments. The first President was Joseph Dawson, principal partner of the Low Moor Iron Works, who was also President of the Association of Iron Masters of Yorkshire and Derbyshire. A former Unitarian minister, Dawson combined in himself nonconformity, science, and industry. Bierley Iron Works was represented by its lessee, Henry Leah, who discovered the hot blast process independently of Neilson. The principal founder of the Society was the craggy Samuel Hailstone, a ranking expert on Yorkshire flora, by occupation a leading local lawyer who was heavily involved in the local iron industry and in a couple of local canal companies. Another leading spirit was Joseph Priestley, chief manager of the Leeds-Liverpool Canal Company. These four worthies were the only performers the Society could muster from a town with a population of 15,000: practising clerics and medics offered no papers and were thinly represented in the membership. The Society expired in 1810 not because of conflict between Tories and Whigs or between Anglicans and dissenters or because of legislative repression, but because it quickly ran out of local intellectual steam: in spring 1809 five consecutive meetings were all adjourned because there was no paper.[40]

[37] *The Bradfordian*, editorial, 1862, **2,** 2; J. Hanson, *Free libraries; their nature and operations: four letters addressed to Mr Alderman Godwin*, Bradford, 1867.

[38] W. Scruton, *Bradford fifty years ago*, Bradford, 1897, p. 97.

[39] M. Tylecote, *The mechanics' institutes of Lancashire and Yorkshire before 1851*, Manchester, 1957, pp. 224–5.

[40] My account is based on: 'The first Bradford Philosophical Society', *Bradford Antiquary*, 1905, **4,** 462–4; minute book of the Bradford Philosophical Society, 1808–10, York Minster Library, Add Ms 204. There were three Yorkshire Joseph Priestleys who are still confused by the unwary: the discoverer of oxygen (1733–1804), *DNB;* the manager of the Leeds-Liverpool Canal (1739/40–1817); and a son (c. 1767–1852) of the Canal manager, author of the still useful *Historial account of the navigable rivers, canals, and railways, throughout Great Britain*, London, 1831. Joseph Dawson (1740–1813); Henry Leah (1772–1846); Samuel Hailstone (1768–1851), *DNB*.

The next attempt to form a philosophical society was made in 1822, with Hailstone again to the fore. This time the industrial motive was mixed with others, such as natural theology, individual moral improvement, and local pride. Bradford's wealth was to be devoted to emulating other northern industrial towns, especially neighbouring Leeds, so that in the glorious race of learning she would not be outstripped by her contemporaries. The aims were correspondingly wide: to promote literature, science, and natural history by erecting a philosophical hall, replete with a library, specimens, apparatus, a news room, a circulating library, and a laboratory. Some 42 affluent locals took seriously Bacon's view that academies, colleges, and halls are the storehouses of knowledge: they subscribed £50 each towards a building which would give permanence to the projected Society and be a local facility worthy of a town of 28,000 people. Unfortunately they started at the wrong end: instead of first cultivating the local taste for science and then paying for an expensive local habitation, they were initially consumed by the vaulting ambition of heroic provincialism (to use Philip Lowe's happy phrase). But some of them soon had second thoughts when Henry Heap, the vicar of Bradford, preached a sermon in which he castigated the irreligious tendency of philosophy: lacking moral and scientific force, they took fright, withdrew their pledged subscriptions, and the whole project collapsed.[41]

Three years later the first Mechanics' Institute failed, even though 1825 was in general a propitious year for the formation of such institutes in the north of England (Manchester, Bolton, Ashton, Hull, Halifax). At the inaugural meeting, held in the parish church Sunday School, local governing and professional élites were sparsely represented: of the town's respectable citizens, only Joshua Pollard, an Anglican manufacturer, and Thomas Beaumont, a Methodist doctor, attended, so that the audience of 200 was composed of mainly mechanics. The chief speaker was Edward Baines, junior, from Leeds, who stressed that all classes could unite in the scheme because they have common interests; accordingly he appealed to the rich, the enlightened, the employers, the ministers, and the magistrates to support the venture. Two speakers referred to a view in the town that a mechanics' institute would promote ideas at variance with religion and the laws of the country. The 1825 scheme foundered on these two rocks of political hostility and religious suspicion. From the start the Institute was

[41] My analysis of the 1822 Society draws on: list of subscribers reproduced in *Bradford Review*, 24 December 1864; *Leeds Mercury*, 21 September 1822; *Leeds Intelligencer*, 25 November 1822; *Leeds Mercury*, 18 and 23 January 1823, giving details of a meeting held on 15 January 1823 at which resolutions were adopted to establish a literary and philosophical Society, John Hustler in the chair; Scruton, *Old Bradford*, pp. 90–91; James, *History of Bradford*, pp. 245–6; Thomas Beaumont's speech, *Bradford observer*, 31 January 1839. John Hustler (1768–1842) of the well-known Quaker family; Thomas Beaumont (1795–1859), a surgeon; Henry Heap (1789–1839), vicar of Bradford 1816–39, was curiously one of the 42 subscribers. For Lowe's characterisation see P. D. Lowe, 'Locals and cosmopolitans. A model for the social organisation of provincial science in the nineteenth century', unpublished MPhil thesis, University of Sussex, 1978.

effectively in the hands of the mechanics themselves and not a paternalistic middle-class coterie. The organising committee was to be elected annually by ballot, with artisans always in a majority. Moreover some of the Institute's supporters were well-known political activists. The Secretary, Squire Farrar, a law-clerk, was especially obnoxious to the middle classes because of his revolutionary republicanism and religious scepticism. Other political radicals involved were: Christopher Wilkinson, a printer and freethinker; and John Jackson, a woolcomber and later a moral-force Chartist.[42] The only clergyman to join such men was the Unitarian Nicholas Heineken who in late 1824 had argued publicly that the Devil did not exist, that scriptural geology was a fable, that the Bible was a mere historical record to be interpreted like other histories, that terms such as redemption and atonement were merely anthropomorphic and figurative terms which did not imply a vicarious sacrifice, and that he was not disposed to trace '*common* events to *supernatural causes*'. Such views appalled local Anglicans and evangelical dissenters who thought Heineken was encouraging secularism, atheism, and materialism. For them Heineken's Socinian scoffing was 'more dangerous than a draught of hemlock'.[43] They had a point: 10 years later Heineken's arguments were being used by Bradford atheists to attack Christianity. Not surprisingly most Anglicans and evangelical dissenters in the town boycotted the Institute which collapsed in the turmoil of the long strike later in 1825. It is significant that Heap, the vicar of Bradford, opposed popular education because he saw it as a vehicle of political and religious subversion; but from 1825 he took a prominent share in establishing and supporting the Bradford Dispensary.[44]

In spring 1832, at the height of reform agitation and with the memory of the 1825 strike still fresh, a permanent Mechanics' Institute was established through the organisational acumen of a group of young tradesmen who saw it was essential to gain the support and money of the accredited wealthy middle class, and to co-opt their clergymen, in order to avoid the political and religious disadvantages which had led to the demise of its short-lived predecessor. In spite of the proclaimed unsectarianism of

[42] James, *History of Bradford*, p. 248; British Library Add Mss 27, 824, ff. 71–2; *The journal of Dr John Simpson of Bradford. 1st of January to the 25th of July 1825*, Bradford, 1981, pp. 13–14, 42; *Rules of the Bradford Mechanics' Institute, established February 21st, 1825*, Bradford, 1825. Joshua Pollard (1794–1887), Tory merchant and manufacturer; Edward Baines (1800–90), *DNB;* Squire Farrar (1785–1873); John Jackson (d. 1873).

[43] For the views of Nicholas Thomas Heineken (1763–1840), and the controversy they provoked see his *A discourse on the supposed existence of an evil spirit, called the devil; and also, a reply to the observations of Mr William Carlisle, of Dudley Hill, near Bradford, the ostensible author of an 'essay on evil spirits', written in opposition to the discourse which was delivered in the Unitarian chapel, Bradford*, London, 1825; W. Carlisle, *An essay on evil spirits; or, reasons to prove their existence, in opposition to a lecture, delivered by the Rev. N. T. Heineken, in the Unitarian chapel, Bradford*, Bradford, 1825, p. 8 (quote); I. Mann, *Strictures on the Rev. N. T. Heineken's reply to Mr William Carlisle, in which is proved the close alliance that exists between Socinianism and Deism*, Bradford, 1826; N. T. Heineken, *Observations on the unity, supremacy, and free unpurchased mercy of God, in answer to the Rev. I. Mann's intemperate and arrogant strictures, on Mr Heineken's reply to Mr William Carlisle's essay on evil spirits*, London, 1826. Isaac Mann (d. 1831) was Baptist minister at Shipley near Bradford.

[44] On Heap, see James, *History of Bradford*, pp. 213–14; Scruton, *Old Bradford*, p. 34.

the Institute, the Anglican clergy and laity and their then allies, the Wesleyan Methodists, generally boycotted it on the grounds that it would favour rabid democracy and infidelity.[45] Their absence meant that from its inception the ostensibly non-sectarian Institute was controlled on a day to day basis mainly by Congregationalists, graced by Baptist clergymen in the Presidency, and supported by Quakers as rich Patrons. These managers knew that public support was contingent upon the exclusion of infidel tendencies: the Institute's rules made it clear that it was Christian and opposed to irreligion, immorality, and scepticism; and moreover, controversial theology like party politics would be excluded. The 1832 Mechanics' Institute enjoyed a continuous life because its managers produced a formula which was both a tactic for survival *and* a means of containing political radicalism and religious scepticism. That was why they repeatedly stressed that the 1832 Institute was not 'a seminary of disaffection, a school for infidelity, and a nursery for political demagogues and anarchists'.[46] These managers also saw that in a town of population 45,000, the vision of science for the workers could sustain middle-class concern and might produce beneficial *class* effects.[47] Leading spokesmen for the Mechanics' Institute were convinced that the improvement of the lower classes was to the advantage of the superior ones, because 'the common people are the ground on which the superior classes, the palaces and pyramids of society are raised'. They also argued that the Mechanics' Institute would preserve rank in society, keep anarchy at bay, and provide the common ground on which different classes and sects could meet without either sacrifice of principle or danger of collision.[48]

The scheme of social and religious insurance embodied in the Mechanics' Institute was quickly questioned when the atheist controversy erupted in 1834, the year which witnessed the start of sustained hostility between church and chapel, in addition to the existing division between Christianity and infidelity. The polemicists were Benjamin Godwin, a Baptist minister and prominent Liberal, and Wilkinson and Farrar, known

[45] My account draws on: J. F. C. Harrison, *Learning and living 1790–1960: a study in the history of the English adult education movement*, London, 1961, pp. 61–2, 174–7; C. A. Federer, *The Bradford Mechanics' Institute. A History*, Bradford Public Library, typescript, 1906; M. Tylecote, *Mechanics' institutes*, pp. 224–240; J. Farrar, *Autobiography of Joseph Farrar*, Bradford, 1889, pp. 45–51; Benjamin Godwin, *Autobiography*, Bradford Public Library archives, typescript, pp. 537–9. For the start of Anglican default, see Bradford Mechanics' Institute minutes book, 1832–1834, 27 March 1832, Bradford Public Library archives: Heap was invited to be a patron but declined.

[46] *Second annual report of the committee of Bradford Mechanics' Institute . . . presented January 31, 1834*, Bradford, 1834, p. 1.

[47] Compare S. Shapin, 'The Pottery Philosophical Society, 1819–1835: an examination of the cultural uses of provincial science', *Science studies*, 1972, **2**, 311–36 (esp. 333).

[48] *Account of the proceedings connected with the inauguration of the Rev. J. Acworth as President of the Bradford Mechanics' Institute, September 26th, 1837*, Bradford, 1837, 7 (quote), 8, 24. Speeches were given by: the Reverend Walter Scott (1779–1858), Principal of Airedale Congregationalist College, Bradford, 1834–58; and the Reverend James Acworth (1798–1883), President of the Baptist College, Bradford, 1835–59. Acworth enjoyed a double succession to the Reverend William Steadman (1764–1837), who was first President of the Baptist College, 1806–35, and first President of the Mechanics' Institute, 1832–7.

secularists who at that time were also active in running the Bradford Radical Association which represented the interests of the labour aristocracy. Godwin had long been appalled by Bradford's 'daring spirit of infidelity' which drew heavily on works popular among sceptics: these were principally Mirabaud's *System of Nature* in English translation (3rd ed., 2 vols., 1817), Hume's *Dialogues on natural religion*, Elihu Palmer's *Principles of nature*, and Richard Carlile's *The Deist*. Given the general drift of these works, Godwin decided to route infidelity by reference to nature and not to the Bible. Early in 1834 he gave a crowded course of lectures in Sion Chapel attacking atheism, drawing heavily on his long experience of teaching science, his advocacy of a liberal and not dogmatic Baptist approach, his conviction that public debate, not fining or jailing, was the best way to defeat infidelity, and above all on his belief in natural theology. Objecting to the way that atheism dressed itself out in the garbs of science, Godwin made a distinction which John Henry Newman was to promulgate later, i.e., that tracing God's hand in nature leads to enlarged and exalted views of God, only if connected with 'the religious principle'; if not so connected, the study of nature, urged on by unaided pride of intellect, can lead to infidelity.[49] Undeterred by this distinction, Godwin's lectures relied on a natural theological approach, using such recent sources as three Bridgewater Treatises (those by Whewell, Kidd, and Roget), and Sedgwick's *Discourse on the studies of Cambridge* (3rd ed., March 1834). Using Lyell's arguments he tried to dispose of Lamarckian evolution and Mirabaudian spontaneous generation, which he rightly saw as impugning inter alia the uniqueness of man. In contrast to many natural theologians of the 1830s, Godwin faced up squarely to Hume's views about the inadequacy of design arguments.[50]

Godwin was soon answered by Wilkinson and Farrar in a publication which was such a defence of 'the most absolute atheism' that booksellers would not handle it and its printer tried to suppress it. Even so 150 copies appeared. Wilkinson and Farrar, drawing largely on Hume and Mirabaud, paid Godwin the tribute of bracketing him with Lord Brougham, whose *Natural Theology* had just been published, in order to show that neither Godwin nor Brougham realised the flaws in analogical and anthropomorphic arguments. Wilkinson and Farrar paraded their materialism and radicalism confidently, arguing that man is a purely material being, and that the relation between mind and matter is like the relation between capital and labour. In their view capital was the mind of labour,

[49] B. Godwin, *Lectures on the atheistic controversy; delivered in the months of February and March, 1834, at Sion chapel, Bradford, forming the first part of a course of lectures on infidelity*, London, 1834, pp. v (quote)–xi; Godwin, *Autobiography*, pp. 577–8; for Newman on scientific pursuits, see his *Letters on an address delivered by Sir Robert Peel on the establishment of a reading room at Tamworth*, London, 1841, esp. p. 41. Godwin (1785–1871) left Bradford in 1836 for ten years. A good general survey of the infidel tradition is E. Royle, *Victorian infidels: the origins of the British secularist movement 1791–1866*, Manchester, 1974, esp. pp. 9–58.

[50] For the attack on Lamarck, Godwin, *Lectures*, pp. 170–80; for that on Hume, pp. 180–6, 190–231.

but could act only through the intervention of labour. Hence they concluded that 'to attribute the works of man to mind or intelligence is like attributing the improvements of the age to capital', and that to claim that mind originated matter is as daft as saying that capital has originated labour.[51]

This atheistic controversy gained for Godwin two American editions in 1835 and 1836, and a Columbia DD in 1842. Nearer home it showed that the promotion and justification of natural knowledge as theological edification could be strongly opposed. Indeed the controversy launched a series of public debates in the town between Christians and non-Christians, culminating in the early 1850s with the ageing Godwin confronting Holyoake, the advocate of atheistic socialism in its new guise of secularism, and giving a repeat performance of the 1835 lectures.[52] Nor did the class aspect of the controversy disappear. The vigour of Owenite socialism in the town from 1837 to 1842 presented a political vision alternative to that of Liberals, Whigs and Conservatives; while simultaneously offering a view of science different from that espoused by the mechanics' institute and lit-and phil movements.

As a Bradford Socialist, Samuel Bower, made clear, Robert Owen had extended the Baconian method of philosophy to the study of man.[53] Moreover Owenite science, the science of the influence of external circumstances over human nature, claimed to be 'the most important science that has yet been discovered by the human faculties'.[54] During the general Owenite ferment from 1838 to 1842, Owenite science and its laws of nature proclaimed a political vision based on equality, brotherhood, collective self-help, and democratic control; it promulgated a related opposition to priestcraft, to the 'mental bondage' it exerted, and to natural theology. Some of its adherents promoted it as identical with practical Christianity as taught by Christ. Others buttressed it with Comte's positivism which provided useful ammunition against the priesthood and against Christian views of nature.[55] Owenite socialists appropriated from Christians such forms as missionaries, sermons, hymns, Sunday schools,

[51] S. Farrar and C. Wilkinson, *An examination of the arguments for the existence of a deity, being an answer Mr Godwin's lectures on the atheistic controversy; with an appendix, containing observations on Lord Brougham's Discourse of Natural Theology*, London, Leeds, Bradford, 1835, p. 33 (quotes). For publication details of the 1835 work see Farrar and Wilkinson, *An examination of the arguments for the existence of a deity; being an answer to Dr Godwin's 'Philosophy of atheism examined and compared with Christianity'*, London and Bradford, 1853.

[52] Godwin, *Autobiography*, pp. 735–42; Godwin, *The philosophy of atheism examined and compared with Christianity. A course of popular lectures delivered at the Mechanics' Institute, Bradford, on Sunday afternoons, in the winter of 1852–1853*, London, 1853.

[53] S. Bower, *The peopling of utopia; or, the sufficiency of socialism for human happiness: being a comparison of the social and radical schemes*, Bradford, 1838, p. 9.

[54] *New moral world*, 1835, **1**, 170. Volume 4 of this Owenite periodical was subtitled 'Manual of science'.

[55] S. Bower, *A sequel to the peopling of utopia; or, the sufficiency of socialism for human happiness: being a further comparison of the social and radical schemes*, Bradford, 1838, p. 13; *New moral world*, 1835–6, **2**, 336–8; 1837–8, **4**, 384–5; 1838–9, **5**, 493.

and baptism, marriage and death services, leading to vehement clerical outrage especially in 1839 and 1840.[56]

The Owenite programme gave cold comfort to respectable and paternalistic science. Lit and phils, and especially the British Association for the Advancement of Science, were deemed inadequate because they focussed on material nature and not on human and social science. For the Owenites, the Association's incomplete hierarchy of science was a good example of the extent to which 'class prejudices, class interests, and, above all, religious and political partizanship' obstructed social reformation. Mechanics' institutes were seen as more useful, as precursors in which the diffusion of physical science was paving the way for the higher concern with moral and social science. But mechanics' institutes, for some Owenite missionaries, had become overgrown with sectarianism, levied an aristocratical price of admission, and burked their lectures to humour popular prejudices.[57]

The Bradford branch of Owen's Association of All Classes of All Nations, opened Sunday 29 October 1837, was soon the subject of clerical denunciation. In late February 1838 Owen himself lectured to a crowd of 700 at exactly the time when the Bradford Temperance Hall was being opened with speeches from the Bishop of Ripon and from Walter Scott, a Congregationalist minister, both of whom were prominent in denouncing socialism that year for its specious doctrine that man was not responsible for his own actions, an idea which they thought destroyed all social order.[58] By November 1839 some Bradford clergy (Scoresby, Bull, Acworth and Glyde) and Anglican laymen (G. Pollard, J. and W. Rand) were so worried that they attended the second anniversary meeting of the Bradford branch in order to deplore its irreligious aspects. Prominent among these clerics was William Scoresby, appointed vicar of Bradford in summer 1839, who was internationally known in scientific circles as a polar voyager and magnetic researcher. In November 1839 he began a series of lectures in the parish church, denouncing atheism and Owenite environmental determinism, and proving that man is essentially evil 'by the method of inductive philosophy as usually applied in science'. Of course Scoresby saved his best shafts for what he regarded as the destructive influence of the sensual system of Owenite polygamy practised by harlots and adulterers.[59]

[56] E. Yeo, 'Robert Owen and radical culture' in S. Pollard and J. Salt (eds), *Robert Owen prophet of the poor: essays in honour of the two hundredth anniversary of his birth*, London, 1971, pp. 84–114.

[57] *New moral world*, 1841–2, **10,** 68–9 (quote); ibid, 1843–4, **12,** 119–20;ibid, 1837–8, **4,** 362; ibid, 1840, **8,** 333.

[58] Ibid, 1837–8, **4,** 20, 171–2; 1838–9, **5,** 74, 478; for the anti-Owenite speeches of Scott and Edward Grubb (1801–78), the total abstinence advocate, see *Proceedings at the opening of the Bradford Temperance Hall*, pp. 70, 74–6.

[59] William Scoresby (1789–1857), *DNB*, was vicar of Bradford 1839–47; Scoresby, *Lectures on socialism: delivered in the parish church, Bradford, on the evenings of the twenty-first and twenty-ninth of November, and the sixth of December, 1839*, London, 1840, pp. 8, 24 (quote); *Bradford observer*,21 November 1839; *New moral world*, 1839, **6,** 923–4. George Stringer Bull (1799–1864), Anglican minister at St James', Bradford; Jonathan Glyde (1808–54), Congregationalist minister, Little Horton chapel, Bradford; George Pollard was the brother of Joshua Pollard; John Rand (1794–1873) and his brother William (1796–1868) were worsted manufacturers.

Undeterred, Wilkinson replied to Scoresby's first lecture and the Bradford Socialists opened their Hall of Science in March 1840. Even though the Bradford Gas Company persistently refused to supply gas and some Owenites were sacked by their employers, the Bradford Socialists believed that their Hall would encourage 'salvation revealed to us by SCIENCE and MIND'. In April 1840 they engaged as district missionary John Ellis, a former Baptist, now a believer in Jesus Christ and Robert Owen. He was immediately on the attack, denouncing 'those intellectual slaughter houses where Methodism is mistaken for religion'.[60]

The third Bradford Philosophical Society, established in April 1839 when the town had a population of 60,000, had two origins. Firstly, the laying of the Foundation stone of the new Mechanics' Institute building on 1 April reinforced a sense of civic embarrassment that in a town of such size, wealth and political importance, no public provision had been made either for the encouragement of science and literature or for a local museum.[61] Secondly, William Sharp, senior surgeon at the Bradford Infirmary and a conspicuous factory reformer, had given a course of lectures in winter 1838–9 with the express intention of cultivating a taste for science among the respectable and establishing a local philosophical society. His general justifications for science were standard for the time: it administers to the wants and comforts of man; it has useful practical applications; it shows the power, wisdom, and benevolence of God; it develops the culture of man's mental and moral character, producing modesty and humility; for those in business it provides valuable habits of application when at work and when not at work relief from the cares of commerce.[62] The primary object of the Society was defined by Sharp, namely, to form a local museum containing natural productions of the Bradford district, an aim which invaded some of the territory already claimed by both the Yorkshire Philosophical Society and the Yorkshire Geological Society.[63] With membership at ½ guinea paid in advance, respectability was ensured. Following the practice of the Mechanics' Institute, local or party politics and controversial divinity were deliberately excluded. Again like the Institute, the Society was a tool of one party, but in this case a Tory/Anglican caucus led first by Sharp and then by Scoresby. Throughout the Society's short history, its managers and performers were mainly Tories. The leading spirits in the Mechanics' Institute, such as James Acworth, a Baptist minister who was its President, and Joseph Farrar, its indefatigable Secretary, never joined the Philosophical Society. Indeed attendance during its first session was a problem for

[60] *New moral world*, 1840, **7**, 1173 (quote); 1841–2, **10**, 159; 1840, **8**, 92 (quote).
[61] *Bradford observer*, 21 and 28 March 1839.
[62] Ibid, 11 April 1839. William Sharp (1805–96), *DNB*.
[63] Ibid, 11 and 18 April 1839; *The laws and regulations of the Bradford Philosophical society, instituted the twelfth of April, 1839*, Bradford, 1839. The Yorkshire Philosophical Society devoted itself inter alia to the geology of the whole of Yorkshire, whereas the Yorkshire Geological Society (founded 1837) concentrated on the geology and technics of the coal-field. Bradford is situated on the northern end of the coal measures and in 1839 was not negligible as a producer of coal and iron.

dissenters because the meetings clashed with the dissenters' missionary prayer meetings.[64] As first President of the Society, Sharp showed 'alert Conservatism' in early 1840, offering his gratuitous services to the Institute and serving as its Vice-president 1840–42, in an attempt to show that science was above party, just at the time of the Chartist uprising and great distress in the town caused by unemployment.[65] He also had taken good care to have his scheme of a local museum approved by leading savants at the British Association in 1839. Though well aware of the difficulties of his undertaking in a town like Bradford, it prospered in terms of membership (172), papers, and attendance in its first session.[66] Then from summer 1840 it began to run into difficulties, even with Scoresby as President from 1841, and with rescheduled meetings to suit the dissenters. For lectures it relied heavily on itinerants, such as James Montgomery, the Sheffield poet, and the odd savant imported from Leeds (Baker, S. Sharp, Nunneley). Contributions to the museum were negligible: by late 1842 Samuel Hailstone sent specimens to the Yorkshire Museum at York, a going concern, the Bradford Museum scheme having folded.[67] In session 1842–3 attendances at meetings were embarrassingly low compared with those at the Mechanics' Institute. The end came at the anniversary meeting on 9 May 1843 when the Society's solitary mourner was John Darlington, its Treasurer and Secretary.[68] The President, the Reverend William Scoresby, FRS, FRSE, Corresponding Member of the Institute of France, doughty survivor of twenty punishing arctic voyages, did not bother to attend to confer the last rites.

The career of the Bradford Philosophical Society, mark 3, may be analysed in terms of audience, performers and local politico-ecclesiastical affairs. The Society attracted a membership of about 200 but the meetings were soon only thinly attended. Gifted members such as Titus Salt and

[64] *Bradford observer*, 6 February 1840. Joseph Farrar (1805–78) was a hatter and later insurance agent of dissenting and Liberal persuasions.

[65] Ibid, 23 January, 12 March, 23 April 1840; Bradford Mechanics' Institute minutes book, 1835–46, 10 March 1840, Bradford Public Library archives. For the notion of alert conservatism see M. Neve, 'Science in a commercial city: Bristol 1820–60', in I. Inkster and J. Morrell (eds), *Metropolis and province: science in British culture, 1780–1850*, London, 1983, pp. 179–204. For the abortive Chartist rising in Bradford in January 1840, see A. J. Peacock, *Bradford Chartism 1838–1840*, York, 1969; for distress in Bradford, see W. Scoresby, *"What shall we do?" or, the enquiry of the destitute operatives considered. A sermon, preached at the parish church, Bradford, on Sunday, the 22nd of December, 1839*, London, 1840.

[66] *The Times*, 27 August 1839; Sharp, 'On the formation of local museums', *Report of the ninth meeting of the British Association for the Advancement of Science held at Birmingham in August 1839*, London, 1840, p. 65; Sharp to Greenough, 16 January 1840, Greenough papers; *Annual report of the Council of the Bradford Philosophical Society, for 1839. Presented to the annual meeting, 4th May, 1840*, Bradford, 1840.

[67] Only two more annual Council reports were produced, i.e. for sessions 1840–1 and 1841–2; they reveal the Council's growing concern about the Society's viability. James Montgomery (1771–1854), *DNB;* Robert Baker, a surgeon; Samuel Sharp (1808–74), an architect; Thomas Nunneley (1809–1870), *DNB*, a surgeon. For Hailstone's donations of specimens in 1842 to the Yorkshire Philosophical Society, see *Annual report of the Council of the Yorkshire Philosophical Society, for MDCCCXLII*, York, 1843, pp. 11, 20–21.

[68] *Bradford observer*, 3 November, 1 and 8 December 1842; Sheppard, *Yorkshire's science*, p. 17; John Darlington (1807–1891) a solicitor and bank manager.

[69] Details of membership have been gained from Darlington's 'Members of the Bradford Philosophical Society 1839', Bradford Public Library archives, case 3, box 4, item 5.

William Edward Forster apparently did not respond positively to Sharp's encomia about the advantages of science.[70] For performers the Society relied on a tiny core of people. Of the 12 local medical members (all but one surgeons), some of whom had formed a short-lived Bradford Medical Association in 1839, only Sharp and Beaumont did anything, perhaps the rest being discouraged by the Society's exclusion of practical medicine. In any event, Sharp left Bradford for Hull in 1843. Crucially there were very few physicians to draw on. For twenty-five years from 1820 the population and the number of surgeons expanded rapidly, but the number of consultant physicians decreased. Compared with all other major West Riding towns, Bradford had the lowest percentage of physicians per population unit. In 1845 there was only one physician for each 45,000 of the population. This clearly was connected with Bradford being bottom heavy socially and with the proximity of well known physicians in Leeds. Until the mid 1850s one suspects that there were not the physicians in the town to do what they had done earlier and elsewhere for provincial science.[71] When we turn to another professional élite, we find that no dissenting ministers, so prominent otherwise in the town, appeared as either performers or managers, though they were happy to lecture gratuitously at the Mechanics' Institute (Glyde, Miall, Scott, Acworth, Ryland). Of Anglican clergymen Scoresby and Joshua Fawcett, abetted by Theodore Dury of Keighley, gave papers. Two solicitors were active but not John James, the distinguished local historian, who was not a member.[72] The local iron, building, textile and chemical industries (56 members) between them offered only J. G. Horsfall, and he was hardly a William Fairbairn. Samuel Cunliffe Lister and Henry William Ripley, two leading industrial innovators, were not even members.[73] All the local gentry joined but were non performing. Of the two aristocratic members, Lord Oxmantown, later third Earl of Rosse, had married into a Bradford family in 1836 but he was busy at Birr Castle, Ireland, with his great reflecting telescope.[74]

[70] For Salt's preoccupations in the early 1840s, see Reynolds, *Titus Salt;* for those of Forster (1818–86), *DNB*, see T. Wemyss Reid, *Life of the Right Honourable William Edward Forster*, London, 1888, i, pp. 128–65.

[71] These conclusions about physicians are drawn from local directories; and they agree with those of Donnelly, 'Technical education in Bradford', pp. 29–30, based on the 1851 Census returns.

[72] James Goodeve Miall (1805–96), Congregationalist minister, Salem chapel, Bradford; John Howard Ryland, Unitarian minister; Joshua Fawcett (1809–64), *DNB*, Anglican minister, Low Moor, Bradford; Theodore Dury (1789–1852), rector of Keighley. The two active lawyers were Darlington and John Crofts, the Society's Curator; John James (1811–67), *DNB*.

[73] In 1826 John Garnett Horsfall, a Tory manufacturer, was the first in Bradford to use power looms; William Fairbairn (1789–1874), *DNB*, the Manchester structural engineer was a competent experimental investigator. Samuel Cunliffe Lister (1815–1906), *DNB*, developed machine combing and velvet power-loom weaving; Henry William Ripley (1813–1882) solved the problem of dyeing mixed fabrics and by mid century owned the largest worsted dyeworks in the world.

[74] In 1836 William Parsons (1800–67), *DNB*, married the elder daughter of John Wilmer Field of Heaton Hall, Bradford, and through her inherited property in the Bradford area; but he took no part in the third Philosophical Society, of which Lord Morpeth was the other aristocratic member.

The question of the relation of the Society to politico-ecclesiastical squabbles is best approached through William Scoresby, vicar of Bradford 1839–47.[75] He arrived in the town in October 1839, next month attending his first meeting of the Society and being repeatedly cheered.[76] Though his fellow Anglicans initially welcomed him as the very man for Bradford, 'a hot-bed of Socialism and Popery', by November 1839 he was at loggerheads with many of them, both clergymen and laymen. He wished to revive Anglicanism in the town; and his vicarship was worth just under £500 pa, from which he had to pay his curates. Accordingly he devised a Plan, approved by the Bishop of Ripon, ensuring adequate finance and authority for the parish church and its vicar. His Plan quickly alienated leading Anglican laymen, such as John Outhwaite, a prominent physician who ran the Infirmary and the Subscription Library, and the Hardy family of the Low Moor Iron-works; Outhwaite was never a member of the Philosophical Society, and Charles Hardy disappeared from its Council when Scoresby became President.[77] Scoresby's stand about church dues led to great dissention with his fellow Anglican clergymen whom he regarded as his subordinates. From 1840 to 1842 there were difficulties with three unconsecrated churches, where Scoresby took the line that no dues meant no consecration. He was at daggers drawn with Parson Bull, the well-known factory reformer, incumbent of St James'. Another minister, Charles Pearson, of St John's, Manchester Road, took the general question of the relation of the vicar to his curates up to the Bishop for a ruling eventually given in 1843. By 1841 Scoresby was on bad terms with William Morgan, incumbent of Christ Church and a leading Temperance supporter, about the extent of Morgan's district. That year Scoresby was reduced to calling a public meeting to justify his removal of John Meridyth, his own curate; and Charles Hardy formally complained to the Bishop about serious evils in the existing state of the church in the parish.[78]

In November 1839 the *Leeds Intelligencer* had concluded that 'Bradford is the stronghold of dissent, whiggism, socialism, chartism, and infidelity', all of which were anathema to Scoresby. In combatting the Owenites, he lectured at the parish church in late 1839 and supported the views of the anti-Owenite John Brindley. Whereas Christopher Wilkinson opposed Brindley's arguments based on contrivance and denounced him as 'one of

[75] Scoresby has been served by two biographies: R. E. Scoresby-Jackson, *The life of William Scoresby*, London, 1861; T. and C. Stamp, *William Scoresby, Arctic scientist*, Whitby, 1975.

[76] *Bradford observer*, 10 October, 7 November 1839.

[77] For this characterisation of Bradford, see ibid, 24 October 1839; Scoresby, *Plan submitted to the Lord Bishop of Ripon by the Vicar of Bradford, for the appointment of districts for spiritual purposes, and for a due and necessary maintaining of the rights and revenues of the mother church within the parish*, n.p., n.d., signed 21 January 1840, approved by the Bishop 6 February 1840; John Outhwaite (1792–1868); Charles Hardy (1813–67). For Scoresby's tribulations in Bradford, see Stamp, *Scoresby*, pp. 140–61, 186–201.

[78] *Retirement of the Rev George S. Bull from St James Church, Bradford, Yorkshire*, Bradford, 1840; *Judgment of the Lord Bishop of Ripon on the charges preferred by the Rev C. J. Pearson against the Rev Dr Scoresby, Vicar of Bradford*, unpublished but signed 11 March 1843; Stamp, *Scoresby*, 148; *Bradford observer*, 1 and 8 October, 1840, 5 and 12 August 1841.

the most unprincipled libellers that ever calumniated humanity', Scoresby hoped in public that Owenite atheism would be 'spued out (as it were) from the land'. In response to Chartism and the distressed condition of the unemployed poor, a time of much trial for Scoresby, he chaired relief meetings, having been peacefully surrounded by a crowd of 1,500 unemployed people on his way home on 16 December 1839. He also preached in response to a request made by the distressed. His practical solution was to urge the Poor Law Guardians to be less severe and the affluent to help voluntarily.[79]

As if this were not enough, November 1839 also witnessed the start of protracted warfare between Scoresby and Baptists and Congregationalists about the imposition of the church rate on dissenters. For Scoresby the church rate was lawful, to be administered, and necessary to re-invigorate local Anglicanism. For the dissenters the church rate was evidence of Anglican dominance and an attack on their civil liberty. Their tactic was to pack the vestry meeting and defer the rate for a year. In 1841 the frustrated churchwardens declared the rate passed on their own authority. Some prominent Liberal dissenters refused to pay and in autumn the bailiffs, known locally as the 'ecclesiastical police', seized goods from them in lieu. John Dale, a printer devoted to the Mechanics' Institute, refused to pay; his case went to the High Court where in 1847 he was vindicated. In 1842 the dissenters retaliated by contesting the elections for churchwardens and returned none other than Dale; and at the vestry again used their adjournment technique for the last time. Scoresby was furious at this defeat at the hands of the dissenters, who at various meetings hissed him, shouted at him, labelled him an enemy, and threatened by letter to assassinate him and to burn his 'bloody old church to ashes'.[80] At the personal level, Scoresby gained the enmity of three Liberals prominent in the Mechanics' Institute, Dale, William Byles of the *Bradford Observer* who chaired the vestry meeting of July 1842, and above all, of James Acworth, President of the Institute. In November 1841 Acworth lectured on the unscripturalness of ecclesiastical impositions to the Bradford Voluntary Church Society, formed in autumn 1840 to nurture religious freedom and to oppose the profane union of church and state. Acworth's polemic deeply hurt Scoresby because as a deliberate argumentum ad hominem it accused Scoresby of belonging to an avaricious priesthood, of being thoroughly secularised, of being indurated by an unhallowed connection with the state, and of supporting coercive interference which was 'the very essence of the spirit of Antichrist'.[81] Presumably this personal attack by Acworth

[79] *Leeds intelligencer*, 30 November 1839; Scoresby, *Lectures on Socialism; Bradford observer*, 12, 19 (quote), 26 December 1839; Scoresby, *What shall we do*.

[80] Reynolds, *Titus Salt*, pp. 107–8; Elliott, 'Municipal government in Bradford', pp. 56–72; Scoresby, *The position of the church, and duties of churchmen to unite for her defence. An address delivered at the formation of the Church Institution at Bradford, July 4th, 1843*, Halifax 1843, pp. 10–11 (quote).

[81] On William Byles (1807–91) see D. James, 'William Byles and the *Bradford observer*', in Wright and

made Scoresby unsympathetic to a proposal made to him in September 1842 by the Mechanics' Institute, which by then was concerned that its middle class support, mainly from dissenters and Liberals, was not wide enough. In order to tap Tory Anglican support it asked Scoresby twice to consider succeeding as President of the Institute none other than Acworth, who had agreed to step down. As the intermediary in these negotiations was Willson Cryer, a doctor and one of the rare Tories who supported the Institute, the proposal to Scoresby was probably conciliatory and not a cynical device for aggravating him.[82]

Scoresby was wounded but not paralysed by the church rate fracas. In 1840 he began his work of extending parochial schools, where his success made for him enemies among the mill-owners and dissenters.[83] In July 1842, stung by the church rate defeat, he engineered the expulsion from the Bradford Workhouse of the dissenting ministers who had previously taken the services, giving himself exclusive Anglican domination. As Joshua Pollard, Scoresby's staunch ally, put it: 'it was not right to preach Christ in the morning and John Wesley in the afternoon'.[84] Most importantly, in July 1843 Scoresby founded the Bradford Church Institute as a union to defend the Anglican church against the combination of Bradford dissenters, the terms 'union' and 'combination' being his. It was partly an Anglican riposte against the Mechanics' Institute and partly Anglican retaliation against the Voluntary Church Society run by dissenters. Scoresby was well aware that the real battle concerned the relations of the Church of England with the state and the monarchy.[85]

Surrounded by uncouth and undeferential Bradfordians, Scoresby was so busy that for two years from 1843 he had no time to correspond with Joule in Manchester. In spring 1844 he suffered a nervous breakdown and was given six months leave of absence by his Bishop. When he returned in Autumn 1844, he renewed his work for the Church Institute, for his parochial schools, for factory reform, and for the Bradford Operative Conservative Society. In a crafty move to outflank the supporters of incorporation of the borough, he acted as chairman in June 1845 of a short-lived Sanitary Committee which was devoted to the solution of public health problems by voluntary means. Though he gave scientific lectures at the Church Institute and the Mechanics' Institute, he did not try to revive the Philosophical Society of which he had been President.

Jowitt, *Victoriam Bradford*, pp. 115–36. For the Scoresby-Acworth polemic: Scoresby, *Position of church*, pp. 8–10; J. Acworth, *On the unscripturalness of ecclesiastical imposts. A lecture delivered in the Exchange Buildings, Bradford, November 30, 1841*, Bradford, 1841, p. iv (quote). See also W. Scott, *The objects of the Voluntary Church Society, stated and defended*, Bradford, n.d. [1841].

[82] Bradford Mechanics' Institute minute book, 6 and 22 September 1842; W. Cryer, *A lecture on the origin and reception of several important discoveries, delivered to the members of the Bradford Mechanics' Institute, in the theatre of their institution, January 2nd, 1843*, London, 1843; Willson Cryer (1805–53).

[83] Stamp, *Scoresby*, 150–4; Scoresby, *Records of the Bradford parochial schools; from the year 1840 to 1846, inclusive. Appendix*, n.p., 1848.

[84] *Bradford observer*, 14 and 21 July 1842.

[85] Scoresby, *Position of church*.

Worn out by interminable trials, difficulties, persection, and contention, Scoresby resigned as vicar of Bradford, left the town in 1847, and promptly had a second breakdown.[86]

In conclusion, I don't think that I find myself in the same situation as Dr Johnson when he gave to the last chapter of his masterpiece *Rasselas* the title 'The conclusion in which nothing is concluded'. It is true that quirky localism remained important in British science as long as centralized state direction was non-existent or ineffective. We all appreciate that different places nourished a public scientific life *sui generis*. Though historians should be aware of la longue durée, they should not be ashamed of responding as sensitively as they can to the specific features of an event or process: the individual and idiosyncratic actions of agents, and their choices from the options available to them are as much the stuff of historical change as long-term preconditions and movements. Arthur Engel's recent book on the rise of the academic profession in nineteenth-century Oxford is *not* vitiated by his conclusion that what occurred there was a distinctive product of Oxford conditions.[87]

That being said, what can we learn from a study of Wissenschaft in Worstedopolis, of science in Coketown, Bruddersford and Grimedale during the industrial revolution? Quite obviously the professionalisation model provides little illumination, and can be dismissed. Again the notion of German influence gives little purchase: up to 1850 there were no Schuncks in Bradford, and subsequently the German migrants were active in philanthropy, music, and medicine rather than science.[88] The idea that provincial science at the savant level either directly served industry, or was directly stimulated by it, takes a heavy beating from the Bradford case. The rapid urbanisation and population growth caused by industrialisation were extremely *dislocating* in ways I have described. Bradford was an extreme example of the general case argued by the radical journalist, Stephen Morley, in Disraeli's *Sybil*, i.e., that the Queen reigned over two nations, the rich and the poor; *and* also that 'There is no community in England; there is aggregation but aggregation under circumstances which make it rather a dissociating, than a uniting, principle.'[89] In Bradford's years of crisis from 1834 to 1850 politico-denominational conflicts within

[86] See especially Scoresby, *American factories and their female operatives; with an appeal on behalf of the British factory population, and suggestions for the improvement of their condition*, London, 1845; and *Position and encouragements of Christian teachers: a discourse to Sunday School Teachers. Preached, March 9th, 1845, in the parish church of Bradford*, London, 1846; *A report of the Bradford Sanitary Committee appointed at a public meeting, held May 5th, 1845*, Bradford, 1845; and generally, Stamp, *Scoresby*, pp. 177, 186–201.

[87] C. Rosenberg, 'Science in American society', *Isis*, 1983, **74,** 356–67; A. J. Engel, *From clergyman to don: the rise of the academic profession in nineteenth-century Oxford*, Oxford, 1983.

[88] On Henry Edward Schunck (1820–1903) see Kargon, *Science in Manchester*, pp. 95–103, and W. V. Farrar, 'Edward Schunk, FRS: a pioneer of natural-product chemistry', *Notes and Records of the Royal Society of London*, 1977, **31,** 273–96. The German contribution to Bradford medicine reached its culmination in the successful work on anthrax of Frederick William Eurich (1867–1945); see M. Bligh, *Dr Eurich of Bradford*, London, 1960.

[89] B. Disraeli, *Sybil or the two nations*, Harmondsworth, 1980, p. 94 (first published 1845).

the middle class and the condition of England question were the results of industrialism. These conflicts and this question together led such a tough nut as Scoresby to two nervous breakdowns. Though he valued the iron specimens from the local Bowling Iron Works for his magnetic researches, Bradford's incessantly wearing version of industrialisation deprived him of time and energy for science, private or public. Bradford's case would seem to indicate that industrialisation could on occasion produce such class hostility, political party spirit, and religious sectarianism, that exclusively middle-class science and access to polite culture had little chance of survival; whereas the Mechanics' Institute endured because it appealed to the Liberal dissenting middle class *and* to the labour aristocracy.[90]

Bradford, I suggest, presents an extreme case. There was a paucity of organised savant and exclusively middle-class science; but, as Ian Inkster has stressed to me, the 1851 Census material confirms the picture of the resilience and buoyancy of mechanics' institutes and mutual improvement societies in the Bradford area in the 1840s. In town which was socially bottom heavy, the third Philosophical Society faded in the early 1840s and the Mechanics' Institute survived because the latter bridged classes, however uneasily, and was not the object of vehement class hostility. It is therefore tempting to see the Mechanics' Institute as preparing the ground for that accommodation between classes which was such a feature of Bradford in the 1850s. More generally, the contrast between savant and artisan science in Bradford reminds us that one can too easily be dazzled by the great successes of the lit and phil movement, say at Manchester and at York, so that one ignores other types of participation in science.[91] It is salutary to bear in mind that at Leeds in 1850 the Mechanics' Institute had seven times as many members and books as the Phil and Lit had; and that at York the Philosophical Society, which in 1831 was capable of fathering the British Association, had slightly fewer members than the Institute of Popular Science and Literature and considerably fewer books.[92]

In recent years there has been an attempt to relate science and industry *indirectly*, via the marginality thesis. On this interpretation, doing or patronising science was a means of upward mobility for marginal men seeking recognition and ultimately Gramscian hegemony in manufacturing areas. Apart from the internal difficulties of this thesis, it is high time that historians took into account those local social, economic, class, political and denominational elements, exacerbated or produced by

[90] *Bradford observer*, editorial, 19 September 1839. Compare the relative fortunes of the philosophical society and the mechanics' institute in the Potteries as recounted in S. Shapin, 'Pottery Philosophical Society, 1819–1835'.

[91] See A. D. Orange, *Philosophers and provincials: the Yorkshire Philosophical Society from 1822 to 1844*, York, 1973.

[92] *Census of Great Britain 1851. Education. England and Wales*, Parliamentary Papers, 1852–3, **90,** pp. 248–9, 251. The figures for Leeds were: Mechanics' Institute, 1848 members, 7747 books; Philosophical Society, 219 members, 800 books. For York: Institute of Science, 496 members, 4053 books; Philosophical Society, 458 members, 1928 books.

industrialisation, which acted as restraints or stimuli on local public science.[93] For example, in the 1830s and 1840s alliances and hostilities apropos such matters as factory reform and civil liberties determined the face of public science in Bradford far more than the alleged marginality of its supporters. It is true that the aim of hegemony was central to local agendas and rivalries; but science could be just one of several vehicles for the display of cultural signals, the acquisition of urban power, and the adjustment of social relations.

It is clear that mono-causal explanations and single factor analyses are now passé. Indeed in a penetrating analysis of provincial scientific culture, Ian Inkster has proposed that no less than twelve factors need to be considered.[94] Slightly transformed by me, these are: population size; population growth; industrial structure; occupational characteristics; class structure; economic stability or vulnerability; geographical location; existing scientific traditions; other cultural or pressure groups, especially competing ones; the relation to the metropolis; the contingent presence of leading savants; and the local political structure. Much of my analysis is compatible with his scheme and indebted to it. Even so, I think we should add two further considerations. Firstly we might combine the Marxist stress on conflict and the Namierite emphasis on interests, without devaluing the intellectual choices made by individuals and the knowledge they produce. Provincial public science, like much else, may be explained in terms of competition between various groups and individuals, who use whatever resources they can to serve whatever interests they have in mind. Secondly, it is useful to be aware of local religious and denominational structure, as well as that of politics, though of course the two were often related. The fragility of scientific culture at the savant level in Bradford shows, above all, that it was all too easy for the bark of science to founder on those religious and political shoals and quicksands which in Worstedopolis in the 1830s and 1840s endangered every cultural project floated for the public weal.[95]

Sir Henry Irving died in Bradford, a renowned graveyard of actors and comedians. In thanking his audiences for their suffrage, he often ended with words which Sir John Barbirolli later used to quote verbatim in his speeches at great musical occasions in this city, the home of the Hallé Orchestra.[96] I wish to maintain that Mancunian tradition: 'Ladies and gentlemen, I am your most humble and obedient servant'.

[93] On Antonio Gramsci see the highly sensible J. Joll, *Gramsci*, London, 1977. For the practical difficulties facing historians in using the marginality thesis, see I. Inskter, 'Variations on a theme by Thackray: comments upon provincial science culture, c. 1780–1850', *British Society for the History of Science Newsletter*, 1982, no. 8, 15–17; for criticism of the social control thesis, C. A. Russell, *Science and social change 1700–1900*, London, 1983, pp. 160–73.

[94] I. Inkster, 'Introduction: aspects of the history of science and science culture in Britain, 1780–1850 and beyond', in Inkster and Morrell, *Metropolis and province*, pp. 11–54.

[95] James, *Bradford*, i, 248.

[96] M. Kennedy, *Barbirolli: conductor laureate: the authorised biography*, London, 1971, p. 288.

INDEX